HOME BUYING

The Complete Illustrated Guide

Henry S. Harrison
Margery B. Leonard

82 7335-2

NATIONAL ASSOCIATION OF REALTORS®
developed in cooperation with its affiliate, the
REALTORS NATIONAL MARKETING INSTITUTE®
of the NATIONAL ASSOCIATION OF REALTORS®
Chicago, Illinois

Library of Congress Cataloging in Publication Data

Harrison, Henry S
  Home buying.
  Includes bibliographical references and index.
    1. House buying—Handbooks, manuals, etc.
I. Leonard, Margery B., joint author. II. Title.
HD1379.H34   643'.12   80-23412
ISBN 0-913652-18-0

International Standard Book Number: 0-913652-18-0
Library of Congress Catalog Card Number: 80-23412
Marketing Institute Catalog Number: 128

Printed in the United States of America
First Printing, 1980, 10,000 copies

To our collective parents, spouses, children; our families—without whom a home is just a house.

This book is also dedicated to the many women who buy and sell homes.
We hope it will be used as an example by others showing how to write a book without any discriminatory masculine pronouns.

"The illusion that times that were are better than those that are has probably pervaded all ages."
Horace Greeley

FOREWORD AND ACKNOWLEDGMENTS

When Margery B. Leonard and I finished writing *HOUSES—The Illustrated Guide to Construction, Design and Systems* in 1973, we knew it would just be a matter of time before we produced a consumer version of that book. We went our separate ways until 1978 when Marge suggested we proceed with the book and I concurred.

Originally we thought the "consumer version" of *HOUSES* would be quite similar to *HOUSES* in substance, with the difference being in how the material was presented.

As we initiated the new project, it became apparent that the material in *HOUSES* would constitute only a small portion of our new book. *HOUSES* covers the subjects of house construction, design and location in depth. Besides these important subjects, the consumer needs to know about the home as an investment, the art of negotiating, as much as possible about sales contracts, financing and insurance, and how to obtain needed help from experts. As a result, our final manuscript contained about 80 percent totally new material and about 20 percent material from *HOUSES* especially reoriented to the consumer. Many of the illustrations in *HOUSES*, drawn by Joseph Jaqua, Ronald Noe and Peter Forbach are used in *Home Buying*.

Much of the time-consuming work for the first draft of *Home Buying* was done by Marge Leonard whose personal acknowledgments follow.

"Considerable personal support sustained me, even when husband Richard Leonard's busy schedule often had to be adjusted and mother Blanche Brennan's delightful daily phone conversations limited to a minimum. Youngest son Zachary did some preliminary sketches and daughter Lisa some very expert first draft typing. The older two children, Nancy and Richard, enriched the telephone companies as well with their frequent calls of encouragement from Boston.

"My sister, Barbara Schaefer, never read a newspaper in the past two years without scissors in hand to clip anything pertinent to the subject. My brother Roger Brennan's authority as a fire marshall was sought, but his and his wife Joan's constant interest was even more welcome. And summer escapes to Cape Cod and Scituate as well as winter weekends in New Hampshire with sisters and brothers-in-law were a blessing!

"Friends and associates who lent their expertise so willingly are also gratefully acknowledged. They are: Francis H. Killorin of Solar Seven; REALTOR® Betty Thomson; Mark Yanarella and Michael Walsh of the Naugatuck (CT) Savings Bank; Ronald Lengyl and Domenic Alegi of the Naugatuck Valley Savings and Loan Association; the late columnist, Sam Shulsky; Earl Lindgren, architect; Joseph Marciano, president, Naugatuck Aluminum and Glass Company; James Usher, security consultant, ADT; Charles A. Cappello, vice president, Security Systems, Inc.; Clem Labine, editor, *Old House Journal*; Bruce Wilbur, Energy Extension Service; Mary B. Smith, executive secretary, Naugatuck chapter, American Red Cross; Stanley Petro, building inspector; John Gunnoud, president, Gunnoud Construction Company; Lois Bryant, Connecticut Department of Consumer Protection; J. W. Bartok and E. L. Palmer, the Cooperative Extension Service, University of Connecticut; and Paul Brennan, security systems installer."

The help I received fell into two categories: general help from my friends, relatives, business associates and employees and specialized help from experts in fields covered by specific chapters in the book.

In this latter category was the comprehensive research compiled by Malcolm Rashba of Liebman, Rashba and Goldblatt on the subject of sales contracts.

My partner in the Harrison-Ross Insurance Agency, Samuel Ross, reviewed the draft of the insurance chapter and made many helpful recommendations.

The REALTORS NATIONAL MARKETING INSTITUTE® review committee for *Home Buying* was headed by REALTOR® John Lane of Chicago and included REALTORS® James Bell of Atlanta and Ed Surovell of Ann Arbor, MI. Aside from reading the entire first draft, the committee reviewed the book's outline and held several meetings with us to help select specific topics and to provide guidance as to where emphasis should be placed.

William D. North, Senior Vice President and General Counsel of the NATIONAL ASSOCIATION OF REALTORS®, reviewed several chapters both for legal accuracy and general organization and clarity. As a result of his recommendations, the insurance chapter was reorganized into a much improved format. He also made many good recommendations that improved the chapters on sales contracts and "people who can help."

Between writing HOUSES and *Home Buying*, I co-authored *Appraising the Single Family Residence* with Dr. George Bloom, MAI, Professor of Real Estate at Indiana University. The chapter on appraising is based on the material in that book.

One of the joys of writing a real estate book is the availability of the NATIONAL ASSOCIATION OF REALTORS® library as a research resource. Librarian Beverly Dordick, besides being a constant and instant source of needed information, also has been a great source of encouragement for my projects. Her excitement about this book was very instrumental in our final decision to go forward.

The glossary-index was prepared with substantial help from Kenneth Ballard and Helen Semplenski. Many of the glossary terms come from the manuscript of *An Illustrated Real Estate and Appraising Dictionary* currently being co-authored by my daughter Julie Harrison.

The bulk of the thousands of manuscript pages were organized and typed by Emily Emerson who transforms illegible script and tapes into pages of beauty. Pat Torino also typed some of the manuscript pages.

It is difficult for us to recognize here all of the REALTORS NATIONAL MARKETING INSTITUTE® staff who helped as we only deal directly with a portion of the people involved. However, their help was inestimable.

Llani O'Connor, Vice President-Publishing, who originally championed the publication of *HOUSES,* again provided the integral leadership to promote this project. She supported our request to again obtain the services of Helene Berlin, editor of *HOUSES,* to edit this book. Helene again demonstrated her great professional editorial skills.

Peg Keilholz was the RNMI Book Editor during most of the time the book was being prepared, and Production Manager Meg Givhan provided much of the technical coordinating.

Writing a book takes a great deal of time, and without people willing to help an author make the needed time available, the book would never be completed. My wife Ruth Lambert and my daughters Julie, Eve and Kate gave up valued time with me to support the project. My parents, Dr. J. M. and Helen Harrison, my sister, Diane Johnson, and her husband, Albert; my brother-in-law and sister-in-law, Dr. Michael and Adena Pliskin; and my mother-in-law, Rochelle Lambert all tolerated broken engagements and turned-down invitations. In addition to this type of support, my father-in-law, Dr. Joseph Lambert, was also a research resource and provided a clipping service.

Barbara Kaye and Judith Fowler produced the appraisals needed to keep the appraisal company going and Florence Milano and Sara Semplenski covered for me at the insurance agency. The responsibility for running our nursing home fell on Marilyn Margolis. Albert Porier and Ruth Loux helped perform many of my functions as President of the Greater New Haven Board of REALTORS.® All of them, again, allowed me the time I needed to research and write.

A special thanks to my friend Walter Dudar for telling the community, in print, about my activities as an author.

Having done our best, Marge and I wish you, the home buyer, the best of luck in your quest for the home of your dreams.

Henry S. Harrison
Margery B. Leonard
New Haven, CT

ABOUT THE AUTHORS

HENRY S. HARRISON

A nationally recognized authority on the single-family residence, Henry S. Harrison is the author of the highly successful *HOUSES— The Illustrated Guide to Construction, Design and Systems.*

Mr. Harrison's feature articles about houses have appeared in *real estate today*® and *The Real Estate Appraiser,* and he has lectured extensively to real estate professionals throughout the country.

Mr. Harrison's earlier book, *HOUSES,* is now a standard text in many colleges where it is used together with *HOUSES—Student Workbook,* co-authored with Ruth Lambert and Bobby Bratton. Both are published by REALTORS NATIONAL MARKETING INSTITUTE®, an affiliate of the NATIONAL ASSOCIATION OF REALTORS®. Mr. Harrison is also co-author (with George Bloom) of the American Institute of Real Estate Appraisers' text, *Appraising the Single Family Residence.*

A real estate professional with 25 years' experience in the sale, appraisal, development and management of residential, commercial and industrial real estate, Mr. Harrison is president of Harrison Appraisal Co., New Haven, CT, affiliated with Real Property Analysts, Inc. He is a graduate in economics of the Wharton School of Finance and Commerce, University of Pennsylvania, and holds a Master's Degree in Adult Education (real estate and appraising) from Godard College in Vermont.

Mr. Harrison's materials are also used extensively to train appraisers in how to make house appraisals for mortgage lenders. They include *Harrison's Illustrated Guide—How To Fill Out a Residential Appraisal Report, Harrison's Illustrated Guide—How To Fill Out a Small Income Property Appraisal Report,* plus a variety of audio-visual seminars and slide shows.

MARGERY B. LEONARD

Margery B. Leonard is an author and freelance writer on a variety of subjects, as well as an experienced newspaper editor and speech writer.

Mrs. Leonard was associated with Henry S. Harrison in the preparation of *HOUSES—The Illustrated Guide to Construction, Design and Systems,* for which she researched and organized the historical material. Her works have been published in several Connecticut newspapers and in *New York* magazine.

A former teacher and educational researcher, Mrs. Leonard is a graduate of Southern Connecticut State College and holds a Master of Arts degree from Yale University.

CONTENTS

Chapter 6 Interior Design and Layout

PART THREE STEPS IN THE BUYING PROCESS

PART FIVE CHECKLISTS

FIGURES

Chapter 7

Chapter 8

Chapter 15

Chapter 16

CHECKLISTS

Chapter 13

Chapter 14

Chapter 15

Chapter 16

Chapter 17

Chapter 18

Chapter 19

INTRODUCTION
HOW THIS BOOK CAN HELP YOU
MAKE AN EFFECTIVE
BUYING DECISION

Now is an excellent time to buy a home! We make this statement to you without knowing when you will be reading this book because experience has shown that it has always been a good time to buy your dream house. Will Rogers is quoted as saying, "Buy Land. They ain't making any more of that stuff." Construction costs keep going up, the population and number of households keeps expanding and home ownership has proven itself to be the single most important step a family can take to improve its way of life.

The projected growth in households from 74.7 million in 1977 to 87.2 million in 1985—an increase of 16.7 percent—is more than double the 7.4 percent projected population growth rate for the same eight-year period. The major reason for this big difference is in the shifts in household formation rates and types of housing demand in response to the projected major changes in the age structure of our nation's population.[1]

This book is intended as a guide to help steer you on the truest, shortest and best route to your goal of buying a home. It will not eliminate the problems you will encounter. But it will help you to foresee them, to anticipate situations, to cut red tape and save precious time, and to surmount your problems with confidence.

Not everyone should buy a house. For example, if you are planning to be in an area only a short time, it may be cheaper to rent rather than buy a house and then have to sell it. Young couples with only small or nonexistent savings and unsettled careers and other temporary plans often are not ready for home ownership. Older people with unsettled plans or poor health may elect to rent until their future plans and health are stabilized. Families in transition because of unsettled domestic relationships, children about to leave home (or return home) or with other prob-

---

[1] R. L. Shrabonek, "A Study of Housing Demand in the Mid-1980s," *REALTORS® Review*, May, 1978.

lems may elect to rent rather than buy. Finally, there are families that simply do not wish to assume the responsibility of home ownership.

However, if you are ready to buy, this book is designed to help you prepare yourself for home ownership. Without proper preparation you are likely to purchase a house based primarily on emotional appeal. While we don't underrate the importance of emotional appeal, we think an informed consumer will stand a far greater chance of having long term satisfaction with the home he or she purchases. It is the purpose of this book to make you an informed consumer armed with the knowledge that will help you buy a home that will provide pleasure and profit for all the members of your family.

This book will take you step-by-step through the home buying process. To help you as you look at and compare houses, a perforated section of 62 checklists is included in this book. Each checklist is keyed directly to material within the text and is designed to help you find the best house for you and your family.

FIRST RULES OF HOME BUYING

Here are some of the first rules you should know about home buying.

1. Before you go shopping for a house, gather the family together and find out what *each* person wants. Ask such questions as do we want a townhouse or a free standing house? To live in the city or the suburbs? A new house or an older one? The worksheet in Figure 2 (Chapter 1) will help you organize your family's needs and desires. After you find out what everyone wants, you then need to establish a list of priorities.

2. Get help from professionals. There are REALTORS®, attorneys, lenders, appraisers, home inspectors, experts in mechanical systems, termite inspectors and many other experts available to help you when needed. (See Chapters 3 and 10 through 15.)

3. Educate yourself about how to buy a house. A good way to start is to read this book. Learn how to inspect a house. This will require that you know basic construction, home design, mechanical systems, etc.

4. Take your time. Don't be stampeded by the seller or salesperson into making a deal before you are ready. It is a time-revered sales technique to try to make a potential buyer think someone else is about to purchase the house he or she is considering. Of course, there are times when there *is* another potential buyer waiting in the wings.

5. Spread the word around that you are looking for a home. Mention it every chance you have. In many areas the demand exceeds the supply. The best houses are shown first to buyers who seem to be serious.

6. Buy the most expensive house you can afford. A home is an excellent financial investment. Your income will probably go up, but inflation is probably here to stay.

7. Shop for the best mortgage available. Shopping often results in

finding a lower interest rate or better terms which might save you hundreds of dollars in payments on a typical mortgage.

8. Be prepared to compromise. There is no such thing as a perfect house or one that will meet all your needs. Most "bargains" turn out to be just that. Long-range happiness and profit is based on paying a fair price for a home that will meet many (but not necessarily all) of your family's needs.

The first step after deciding to buy a home is to figure out how much you can afford to pay. The next chapter tells you everything you need to know to determine what price house you can afford to buy and maintain.

In a typical year nearly five million families will buy homes. Many will receive years of happiness, satisfaction and profit. We sincerely hope you will be one of this group.

PART ONE
THE PLANNING STAGE

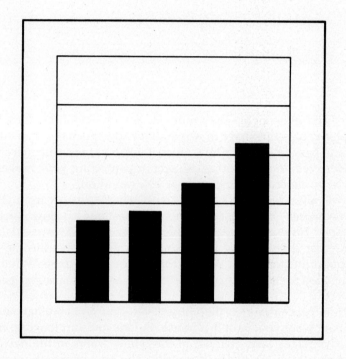

CHAPTER 1

HOW MUCH CAN YOU AFFORD
TO SPEND?

In their lives few people spend more for any one item than for a home. The majority of people have to worry about how much they can afford to spend and have to consider how much it will cost to run a house. Therefore before reading the real estate ads or contacting your broker, it is very wise to determine exactly what you can afford.

You will always get the best and most reliable answer from the best source—yourself. You must answer such questions as: How much cash is available? How much equity is there in our other investments? What are our other assets? What is the single (or double) net income which will support the financing? What is the sum of all our debts? What is our monthly need for cash to pay off debts such as auto loans and personal notes?

But first, concentrate on the house itself. You probably have definite ideas about what you want in a house. Before you start looking, make a list of advantages each member of the family wants in the new home and arrange the list in order of priority. The next step is to investigate the market to find out how many of the desired items can be found in a house that is affordable to you. What is available and what you can afford are the next two factors to consider.

INCOME MEASUREMENTS

Much has been written about how much a family can afford to pay for a home.

In 1975, *Fortune* magazine used the rule that a family's gross income should be at least five times its mortgage payments. Few families now could afford the house they need if they used this formula, however. In her popular book Sylvia Porter[1] states, "You can afford to buy a house roughly two and one-half times your gross (before taxes) yearly income."

This is a good general rule of thumb for preliminary estimates. Lower income families probably should pay closer to two times their annual income. However, other long-term debt or unusual long-term payments that come from annual income rather than savings must be deducted from the gross income to make this a reliable measure.

That old rule still applies: The more money you put down, the lower your interest costs over the 15, 20, 25, or 30 years, and the faster the equity builds up in your own home. And the larger the down payment, the easier it will be for you to obtain the lowest possible interest rate on your mortgage loan. On the other hand, beware of getting in over your head so that there is little money available for emergencies, recreation and other family needs. Don't lose sight of the fact that you want to enjoy and *live* in your new home.

USING THE 40-PERCENT FORMULA

A more acceptable guideline is that a family can afford to spend about 40 percent of its after-tax income for shelter. The cost of shelter can be defined as the mortgage payment, real estate taxes, property insurance, repairs and maintenance, utilities and commuting costs. It is customary when using this method to deduct from current after-tax income all other debt payments that will continue for more than a year. Many families, for example, are almost always making automobile loan payments. The forecasted amount of these payments should be deducted from the after-tax income before the 40 percent formula is applied. The same would be true for any other unusual long-term payments such as education expenses and alimony.

You still have to figure one more set of considerations—those of your family's life style. Included here are all those major expenses of food, clothing, medical expenses and charitable and church obligations. Do you need two cars? Do you entertain frequently? Lavishly? How much emphasis do you put on recreation? This includes an annual vacation and other trips, long weekends, books, records, concerts, movies and hobbies. Will you be going from a two-income family to a one-income family in the future (or vice versa)? Do you have future college tuition or private school tuition to consider? Are you (or will you be) supporting an elderly parent? Are you paying alimony and/or child support?

When any of these needs for money are greater than those of a typical family, your income available for mortgage payments will be reduced

---

[1] Sylvia Porter, *Sylvia Porter's Money Book*, (Garden City, New York: Doubleday & Co., 1975).

accordingly. When this happens the typical 40 percent of income available for shelter should be revised to reflect the actual amount of after-tax income available.

Here is an example of how the formula works:

Husband's annual income	$26,000
Wife's annual income	+ 13,000
Gross income	$39,000
Income taxes	− 7,000
After tax income	$32,000
Annual car payments	− 2,000
Income Analysis after taxes and long-term debt payment	$30,000
Maximum income available for shelter	× 40%
	$12,000
Est. property taxes, insurance, repairs, maintenance, utilities and commuting costs:	− 5,000
Annual dollars available for mortgage payment:	$ 7,000

If a typical mortgage for the house being contemplated is a 25 year, 12%, level monthly payment mortgage, $7,000 would pay off about a $55,385 mortgage. If these buyers had $12,500 to invest as a down payment, they could afford to pay about $68,000 for a house.

Use the above calculations on your own income, tax and expense figures. Then refer to Figure 1 to obtain the amount of mortgage you can afford.

Use Figure 2 as a detailed worksheet to determine what your true available income is for buying a house. After you have made these calculations for several houses that you have considered buying, you will have a good idea of what you can seriously afford. Then go on to Chapter 2 to see just how good an investment a house is, regardless of how much you can afford to pay.

FIGURE 1
AMOUNT OF INCOME NEEDED TO PAY OFF EACH $1,000
OF A LEVEL MONTHLY PAYMENT MORTGAGE

Interest Rate	Term of Mortgage			
	15 Yrs	20 Yrs	25 Yrs	30 Yrs
10	128.95	115.80	109.08	105.36
10 1/4	130.79	117.84	111.12	107.52
10 1/2	132.65	119.76	113.28	109.80
10 3/4	134.51	121.80	115.44	111.96
11	136.39	123.84	117.60	114.24
11 1/4	138.28	125.88	119.76	116.52
11 1/2	140.18	127.92	121.92	118.80
11 3/4	142.10	130.80	124.20	121.08
12	144.02	132.12	126.36	123.48
12 1/4	145.96	134.23	128.61	125.75
12 1/2	147.90	136.34	130.84	128.07
12 3/4	149.86	138.46	133.90	130.40
13	151.83	140.59	135.34	132.74
13 1/4	153.81	142.73	137.60	135.09
13 1/2	155.80	144.88	139.88	137.45
13 3/4	157.80	147.05	142.16	139.81
14	159.81	149.22	144.45	142.18
14 1/4	161.82	151.41	146.75	144.56
14 1/2	163.90	153.60	149.06	146.95
14 3/4	165.90	155.80	151.38	149.34
15	167.95	158.01	153.70	151.73
15 1/4	170.01	160.24	156.03	154.14
15 1/2	172.08	162.47	158.37	156.54
15 3/4	174.16	164.70	160.71	158.95
16	176.24	166.95	163.07	161.37

How To Use This Table:

1. Select the interest rate and mortgage term for the house you are planning to buy.

2. Divide the amount shown on this Table into the annual dollars you have available for mortgage payments to obtain the amount of the mortgage (in thousands of dollars) which can be paid off with available income.

Example:

If a family has $7,300 available for mortgage payments and a mortgage for the house they are seeking is a 20-year, 12% mortgage, they would divide $7,300 by 132.12 which gives 55.252 thousands or a $55,252 mortgage.

Figure 1, continued

Here are some other examples:

Available Income	Mortgage Term	Interest	Amount of Mortgage
$6000	20 yrs.	12%	$45,413
$7000	30 yrs.	11.5%	$58,923
$8500	25 yrs.	11%	$72,279
$9000	20 yrs.	12.5%	$66,011

FIGURE 2

WORKSHEET: HOW MUCH CAN YOU AFFORD TO PAY FOR A HOUSE?

Family Annual Income:

Husband's	$_____
Wife's	_____
Total	$_____
minus income taxes	=_____
Total after-tax income	$_____
minus automobile payments	=_____
minus other long-term expenses	=_____
Annual income after taxes and payments	$_____
	$\times$ 40%[4]
Maximum income available for shelter	$_____

Estimated Operating Expenses:

Property taxes[1]	$_____
Homeowner insurance[2]	_____
Trash & garbage collection[2]	_____
Repairs & maintenance	_____
Commuting cost[3]	_____
Heating, cooling, domestic hot water[2]	_____
Electricity[2]	_____
Grounds maintenance[2]	_____
Snow removal[2]	_____
Total	$_____

Income available for shelter (see above)	$_____
minus estimated operating expenses	−_____
= Annual dollars available for mortgage payments	$_____
Divided by annual payment per $1,000 for mortgage payment[5]	÷_____
= Amount of mortgage feasible	$_____
Add amount down payment	+_____
= Total Amount You Can Afford To Pay	$_____

[1] If you are moving to a new community find out how the property taxes are charged. In some communities one tax covers everything. In other places, there are several separate taxes such as school taxes, water taxes, etc.

[2] Estimates for some of these costs—taxes, utility and heating bills, and others—can usually be obtained from your real estate agent or from the seller. If you wish verification of the property tax bill, you need only to go to your tax office in the city or town hall, as tax payments are a matter of public record.

Figure 2, continued

[3] Some people might not include this as part of "housing" expenses—however, it is a fact of life and must be included somewhere.

[4] Maximum percentage of after-tax income many families can pay for shelter.

[5] Find amount on table shown in Figure 1.

For your convenience, a perforated copy of this worksheet is on page C-1.

CHAPTER 2
A HOME AS AN INVESTMENT

One of the few concepts almost all investment counselors agree on is that investors should own their own homes. Ownership of a home becomes the foundation upon which a family can build an investment program that will create financial security. It can provide a source of emergency funds and can be an important part of future retirement planning.

Almost half the families in the United States own their own residences. Most of them have enjoyed seeing their houses increase in value at a rate greater than the rate of inflation; they have made a profit in "real" dollars as well as a "paper" profit in dollars that have become worth less and less because of their decrease in buying power. Because most of these houses were financed with long-term fixed payment mortgages, the rate of profit of the down payment invested was multiplied many times as we will explain later in this chapter. Figure 3 shows exactly how the purchase of a house has compared with other investments in the late 1960s and 1970s.

In general, the price of single family houses has been going up for years. Even in those years when the economy has been in a state of recession, most houses did not go down in price significantly. (See Figure 4 for an overview of median sales prices in recent years.)

There are, of course, some cases where houses have gone down in value. Fortunately, the careful buyer can often foresee the circumstances that cause isolated houses to decrease in value at the same time that home values in general are increasing.

INCREASES AND DECREASES IN HOME VALUES

Some of the reasons houses in general keep increasing in value are:

1. A constantly increasing number of families wanting to buy single family houses.

FIGURE 3

PURCHASING POWER OF DOLLAR INVESTED IN 1967

Year	Single-Family Homes	Corporate Bond[1]	Passbook Savings Account[1,2]	Common stock[2]	Cash
1967	$1.00	$1.00	$1.00	$1.00	$1.00
1968	1.02	1.02	1.01	1.08	.96
1969	1.03	1.03	1.01	1.14	.91
1970	1.05	1.06	1.00	1.00	.86
1971	1.10	1.09	1.01	1.06	.82
1972	1.14	1.13	1.03	1.26	.80
1973	1.18	1.14	1.02	1.38	.75
1974	1.15	1.12	.97	1.11	.68
1975	1.15	1.12	.93	.96	.62
1976	1.18	1.14	.93	1.01	.59
1977	1.26	1.16	.92	1.04	.55
1978	1.35	1.17	.90	1.07	.51
1979	1.39	1.17	.85	1.16	.46

(All items deflated by Consumer Price Index.)

[1] Includes interest/dividends.

[2] Based on a savings rate of 5 1/4 percent from 1967–mid 1979; 5 1/2 percent since then.

Source: Economics and Research Division, NATIONAL ASSOCIATION OF REALTORS®

FIGURE 4
MEDIAN SALES PRICE OF EXISTING SINGLE-FAMILY HOMES:
1972–1980

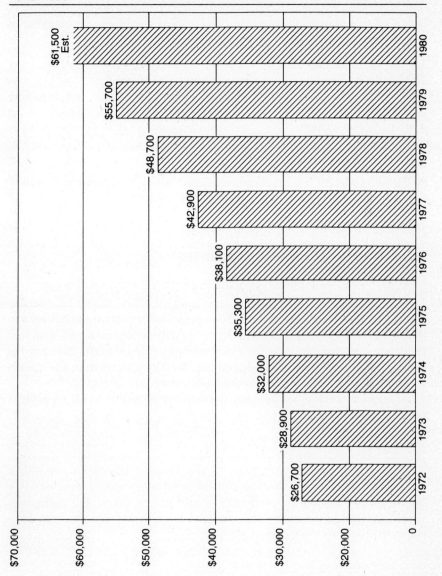

Source: Economics and Research Division, NATIONAL ASSOCIATION OF REALTORS®

2. Increase in building materials cost at least at the rate of inflation.
3. Increase in labor cost at least at the rate of inflation.
4. Increase in cost of suitable land for new houses.

Some of the reasons specific houses go down in value or increase in value slower than houses in general are:

1. Declining neighborhood.
2. Cut-back of employment opportunities in the area.
3. Nuisances in the area such as heavy traffic, pollution, incompatible land uses.
4. Poor house design.
5. Poor quality of construction.
6. Poor maintenance.

Another important reason people can lose money on a house is that they just pay too much for the house to begin with.

TAX ADVANTAGES OF HOME OWNERSHIP

TAX REDUCTION

It is no secret that our income tax laws provide for substantial benefits to taxpayers who are homeowners. Many first-time homeowners discover that they can now itemize their deductions on their Form 1040 tax return. The total of itemized deductions is usually greater than the standard unitemized deduction they had been formerly using.

The tax advantages of homeownership are available to all regardless of economic strata.

MORTGAGE INTEREST

The interest a homeowner pays to the lending institution (or other holder of the mortgage on the house) is an allowable deduction. If a family rents a house, the deduction could not be taken· the deduction would instead be taken by the landlord who would use the rent payments to pay the mortgage.

REAL ESTATE TAXES

All the property taxes a homeowner pays are allowable deductions on an income tax return. When you own your home you get this deduction. When you are renting the landlord uses your rent to pay the taxes and the landlord takes the tax deduction. Typically about 20 percent of a rent payment goes directly to paying the landlord's taxes.

CAPITAL GAINS

The sale of your home for a profit is one of the few capital gains that can be made tax free. One simple way to do this is to invest the money received into another home. To qualify for this tax-free treatment, the replacement home must be purchased within 18 months from the sale of the original home. If you build a new home you must start within 18 months after the sale of your home. (You must occupy the new home within 24 months of the sale of your old home.) This tax-free advantage applies to single family residences including mobile homes, cooperative apartments, condominium apartments and houses and houseboats. An important condition of this tax exemption is that both the new and old residence must be the principal residence.

Whenever you are considering taking advantage of the sale of your home, you should consult your accountant before you sell and buy. These tax laws are not as simple as they seem. A simple mistake such as timing might cost you the benefit of the deduction. If you were 55 or over before the date of sale, you may elect a one-time-only tax exclusion on your gain.

There are special ways for people over 65 to avoid capital gains taxes on houses they sell at a profit even if they do not reinvest in another residence. Again, a competent accountant or tax lawyer is the best source of information on these complicated laws.

LOCAL TAX CREDITS

Some states and communities have special laws that provide for tax benefits to homeowners. You should inquire about such local benefits.

SPECIAL TAX CREDITS

There are special income tax deductions allowed for qualified types of improvements made to historic properties and for the purchase of energy efficient and solar home components.

DOWER RIGHTS OF SPOUSES

The laws of many states give the surviving spouse special rights to inherit property. Often these rights give the surviving spouse protection against creditors. This often provides assets for the survivor that would not be available without this special protective legislation.

OTHER ADVANTAGES OF HOMEOWNERSHIP

There are many other advantages of homeownership. An improved credit rating is one example. Social prestige is another. There are a variety of intangible benefits too. Most homeowners will tell you that it feels good to own a home and to have a place to call your own.

HOW HOME INVESTMENT WORKS

The advantages of homeownership are illustrated by the following three hypothetical examples of families who invested their available money in three different ways 10 years ago. Each family had $10,000 available for an investment and was in approximately the 30 percent income tax bracket.

Family No. 1: This family invested its money in a savings account that paid an average of 6.5 percent interest over the years.

Original investment	$10,000
Interest @ 6 1/2% = $1,391[1]	
less: 30% tax − 471[1]	973
Total Investment at end of 10 years	$10,973

If the purchasing power of the dollar had been going down at the average annual rate of 4 percent per year over this period of time, the $10,973 would actually be worth in real dollars $6,584.

Family No. 2: This family invested its money in stock. The stock went up at the rate of 2.5 percent per year over the 10-year period (much better than the average increase of stocks) and they received average annual dividends of 5 percent (again above-average performance).

Original investment	$10,000
Dividends: 5% × $11,250 (average value of stock over the holding period)	5,625
Income tax on dividends	−1,687
After-tax dividends	$ 3,938
Appreciated value of stock	12,250
Value of Investment at end of 10 years	$16,188

If the purchasing power of the dollar had been going down at the average annual rate of 4 percent per year over this period of time, the $16,188 would actually be worth $9,712.

Family No. 3: This family invested its money in a $40,000 house. They put $10,000 down and financed the house with a $30,000, 20-year, 7.5

---

[1] These figures are approximate. If income tax was taken annually, even less money would be available to earn compound interest.

percent level monthly payment mortgage. They figured it cost them about the same (35 percent of their after-tax income) to live in this house as it would have cost them to rent a similar suitable house or apartment. Houses in this market increased in value at an average rate of 4 percent per year.

Original investment		$10,000
Cost of house	$40,000	
Value 10 years later	$56,000	
Profit		16,000

Tax savings on portion of shelter cost
that was real estate taxes and mortgage interest:

Annual average property taxes	$ 800	
Annual average interest on mortgage	2,000	
	$2,800	
Tax bracket	×.30	
Annual tax savings	$ 840	
Holding period	×10 years	
		8,400

Reduction of mortgage debt in 10 years

Original mortgage	$30,000	
Balance at end of 10 yrs	20,360	
Debt reduction		9,640
Total equity and tax savings at end of 10 years		$44,040

Assuming the same 4 percent decline in purchasing power, the $44,040 would actually be worth $26,424.

SUMMARY

Family	Investment	Profit	Taxes (tax savings)	Total Profit	Equity Value In Real Dollars
No. 1	$10,000	$ 1,391	− $471	$ 973	$ 6,584
No. 2	10,000	7,875	− 1,687	6,188	9,712
No. 3	10,000	25,640	+ (8,400)	34,040	26,424

- **Family No. 1** Profit consists of interest
- **Family No. 2** Profit consists of dividends and stock appreciation
- **Family No. 3** Profit consists of appreciation in value and mortgage debt reduction

This illustration clearly demonstrates that a house can be an excellent investment when compared to a savings account or to stocks.

Now let's assume in this example that the home Family No. 3 purchased did not increase in value at the average rate of 4 percent per year. Assume it did not increase in value at all over the 10-year projection period.

Original investment		$10,000
Cost of house	$40,000	
Value 10 yrs. later	$40,000	
Profit		–0–
Tax savings on portion of shelter cost that was real estate taxes and mortgage interest:		
Annual average property tax	$ 800	
Annual average interest on mortgage	2,000	
	$2,800	
Tax bracket	× .30	
Annual tax savings	$ 840	
Holding period	× 10 yrs	$ 8,400
Reduction of mortgage debt in 10 years		
Original mortgage	$30,000	
Balance at end of 10 yrs	20,360	
Debt reduction		$ 9,640
Total Equity and tax savings at end of 10 years:		$28,040

If the purchasing power of the dollar had been going down at the average annual rate of 4 percent per year over this period of time, the $28,040 would actually be worth $16,824. However, the investment in a home would still produce a better return on the investment, even without any appreciation, than the investment in a savings account or stocks.

CHAPTER 3
PEOPLE WHO CAN HELP

Some people like to do everything themselves. They often operate on the theory that the value of the services they receive is seldom worth what it costs. Others like to obtain free advice from whomever will give it to them. They obtain advice from friends, relatives and professionals, often from the latter at social functions. They do not believe in the old saying "Free advice is worth what you pay for it."

A smart home buyer, in the process of making decisions that will affect his or her family's way of life and budget, would be wise to seek and pay for good professional advice from a variety of sources.

In this chapter we explain the kinds of advice you need and how help can be obtained.

REALTORS®

The person who will be of the most service to you throughout the home buying process is your real estate broker. A REALTOR® is a real estate professional who is a member of the NATIONAL ASSOCIATION OF REALTORS® and his or her local real estate board, as is a REALTOR-ASSOCIATE® (salesperson). Only members in good standing of the NATIONAL ASSOCIATION OF REALTORS® may use these trademarks. This organization devotes itself to the education of its members. Each member voluntarily subscribes to a strict Code of Ethics which is enforced by a local Board of REALTORS® in the area where the REALTOR® conducts his business.

DESIGNATIONS

REALTORS® and REALTOR-ASSOCIATE®s can hold designations offered through the Institutes of the NATIONAL ASSOCIATION OF REALTORS® denoting advanced education and professional standing.

The designations offered by the REALTORS NATIONAL MARKETING INSTITUTE® (RNMI®), an affiliate of the National Association, are:

- CRS—Certified Residential Specialist. Awarded to those individuals passing prescribed courses and meeting professional standards in the field of residential marketing.
- CRB—Certified Real Estate Brokerage Manager. Awarded to those who have taken prescribed courses and have proven competence in the management of a real estate brokerage.
- CCIM—Certified Commercial-Investment Member. Awarded to those who have passed prescribed courses and have met professional standards in the field of commerical and investment real estate.

It is important to note that not all real estate brokers and salespeople are REALTORS® or REALTOR-ASSOCIATE®s. The real estate industry is a vast business and it encompasses many kinds of people, some of which, for a variety of reasons have not elected to become REALTORS®. While many of these people have good reputations, they do not have behind them the backing of the NATIONAL ASSOCIATION OF REALTORS®, its Code of Ethics to which each member must subscribe and the comprehensive informational and educational resources of Boards of REALTORS®.

Chapter 12 describes designations offered by the American Institute of Real Estate Appraisers, another institute of the National Association.

MLS AND OTHER SERVICES

The Multiple Listing Service (MLS) is a service of REALTORS® and the local real estate boards to which they belong. This is a service that is designed to benefit the seller by bringing into play the services of many REALTORS®.

When a REALTOR® who is a member of an MLS system lists a house for sale it is just the first step in what will be an extensive marketing effort. The MLS is a vehicle whereby a REALTOR® with an exclusive listing can make a "unilateral blanket offer of subagency" to the other participants in the MLS. Each member of the service becomes actively engaged in trying to find a satisfactory buyer for the property. This means that the seller receives the services of many REALTORS® each of which have the legal right to show the property and make representations about it to prospective buyers.

As part of this service, information about each property offered through the MLS is sent to each participating REALTOR® office. Each office is kept current about any changes in the offering price or other information that may help the REALTOR® more effectively offer the home for sale.

It is very important for the home buyer to understand that the MLS is much more than just an information-sharing service. Information alone can be communicated by advertisements, flyers or magazines. But the MLS makes each member a subagent of the listing agent. Therefore each

PEOPLE WHO CAN HELP 23

member can actively seek customers to show the property to and can make representations to these potential buyers about the property.

REALTORS® are attuned to many factors that make up the market in which they operate. They have current information about houses that have recently sold and houses that are being offered for sale in the market. In addition, REALTORS® are able to show prospective buyers why they feel the properties they are offering for sale are "good buys." They do this by offering comparisons of the house with other houses in the marketplace.

While it is true that REALTORS® frequently comment on houses in this way, it must be clearly understood by the potential buyer that the real estate broker is either the agent or subagent of the seller and is legally bound to obtain the highest reasonable price obtainable for the property. It is a mistake for the buyer to consider the real estate broker as an independent third party who is representing both buyer and seller in the transaction. The broker, by virtue of the listing agreement, owes a fiduciary duty to the seller. He or she also has a duty of honesty and fair dealing to the buyer.

A REALTOR® is an excellent source of information on where mortgage money is and how to obtain the best possible financing. By helping the buyer with his or her financing, the seller is also being helped in making the best sale possible. REALTORS® know alternative lending sources available in their communities. They understand the advantages of purchase money mortgages and other methods of creative financing (see Chapter 11).

Experience has shown that time and time again a skilled real estate broker helping in the negotiation process will substantially increase the chances of the buyer and seller reaching agreement. Few of us are experienced in the techniques of negotiating anything as large or important as a house. Indeed, most of us have never purchased anything more expensive than a car. For a complete discussion of the negotiating process and the part the real estate broker takes in it, see Chapter 10.

Most local real estate boards (which are listed in the telephone directory) will send you a list of their members free of charge. However, as you do with other professionals, the best way to choose an agent to work with is often by a recommendation from someone in whom you have trust and confidence.

ATTORNEYS

There is an old saying, "Anyone who is his own attorney has a fool for a client." We believe this saying is especially true when it comes to buying a home. It is almost impossible (and in our opinion certainly not wise) to complete a real estate closing without the use of an attorney.

We realize, however, that many real estate transactions are completed without the use of an attorney and that many people use an attorney only at the closing. Most REALTORS®, when directly asked, will recommend the use of an attorney. But it is important that the attorney be the type who contributes to the efficiency of the transaction and does not obstruct or delay it through inattention.

BINDER OR OFFER TO PURCHASE

A binder or offer to purchase on a house is designed to appear simple and non-threatening but it can be the most important document you will ever sign. When you sign the binder and give the REALTOR® your earnest money deposit you usually have committed yourself and your family to buying a house. All the other documents you will sign are more or less routine. A binder usually covers all of the major conditions of the sale, including the price, mortgage amount, term and interest, when and where the closing will be and any other special conditions agreed to about the sale. Items that binders often do not cover adequately are your rights to have a variety of inspections made such as a termite inspection, roof inspection, inspection of the mechanical systems, etc., and what happens when you are not satisfied with the results of one or more of these inspections. There are other options possible besides just voiding the sale if an inspection is not satisfactory; a binder may require, for example, that the seller correct the deficiency.

Some other items binders often do not cover is what happens if the house is damaged by fire, flood, earthquake or storm before the closing; what happens if the seller delays the closing or refuses to close at all; what happens if a minor defect in title is discovered and you still want to go ahead and buy the house, etc. Here is where the services of an attorney can be the most advantageous to you.

Attorneys can see that some of these items indeed are included in the binder. They might also require the purchase price be included as well as how the purchase will be financed, what will happen if you are unable to obtain the needed financing, how much the down payment will be, who will hold the down payment, when it will be turned over to the seller and when and under what circumstances it will be returned to you.

An attorney will determine if the description of the property is adequate so that there will be no question as to what you are buying. Sometimes it will be necessary to obtain a survey in order to get a satisfactory description.

Often there are items in and around the house the buyer believes to be part of the real estate and therefore included in the sale. However, they may not technically be real estate and the seller intends to remove them prior to the closing. (We remember once when we arrived after a closing at a house with the buyer to find the outdoor barbecue had been removed, much to the buyer's surprise.) The whole matter of what personal property is going to be included in the sale should be agreed upon prior to the signing of the binder or sales contract, with the help of your attorney.

Special attention should be paid to the appliances such as the stove and oven, dishwasher, washing machine, dryer, freezer, any built-in electrical equipment, bookcases, rugs and carpets, and irons and fireplace equipment, cook-out equipment, porch furniture, ground care equipment, equipment used to run the pool or courts, hobby equipment such as workbenches, darkroom sinks and fans.

Sometimes special agreements can be worked out that are mutually advantageous. For example, rather than delay the closing of a house to allow the seller to find new housing, it may be better for the buyer to take over the property and allow the seller to continue occupancy.

HOW TITLE IS HELD AND TRANSFERRED

How the title is going to be transferred should be set forth carefully, again with the help of your attorney. Who is going to do the title search and who is going to have it made? Often a form contract will state that the closing costs will be paid according to the custom of the area. This may not always work. For example, in one area, within just 10 miles of each other, there are two completely different local customs. A buyer in one town pays a much larger portion of closing costs if left to local custom unless different arrangements are agreed upon. Often just by the contract asking that the seller share equally in the costs of the title search and closing costs, the savings to the buyer will be more than ample to pay the cost of an attorney.

SOLE OWNERSHIP

When you decide to buy a house you must decide how you will take title. If there is just one purchaser it is relatively simple. When you take title alone it is called a "tenancy in severalty."

CO-OWNERSHIP

When a person is married and desires to own a property as a sole owner, an attorney should be consulted. Various states have complex laws that affect title held severally by married people. In some states it is necessary to have the non-owning spouse sign special papers. When either spouse is a minor, additional steps must be taken. Dower rights, courtesy (rights of widows) and homestead rights all must be considered.

When there is more than one owner, you must choose among several possible ways to take title. The most common forms of co-ownership:

- Tenancy in common
- Joint tenancy
- Tenancy by the entirety
- Community property
- Partnership and corporation ownership

Briefly, here is a description of each of these common forms of ownership.

Tenancy In Common. This is a form of ownership where two or more owners each have an undivided interest in the whole property. The portion owned by one person is not distinguished physically from the portions owned by the co-owners. Each owner can sell, convey, mortgage or transfer his or her interest with the consent of the co-owner. Upon the death of a co-owner, his or her undivided interest passes to heirs. It is especially important that married people who wish to own property as tenants in common seek the advice of an attorney. In many states, the spouse of a married tenant in common must sign the deed even though he or she does not have a direct ownership in a property in order to release the dower or homestead rights.

Joint Tenancy. This is a popular way for married people to own property. The basis of joint tenancy is unity of ownership. The death of one of the joint tenants does not destroy the unit. The remaining joint tenants receive the interest of the deceased owner by what is known as right of survivorship.

The creation of a joint tenancy must be carefully accomplished by a conveyance that specifically states exactly how the joint tenancy is to be created. An attorney experienced in real estate law should be consulted. Before you decide to own property as a joint tenant, you should also consult your tax advisor.

Tenancy by the Entirety. This is a special joint tenancy between husband and wife. It is permitted in about half of the states. Some unique features of this form of ownership are that the owners must be married to each other; during their lives title can be conveyed only by a deed signed by both parties, and in most states there is no right to petition. This form of ownership is based on the historical common law concept that husband and wife are considered to be one person. Before you select this form of ownership, you should explore your own feelings and then consult your attorney and tax advisor.

Community Property. Eight states have various forms of community property laws which affect the ownership of real estate. In these states, spouses of property owners automatically acquire some rights in property owned by their spouses. These rights include the automatic right to inherit half the property. Estate planning is complex and especially important in community property states; adequate advice is especially important.

Partnerships and Corporations. Occasionally, usually for business or tax purposes, homes are owned by partnerships or corporations.

A partnership is an association of two or more people joined together for the purposes of conducting a business. They share the business's profits and losses.

There are two kinds of partnerships. In a general partnership all of the partners participate in the operation and management of the business (but not necessarily equally). The partners may be held personally liable for the losses and obligations of the partnership.

A limited partnership is made up of two classes of partners: The general partners run the business and may be held personally liable for the losses and obligations of the partnership. The limited partners invest in the partnership but do not participate in the management of the partnership in any way. They can be held responsible for losses and obligations of the partnership only to the extent of their individual investments.

A corporation is a legal entity that is created according to special statutes existing in each state. A corporation is owned by its stockholders and managed by its officers and directors. Each corporation has a charter that it receives from a state. A corporation can only buy and sell real estate if it is permitted in its charter. If permitted by its charter, a corporation may own one of many pieces of real estate as well as engage in other business activities. Individuals invest in a corporation by purchasing stock. Their individual liability is limited by their investment.

Before you elect to own a home in either a partnership form of ownership or corporate form of ownership, you should seek advice from your accountant and attorney. The entire subject of corporate taxation is very complex and beyond the scope of this book.

IS JOINT OWNERSHIP BEST?

Many husbands and wives select a form of joint ownership to own their home without giving the matter much thought and without getting professional advice. Many of these people would have made this same decision after thought and advice. However, many others would have selected a different form of ownership because they would have discovered that some of their estate assets might end up in the hands of the wrong people, that the property might be subject to mismanagement or poor judgment and that thousands of dollars may be lost due to overpayment of federal and state estate taxes.

Professional estate planners point out that joint ownership is a poor substitute for a will. Many married couples think that because they own everything in both names if anything happens to one of them, the other gets everything automatically.

It is important to remember that property held in joint ownership passes directly to the survivor. If the survivor is the husband or wife none will pass to the children. If you have become separated from your spouse but are not divorced, the surviving spouse still gets everything and the children nothing.

When the survivor is a minor or an adult incapacitated by advancing age or poor health, the property he or she receives may have to be managed by a guardian. This can mean court costs and red tape.

The answer to estate planning for many families is some kind of a trust. It is much easier to establish a trust before you put a property in joint ownership than it is afterwards. If for no other reason than for potential tax savings, you should get professional advice on how to hold title to your home *before* you buy it.

OTHER FORMS OF OWNERSHIP

When appropriate, a home can also be owned by a trust, syndicate or a variety of other complex forms of ownership. Particularly when any unusual form of ownership is considered, adequate legal and tax advice is a must.

An attorney often either makes a title search or examines the title abstract or title insurance commitment prepared by a professional title searcher or title insurance company.

The abstract is a legal history of the property that describes all the former owners, financing, liens, attachments, easements, etc. It also spells out the releases of most of these documents if they are no longer in effect. It is the document that shows that the present owner has the right to convey the title to you. (These items are covered in more detail in Chapter 15, on Closing.)

SELECTING AN ATTORNEY

The best way to select an attorney is through the recommendation of someone familiar with the attorneys in your area and in whom you have confidence. REALTORS®, appraisers, lenders, accountants and insurance agents often deal with attorneys who handle real estate matters and are often good people from whom to seek recommendations.

Finally, ask the attorney approximately what he is going to charge you right at the beginning. Most attorneys are happy to provide you with this information. They know that their relationship with their clients will be much sounder when the client is not wondering about how much the attorney's fee is going to be.

HOME INSPECTORS

In most areas of the country the home inspection business is relatively new. Often home inspectors are confused with real estate appraisers. There is some overlap in what home inspectors and appraisers do but basically they concentrate on different things. The real estate appraiser is primarily interested in estimating the value of the property. The home inspector is primarily concerned with the condition of all the improvements. Most home inspectors do not estimate the property's value.

Few, if any, houses are perfect. Inherent in the aging process of a home is a deterioration in its basic structure and mechanical systems. Some of these defects will merely cause the occupants to be inconvenienced. Examples of such defects are squeaky floors, windows that stick, a noisy heating system, minor cracks in plaster, cabinet doors and drawers which open and close with difficulty, etc. Most homeowners are prepared to live with a reasonable number of such problems or fix the most annoying of these themselves.

Many other problems are much more serious and may cost substantial sums of money to correct, if they can be corrected at all. Some examples of serious problems are inadequate heating, hot water systems, or any system for that matter which will need repairs, inadequate electrical service, wiring and outlets, worn-out roof, poor ventilation, poor framing, poorly functioning water supply or waste disposal system, and worn-out plumbing.

Until recently buyers had either to depend on their own knowledge about house construction and mechanical systems or they sought the help of contractors, architects, friends and anyone else they could find to give them the help they needed. Many buyers did not have access to such help so they had to buy a house without clearly knowing about its defects and what problems they could expect to face in the future.

It is from these needs that the home inspection industry has developed. The purpose of home inspectors is to determine the structural quality of a house. Unfortunately, because of the newness of the field it operates without many established standards. In most states home inspectors do not have to be licensed. Recently, however, the American Society of Home Inspectors has been formed, and has developed a code of ethics and some performance standards.

Again, the best way to find a competent, honest home inspector is to check with others in whom you have confidence, such as your REALTOR®, attorney, appraiser or insurance agent.

A possible problem you may encounter is that some inspectors also have home improvements and contracting businesses. They are often more interested in getting work for these businesses than they are in doing the inspection report. Sometimes these so-called inspectors will charge only a nominal fee in hopes that the inspection will lead to work.

Some inspectors work with home warranty companies and as part of the inspection service (usually at an additional charge) they will provide you with a home warranty policy (see Chapter 13 on Insurance).

A conscientious home inspector will take several hours going through the house and charge somewhere between $100 and $300 for the service. He or she will carefully check all of the mechanical systems, the water and waste disposal systems, the foundation, framing, doors, walls, ceilings, trim, outside walls, stairs, fireplaces and chimneys, roofs, gutters and leaders, storm water drainage, etc. If possible, you should accompany the inspector during this inspection process as you will learn much more than you would just from the written and/or verbal report.

When you hire a home inspector, obtain an agreement as to when the inspection will be made (preferably at a time convenient to you so you can accompany the inspector) and when the report, both oral and written, will be delivered. This is especially important if you are going to hold up making an offer until you have received the report or if your binder or sales contract has a deadline for the inspection to take place. A report received after you have a firm committment to buy the house is not nearly as useful as one which, if not satisfactory, will let you either void the sale or renegotiate with the seller as to who will make needed repairs. A well-written contract prepared by your attorney should contain such provisions.

Finally, be wary when a seller or anyone else discourages an inspection. After all, you are the one who is going to have to live in the house and make any necessary repairs.

OTHERS WHO CAN HELP YOU

Besides REALTORS®, attorneys, inspectors and appraisers (who are discussed in later chapters) there are a variety of other people who can help you buy a home intelligently.

Some people consult architects even when they are buying a used house (how they can help you build a house is discussed in Chapter 17).

Contractors are often asked to look at houses to advise buyers about their construction and condition.

Termite inspectors (who are often exterminators) should routinely be consulted whenever a house is purchased. There are few areas left where termites are not a potential problem. Indeed some states require a termite inspection before title can be transferred. A good sales contract might contain a provision that makes the sale conditional upon there being a termite inspection certificate which shows the house is free of termite infestation. Termite inspectors will often also inspect the house at the same time for other possible vermin infestation.

It is almost impossible to tell just by looking at a heating, plumbing or electrical system if they are in good working order and of sufficient size to provide the services needed by a family. There are experts in most areas who will inspect these systems for you at a reasonable cost. (Again, it is a good idea to have your sales contract conditional upon satisfactory inspections by experts.)

Septic systems often malfunction. If the problem has been left uncorrected in the past, there may be permanent damage to the leaching fields. The cost to replace a septic system and/or the leaching fields can run into thousands of dollars. Some septic systems have never worked from the day they were constructed because the soil does not have the capacity to absorb the water. Whenever the house you are buying has a septic system, you should have it inspected.

A good water supply is critical. A well that flows freely in January may only provide mud in August. Again, only a professional inspection will protect you from future problems.

Unless the roof is new, it is often advisable to have a roofer look at it and tell you about its condition and how long you can expect it to last before it will need to be replaced.

Many insurance agents are very knowledgeable about houses. They can tell you what adequate insurance will cost, how much insurance to carry and if there will be any unusual problems obtaining adequate insurance for the house. (See Chapter 13 on Insurance.)

The estate tax, income tax and capital gains tax laws are becoming more and more complex. It is certainly prudent to discuss with your accountant or estate planner the tax consequences of buying your home. Sometimes the timing is important, especially if you have recently sold another home. Also, they can tell you the special tax advantages you will enjoy by owning a home.

There is an almost endless list of others who will offer you advice about the house you plan to buy. Generally, the best advice is obtained from trained, objective professionals. A smart home buyer makes the sales contract conditional upon whatever inspections and appraisals are needed and then seeks the best advice obtainable, thereby substantially reducing the chance of costly unanticipated problems. See Chapters 10 through 15 for more detailed information on these professionals.

For a complete checklist on the material in this chapter, see Checklist 1, People Who Can Help You, page C-3.

PART TWO
COMPARING HOUSES AND THEIR FEATURES

CHAPTER 4
LOCATION, LOCATION, LOCATION

The value of a home is influenced more by its location than by any other factor. We know a builder in Connecticut who simultaneously built two houses from the same set of plans. For all practical purposes the houses were identical, yet one house sold for almost 100 percent more than the other. Nobody was surprised—the reason was obvious. One house was located in Fairfield County, a section of Connecticut that attracts many affluent New York City commuters. The other was located in upstate Connecticut in an area too remote for easy commutation to New York. In one location houses are worth almost double what they are worth in the other location.

Choosing the location of the family home can be the most important decision a homeowner can make. It will affect the family happiness by playing a major role in shaping its life style. From a financial point of view, people profit from an investment in a house, in a community and in a neighborhood which are growing in value and community spirit.

Most families are attracted to a region because of available employment, proximity to relatives, or the climate. It is beyond the scope of this book to explore relative advantages and disadvantages of the many regions of the United States. This chapter, however, will explore the factors that should be taken into consideration when selecting a community, neighborhood and site within a specific region.

COMMUNITY

Usually a potential home buyer has a choice of communities in which to locate within a particular region. These communities each have unique characteristics which are advantages or disadvantages depending on the person doing the home shopping.

Ironically, many home buyers do not select a community objectively and thereby diminish the potential advantages of home ownership.

Sometimes it is of the utmost importance to your family to live in the same community as your relatives, your place of employment, some recreational facility or some other factor that predetermines your community selection. Under these circumstances you may skip this section and proceed to learn how to select a neighborhood within the chosen community. If you are open-minded about community selection, here is what you need to know to help you select the best community for your family.

The two primary reasons for selecting a community are economic factors and the community's facilities. These factors are usually interrelated and both must be weighed in making the final selection.

ECONOMIC FACTORS

The economic health of a community depends upon its economic base. Basic employers are those industries, businesses and institutions which export goods and services out of the community. It is the money received by them from outside the community that supports the non-basic employers who provide local goods and services. Economists generally agree that the higher the ratio of basic employment to non-basic employment, the better the economy of the community.

Another factor that must also be considered is the diversity and stability of the basic employers. It is best for the community to have a variety of basic employers including several different industries, businesses, government agencies (regional, state or federal). The base is further enhanced if the community has educational facilities that draw students from a wide area or if it is a regional trade center, a farm trade center, a tourist trade center or a transportation hub.

By having a diversity of basic employers, the economic health is not tied to one source which, if it should fail, would have a major depressing impact upon the community.

For a complete checklist on the economic health of a community, see Checklist 2, How To Rate the Economic Health of a Community, page C-5.

PROPERTY TAXES

The relationship between the property taxes in a community (known as ad valorem tax) and the services provided by a community affects the value of houses. Generally speaking, communities that must obtain the majority of their property taxes from homeowners will provide fewer services per dollar of taxes received than communities that have substantial non-residential properties to derive tax income from.

These non-residential tax payers are industries, commercial and investment properties and institutions (excluding tax-exempt schools, places of worship, government owned property and other properties that do not have to pay property taxes). The reason for this is that in most communities the bulk of the tax dollar goes into the cost of education. Non-residential properties cost less for the community to service in relationship to the taxes they pay, thereby reducing the burden of taxes on the homeowners.

The traditional language of the tax collector and assessor has always made it unnecessarily complicated to compare the tax structure of a community with that of a competing community. The tax collector and assessor use the terms *assessed value*, which is some percentage of market value (often the claimed percentage differs from actual percentage), and *mill rate*, which is an obsolete term referring to the tax rate per dollar of assessed value. Both of these terms confuse people.

To really understand how a community is taxing the property, it is necessary to think in terms of what percentage the annual real estate taxes are compared to the actual value of the property being taxed.

For example, a house in Community "A" has a market value of $75,000 and is assessed at 50 percent of value. Its assessment would be $37,500. The tax rate in the community is 35 mills (a mill is 1/10th of a cent which means that the tax rate is $.035 per $1.00 of assessed value, or $3.50 per $100 of assessed value, or $35 per $1,000 of assessed value[1]) The annual property tax is $1,312.50.

In competing Community "B" another house has a market value of $55,000. It is assessed at 75 percent of value. Its assessment would be $41,250. The tax rate in this community is 29 mills. The annual property tax is $1,196.30.

Based on a comparison of just the mill rate or tax rate it appears that the tax rate in Community "B" is less than the tax rate in Community "A". Actually, the opposite is true as the taxes are based on both the mill rate and the assessed value percentage.

The worksheet in Figure 5 shows how to compare taxes by converting the actual taxes into a percentage of market value.

The percentage of taxes to market value is known as the effective tax rate. It can be used to compare taxes on different properties within a community or the taxes in different communities. However, despite its importance, analyzing the tax rate is not sufficient. Taxes must be analyzed together with the services they purchase.

The biggest portion of the property tax dollar goes toward financing education. In many areas, the quality of education offered in a community has a substantial effect upon home values. Often the competitive

---

[1] In some communities the tax rate is broken into separate rates for school taxes, utilities, county taxes, etc. When this is the situation, just add the rates together.

FIGURE 5
TAX COMPARISON WORKSHEET

Market value of property	$_____
Actual taxes	
mill rate × assessed value	$_____
Percentage of taxes to market value	
actual taxes ÷ market value	_____ %

Using this worksheet, here is how the taxes* on the house in Community "A" compare with the taxes on the house in Community "B."

HOUSE IN COMMUNITY A

Market value of property	$75,000
Actual taxes	
35 mills × $37,500	$1,312.50
Percentage of taxes to market value	
$1,312.50 ÷ $75,000	.0175 or 1.75%

HOUSE IN COMMUNITY B

Market value of property	$55,000
Actual taxes	
29 mills × $41,250	$1,196.30
Percentage of taxes to market value	
$1,196.30 ÷ $55,000	.0217 or 2.2%

It now becomes apparent that the taxes in Community "B" are substantially greater than the taxes in Community "A" based on the two houses.

---

* Some communities utilize an equilization factor which attempts to reduce the difference between the assessments in various communities in the state. When it is determined that the assessments in one community vary from the established norm set by the state, the community is required to adjust its assessments based on a factor determined by a state agency.

advantage a community enjoys because of its low taxes is a result of economics in the school system which result in poor schools. Even buyers with no school-age children will often consider the school system when selecting a house, since they know it will be an important factor when they sell.

It is becoming more difficult to ascertain the quality of a community school system. Real estate brokers, appraisers and lenders are sensitive to potential criticism when commenting on school systems. Often state boards of education issue reports that rank the schools in their state. Admissions personnel of colleges will often freely discuss the quality of various school systems. And parents whose children attend the local schools are, of course, good sources.

A personal visit to the schools often is an effective way to begin assessing the quality of available education. One item such a visit will indicate is the condition of the facilities. The buildings should be in good repair. There should be an indoor gym, a playground outside and lunch facilities. Whether or not the school, for lack of funds or facilities, is on double session or is scheduled for them in the foreseeable future is also significant.

A call to the superintendent of schools will answer one very important question: How many dollars per student are allocated? The more money spent per pupil, the better the teachers and facilities are likely to be, although this is not the sole factor to consider by any means.

GOVERNMENT AND COMMUNITY SERVICES

There is usually a relationship between the effective tax rate and the quality of services provided by the community. And the quality of the services provided by the community to its residents affects the value of the house within the community. All other things being equal, a community that has a municipal sewer system, free rubbish and garbage removal and good fire and police protection would be expected to have a higher effective tax rate than a competing community without some or all of these services or with a lower quality of services.

A stable, well-run city administration will provide easily understandable and strictly enforced codes, a good inspection program (building, plumbing, etc.), effective zoning regulations, efficient fire and police protection and maintenance (street repairing and cleaning, garbage pickup).

The quality of fire and police protection is not easy to evaluate, but the quantity is not hard to ascertain, and quantity can be important. Usually, the more vehicles the police and fire departments have, the larger they are and, theoretically, the better equipped to cover the city and its neighborhoods. Quality of police and fire protection can be checked by talking to local residents. A check of fire insurance rates in the area is one way to evaluate the quality of the fire protection.

CONVENIENCE OF SERVICES

In heavily populated communities most services required by typical homeowners are readily available. However, in remote, less populated areas, the availability or lack of services can influence the value of a home.

The list of such services is practically endless but it might include some of the following: airport, gas station, regional shopping centers (one with at least one department store), doctor's office, dentist's office, hospital, etc. The important factor to be aware of is not necessarily how far away any of these may be but rather how long it takes to get to them, either by car or by public transportation.

RECREATIONAL FACILITIES

The nearness of recreational facilities is another important value factor in many communities. Some communities owe their very existence to their proximity to bodies of water, mountains, and other recreational facilities. Traditionally homes close to water, golf courses, ski slopes, yacht clubs, etc. sell for substantially more money than similar houses farther away from the recreational facilities.

Even values in communities that are not associated with major recreational facilities are influenced by the general recreational facilities that are available such as concert halls, legitimate theaters, museums, skating rinks, sports stadiums, municipal swimming pools, municipal golf courses, country clubs, playgrounds and parks.

In rating a community, it is most important how the community's facilities compare with competing communities in the same region rather than how they compare with available facilities in remote cities.

**For a complete Community Rating checklist,
see Checklist 3, page C-7.**

NEIGHBORHOOD

A neighborhood was once defined as a segment of a community that gave a noticeable impression of unity. The unity might have been reflected in similar types of buildings or similar economic, religious, racial or ethnic status of most of the neighborhood residents. Some neighborhoods were occupied predominantly by workers from a local industry.

Today these characteristics still define some neighborhoods, but as indicators they are becoming less reliable. Today a neighborhood often will have residences mixed with industrial and commercial buildings. Likewise, people with a variety of economic, ethnic, racial and religious backgrounds are increasingly integrated together in the same neighborhood.

A neighborhood has recently been defined as "any separately identifiable cohesive area within a community with some community of interests shared by its occupants. It usually has recognized boundaries, which may be natural or man-made, and its own name, such as Old Town or Pidgeon Hill."[2]

When the neighborhood has been identified and its boundaries determined, it should then be analyzed. The purpose of the analysis is to determine its desirability as a place to live that will adequately fulfill the needs of the homeowner's whole family. The analysis will also help to forecast the future of the neighborhood in order to estimate the effect changes in the neighborhood may have on the value of the properties within its borders. Appraisers often divide the analysis of a neighborhood into four parts:

1. Physical or environmental
2. Social
3. Economic
4. Governmental

This same kind of analysis works equally well for home buyers.

PHYSICAL AND ENVIRONMENTAL FACTORS

There are 12 physical or environmental factors:[3]

1. Location within the community
2. Barriers and boundaries
3. Topography
4. Soil, drainage
5. Services and utilities
6. Proximity to supporting facilities
7. Street patterns
8. Pattern of land use
9. Conformity of structures
10. Appearance
11. Special amenities
12. Nuisances and hazards
13. Age and condition of residences and other improvements

For a complete Neighborhood Physical and Environmental Factors checklist, see Checklist 4, page C-9.

---

[2] George Bloom and Henry S. Harrison, *Appraising the Single Family Residence* (Chicago: American Institute of Real Estate Appraisers, 1979).

[3] Bloom and Harrison.

SOCIAL FACTORS

There are three primary social factors to consider:[4]

1. Population. The U.S. Census provides detailed information about most residential areas in this country on a block-by-block basis. This information can be used to provide data on any neighborhood once you have determined the boundaries of the neighborhood you are interested in. The data can be obtained from many libraries and, of course, census offices.

The population characteristics of a neighborhood do not provide an accurate means of measuring value trends. However, they may be useful to an individual home buyer in selecting a neighborhood.

2. Neighborhood Associations. Neighborhood associations are often formed on a voluntary basis by residents. Some consist of just tenants and some are a mixture of both owners and tenants. Block clubs are a typical form of this kind of association.

Some associations may be legal entities formed by the original developer as part of a Planned Unit Development or condominium development. This type of association may include all the property owners within defined boundaries. It often owns the open space land and the recreational facilities such as the swimming pool, club house, courts, golf course, etc. And it often has the right to assess each homeowner his share of the maintenance cost of the commonly owned property and facilities. (See Chapter 16 for further information on these associations.)

In addition to the maintenance of the common facilities, some neighborhood associations hire guards for security purposes. Other functions that some associations perform are collecting rubbish and garbage, removing snow, sweeping streets, providing and maintaining sewer disposal and water supply systems, providing police and fire protection and providing lifeguards at swimming facilities.

Another function of some neighborhood associations is to enforce private deed restrictions and covenants. Some such covenants give the association the right to approve the transfer of title of the property within the boundaries of the association and to control the rental of the property. The association may also have the right to approve the style and size of any new improvements. However, the courts have ruled that any restriction based on race, religion or national origin is completely unenforceable.

Some neighborhood associations are primarily interested in promoting social interaction among the neighborhood or block residents. Others are interested in neighborhood preservation and enhancement and

---

[4] Bloom and Harrison.

political lobbying efforts to prevent changes in property use and zoning laws believed to be detrimental to the neighborhood. Other activities include neighborhood improvement projects where members of the association perform all or some of the work on a voluntary basis, social gatherings, block parties, fairs, parades, etc. Obviously the level of activity of these organizations varies considerably. Some meet only occasionally and are very non-structured. Others meet quite frequently and are very structured with officers, directors, committees, etc.

The importance of these associations varies from neighborhood to neighborhood. Where the association controls important recreational facilities and/or provides substantial needed services, it can substantially affect the value of the property and the happiness of the residents within the neighborhood. On the other hand, those whose function is primarily social may have little or no effect on values.

3. Crime. The safety of personal property and the freedom from fear of physical violence is becoming an increasingly important matter. Today, the level of crime in a neighborhood and the adequacy of police protection provided by the community are factors that affect the value of property. Some neighborhoods have a reputation as places where a high crime level exists. This may cause some residents to flee the neighborhood and discourages others from buying homes there. Residents can work together to demand better police protection, increased street lighting and they can increase their own vigilance and reporting of suspicious activities to the police.

For a complete Neighborhood Social Factors checklist, see Checklist 5, page C-13.

ECONOMIC FACTORS

There are four important neighborhood economic factors:[5]

1. Relationship to Community Growth. Communities do not grow evenly in all directions. Houses in neighborhoods that are in the growth area of the community usually will increase in value faster than those in areas where there is little or no community growth.

2. Economic Profile of Residents. The income level of residents within a neighborhood tends to be reflected in the value of properties in that neighborhood. A large, well-maintained house in a low income neighborhood will be penalized for its location. On the other hand, an inferior house in a high income neighborhood will sell at a premium because of its location.

---

[5] Bloom and Harrison.

Probably one of the single most objective indicators in comparing neighborhoods is the median income of the neighborhood residents. This information can be obtained from the U.S. Census Bureau or a local library. In neighborhoods where the residents primarily receive their income from one or just a few sources, the value of property in that neighborhood is linked to the economic health of the employer or employers. Changes in the residents' purchasing power may result in changes in property values in the neighborhood.

3. New Construction and Vacant Land. Some neighborhoods are almost 100 percent developed. Construction on the few vacant lots probably will have little effect on the neighborhood. Other neighborhoods contain large tracts of vacant land, and what is built on these tracts may substantially affect the whole neighborhood. Good zoning regulations and/or deed restrictions can control the use of vacant land. However, if land is spot-zoned non-residential or if variances are granted permitting non-residential or high density residential construction, the new use may (but not always) have an adverse effect on the other properties in the neighborhood. Before buying a house in a neighborhood with a lot of vacant land, it is wise to find out what the proposed future uses are.

4. Turnover and Vacancy. Another objective tool to indicate the economic health of a neighborhood is the property turnover rate. Some turnover is a healthy sign. A stable neighborhood tends to hold the majority of its residents. The average marketing time of properties for sale is a useful indicator. When there is a significant number of houses that have been on the market over three months, it usually indicates a weak real estate market in the neighborhood especially if real estate activity in general is good. Another indicator of a weak market is when a significant number of houses are rented rather than sold.

For a complete Neighborhood Economic Factors checklist, see Checklist 6, page C-15.

GOVERNMENTAL FACTORS

There are four governmental factors:[6]

1. Taxation and Special Assessments. Government continues to play an increasingly important part in the quality of life in a neighborhood and the value of property. Property taxation may vary not only from community to community but also between neighborhoods within a community. In some neighborhoods there are special tax assessments for special services provided to the neighborhood such as sewers, private

[6] Bloom and Harrison.

beach associations, special fire protection, etc. Although generally higher taxes tend to reduce values, the value reduction may be offset by the extra service or facility which resulted in the higher taxes.

2. Public and Private Restrictions. Zoning regulations can be an important factor in maintaining the character of a neighborhood. Traditionally, politics play an important role in the zoning process and some zoning changes, variances and special exceptions have been based more on political expediency than on what was best for the existing residents of the neighborhood involved. The strict enforcement of zoning regulations and deed restrictions provides legal protection for the neighborhood against outside interests, nuisances and hazards.

3. Schools. The schools that serve a neighborhood often are an important factor to many potential home buyers. These buyers are attracted to neighborhoods which have the reputations for good schools. When the quality and reputation of schools decline, it is usually followed by a relative decline in housing values.

Schools have already been discussed in our community analysis earlier in this chapter. However, even within a community there may be a wide variety of school facilities. For example, one neighborhood may be served by a new, well-equipped grammar school while another neighborhood is served by an old school with poor equipment and lack of recreational areas.

The quality of a school's physical plants is easily judged by personal inspection. The quality of the education being offered within the physical plant is a more difficult item to judge objectively. The techniques discussed in the community analysis section can also be used to judge the quality of education being offered in neighborhood schools.

Whether the prospective home buyers have school-age children or not does not matter when it comes to a school quality investigation. The quality of schools will affect the property value regardless whether they have children attending or not.

4. Planning and Subdivision Regulations. When a neighborhood is still growing, the municipal government should plan for the growth. The plans should include a land use plan coupled with zoning regulations that will protect the integrity and character of the neighborhood. Plans are also needed for additional recreational facilities, schools, service areas, utilities, open spaces and other municipal services such as police and fire protection, and garbage removal. Poor planning and failure to provide increased services may lead to neighborhood disintegration.

For a complete Neighborhood Governmental Factors checklist, see Checklist 7, page C-17.

NEIGHBORHOOD LIFE CYCLES

GROWTH PERIOD

Over a period of years, neighborhoods go through cycles. The first cycle begins when the first buildings are constructed and the streets, utilities and other services are first installed. This cycle is known as the growth period. The growth period may last for only a year or two or it may continue for many years. It may continue until all the available land is used up or it may stop when, because of market conditions or financing factors, it is no longer possible for developers to make a profit on new construction in the neighborhood. Developers and builders will continue to build as long as they can make a profit on what they are building.

Land remains vacant usually because the cost of the land plus the cost of proposed improvements add up to a figure higher than what the finished property will sell for in the market. When a neighborhood is successfully developed new inhabitants are attracted and the neighborhood gains recognition. During this period values often increase at a rate greater than the average rate of increase in the community.

STABLE PERIOD

When the growth period ends, many neighborhoods enter into a long period of relative equilibrium. (Of course, if the forces that affect value change significantly, the neighborhood may start to decline shortly after the end of the growth period.) During this period of stability, change slows down but rarely stops completely. New construction may still continue on a limited basis as the relationship between costs, demand and financing fluctuate and from time to time make additional construction profitable. There is no automatic end to this period of stability. Historically, neighborhoods have remained stable 40 years, 50 years and some for even longer periods of time. Decline is not imminent in all older neighborhoods.

DECLINING PERIOD

The creation of new neighborhoods in the same or nearby communities or a change in the factors that affect value may put an existing neighborhood at a competitive disadvantage, and it may enter a period of decline. When this happens prices may be lowered to attract buyers to the neighborhood. When existing houses are too large they are often converted into multiple family dwellings. Often zoning enforcement will slacken and a variety of commercial uses will infiltrate the neighborhood. Another characteristic of a declining neighborhood is an overabundance of poorly maintained properties.

There are other warning signs that foretell a neighborhood's period of decline. The population may consist of a high percentage of unskilled workers and workers representing only one industry. Another sign may be a high percentage of older couples who are long-time residents and whose children are grown and have left home. Additional factors are many absentee owners, houses in foreclosure, an overabundance of "For Sale" signs and a decrease in rental rates.

When a new transportation system (such as a throughway or a subway) or a new industry is introduced into an area, it is certain to have a major impact on any nearby residential neighborhood. Often it is difficult to tell in advance whether the impact will be to stimulate neighborhood growth, slow it down or reverse it. For instance, a throughway that provides new access to a metropolitan area may make new job markets available to residents, but if the new highway cuts the neighborhood off from its own city center, there will be negative ramifications. A neighborhood, in a situation like this, will probably benefit and suffer at the same time.

The period of decline may end in several ways. Changes in the area may change the property use into commercial or industrial uses. When this happens the existing houses are either razed or converted into the new uses. This change may create a mixed use neighborhood where residential, commercial and industrial uses all co-exist. Or a neighborhood may enter a period of rebirth as a residential neighborhood.

REBIRTH

A period of neighborhood rebirth or rejuvenation may be the result of a change in the economic, social, physical, or governmental forces that affect the neighborhood. For example, a community may experience growth because of the expansion of its institutional, commercial or industrial facilities. This in turn may increase the demand for housing in neighborhoods near the expanded activity. Demand for housing in a neighborhood may also be increased by the introduction of new nearby transportation facilities such as a rapid transit line, new highway or public bus route. The increase in demand may also be caused by new schools, shopping facilities, hospitals, and recreational facilities.

Neighborhood rejuvenation may also be the direct result of organized activities by the government and private organizations. Redevelopment programs and historic renovations are examples of this type of activity.

We are starting to see more and more neighborhood rebirths—the end of periods of decline in our older neighborhoods. In addition to the above factors causing rejuvenation, changing life styles and the personal preferences of many people to live inside our older communities rather than in the suburbs are responsible for this phenomenon.

The neighborhood life cycle does not stop with a period of rebirth, however. Although there are few actual examples to go by, it is reasonable to assume that after a period of rejuvenation the neighborhood will again stabilize, may again go into a period of decline and again be rejuvenated, thus repeating the cycle all over again.

No one neighborhood is going to be superior in all ways when compared to other neighborhoods within the communities that your family has selected as suitable places to live. The use of the checklists referred to in this chapter will provide an objective evaluation of a neighborhood and will demonstrate how one neighborhood compares with another competitive neighborhood.

The final step in neighborhood selection is to consider the specific needs and desires of your family. If, for example, the family is more interested in a neighborhood with good schools than good recreational facilities, then obviously more weight in the selection process should be given to the schools.

CHAPTER 5
SITE

Once the region, community and neighborhood have been selected, the final location decision is the actual site[1] on which your new home is located. Choosing a site is, of course, a critical decision when you are building a home, but it is a genuine factor to consider even when looking at existing houses. Although this chapter deals primarily with considerations of vacant sites, the points made are also germane to buying an already-built house.

Site analysis can be divided into four parts:

1. Relationship to surroundings
2. On-site physical characteristics
3. Economic factors
4. Title and record data

The first step in selecting a site is to decide if it provides the amenities the family considers important. Start by considering the site's relationship to its surroundings. Because the location of the site is fixed, its surroundings have a significant effect both on the value of the site and the improvements constructed on it.

RELATIONSHIP TO THE SURROUNDINGS

What is happening in the immediate vicinity is of great importance. If most of the surrounding lots are improved with low-priced, one-story

---

[1] "In the specialized vocabulary of the real estate professional, *land* and *site* are *not* synonymous. *Land* means the surface of the earth which is unimproved by humans, plus a wedge-shaped subsurface piece that theoretically extends to the center of the globe and air rights extending upward to the sky. . . . *Site* is the land plus improvements that make it ready for use, including streets, sewer systems and utility connections."
From George Bloom and Henry S. Harrison, *Appraising the Single Family Residence* (Chicago: American Institute of Real Estate Appraisers, 1979), p. 104.

ranch style houses and the house on the site you are looking at is or will be a medium-value, two-story Colonial style house, it will be nonconforming to its neighbors. In general, maximum value will be achieved when your house reasonably conforms to those nearby in the neighborhood, although too much similarity is not good either.

The same principle applies to the orientation of the house on the site. If most of the houses in the neighborhood are set back 75 feet from the street and face the street, a site that requires, because of its physical characteristics, that the house be located 25 feet from the street and face the side of the lot might be less desirable.

Traffic flow also affects value and safety. Families with small children are often fearful about living on streets with fast-moving through traffic. Older neighborhoods tend to have streets that are arranged in grid patterns. Some of these streets become thoroughfares that carry fast, heavy traffic through the neighborhood. In newer neighborhoods the streets are often curved and many have dead ends. Heavy traffic is routed away from the interior streets. In some areas access to a site by a back alley or special service road adds to the site's value.

In any given neighborhood there is usually a variety of different types of buildings and activities that are desirable features. However, located too close to a home site, some of these uses create nuisances and thereby detract from the value of the site and its improvements. "Values of properties tend to be higher in neighborhoods that have accepted standards of public health, comfort and safety than those that do not. A nearby factory complex or the flight path of an adjacent airport can have a marked negative effect on the property values in a residential neighborhood. Effective barriers against such disturbances tend to create a premium."[2]

The following is a list of buildings and utilities that, when too close to a house, may decrease its value. On the other hand, having them a few blocks away may be very convenient:

1. Fire stations
2. Vacant houses
3. Schools
4. Funeral homes
5. Stores
6. Apartment houses
7. Motels
8. Restaurants and bars
9. Utility wires and poles
10. Noisy highways

---

11. Hospitals
12. Offices
13. Commercial buildings
14. Gas stations
15. Industries[3]

Access from a specific site to places of work, shopping and recreation by both automobile and public transportation should be considered, especially if there is some unique feature not typical of other houses in the neighborhood. For example, the site may be near the grammar school or a park or other recreational facility, making it easy for children to come and go without adult supervision.

ON-SITE PHYSICAL CHARACTERISTICS

Buying vacant sites can be very treacherous. Most architects, builders, REALTORS®, appraisers and others in the housing field can tell you personal experiences of people who have purchased sites for their homes and then run into all kinds of unexpected problems. Some of the problems were so bad that the sites turned out to be unusable for their intended purposes.

WATER

In order for a site to be usable for a home, there must be a suitable source of water. The best source of safe, pure water is from a municipal or public water company. It is "penny-wise and pound-foolish" to endanger the health of your family by not using public water when it is available. Also, FHA Minimum Property Standards (FHA-MPS) require that when a public water supply is available, it must be used, even when there seems to be an adequate well. Even the best well may not provide adequate water during a prolonged dry spell or may become polluted without the users being aware of the pollution.

When there is a public water supply in the neighborhood, it is necessary to determine whether it can be brought to the site and if there will be sufficient pressure. When there is not a public water supply it will be necessary to drill a well if one does not already exist. It is not considered satisfactory to obtain water from rivers, streams, lakes or rain catches as these sources will not provide a dependable supply of pure water on a year-round basis.

The FHA-MPS state, "A well shall be capable of delivering a sustained flow of five gallons per minute. The water quality shall meet the chemical and bacteriological requirements of the health authority having jurisdiction."

---

[3] Henry S. Harrison, *Houses—The Illustrated Guide to Construction, Design and Systems,* (Chicago: REALTORS NATIONAL MARKETING INSTITUTE®, 1976).

An artesian well is one drilled through impermeable strata, deep enough to reach water that is capable of rising to the surface by internal hydrostatic pressure. It still requires a pump to develop sufficient pressure for household use.

The only way to be sure a well meets these important standards is to have it tested professionally. Unfortunately, in spite of all of our scientific advances, there still is no reliable way to predict how deep it will be necessary to drill to reach water of sufficient quantity and purity to meet household needs.

WASTE DISPOSAL

Waste disposal is best accomplished through a municipal sewer system. This is the only way that anyone can be sure the waste is being disposed of without polluting the environment. It comes as no surprise to most people who have had to depend upon a septic system or a cesspool for waste disposal to learn that a U.S. Public Health Survey indicates that 50 percent of the existing systems are not continuously operating properly. How these systems operate is explained in more detail in Chapter 9.

It is possible to test whether a site will be satisfactory for a waste disposal system by digging a hole at least eight feet deep during the wettest month of the year. This is to test for a water table, which will affect the filtration capacity of a septic system. If the hole fills itself with water the location is not suitable for a waste system.

Another necessary test is a percolation test which measures the rate at which the soil will absorb water. One method is to dig a hole at least 36 inches deep and fill it with water. Each hour the depth of the water is measured. Anything less than an inch decrease in depth each 30 minutes is substandard. Again, this test should be done during the wettest season. The best sources to go to for professional information and testing of soil capabilities are qualified land brokers and engineering firms and the county or municipal sanitarian.

BEARING QUALITIES

Try to learn if the site was a land-fill. Also, test for the bearing quality of the subsoil. You hardly need to be reminded that you wouldn't want your house to settle before—or after—you do!

Another test that can be made on an undeveloped lot determines if the soil has the capacity to support the landscaping. This is a simple test and is a free service of the agricultural station of the U.S. Dept. of Agriculture. Either find the address in the yellow pages or contact your health officer.

LOT SIZE

So far we have discussed the ability of the site to bear the weight of the house, support landscaping, provide water and as a means of waste disposal. All of these factors must be considered in deciding how large the lot must be. In order to estimate a minimum satisfactory site size, first locate where the house will be, then establish the location of the septic system, together with its leaching fields (explained in Chapter 9) if there is no municipal sewer connection. If there is no public water, a location must be found for the well that will ensure it will not be polluted by yours or your neighbor's septic system.

LAYOUT

Mentally, lay out your terrace/patio, where you hope to entertain without the neighbors knowing the brand names of the refreshments you serve. Perhaps a swimming pool or tennis court fit into your plans— now you have to fit them into the lot, all the while trying to retain already-established trees and plantings.

DRAINAGE

Another overall consideration is how storm water will be carried off the site. Land that retains large puddles of water for days after a storm can present problems for your basement or even your slab foundation. Too much moisture retention affects many parts of the house including the exterior paint or finish.

OTHER CONSIDERATIONS

The analysis of a site's physical characteristics should also include consideration of its width and frontage, depth, size, shape and where there will be any excess land.

Consideration should also be given to how the street is or will be improved. Is the pavement in good condition and who is responsible for keeping it in good shape? If it is a private street, check into the details of how it is to be used and maintained.

It is vital that you know exactly what the flood hazard is of any site you are considering. You can determine this by looking up the site on a Flood Hazard Boundary Map (FHBM) which is prepared by the Federal Insurance Administration, a part of the Department of Housing and Urban Development. This agency also works closely with local governments, helping them to adopt and enforce land use and control measures aimed at avoiding or reducing future flood damage.

Many insurance agents, REALTORS®, appraisers and other real estate professionals have flood maps for their areas in their offices. Maps can also be found in the local government center in the building department, engineering office or town or city clerk's office. The FHA office that covers your region will have current maps as will lenders who often make them available to the public. If you cannot locate a map locally, contact the National Flood Insurance Program, Federal Insurance Administration, Department of Housing and Urban Development, Bethesda, Maryland 20034.

If the site or house you are considering is located in a designated flood zone it is subject to controls as to what can be constructed. Many lenders who give mortgages on houses in such areas will require that the property be insured with flood insurance (see Chapter 13).

Other potential hazards that should be investigated are potential earth and rock slides, earthquakes, dangerous ravines and dangerous bodies of water. In some areas there is an unusually high fire danger (the case in many areas of Southern California, for example).

ECONOMIC FACTORS

Most of the economic factors that affect the value of a site and the house constructed on it were previously discussed in Chapter 4. In addition to these factors, there may be some considerations that affect only a specific site.

A temporary factor that affects a property's value is the tax burden on the lot as compared to other similar lots in the neighborhood. When taxes are substantially higher or lower than on neighboring lots the differential can have an effect on the house's and/or lot's value and saleability.

Sometimes because of the lot's location or shape, the cost of connecting the utilities will be excessive as compared to similar services to other houses in the neighborhood. In extreme situations because of difficult topography, subsurface conditions or distances, utilities that are available to other houses in the neighborhood are not available to a specific site or if they are, they may not be as adequate. For example, because of the elevation of a site the water pressure may be lower than the pressure to other nearby houses.

When the house is on a private street, rather than a public street, besides the cost and responsibility of street maintenance, there may be extra costs for snow removal, rubbish and garbage collection and utility services. There may even be limited police and fire protection.

TITLE AND RECORD DATA

Closing and title data are covered in detail in Chapter 15. In this section we explain how a site is described, the zoning, easements, encroachments and other restrictions.

LEGAL DESCRIPTION

The legal description of the site needed for official documents may be based on one of four systems or, maybe a combination of several of these systems. The Metes and Bounds System was the first system used in this country. It is still the principal system used in the original 13 states. It identifies the property by delineating its boundaries in terms of a series of directions and distances. Each boundary line is described in succession, using a compass bearing and distance, until the entire parcel has been enclosed. Here is an excerpt from a typical metes and bounds description:

"North starting at a large rock on the edge of the highway 355 degrees, 30 minutes for a distance of 233 feet . . ."

The Geodetic Survey was originally done by the government to identify tracts owned by the federal government. It has been expanded to cover most of the country. The basis of the system is a network of "benchmarks" throughout the country which are precisely located by latitude and longitude.

The Lot and Block System applies in many urban communities. It grew with the communities where the developers had their tracts surveyed and platted into rectangular blocks and lots. Copies of the plat were filed in local government record offices for permanent reference. Individual sites were identified by the use of lot and block numbers.

The most exact system, used in all except the 13 original states, is the Government Survey System. It divides an area into units approximately 24 miles square. Because of the curvature of the earth each unit is slightly different in size and shape. The 24-mile square unit is divided into areas six miles square called townships which in turn are divided into 36 one-mile squares called sections which are numbered consecutively, beginning with the northeast corner. Base lines running east and west and meridians extending north and south are used. This system allows for an accurate, precise description of property which is more difficult to obtain with the other three systems.

ZONING AND OTHER PUBLIC RESTRICTIONS

Zoning regulations control the general use to which property is put. They vary considerably from community to community. If the site is undeveloped, these regulations must be checked to see if the proposed improvement is permitted on the site. Sometimes it is possible to get a variance to permit a use not otherwise allowed by the zoning regulations if it can be proven to the zoning authority that a hardship would be incurred if the proposed improvement is not permitted.

Besides use, zoning ordinances often control the distance improvements must be from each edge of the lot. These restrictions are known as front, side and rear yard requirements. Zoning regulations also often control the size of the improvements, parking requirements and a variety of other factors that vary from community to community.

Sometimes the zoning of an area will change after the improvements have already been constructed. The improvements which do not comply with the new zoning regulations then become known as nonconforming uses. This means that the present use usually can be continued. However, when a nonconforming use exists the regulations should be checked to see what happens in the event of a major fire or other interruption of the use.

Each site has other public restrictions and regulations which are special for every community. There may be a general building code, plumbing code, electric code and special fire regulations. Environmental regulations govern inland wetlands, tidal wetlands and flood plains.

Riparian rights deal with the rights of owners whose lands abut a body of water. It controls the use of this water by the adjoining land owners. Riparian rights may have a significant effect on the value of a site. Communities' health codes usually have jurisdiction over the water supply, including wells, sewers, waste removal and septic tank systems. All of these factors affect the usability of your property.

PRIVATE RESTRICTIONS

In addition to the public regulations, many deeds contain private restrictions and stipulations. A title search will reveal all of the private restrictions. In more than one instance a title search has saved a would-be owner from a fate worse than death! Some deeds contain such elements as the type of structure which can be built; size and design; the price or value of the structure; minimum two or four-acre lots; whether or not you can park your truck in your driveway or hang your laundry out to dry on a backyard clothesline—all these and more may have been already regulated by the prior decisions of someone else.

Private covenants are agreements made between property owners to restrict the use of their properties, resulting in mutual advantage. When a restrictive covenant is entered into, each property owner is required to comply with the covenant's restrictions. One owner has the right to enforce compliance with the restriction by the other parties to the agreement. Usually, these restrictions are established by a developer of a residential subdivision, a redevelopment agency or by members of a neighborhood association.

Normally it is the intention of those who enter into such agreements to make them "run with the land," meaning the agreement is binding not only on the parties who sign it but also on successive owners.

Restrictive covenants usually must be negative in nature rather than affirmative—they can stop the property owners from doing certain things but cannot place a burden upon them to take any kind of positive action. However, a party wall agreement may require some positive requirement should you elect to raze your improvements.

EASEMENTS

Easements are rights extended to non-owners of a property to use the property for some specific limited purpose. Typical easements give public utilities the right to cross the property with utility poles and wires, pipes and tracks. Other types of easements give non-owners the right to remove soil, mine minerals and use the air above the surface.

Sometimes an easement exists that has not yet been used. For example, you might purchase a property with no visible easements only to find that a high voltage power transmission line will soon be constructed which will cross your property.

ENCROACHMENT

An encroachment exists when the improvements on one property extend over the property line onto an abutting property. It is a two-way street. Your improvements may be on your neighbor's property or theirs may be on yours. Unless steps are taken to have these improvements removed, they eventually may have a permanent right to stay where they are.

A survey of the site by a registered surveyor is the best way to determine if there are any encroachments. The surveyor, for a small extra charge, will put markers on the boundaries so you will know where they are. The surveyor will also indicate the position of any existing improvements, and will determine if their location conforms to the existing zoning regulations. Often a mortgage lender will insist upon a current survey as a condition to granting a mortgage loan. Every home or site buyer should seriously consider obtaining a current survey prior to taking title to the property.

For a complete checklist on the material in this chapter, see Checklist 8, Site, page C-19.

CHAPTER 6
INTERIOR DESIGN
AND LAYOUT

The interior design of a house means different things to different people. Utility requirements and budget allowances of families vary as does what aesthetically appeals to them. Therefore, house designs will also vary to meet these needs, tastes and budgets.

However, just as house designs vary, they are also similar. Regardless of the size or cost of the house, from cottage to castle, each contains certain common characteristics. Usually there is a kitchen, living room, possibly a dining room, bedrooms and bathrooms. The way in which these rooms are arranged within the house is referred to as the interior design or layout, and like the "little girl who had a little curl," . . . it can be "very, very good" or it can be "horrid."

One definition of interior design is the method by which we enclose living space in such a way as to provide maximum utility to satisfy our needs, together with maximum amenities to please the senses, on the selected site within the budget available.

In good design there is a delicate balance between reason and aesthetics. This can be best demonstrated by the concept of zones.

Looking at homes on the market, you should pay particular attention to the interior zoning concepts discussed in this chapter. And if you are planning to design your own home, no matter how original and uniquely yours the ideas are, you should not stray from the concept of zones.

Unfortunately, even new homes are not always laid out to utilize space well. Even worse are the older homes which appear to have been modeled after a maze.

It is, of course, not necessary to buy or build a house that subscribes to every zoning concept in this chapter But you will find that a house conforming to as many of the basic zoning tenets will be a comfortable, easy, unstressful place to live.

ZONES WITHIN A HOUSE

A house can be divided into several basic zones. The private/sleeping zone contains the bedrooms, bathrooms and dressing rooms. The living/social zone consists of the living room, dining room, recreation room, den or enclosed porch. The working/service zone consists of the kitchen, laundry, pantry and other work areas. Ideally, the three zones should be separated from each other so that activities in one zone do not interfere with activities in another. In addition to the three zones there are circulation areas consisting of halls and stairs plus guest and family entrances.

The private/sleeping zone should be located so that it is insulated from the noises of the other two zones. It should be possible to move from the bedrooms to the bathroom in this zone without being seen from the other zones.

The working/service zone is the nerve center of the house. From here household activities are directed. In fact, the relationship between the kitchen and the rest of the house is the key to good interior layout. From the kitchen it should be possible to control both the guest and family entrances, activities in the sleeping/private and living/social zones plus activities in the porch, patio and backyard areas. This is a difficult bill to fill, but we'll show how it is done in well-zoned houses.

The guest entrance should lead into the center of the house. From here there should be direct access to living areas, the guest closet and the guest lavatory. A noise and visibility barrier should exist between the guest entrance and the sleeping/private area.

The family entrance ideally should be from the garage, carport or breezeway into the kitchen. It should be possible to carry the groceries from the automobile into the house without getting wet in inclement weather. However, traffic from this entrance should not have to penetrate the work triangle of the kitchen. And the circulation should be such that it is possible to move from the work/service zone to the private/sleeping zone without going through the living/social zone.

If the house has a basement it should have a separate outside entrance. The inside entrance should lead into a circulation area that in turn has access to the private/sleeping zone and living/social zone and both the guest and family entrances without going through the living room or the kitchen work triangle.

POOR FLOOR PLAN

Here is a list of some of the most common floor plan deficiencies (based on a large national survey of homeowners):

1. Front door entering directly into living room.
2. No front hall closet.

FIGURE 6
ZONING: ONE-STORY HOUSE

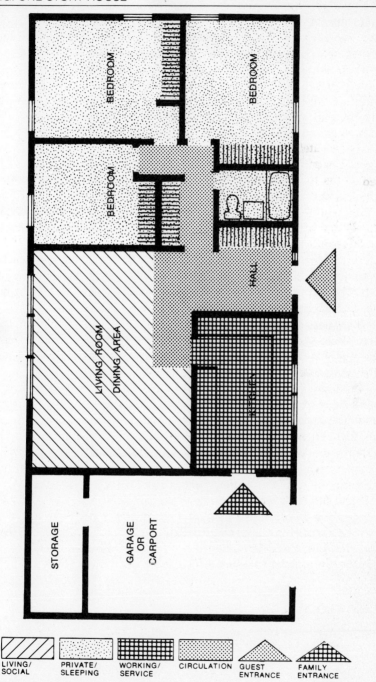

BEDROOM

BEDROOM

BEDROOM

HALL

LIVING ROOM
DINING AREA

STORAGE

GARAGE
OR
CARPORT

LIVING/
SOCIAL PRIVATE/
SLEEPING WORKING/
SERVICE CIRCULATION GUEST
ENTRANCE FAMILY
ENTRANCE

FIGURE 7
ZONING: TWO-STORY HOUSE

First Floor

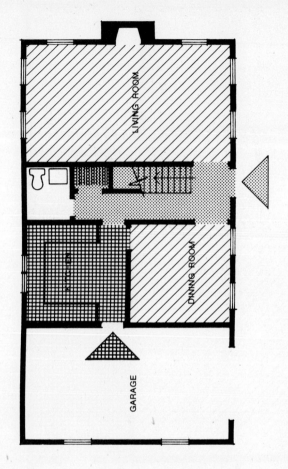

LIVING/
SOCIAL

PRIVATE/
SLEEPING

WORKING/
SERVICE

CIRCULATION

GUEST
ENTRANCE

FAMILY
ENTRANCE

Figure 7, continued

Second Floor

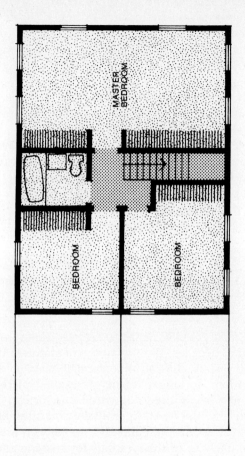

3. No direct access from front door to kitchen, bathroom and bed-rooms without passing through other rooms.
4. Rear door not convenient to kitchen and difficult to reach from street, driveway and garage.
5. No comfortable space for family to eat in or near kitchen.
6. A separate dining area or dining room not easily reached from kitchen.
7. Stairway off a room rather than a hallway or foyer.
8. Bedrooms and bathrooms so located as to be visible from living room or foyer.
9. Walls between bedrooms not soundproof (best way to accomplish this is to have them separated by a bathroom or closets).
10. Recreation room or family room poorly located.
11. No access to the basement from outside the house.
12. Outdoor living areas not accessible from kitchen.
13. Walls cut up by doors and windows making it difficult to place furniture around room.

For a complete Interior Zoning checklist, see Checklist 9, page C-21.

LIVING ROOM

In the past several decades, the function and status of the living room have undergone a slow, almost imperceptible change. The realization that the living room no longer retains its exalted place as the family living center is just beginning to dawn on our society. The old "front room" is no longer in the front, figuratively and often literally as well.

Today, the family room, the patio and the kitchen are more lived-in and much more likely to be the locations for relaxing and entertaining. As these grew and developed, the size and importance of the living room diminished proportionately.

However, graceful living is still very much a part of the cherished traditions of many families and the living room still holds its place of importance for them.

As is the case with the other rooms in the well-planned house, the size and use of the living room should be determined by the size, make-up and attitudes of the family—hence, by its needs. If there is also a family room, this must be considered in relationship to the living room.

LOCATION

The old custom of always locating the living room in the front of the house has all but been discarded since the family room has become so overwhelmingly popular.

The location should be appropriate to the house and family. It should

FIGURE 8
MINIMUM SIZE LIVING ROOM

For a typical three-bedroom house a living room should have minimum dimensions of 11 by 16 feet (170 square feet). The width should never be less than 11 feet. Recommended living room size is 12 by 18 feet.

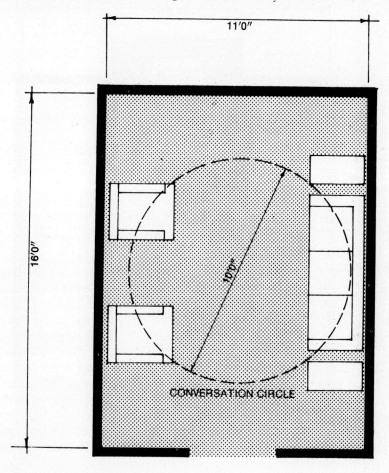

FIGURE 9
LONG LIVING ROOM

A dining area at one end of a living room demands that the dimensions of the room increase to 16 by 26 feet or more. A width of 14 feet is recommended for good furniture arrangement.

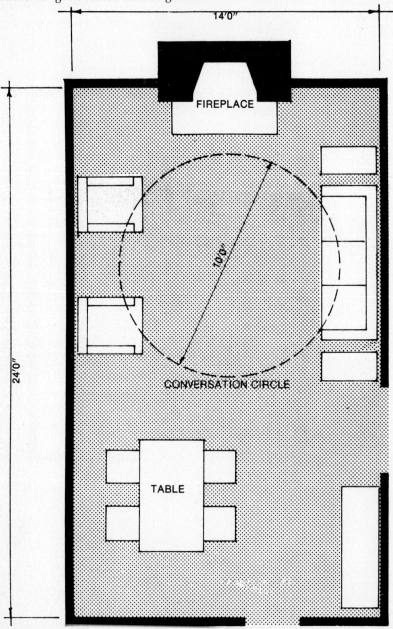

FIGURE 10
LONG AND WIDE LIVING ROOM

Ideally, there should be no traffic through a living room. However, when the layout of the house demands living room traffic, a long and wide living room, with a width of 15 or 16 feet, is necessary in order to route traffic outside the conversation area.

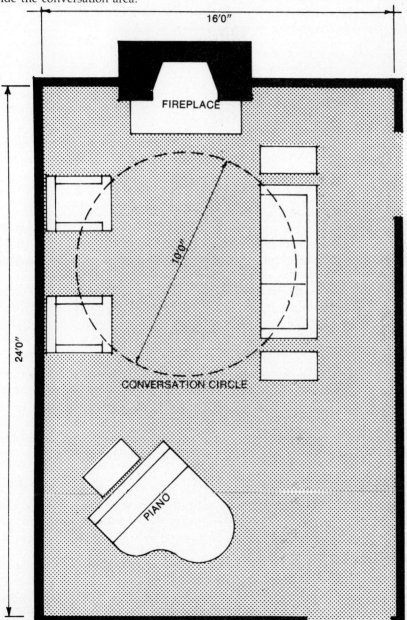

not be a passageway for traffic, but normal circulation should be easy. The room should be in a position to supplement the dining and outdoor entertaining areas. In many houses, one end of the living room is the dining area, so it must have good juxtaposition with the kitchen/service area.

If there is a fireplace it should be out of the way of traffic. And the area immediately adjacent to the fireplace should allow enough space for conversational furniture groupings.

SIZE AND LAYOUT

Because the living room concept has become vague and varied, it is difficult to recommend specific room dimensions. Shape, layout and special interest considerations are every bit as important as square footage.

Figures 8, 9 and 10 show various sizes and shapes of living rooms. The "recommended" sizes are those guidelines set by the Federal Housing Administration in its Minimum Property Standards.[1]

STORAGE

Storage for the living room should include a closet outside the main entrance for coats and other street clothing, umbrellas and raincoats. It should be spacious enough to accommodate guests' clothing, particularly outerwear.

Many living rooms have storage space for books, radio, stereo, records, newspapers and magazines, ash trays and coasters and stationery and writing equipment.

VENTILATION

Ventilation areas should exceed 10 percent of the floor area. Proper ventilation is particularly important where there is a fireplace, for both proper draw and fresh air circulation. Cross ventilation in the living room is desirable but, where there are large glass doors which slide open, not always necessary. A door may be considered part of the cross ventilation system since it too creates desired air circulation.

HEATING

Baseboard and other similar types of heating units do not interfere with furniture arrangements. Where there are forced hot air vents and cold air return ducts they should not be blocked by large furniture pieces like chairs, divans or chests.

---

[1] Throughout this chapter "FHA-MPS" minimum and recommended room sizes refer to the Minimum Property Standards set by the Federal Housing Administration of the Department of Housing and Urban Development.

LIGHTING

Natural lighting can be achieved best by correct and attractive window treatment. The newest innovations in artificial light add tremendously to the aesthetics of the living room. Ideally lighting is done best if it can be incorporated into the room during the building stage.

Adequate electric outlets should be readily available in the living room so that there is flexibility in arranging furniture and lamps to serve the seating plans. Nothing detracts more from good decor than lengthy wires running along the floor.

CONVERSATION AREAS

The ideal conversation area is a circle approximately 10 feet in diameter. Furniture groupings should be arranged with this in mind. The family and/or guests are more comfortable when seated within this range since most people like to congregate in small groups whether in a large or a small room. Within the 10-foot circle they can see each other easily and communicate comfortably without shouting. A large room may require several conversation centers of this size if this principle is followed. When the living room has a fireplace it is desirable to make it the focal point of furniture in one of the conversation circles.

For a complete Living Room checklist, see Checklist 10, page C-23.

KITCHEN

Today's kitchen is essentially a result of the comparatively recent revolution in kitchen equipment. With the exception of the same mouth-watering odors which emanate from it, the modern kitchen bears little resemblance to one of even 25 years ago. The preparation of food has become only one of the kitchen's many functions. It is a gathering place for the family and most likely the place where the family eats. The kitchen is often a laundry center. And it can also serve as an "office" or business center for family financial planning.

The kitchen can be a marvel of versatility, constituting the major part of the work area in the average house. As such, it deserves the greatest attention as you inspect houses or plan to build a new one.

LOCATION

The location of the kitchen in the house should be planned to fit into your family life. Whether it should be in the front or back of the house should be determined by style, site, view, exposure or other variables. There should be direct access from the kitchen to the dining area and to the front or guest entrance. Access to an outdoor eating area, patio or

FIGURE 11
PARALLEL WALL (GALLEY) KITCHEN

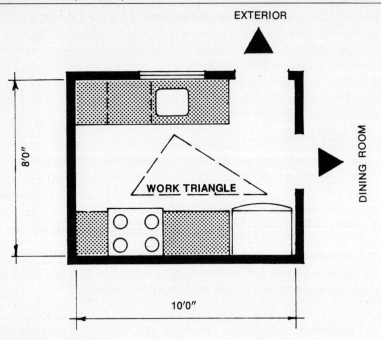

FIGURE 12
SINGLE WALL (GALLEY) KITCHEN

The total of the three sides of the Work Triangle should not exceed 22 feet.

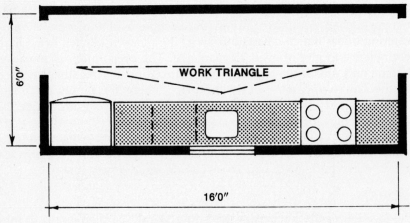

FIGURE 13
"L" KITCHEN

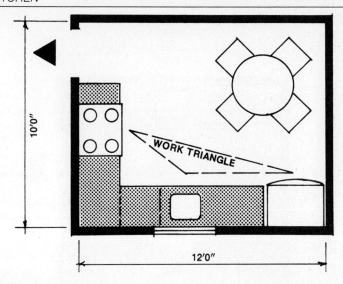

FIGURE 14
"U" KITCHEN

The total of the three sides of the Work Triangle should not exceed 22 feet.

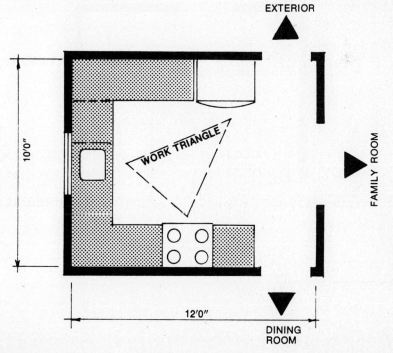

FIGURE 15
BROKEN "U" KITCHEN

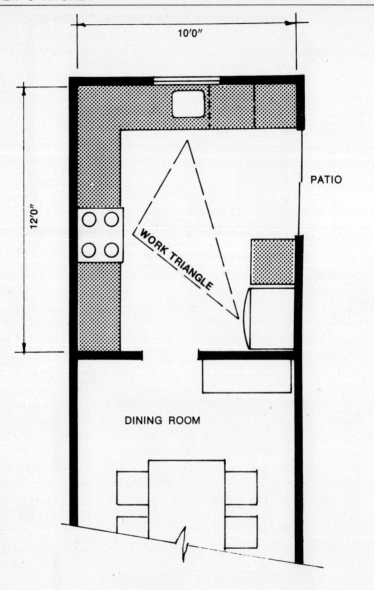

The total of the three sides of the Work Triangle should not exceed 22 feet.

porch should be from the kitchen and/or dining room. If there are children in the family, the kitchen should be located adjacent to or have a good view of the play area. Psychological studies of children's play habits have proven that small children want and need to have an adult within their view. It is also desirable that the kitchen entrance be close to the garage, breezeway or carport.

If there is a family room, the kitchen should be open to it wherever possible. Space for storage, utility cabinets, eating, laundry facilities, a serving counter and a planning area with a desk all should be incorporated whenever possible.

What a kitchen should not be is a main thoroughfare for the rest of the house. Any through-traffic should bypass this important work area.

SIZE AND LAYOUT

The size of the kitchen depends on factors such as the space available, the number of people in the family, the kind of equipment desired and what activities other than those directly associated with food preparation will be carried on there.

For houses with a floor area of less than 1,000 square feet, the recommended standards are for a small kitchen of 8 by 10 feet to 10 by 10 feet. The standards for houses with 1,000 to 1,400 square feet are 10 by 10 to 10 by 12 feet. Liberal standards for houses over 1,400 square feet in area are 10 by 12 feet and over.

When kitchen layout finally caught up to the progress made in kitchen equipment, the concept of "work triangle" emerged. It has yet to be improved upon. The triangle is applicable to each of the five basic kitchen shapes: the L-shape, the U-shape, the corridor (galley) shape, the broken U-shape and the straight line shape. Other good kitchen shapes are possible as long as there is sufficient wall space for appliances and the necessary cabinet and counter space.

There are three essential work areas of use and activity which comprise the kitchen triangle. These "centers" are the refrigerator area, sink-wash-preparation area and range-serve area. The centers can be arranged in any logical way, determined by the space available and the personal preference for one particular center over another. A fourth separate center is often added, for "planning." This usually includes a desk for menus, cookbooks, stationery, a family activities calendar and the telephone. Generally this area is located outside the triangle.

However the kitchen is arranged, work should flow in a normal sequence from one center to another. Ideally, no traffic should move through this work triangle. Properly establishing the location of the windows and doors and the traffic pattern ensures efficient use of the work centers. The counters of two or more centers can be combined, but dual-use counters should be wider wherever possible. The amount of wall space available for cabinets in the kitchen is affected by the placement of the windows. Most building standards require that the glass area should equal at least 10 percent of the floor area of the room. The window-over-the-sink concept is still the best plan, aesthetically and otherwise. It is unsafe to place a window over a range.

COUNTERS AND CABINETS

Cabinet space should be planned with care and thought. It takes little extra effort to make the difference between good utilization of space or expensive waste. Some common and glaring errors found in a sampling of kitchens (mostly in smaller homes) are insufficient base and wall cabinet storage, too little cabinet space, wasted wall space, no counter beside the refrigerator and insufficient space in front of the cabinets and appliances.

Kitchen storage is judged by its "base cabinet frontage," the length of accessible cabinet space in total. Space under the sink, although useful, is not included in base-cabinet frontage since it does not have multiple shelves. Turn-around or lazy-Susan corner cabinets add extra storage space equal to an additional six inches in base-cabinet length. General recommended standards for base cabinet frontage area are: minimum, six feet; medium, eight feet and liberal, 10 feet. The standard counter width is 25 inches.

Wall cabinets should be installed 15 inches above the counter top of the base cabinet. This provides sufficient room for blenders, toasters, mixers and all the other luxury items-turned-necessities which the modern homemaker enjoys. Cabinets should be located above the counter for each work center in the kitchen.

For a complete Kitchen checklist, see Checklist 11, page C-25.

DINING ROOM AND DINING AREA

The question today is not where to put the dining room but whether to have one at all. If space permits, it is a room desired by many homemakers. However, the trend is toward "space in which to dine" and the separate dining room is now often considered an amenity. Now Grandma sets a table for 12 or more comfortably on Thanksgiving in space which the rest of the year serves as a living area for her sewing, bridge and social activities. When the budget is tight in building a new home, it is usually the dining room which is most expendable.

Acceptable alternatives to the dining room are dining areas, extra-large kitchens which provide space for family meals, and possibly the family room or living room and the patio in season. A common compromise is a dining "L" between the living room and kitchen. This is usually furnished with a drop leaf or other expandable type of table, several

FIGURE 16
MINIMUM SIZE DINING ROOM—TWO-BEDROOM HOUSE

FHA minimum dining room size for a two-bedroom house is 100 sq. ft.

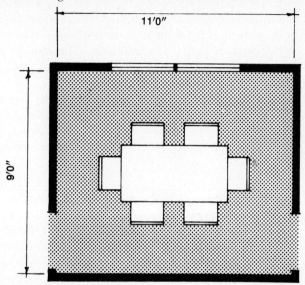

FIGURE 17
MINIMUM SIZE DINING ROOM—THREE AND FOUR-BEDROOM HOUSE

FHA minimum dining room size for three and four-bedroom houses are 110 sq. ft. and 120 sq. ft. respectively.

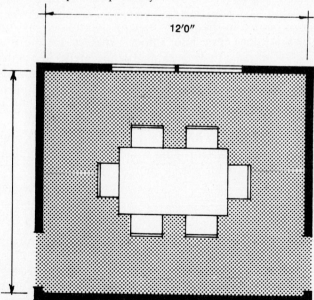

chairs, and, if possible, one other piece of furniture such as a serving cart, cabinet, hutch or lowboy to provide storage space for linens, dishes and silverware.

Requirements for a dining room or a dining area are identical. Access from the kitchen service area to the dining table should be short and direct. Ten to 15 percent of the floor area should be given to windows in order to provide adequate light and ventilation. One wall should be free of windows or doors to ensure that not all of the wall area is cut up, thereby precluding good furniture arrangement.

The size of the separate dining room or area obviously depends upon what circulation exists through the room, as well as its function for dining. Since the ideal seating situation is to have a clear three and one-half feet on all sides of the dining room table, it is best for the dining room to be at least 12 feet wide.

For a complete Dining Room and Dining Area checklist, see Checklist 12, page C-27.

BEDROOMS

A bedroom is no longer just a place in which to sleep or dress. It is a place where one enjoys reading or lazy contemplation, a place to unwind and relax during the waking hours. For children it harbors games, books and other treasures.

NUMBER OF BEDROOMS

The number of people in the family usually determines the number of bedrooms in the house they buy. Other variables are the number of adults and children, what their particular requirements in a bedroom are and, of course, the budget. As construction costs have escalated, the size of the bedroom has diminished. Therefore, the most important consideration is still that of its main function: to accommodate beds for sleeping.

In many markets houses with fewer than three bedrooms often sell at a substantial discount. Therefore, three is the minimum number of bedrooms all except very small houses should have.

LOCATION

Location of bedrooms shares equal importance with size in good planning. The relationship of the bedrooms to the other areas of the house and to each other varies with the type of the house.

Whatever the house plan, however, bedrooms should be reached directly from a hall, be removed from the living/social zone and working/ service zone and be directly accessible to at least one bathroom without observation in ordinary circumstances.

FIGURE 18
MINIMUM SIZE BEDROOM—SINGLE BED

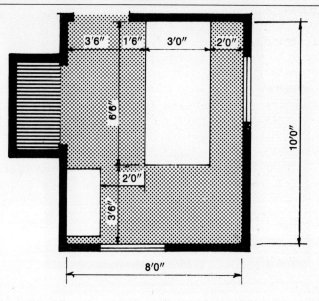

FIGURE 19
RECOMMENDED SIZE BEDROOM—SINGLE BED

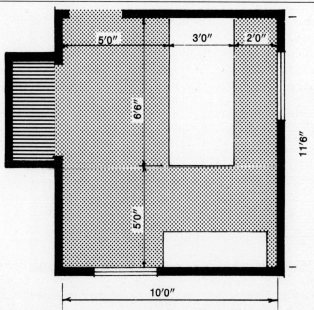

FIGURE 20
MINIMUM SIZE BEDROOM—DOUBLE BED

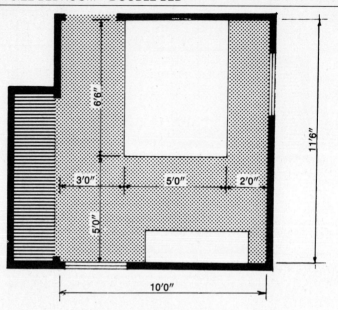

FIGURE 21
RECOMMENDED SIZE BEDROOM—DOUBLE BED

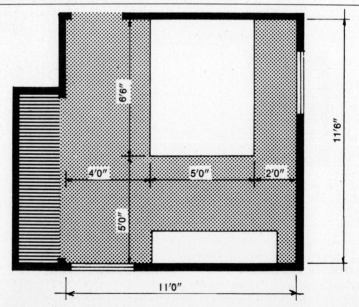

FIGURE 22
MINIMUM SIZE BEDROOM—TWIN BEDS

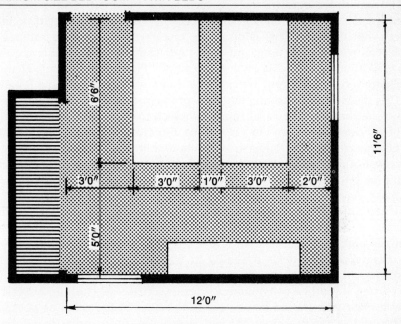

FIGURE 23
RECOMMENDED SIZE BEDROOM—TWIN BEDS

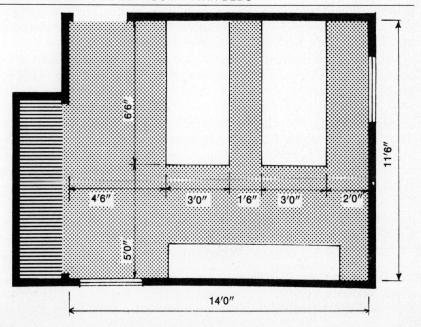

SIZE AND LAYOUT

The square footage will vary in each room, but the need for space for adequate movement and circulation is a minimum requirement no matter what the size. This is also true of clearances, general outlines of closets, window locations and entry. A bath in the master suite requires a wall interruption of its own, for example. Figures 18 through 23 show illustrations of different types of bedroom sizes and possible layouts.

As the size of the room increases, problems of layout decrease. There is more uninterrupted wall space in which to place furniture and allow for windows, doors and in some cases, radiators. The wall area or usable room perimeter length has to accommodate the bed or beds and usually a chest of drawers, a dresser and a chair. Other furniture often includes one or two night tables, a dressing table and perhaps a desk and a chaise.

Space allowance must be added for making the bed and for cleaning under it. Therefore, specific clearance distances for use and circulation are as important in considering the layout as are furniture dimensions.

Clearance should be provided in front of the dresser or chest for movement in pulling out drawers. The space and floor area required for dressing should be convenient to closets, dresser or chest and dressing table/chair and should be as near to the door of the room as possible. This allows for the most efficient use of the traffic area. It has been determined that the average adult needs an area of 42 inches in diameter for dressing. Some larger new homes accommodate this with the luxury of a dressing room in combination with the bedroom and bath.

Doors should never be placed so as to open back against the wall and should never interfere with other doors. They also should be placed so as not to interfere with beds and other furniture.

Minimum code requirement of MPS for window area in relation to the bedroom area is 10 percent. Windows should be placed to provide for the best use of light, sun and ventilation. They should be located to allow free wall space for the furniture and doors. The increase in popularity of bedroom air conditioners might be a factor where window planning would be affected by installation of a cooling unit. Some of the more expensive homes today feature entire bedroom walls of glass which are designed to slide open with screen protection, thus providing excellent ventilation.

For best ventilation, windows on adjoining walls should be placed away from corners on as long a diagonal as possible with one another. Cross ventilation wherever possible is most desirable.

LIGHTING

Proper lighting enhances the desired climate of relaxation. At the same time it must illuminate different areas more than others. There are three general sources of artificial light in a bedroom: the ceiling light, which should be of low intensity; brighter intensity lights for the dressing table or, if there is none, for the dresser mirror; and a light for the night table or tables. A switch control at the room entrance should turn on one of these sources. Different intensities of light make the room more interesting and attractive. Glare and reflection are eliminated and the walls and draperies have a softer glow.

In more sophisticated and expensive houses, use of structural lighting, such as soffit lighting, luminous ceiling panels or lighting under valances is both attractively decorative and functional. Lighting can be controlled by dimmers to achieve the proper intensity desired at any given time. Diffused lighting directs light to the ceiling or uses one of the many new types of diffusing materials along with structural lighting.

CLOSETS

Each bedroom should have at least one closet with these recommended minimums:

1. Depth, two feet clear for required area.
2. Width, three feet clear.
3. Height, (a) minimum: adequate to permit five feet clear hanging space for at least the required width; (b) maximum: lower shelf should not be over 74 inches above the floor of room.
4. One shelf and rod with at least eight inches clear space over shelf.

Bedroom closets serve as clothing storage primarily but also store hobby or special articles, books, radios and built-in TVs. The children's bedrooms, ideally, should have clothes closets with movable hooks and shelves, a rod which can be elevated as children grow and their clothing becomes larger, plus storage for hobbies, games, books and equipment.

If sliding doors are used, half of the closet can be exposed at once. Swinging or hinged doors (either singly or in a pair) expose the entire closet at once, but they open into the room and take up space. Care must be taken that they do not hit the furniture or another door.

Bedroom closets should have an electric light installed—preferably one that automatically turns off and on as the door is closed and opened. To avoid a fire hazard the light should be placed so that flammable material (i e , plastic cleaner's bags) cannot come in contact with the bulb.

For a complete Bedroom checklist, see Checklist 13, page C-29.

BATHROOMS AND LAVATORIES

The American bathroom continues to grow in size and splendor. It has become a major selling point in new homes, and next to the kitchen is the most important interior influence in selling houses. Features that were once considered major luxuries and found only in expensive custom homes are becoming more commonplace. These include partitioned toilets, twin wash basins, sunken tubs, bidets and ultraviolet lamps among other amenities.

NUMBER AND LOCATION

There is no universally accepted formula to establish the number of bathrooms and lavatories considered adequate for any given house. Such factors as regional customs, social status, ethnic background, size, shape and layout of the house as well as the individual family size and habits must all be taken into consideration.

In most areas the minimum acceptable standard for a three-bedroom house is one full bath with a tub and shower combination plus a lavatory. Many three-bedroom houses have a bathroom off the master bedroom, another full bath off the hallway in the bedroom area of the house and a lavatory near either the front or rear entrance. Another minimum standard is a bathroom or lavatory on each floor. If there is a maid's room or guest room there should be a separate bathroom in that area too. Custom-built luxury houses often have a full bathroom for each bedroom.

Interior bathrooms (bathrooms with no windows) are growing in popularity and have many advantages. Ventilation must be mechanical and therefore does not depend upon an open window which is drafty and during part of the year must be kept closed anyway. Cold and dirt will not come in through windows, and no curtains, shades or blinds are needed. Additional wall space is available for cabinets, mirrors and towel bars.

Entrances to bathrooms should be private. It should be possible to get from each bedroom to a bathroom without being seen from another area of the house, especially living areas where guests are entertained.

The soundproofing of the bathroom can be accomplished in several ways. If possible, walls between bathrooms and bedrooms should contain closets which make excellent sound barriers (see Figure 28). If this is not possible, soundproofing can be accomplished with an extra layer of Sheetrock, staggered studs or insulation batts nailed between the studs—or ideally, all three of these methods.

SIZE AND LAYOUT

Figures 24 through 28 show the FHA minimum size bathrooms and some recommended sizes and layouts for compartmented bathrooms and a bathroom using closets as sound barriers. Ideally, the bathroom should have one wall long enough to allow the toilet to be on the wall opposite the tub rather than between the tub and basin, which is unsatisfactory. The door should be able to swing in without hitting a fixture.

The utility of the bathroom is increased when a separate toilet compartment is created or two sinks are built into the vanity counter and a separate dressing room or dressing table is included.

VENTILATION, HEATING AND WINDOWS

The bathroom requires the most heat and the best ventilation of any room in the house. Ventilation of an interior bathroom or lavatory must be accomplished with a mechanical ventilation fan ducted to the outside. This fan should be wired to the light switch so it automatically goes on when the room is in use and turns off automatically when the lights are turned out. There are combination electrical fixtures being marketed that include the ventilation fan, a radiant heater and a light.

When the lavatory or bathroom is on an outside wall, natural ventilation and light are supplied from windows. Because windows are usually kept closed during cold and inclement weather, it is a good idea to have a ventilation fan in an outside wall location as well.

The window location is very important. When over the tub, windows produce drafts and radiate cold which feel uncomfortable to a wet body in the process of taking a shower or bath. These windows are difficult to cover since the steam from the bath or shower wets the blinds, shades and curtains. Windows directly behind toilets also produce uncomfortable cold drafts and interfere with privacy. The best light and ventilation come from a single window away from the tub and toilet that is air tight, opens from both the top and bottom to provide ample ventilation and has a good screen.

ACCESSORIES AND STORAGE

Besides a toilet, bathtub and shower and basin, every bathroom also must have a medicine cabinet with a mirror, towel racks, toilet paper holder, soap holder, glass and toothbrush holder, linen storage space, dirty laundry storage and hooks for clothes. There are a myriad of ingenious and attractive ways of incorporating these essentials into the bath decor.

Ceramic tile fixtures on a ceramic wall are excellent. They should be installed so as to withstand 300 pounds of pressure. The more towel bars the better. At least one for each person using the bathroom, plus one extra, is preferable. There should be a soap holder at the tub and sink and in the shower. A shelf on brackets is also a handy extra. The toilet paper holder should be on the wall at the side of the toilet and not behind it.

The door should have hardware with an emergency device on the outside to permit entry if a child gets locked in or an adult has an accident. An important safety feature is a firmly anchored grab bar in the shower stall and tub enclosure to help prevent falls.

A linen storage closet may be in the bathroom or in the hall directly

FIGURE 24
MINIMUM SIZE BATHROOM

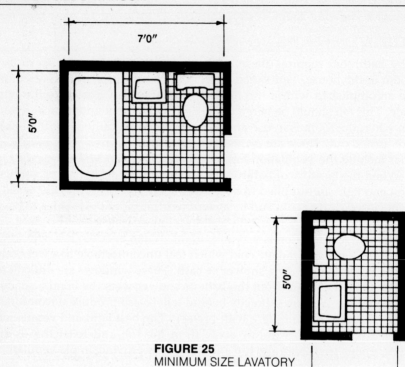

FIGURE 25
MINIMUM SIZE LAVATORY

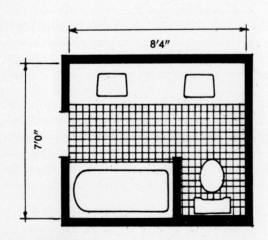

FIGURE 26
BATHROOM WITH TWO LAVATORIES

FIGURE 27
COMPARTMENTED BATHROOM

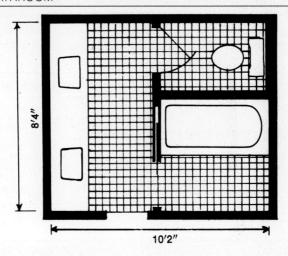

FIGURE 28
BATHROOM WITH CLOSETS AS SOUND BARRIERS

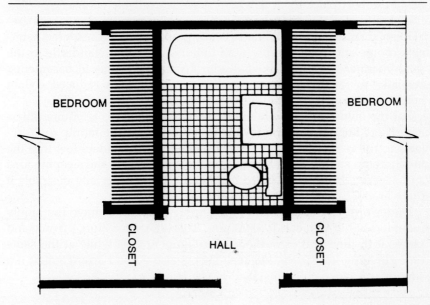

outside. A hamper for dirty laundry can either be built-in or free standing, if there is room. There must also be ample storage for medicine and beauty aids. This can be on shelves in the vanity or medicine cabinet or on bracketed shelves. If space is lacking, these items will end up on the window sill, toilet tank top, bathtub edge and vanity counter top.

For a complete Bathroom checklist, see Checklist 14, page C-31.

FAMILY OR RECREATION ROOM

The family room, as we have come to know it in twentieth century America, is almost totally peculiar to our culture. It is alternately a den, a TV room, an entertaining center, a study, a guest room and perhaps a library or a hobby center. Whatever, it is an asset.

LOCATION

Wherever is a question of space and finances. Many homeowners in older houses have utilized the cellar area where there is the most available space. Others have converted attics and garages or added a room to the house. It is really difficult to say what is the ideal location for the family room in homes that did not originally include one, because, obviously the best place for it is where space is available.

It should be noted that the FHA has some minimum standards here. "Finished rooms in basements or below grade . . . are considered habitable rooms and shall comply with building planning standards in the same manner as rooms above grade. Recreation rooms in basements, auxiliary to the living unit, may be permitted with reduced ceiling height, light and ventilation and outside grade standards."

For the owner of a new home, however, the options are quite different. There are now criteria for the best location as the family room relates to the rest of the house. Most planners and builders feel that the family room should be in the kitchen area, away from the sleeping area and separate from the living-dining area. This is especially desirable if there are teen-aged family members.

Under ordinary circumstances it is more practical to have the family room located in the rear of the house. This allows for more privacy and places it in the patio or outdoor entertainment area while at the same time situating it near the kitchen. This is also a good arrangement if a sink or wet bar is to be installed in the family room.

SIZE AND LAYOUT

A good size family room for a small house is approximately 12 by 16 feet to 13 by 18 feet but, whatever the room area, the smallest wall dimension should not be shorter than 10 and one-half linear feet. There is no maximum size and a larger home could conceivably have a family room of 16 by 26 feet, 18 by 30 feet or more.

If the room is to serve as an occasional guest room, provision should be made for a studio or convertible divan, figuring in plenty of space for when it is open as well as closed.

A clothes closet should be included in the overall plan for the family room. The dimensions of the average size bedroom closet are adequate as a guide. If a larger closet is possible, some of it should be for clothes and some for shelves or built-ins.

No attempt will be made to recommend cabinet size or counter space. A cabinet or wall unit is best built to suit its use. Measurements and guides are available at any reputable hardware or lumber store to aid in producing a tailor-made family unit. Stamp albums, music albums, photograph albums, cassettes, paint brushes and canvasses, clipboards, file cabinets and paper—each has a particular dimension and can be neatly housed with a little forethought.

LIGHTING

Good lighting is always a minimum requirement for health, safety and efficient use. Each area in the family room should have its own lamp—one or two for close intensity work. A cove light over work or game areas produces good lighting. Thoughtful lighting can be the "frosting on the cake" in the warm, friendly, truly recreation-oriented room.

For a complete Family and Recreation Room checklist, see Checklist 15, page C-33.

PATIO

In America today, where we have become geared to leisure time and long weekend holiday entertaining, the patio or terrace has become an integral part of the house although it is actually outside the walls. A majority of our houses have one, be it an elaborate terrace, a side porch, a slab of concrete in the backyard or 100 square feet of grass with a grill. Whatever it may be, it is affectionately referred to as the patio and we cherish and care for it as much if not more than other areas of the house.

LOCATION

There are certain basics recommended for patio location. The patio should be removed from the noise of the street by being in the back of the house. This ensures the necessary privacy. The most important consideration in locating the patio is that there be direct passage from the service area to the patio for serving. The fewest steps from the kitchen for the transporting of food, drink, dishes and other cookout supplies should be the top priority. If this area can be "tied" to the house by extending the flooring material of the terrace to the interior of the house for an indoor-outdoor effect, so much the better. Slate flooring, for example, is often used. Glass doors are usually installed to achieve the proper effect and to give good access.

SIZE AND LAYOUT

Some patios have clearly defined areas for different functions: the cooking area, the eating area and the relaxing or sunbathing area. There is no hard and fast rule for arrangement. Sometimes it is dictated by trees or the landscape, the view or simply by the number of people in the family. An adjacent swimming pool can influence the set-up. The arrangement is purely individual and the possibilities for making the area a haven are endless.

Occasionally wind control is necessary for patios in certain areas of the country. The erection of screens such as dense plantings, certain types of fencing or a combination of both usually eradicates the problem adequately; where practical, glass may also be used.

The material selected for the "floor" of the patio should combine durability with economy for the average homeowner. Concrete fits these specifications best. Patterns can be created with it; it can be colored or not, yet it provides an even, inexpensive, long-lasting surface for the least amount of money. There are variations on the use of concrete such as adding pebbles or other decorative materials to the surface but these do add to the cost.

Brick makes an attractive patio flooring but takes more time and money. Used brick is slightly cheaper and very effective. Brick flooring can also be carried into the house area as discussed above. Slate and flagstones are among the more popular surfaces used. They come in a variety of shapes, sizes and colors, and can be installed by the homeowner.

One of the newer surfaces is the round wooden block. The blocks are literally sliced from the tree trunk just as one would slice up a carrot. They are treated to resist rot, moisture and insects and are very attractive when set into the ground. Some kind of "fill" is necessary to go with them because of their circular shape.

Where the architecture of the house or the slope of the land is a factor, a popular patio is the wooden deck. Quite frequently this is an extension of the living room although it may also be an integral part of the family room or kitchen, since it goes across the entire side of the house. Here, glass doors are a frequent companion feature.

The more expensive patio flooring materials are ceramic tiles (usually near the pool), terrazzo, slate, unglazed quarry tile and a number of new composition materials. All these require expert if not professional installation but, where finances allow, repay the owner in beauty and "mileage."

Occasionally one will find a homeowner who wishes to have a patio entirely screened. There are other methods of insect control besides this one, such as special electric light bulbs which repel insects and a particular blue light which attracts and exterminates with an electric shock. Careful placement of either of these two types of lighting can achieve the desired effect of an insect-free area, for evening entertaining in particular. It is advisable to have such lighting since much of our outdoor living takes place in warm weather and in the evening, both of which beckon the uninvited bug.

A waterproof electrical outlet for the patio area provides versatile use and ultimately, successful entertaining.

PORCH

Millions of older Americans living today would have been appalled and unbelieving if, when they were children, someone had told them that porches would all but disappear from houses by mid-century. But it has happened, for several reasons.

The great housing boom, the population explosion and the mushrooming development of the ranch-split level community have conspired to eradicate the porch from the drawing board. The disappearance of the porch is in direct ratio to the appearance of the patio. The small, token porch, usually formed from the deep overhang above the front door and the one or two-step concrete slab just below it, is about all that remains.

There are exceptions, of course. In the larger, more expensive homes the "side porch" (covered or not) off a living, dining or family room is not unusual, nor is the sun porch. Often these have to double as patios where lot size and other considerations make it necessary or just desirable. In Hawaii, the lanai, a covered patio (or an open porch), continues to be popular.

Many young people who are seeking the most house space for the least amount of money are buying older houses and remodeling them. When finances permit, the first thing to go usually is the front porch. Occasionally it is transformed into another room. Again, there are exceptions and occasionally a young family will discover the joys of sitting, rocking and watching the neighbors or cars go by. Another exception is the beach or summer house, particularly in the northern areas of the United States. Here, the screened-in porch is common and popular, frequently doubling as sleeping space. But, because styles in architecture, as in other art media, have a way of coming full circle every now and then, it is unlikely that the porch will ever disappear completely.

For a complete Patio and Porch checklist, see Checklist 16, page C-35.

LAUNDRY

The average house has four general areas in which the laundry facilities may be installed: the kitchen or service area; the utility room; the bedroom-bath area; or an attached garage, enclosed porch, basement or other utility space.

The location is determined by space, practicality and preference, not always in that order. In new houses the kitchen is a commonly used location. Because the automatic washer and dryer are compact and attractive they fit in well with the decor of any kitchen. The plumbing is already there, as is cabinet space to house the necessary laundry supplies. Occasionally machines have to be installed under a counter, but the front loading machines eliminate this difficulty. The counter top serves as a useful holding and folding area.

The attached garage can provide an excellent utility room situated between the garage and the kitchen and easily accessible to both. This arrangement gives easy access to the backyard play area and if there is no dryer, to the clothes line. When the children come in from play they can shed their muddy clothes within inches of the washing machine.

Larger, more expensive houses often permit the luxury of a separate utility room off the kitchen, with its own lavatory, counters, cabinets, appliances, ironing board and perhaps a sewing machine.

The basement is a good solution for laundry placement. Space here is not in short supply as it is upstairs and soiled linen and laundry supplies do not interfere with the aesthetics of the home decor. Many new houses with basements have a walk-out entrance. In a multi-level house, a clothes chute from the bedroom-bath area to the basement is desirable. Some larger homes have laundry centers in the bedroom area.

SIZE

The size of the laundry is not as fundamentally important as are the other room sizes; efficiency and location are. The neat, compact washer and dryer can be housed within a very small space. Nevertheless, it is advantageous to have some counter space and shelves.

It should be noted that there are some non-automatic washers in use and these require a large tub or two. This necessitates a larger area. A space roughly seven and one-half by eight and one-half feet is adequate.

Proper ventilation in the laundry room or area is important both within the room and for the dryer. The dryer vent, be it for an electric or gas dryer, removes mositure and humidity to the outside and is highly recommended. Counter surfaces and flooring should be of finishes that withstand high humidities and moisture from liquid laundry supplies, which occasionally get dropped or spilled. Where the walls are covered or decorated these too should be moisture-resistant.

Most new houses come with the necessary water and electrical hook-ups for the automatic washer and provide for the elimination of waste water. In most new houses the wiring provides for the necessary outlets and electric lights. Good artificial light is also a requirement. A well-lighted laundry room is attractive and makes the usual laundry routine not only more pleasant but also much safer.

STORAGE AREAS

Storage has become a complex problem; each family's needs are individual and should be carefully considered. Convenience, accessibility and organization are the objectives. "Everything in its place" is fine, but the place must be provided and planned for in order that the family live in a well-ordered existence. The days of storing *everything* in the basement or attic have long gone.

INDOOR STORAGE

Still, the basement is one of the best and most popular storage areas because it provides a lot of leeway in arranging for storage of large articles. This is possible only if the basement is dry and well ventilated. Good lighting on the stairs and near the door to the outside is necessary.

Basement storage in general often houses skis, skates and archery, fishing, camping and other sporting equipment. Seasonal items like suitcases and trunks, Christmas and other holiday decorations, screens, storm doors and summer furniture are also found here. Occasionally there is a pool table or ping-pong table and several bikes. The basement is also a favorite spot for unused furniture, children's toys, frames, old clothes, family treasures and just junk.

Regardless of the bulk or variety, if things are properly stored to utilize every available space, there will be much more living space within the home. Wall shelving units, racks and cabinets are ideal. Remember, storing things close to where they are to be used is the ideal situation.

Utilizing existing space in a house is always more economical and easier than building an addition. The attic makes an excellent storage area and where existing conditions permit, it can be attractively remodeled into a bedroom, a study or a hobby center in combination with storage. Lockers and cabinets fit ideally under the lower portions of the roof. Closets for items other than clothing need not be at regulation height in order to hold storage shelves.

OUTDOOR STORAGE

Outdoor storage sheds have been increasing in popularity at the same rate as we acquire sophisticated equipment for the care of the home and its environs. A shed is also a good answer to the storage problem in a house without a basement. A handyman may construct a shed of wood fairly inexpensively or assemble a precut one which is slightly higher in initial cost and upkeep. Perhaps cheapest in the long run is the popular steel shed which is dotting the landscape in ever-increasing numbers. It is attractive, practical, inexpensive, requires little maintenance and provides good space without taking up too much of the yard area.

Besides yard tractors, power mowers, snow blowers, leaf compactors, tools and bicycles, it may be necessary to store patio furniture and game equipment like badminton or croquet sets, the inevitable grill or habachi, tree sprayers and ladders. The list expands with each subtle change in our technology.

GARAGE STORAGE AREA

The garage is a logical place to find extra storage space. The first garages were built solely to house the automobile and protect it from the elements. Today that is only one of its functions. The modern garage is often attached directly to the house with an open or enclosed breezeway, or is incorporated into the house structure.

Garage storage is particularly desirable where there is no basement to solve many of the storage problems. Many garages built in the last decade or two are usually longer and wider than is necessary for car space, allowing for adequate traffic and movement around the car. This also provides space for closets and shelves along the sides.

When laundry equipment is installed in the garage, adequate space must be provided for its use. Other than laundry equipment, the most frequently stored mechanical equipment in a garage is a freezer. It is a good idea to enclose such equipment within doors such as the shutter type which fold back and use minimum space. The garage should be easily accessible to the service area of the house so laundry and supplies can be carried directly to and from the kitchen.

The garage makes excellent storage for unused equipment, in or out of season garden tools, storm windows, ladders, a workbench, fireplace wood, bicycles and baby carriages. When there are rafters or some type of a ceiling, overhead garage storage space can be utilized.

OTHER STORAGE AREAS

There are a variety of other types of storage space.

The cedar closet, admittedly a luxury, is fast being phased out, even where money allows. Except for those purists who like the odor and the nostalgia of a cedar closet, the best storage protection against moths is the average bedroom closet.

A wine cellar is the ultimate in storage considerations and is fast growing in popularity as the wine rage sweeps the country. The wine cellar may range from a very small closet to a small room. The "cellar" may not be in the cellar at all, but wherever its location, the prime concern must be steady temperature.

The old root or vegetable cellar below ground or cellar level has all but disappeared. Some houses built in the nineteenth century or before still have them, but they are rarely used for food storage anymore except in farm houses or rural areas. Such a space would make an excellent wine cellar or darkroom, given the proper temperature controls.

For a complete Laundry and Storage Area checklist, see Checklist 17, page C-37.

GARAGES AND CARPORTS

Many families owning houses also own two or more cars. Americans like their cars and they like to keep them under cover in garages and in carports. Their desire to do this varies from area to area. In many northern parts of the country any house without a two-car garage is substandard. In parts of the West and South the demand for garages and carports is more flexible and often a one-car carport with an additional parking area for the second or third car is acceptable.

A garage built only to shelter one car should be 10 feet wide and 20 feet long, measured from the inside of the studs and door to the edge of the opposite wall, stair platform or any obstruction, whichever is the narrowest dimension.

However, to build a garage to these minimum standards is false economy. For only a small additional amount of money, the garage can be built about three feet longer and wider. Here is the cheapest and most convenient place to store all of the paraphernalia of outdoor living. If built even bigger, it can house the laundry and drying equipment and also serve as a workshop and a place for the children to play on cold or wet days.

The choice between a carport or a garage is mainly influenced by local custom and climate. A carport is a good choice when it fits into the neighborhood and the prime purpose will be to shelter the automobile from the sun and rain.

A garage has the advantage of providing shelter from the cold, ice and snow in the northern climate. Even in the South and West, garages are selected by many who wish complete protection of their automobiles plus the other advantages of the garage.

There has been a definite trend away from the detached garage and towards an attached garage or carport or, if detached, connected to the house by a covered breezeway.

Garage doors come in several styles, the most popular being the overhead door which is raised and lowered on a track and is counterbalanced with a spring to make it easier to handle. The minimum acceptable width is eight feet, but nine feet is much better. On a double garage a 16-foot door is the minimum acceptable size. These double doors tend

FIGURE 29
MINIMUM ONE-CAR GARAGE

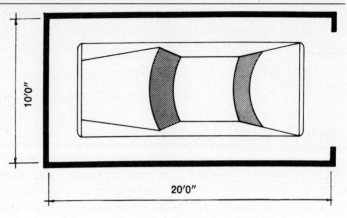

FIGURE 30
RECOMMENDED ONE-CAR GARAGE WITH STORAGE

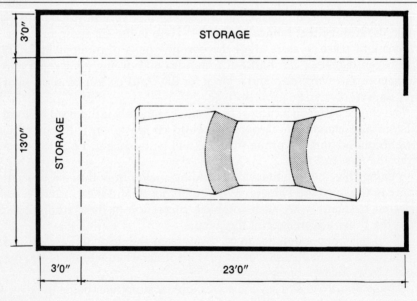

FIGURE 31
MINIMUM TWO-CAR GARAGE

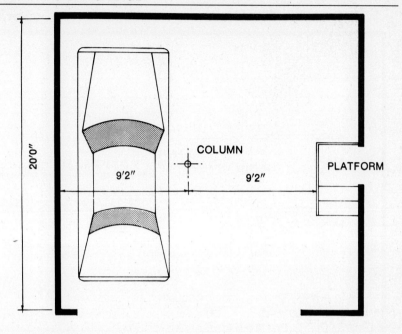

FIGURE 32
RECOMMENDED TWO-CAR GARAGE WITH STORAGE

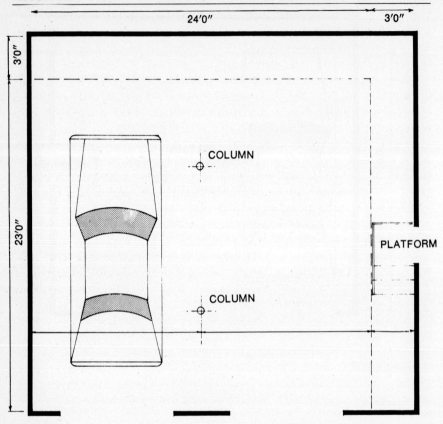

FIGURE 33
CARPORT

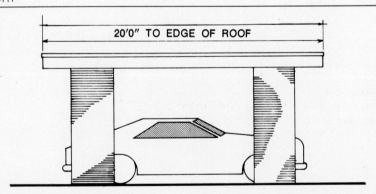

to be heavy and hard to open and close unless you have an electric door opener. Two single doors eight or nine feet wide offer a much better arrangement. The minimum height for the door should be six feet, four inches. This will prove inadequate for a wagon with a rack of luggage or some recreation vehicles or trailers, however. A better height is seven feet or more, particularly if you are a "van" fan.

Automatic door openers and closers are very appealing. These devices open and close the door by power from an electric motor. They can be controlled with switches on the inside or outside of the garage or from a radio transmitter in the car or in the house.

A small door from the garage to the backyard is also a great convenience. At least one window is desirable for light and ventilation, especially if the garage is to be used for a work, play or laundry area. Some garages are built with some unfinished storage area under the roof eaves which can be reached via pull-down stairs or a ladder.

The wall between the house and an attached garage should have a one-hour fire resistance rating. This is required by many building codes.

In some of the northern parts of the country garages are heated, usually to heat the garage to just above freezing rather than to 70 degrees. If the garage is insulated, a lot of heat is not required. Care must be taken to insulate all water pipes so they will not freeze. If a hot air system is used, no cold air return into the garage should be installed as this would provide an inlet for fumes into the rest of the heating system.

A concrete slab provides a good garage floor. It should be one or two inches above the driveway level to prevent water from running into the garage. The floor should either be pitched to a central floor drain or to the driveway to allow the water from melting ice and snow to flow away.

The garage and carport should be lit and have electric outlets. The lights should be controlled from both inside the garage and inside the house. The garage light switch should be located at the front so it can be turned on without having to walk into a dark garage.

It is dangerous to have a driveway that enters the public street at a blind curve. A driveway that slopes upward to the street may also be dangerous, especially in the winter.

**For a complete Garage and Carport checklist,
see Checklist 18, page C-39.**

CHAPTER 7
EXTERIOR DESIGN

In terms of exterior design American houses range from houses with no recognizable design features to homes that are exact replicas of historical houses from around the world.

Different styles developed in different regions of the country. Many of the early colonists copied styles from their homelands. Some copied the classic Gothic, Greek and Roman designs, while others developed truly indigenous American styles. Most pre-World War II houses reflect in some way these traditional styles of the past. Many represent easily identifiable styles.

Today more than 50 million American homes reflect such traditional styles. They range from original Colonials and authentic Colonial reproductions and painstakingly restored Victorian villas to inexpensive tract speculation houses that adopt one or more style features of the past.

Much confusion exists as to the identification and origin of these styles.

Using traditional style features diminished in popularity after World War II. At that time the one and one-half story Cape Cod style house was replaced as the national favorite by the one-story Ranch style house.

New houses such as the Split Level, Raised Ranch (split foyer or bi-level) and the Hillside Ranch evolved. Sometimes these new types were decorated with traditional style features. Sometimes, to the shock of the purists, several different style features and a combination of unrelated materials were all combined in the same house.

Following World War II speculators developed large tracts of homes with only the nominal help of architects. Millions of houses were built by small builders often without formal sets of plans. Many of these houses were very poorly designed.

Gradually there has been a trend away from these poorly designed houses. Large tracts of land were built up by development companies who employed land planners and architects. These architects often elected to use new materials and contemporary designs rather than those based on our historical past. The overall quality of house design began to improve. A substantial portion of the home-buying market would not accept the poorly designed houses of the late 40's, 50's and 60's.

Another development increased our awareness of historical design. This was our Bicentennial Celebration. And, as housing in the suburbs became more and more expensive, there was renewed interest in the cities. Here, houses built in the eighteenth and nineteenth centuries were recognized as excellent values. They could be renovated into homes with high ceilings and large rooms, providing living space unavailable in most suburban homes. Historic districts have been established in many cities and the restoration of older homes has become a new national pastime.

THE CTS SYSTEM

The CTS System (Class, Type, Style) was developed for the REALTORS NATIONAL MARKETING INSTITUTE® to provide a uniform method of describing residential construction. This system provides a precise method of describing houses. The description is divided into three components: Class, Type and Style. A uniform narrative description, standard abbreviation and computer code are provided for each part of the system.

The system starts by dividing all houses into one of nine basic classes:

Code	Description	Abbreviation
1	One-family, detached	1 FAM D
2	Two-family, party wall	2 FAM D
3	Three-family, detached	3 FAM D
4	Four-family, detached	4 FAM D
5	One-family, party wall	1 FAM PW
6	Two-family, party wall	2 FAM PW
7	Three-family, party wall	3 FAM PW
8	Four-family, party wall	4 FAM PW
9	Other	OTHER

Class is used to denote the number of families the unit being described will accommodate and whether the units are detached or have a party wall.

For example, a one-family town house would be described "one-family, party wall." This same description would also describe a single unit in a 20-story condominium highrise.

Another example is a two-family house on its own lot which would be described as a "two-family, detached."

If the house being described was a fourplex or quadro and the title included all four units, it would be described as "four-family, party wall." On the other hand, if the title was to only one of the four units, it would be described as "one-family, party wall."

The CTS System in its present form does not include apartment houses except as single units that are sold individually in condominium or cooperative forms of ownership (See Chapter 16).

After describing the class a house falls into, the CTS System refers to the structural nature of the house. All houses can be classified into one of these nine types:

Code	Description	Abbreviation
1	One-story	1 STORY
2	One and one-half story	1 1/2 STORY
3	Two-story	2 STORY
4	Two and one-half story	2 1/2 STORY
5	Three or more stories	3 STORY
6	Bi-level	BI-LEVEL
6	Raised Ranch	R RANCH
6	Split Entry	SPLT ENT
7	Split-level	SPLIT LEV
8	Mansion	MANSION
9	Other	OTHER

Figure 34 shows illustrations of the different types of houses.

The third step of the CTS System is to identify any style feature the house may have. All houses can be identified by one of nine style groups (see Figures 35 to 43 for illustrations):

Code	Description	Abbreviation
100	Colonial American	COL AMER
200	English	ENGLISH
300	French	FRENCH
400	Swiss	SWISS
500	Latin	LATIN
600	Oriental	ORIENT
700	19th Century American	19th CTY
800	Early 20th Century American	EARLY 20 C
900	Post World War II American	POST WW 2

Some houses are good examples of one of these specific historical periods. The user of the CTS System elects whether to identify the house by

FIGURE 34
NINE BASIC HOUSE TYPES

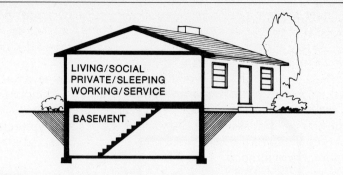

ONE STORY (1 Story — 1)*

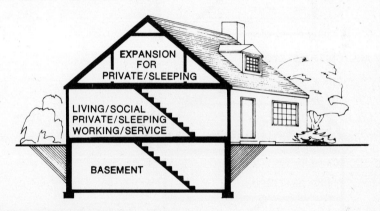

ONE AND ONE-HALF STORY (1 1/2 Story — 2)

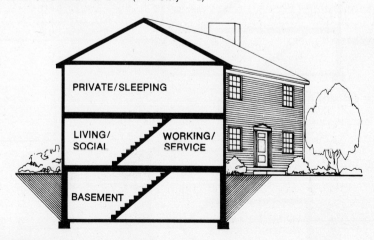

TWO STORY (2 Story — 3)

* CTS Code and Abbreviation

FIGURE 34
NINE BASIC HOUSE TYPES (continued)

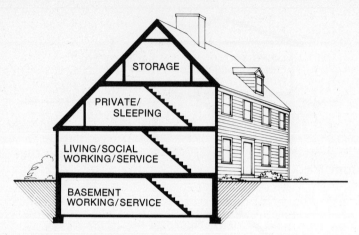

TWO AND ONE-HALF STORY (2 1/2 Story — 4)

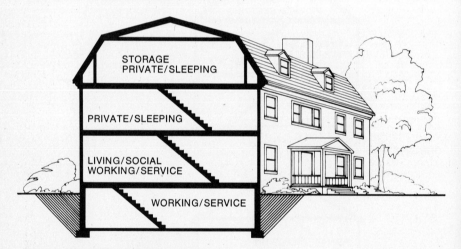

THREE OR MORE STORIES (3 Stories — 5)

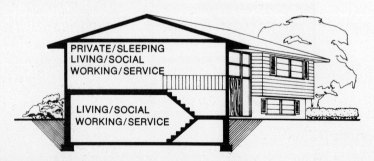

BI-LEVEL/RAISED RANCH/SPLIT ENTRY/SPLIT FOYER
(Bi Lev/ R Ranch/Split Ent/Split Foy — 6)

FIGURE 34
NINE BASIC HOUSE TYPES (continued)

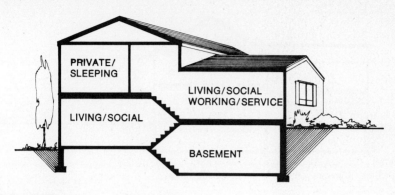

SPLIT LEVEL (Splt Lev — 7) Side to Side

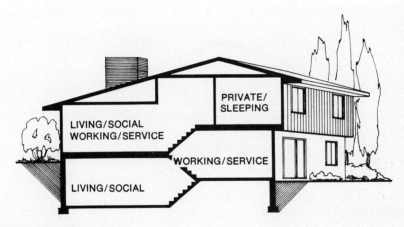

SPLIT LEVEL Back to Front

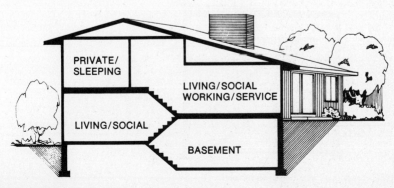

SPLIT LEVEL Front to Back

FIGURE 34
NINE BASIC HOUSE TYPES (continued)

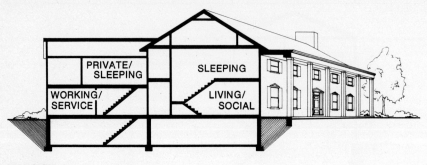

MANSION (Mansion — 8)

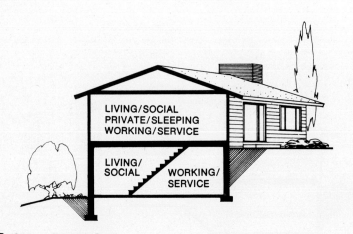

OTHER (Other — 9) Hillside Ranch

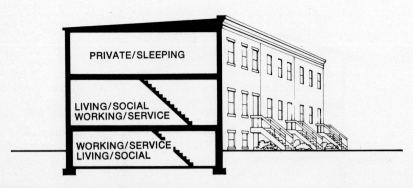

OTHER Townhouse with English Basement

FIGURE 34
NINE BASIC HOUSE TYPES (continued)

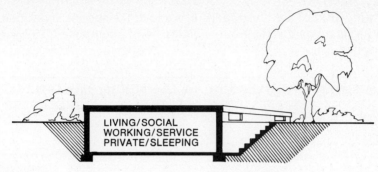

LIVING/SOCIAL
WORKING/SERVICE
PRIVATE/SLEEPING

OTHER Cellar

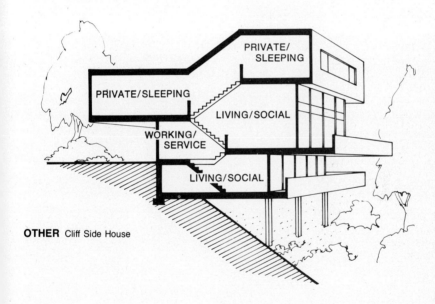

PRIVATE/
SLEEPING

PRIVATE/SLEEPING

LIVING/SOCIAL

WORKING/
SERVICE

LIVING/SOCIAL

OTHER Cliff Side House

one of these nine groups (all houses can be classified into one of these nine groups) or whether to choose one of the 58 specific style descriptions.

Figures 35 to 43 are illustrations of some of the specific styles that fit into the nine broad style groups. Figure 44 is a complete CTS System description list.

For an Exterior Design checklist, see Checklist 19, page C-41.

FIGURE 35
COLONIAL AMERICAN STYLES

CAPE COD (Cape Cod — 104)*

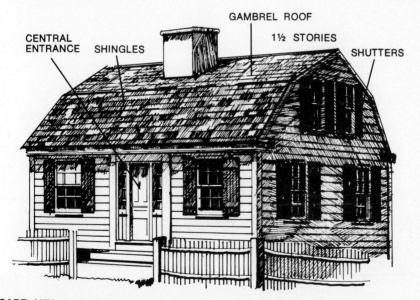

CAPE ANN (Cape Ann — 105)

* CTS Code and Abbreviation

FIGURE 35
COLONIAL AMERICAN STYLES (continued)

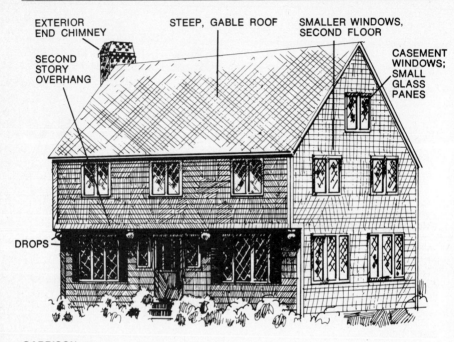

EXTERIOR
END CHIMNEY

SECOND
STORY
OVERHANG

STEEP, GABLE ROOF

SMALLER WINDOWS,
SECOND FLOOR

CASEMENT
WINDOWS;
SMALL
GLASS
PANES

DROPS

GARRISON (Garr Co — 106)

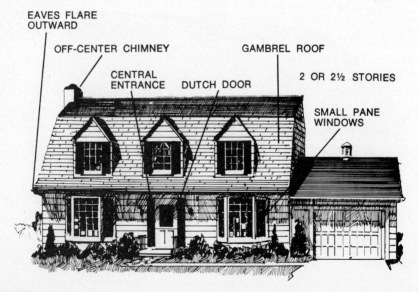

EAVES FLARE
OUTWARD

OFF-CENTER CHIMNEY

CENTRAL
ENTRANCE   DUTCH DOOR

GAMBREL ROOF

2 OR 2½ STORIES

SMALL PANE
WINDOWS

DUTCH (Dutch — 108)

FIGURE 35
COLONIAL AMERICAN STYLES (continued)

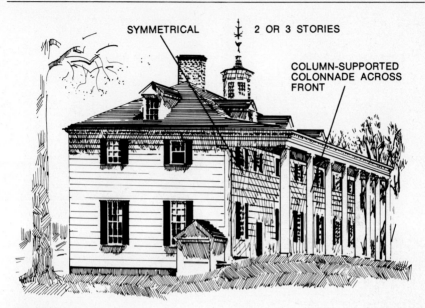

SYMMETRICAL   2 OR 3 STORIES

COLUMN-SUPPORTED
COLONNADE ACROSS
FRONT

SOUTHERN (South Co — 113)

OTHER COLONIAL AMERICAN STYLES

Federal
New England Farm House
Adams
New England
Salt Box/Catslide
Pennsylvania Dutch/Pennsylvania German Farm House
Classic
Greek Revival
Front Gable New England/Charleston/English Colonial

FIGURE 36
ENGLISH STYLES

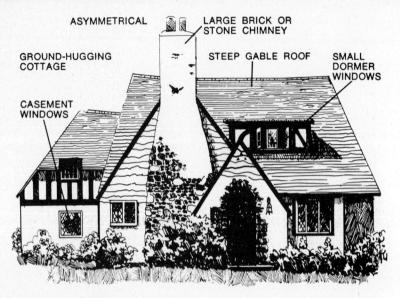

ASYMMETRICAL

LARGE BRICK OR STONE CHIMNEY

GROUND-HUGGING COTTAGE

STEEP GABLE ROOF

SMALL DORMER WINDOWS

CASEMENT WINDOWS

COTSWOLD COTTAGE (Cotscot — 201)

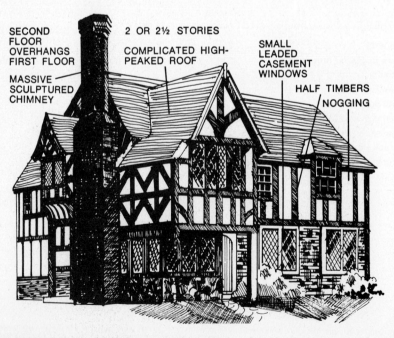

SECOND FLOOR OVERHANGS FIRST FLOOR

2 OR 2½ STORIES

SMALL LEADED CASEMENT WINDOWS

COMPLICATED HIGH-PEAKED ROOF

MASSIVE SCULPTURED CHIMNEY

HALF TIMBERS

NOGGING

ELIZABETHAN/HALF TIMBER (Eliz/Halftim — 202)

FIGURE 36
ENGLISH STYLES (continued)

FORT-LIKE APPEARANCE

2 TO 3 STORIES   HIGH CHIMNEY

SEMI-HEXAGONAL   CHIMNEY POTS
BAYS

BRICK OR
STONE WALLS

MOULDED
STONE TRIM

STONE
MULLIONS

TUDOR (Tudor — 203)

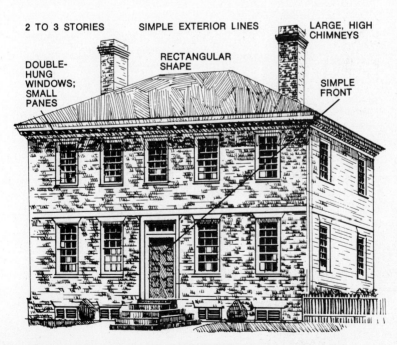

2 TO 3 STORIES   SIMPLE EXTERIOR LINES   LARGE, HIGH
CHIMNEYS

DOUBLE-
HUNG
WINDOWS;
SMALL
PANES

RECTANGULAR
SHAPE

SIMPLE
FRONT

WILLIAMSBURG GEORGIAN/EARLY GEORGIAN (Williams/E Georg — 204)

FIGURE 36
ENGLISH STYLES (continued)

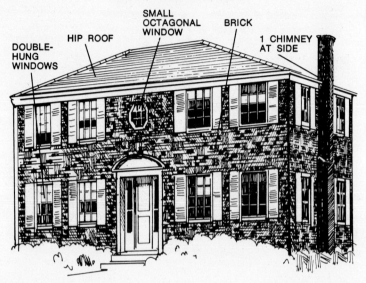

SIMPLE, INFORMAL STYLE

SMALL OCTAGONAL WINDOW

HIP ROOF

BRICK

1 CHIMNEY AT SIDE

DOUBLE-HUNG WINDOWS

REGENCY (Regency — 205)

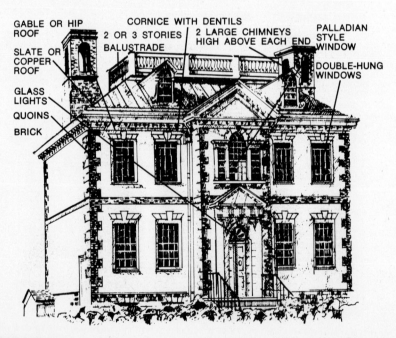

GABLE OR HIP ROOF

CORNICE WITH DENTILS

2 OR 3 STORIES

BALUSTRADE

2 LARGE CHIMNEYS HIGH ABOVE EACH END

PALLADIAN STYLE WINDOW

SLATE OR COPPER ROOF

DOUBLE-HUNG WINDOWS

GLASS LIGHTS

QUOINS

BRICK

GEORGIAN (George — 206)

FIGURE 37
FRENCH STYLES

DORMERS
BREAK
THROUGH
CORNICE

LARGE CHIMNEY

1½ TO 2 STORIES

HIGH HIP OR
GABLE ROOF

VARIETY OF
BUILDING
MATERIALS

HALF
TIMBERS

FRENCH FARM HOUSE (Fr Farm — 301)

1½ TO 2½ STORIES

CURVE-HEADED
UPPER
WINDOWS THAT
BREAK THROUGH
CORNICE

BRICK

PERFECTLY BALANCED

FORMAL LOOKING

HIGH, STEEP
HIP ROOF

SOME HAVE
2 SYMMETRICAL
1-STORY WINGS

FRENCH
WINDOWS
AND
SHUTTERS

FRENCH PROVINCIAL (Fr Prov — 302)

FIGURE 37
FRENCH STYLES (continued)

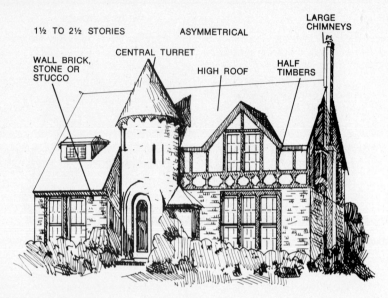

1½ TO 2½ STORIES   ASYMMETRICAL   LARGE CHIMNEYS

WALL BRICK, STONE OR STUCCO

CENTRAL TURRET

HIGH ROOF

HALF TIMBERS

FRENCH NORMANDY (Fr Norm — 303)

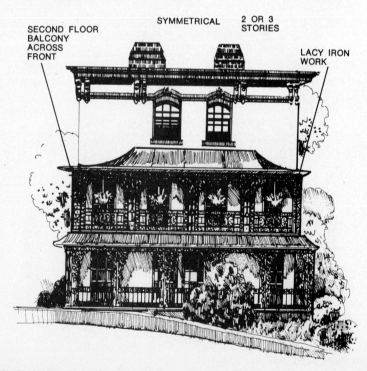

SECOND FLOOR BALCONY ACROSS FRONT

SYMMETRICAL   2 OR 3 STORIES

LACY IRON WORK

CREOLE/LOUISIANA/NEW ORLEANS (Creole/Louisia/New Or — 304)

FIGURE 38
LATIN STYLES

1 TO 3 STORIES

PAINTED STUCCO
EXTERIOR WALLS

RED TILE ROOF

OVAL-TOP DOORS

SPANISH VILLA (Sp Villa — 501)

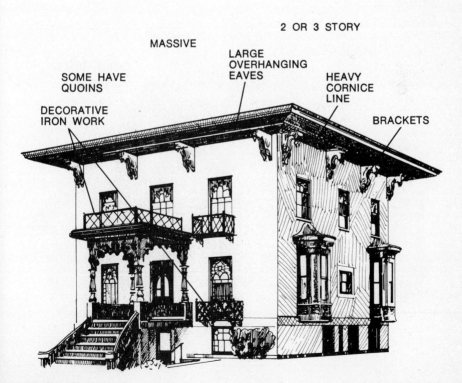

2 OR 3 STORY

MASSIVE

LARGE
OVERHANGING
EAVES

HEAVY
CORNICE
LINE

SOME HAVE
QUOINS

BRACKETS

DECORATIVE
IRON WORK

ITALIAN VILLA (It Villa — 502)

FIGURE 39
ORIENTAL STYLE

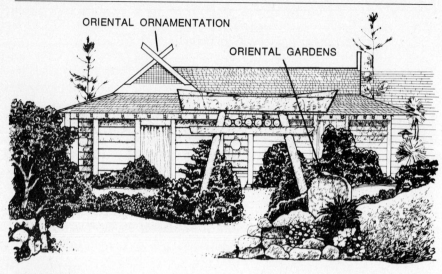

ORIENTAL ORNAMENTATION

ORIENTAL GARDENS

JAPANESE (Japan — 601)

FIGURE 40
SWISS STYLE

1½ TO 2½ STORIES

GABLE ROOF

NATURAL
WOOD
LOOK

DECORATIVE
WOOD WORK

LARGE GLASS
WINDOWS

OPEN
PORCHES

CURVED
CORNICE

SWISS CHALET (Swiss Ch — 401)

FIGURE 41
19TH CENTURY AMERICAN STYLES

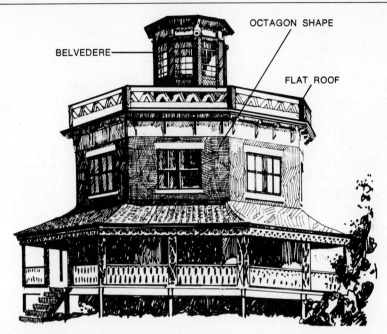

BELVEDERE

OCTAGON SHAPE

FLAT ROOF

OCTAGON HOUSE (Octagon — 704)

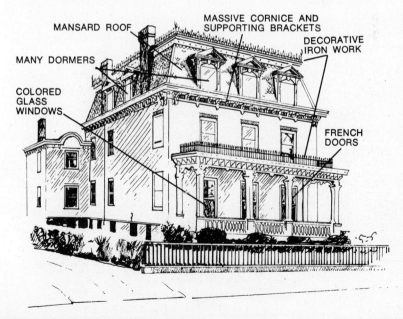

MANSARD ROOF

MASSIVE CORNICE AND
SUPPORTING BRACKETS

DECORATIVE
IRON WORK

MANY DORMERS

COLORED
GLASS
WINDOWS

FRENCH
DOORS

AMERICAN MANSARD/SECOND EMPIRE (Mansard/2nd Emp — 707)

FIGURE 41
19TH CENTURY AMERICAN STYLES (continued)

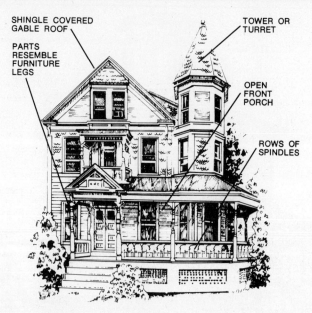

SHINGLE COVERED
GABLE ROOF

PARTS
RESEMBLE
FURNITURE
LEGS

TOWER OR
TURRET

OPEN
FRONT
PORCH

ROWS OF
SPINDLES

EASTLAKE (East L — 709)

PROJECTING
UPPER STORIES

UNIQUE LOOKING

MULTI-STORY

TURRETS

BAY WINDOWS

BIG CHIMNEYS

VARIETY OF
SURFACE TEXTURES

VARIOUS FORMS
OF WINDOWS

IRREGULAR SHAPE

MANY
SMALL
DETAILS

QUEEN ANNE (Q Anne — 712)

FIGURE 41
19TH CENTURY AMERICAN STYLES (continued)

STOOP UP TO FIRST FLOOR · BROWNSTONE TRIM · 4 OR 5 STORIES · COMMON WALLS · BRICK · FLAT ROOF · SIMPLE DOUBLE-HUNG WINDOWS

BROWNSTONE/BRICK ROW HOUSE/EASTERN TOWNHOUSE (Brown S/Br Row/E Town — 713)

**OTHER 19TH CENTURY
AMERICAN STYLES**

Early Gothic Revival
Egyptian Revival
Roman Tuscan Mode
High Victorian Gothic
High Victorian Italianate
Stick/Carpenter Gothic
Shingle
Romanesque
Western Row House/Western Townhouse
Monterey
Western Stick
Mission

FIGURE 42
EARLY 20TH CENTURY AMERICAN STYLES

PRAIRIE HOUSE (Prairie — 801)

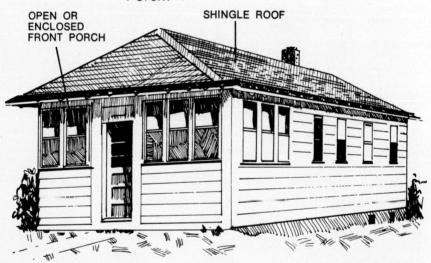

BUNGALOW (Bungalow — 802)

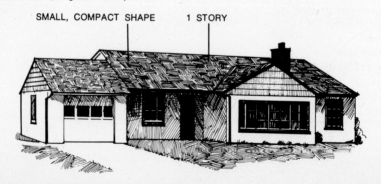

CALIFORNIA BUNGALOW (Cal Bung — 803)

FIGURE 42
EARLY 20TH CENTURY AMERICAN STYLES (continued)

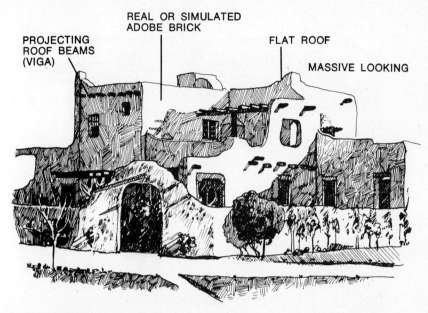

PROJECTING
ROOF BEAMS
(VIGA)

REAL OR SIMULATED
ADOBE BRICK

FLAT ROOF

MASSIVE LOOKING

PUEBLO/ADOBE (Pueblo/Adobe — 804)

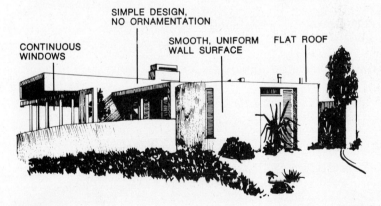

SIMPLE DESIGN,
NO ORNAMENTATION

CONTINUOUS
WINDOWS

SMOOTH, UNIFORM
WALL SURFACE

FLAT ROOF

INTERNATIONAL (Internat — 805)

FIGURE 43
POST WORLD WAR II AMERICAN STYLES

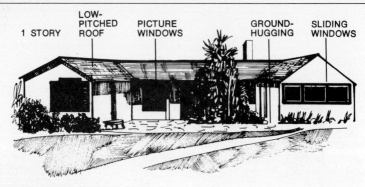

CALIFORNIA RANCH (C Ranch — 901)

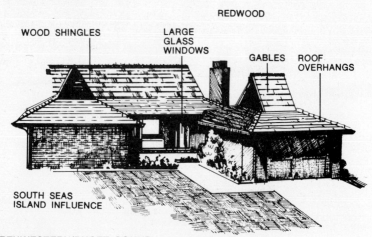

NORTHWESTERN/PUGET SOUND (North W/P Sound — 902)

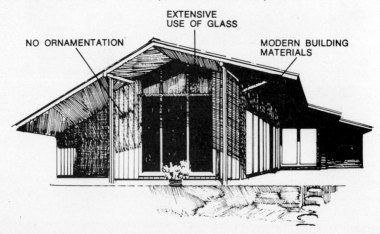

FUNCTIONAL MODERN/CONTEMPORARY (Fun Mod/Contemp — 903)

FIGURE 43
POST WORLD WAR II AMERICAN STYLES (continued)

LARGE GLASS WINDOWS AND DOORS

LARGE OVERHANGING EAVES

SOLAR HOUSE (Solar — 904)

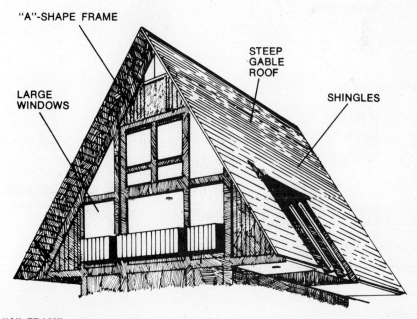

"A"-SHAPE FRAME

STEEP GABLE ROOF

LARGE WINDOWS

SHINGLES

"A" FRAME (A Frame — 905)

FIGURE 43
POST WORLD WAR II AMERICAN STYLES (continued)

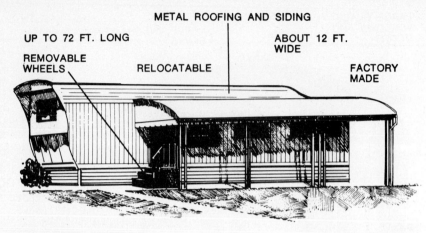

UP TO 72 FT. LONG

METAL ROOFING AND SIDING

ABOUT 12 FT. WIDE

REMOVABLE WHEELS

RELOCATABLE

FACTORY MADE

MOBILE HOME (Mobile — 906)

PLASTIC EXTERIOR SIDING

CLEAN, MODERN LINES

PLASTIC HOUSE (Plastic   007)

FIGURE 44
THE CTS SYSTEM (CLASS, TYPE, STYLE)
A UNIFORM METHOD FOR DESCRIBING HOUSES

CODE #	DESCRIPTION	ABBREVIATION
	CLASS	
1	One-family, detached	1 FAM D
2	Two-family, detached	2 FAM D
3	Three-family, detached	3 FAM D
4	Four-family, detached	4 FAM D
5	One-family, party wall	1 FAM PW
6	Two-family, party wall	2 FAM PW
7	Three-family, party wall	3 FAM PW
8	Four-family, party wall	4 FAM PW
9	Other	OTHER
	TYPE	
1	One-story	1 STORY
2	One and one-half story	1 1/2 STORY
3	Two-story	2 STORY
4	Two and one-half story	2 1/2 STORY
5	Three or more stories	3 STORY
6	Bi-level	BI-LEVEL
6	Raised ranch	R RANCH
6	Split entry	SPLT ENT
7	Split-level	SPLT LEV
8	Mansion	MANSION
9	Other	OTHER
	STYLE	
100	COLONIAL AMERICAN	COL AMER
101	Federal	FEDERAL
102	New England Farm House	N E FARM
103	Adams	ADAMS CO
104	Cape Cod	CAPE COD
105	Cape Ann	CAPE ANN
106	Garrison Colonial	GARR CO
107	New England	N E COL
108	Dutch	DUTCH CO
109	Salt Box	SALT BOX
109	Catslide	CATSLIDE
110	Pennsylvania Dutch	PENN DUT
110	Pennsylvania German Farm House	GER FARM
111	Classic	CLASSIC
112	Greek Revival	GREEK
113	Southern Colonial	SOUTH CO
114	Front Gable New England	F GAB NE
114	Charleston	CHARLES
114	English Colonial	ENG COL
115	Log Cabin	LOG CAB
200	ENGLISH	ENGLISH
201	Cotswold Cottage	COTSCOT
202	Elizabethan	ELIZ
202	Half Timber	HALFTIM
203	Tudor	TUDOR
204	Williamsburg	WILLIAMS
204	Early Georgian	E GEORG
205	Regency	REGENCY
206	Georgian	GEORGE

FIGURE 44
THE CTS SYSTEM (continued)

CODE #	DESCRIPTION	ABBREVIATION
300	FRENCH	FRENCH
301	French Farm House	FR FARM
302	French Provincial	FR PROV
303	French Normandy	FR NORM
304	Creole	CREOLE
304	Louisiana	LOUISIA
304	New Orleans	NEW OR
400	SWISS	SWISS
401	Swiss Chalet	SWISS CH
500	LATIN	LATIN
501	Spanish Villa	SP VILLA
502	Italian Villa	IT VILLA
600	ORIENTAL	ORIENT
601	JAPANESE	JAPAN
700	19th CENTURY AMERICAN	19th CTY
701	Early Gothic Revival	E GOTH
702	Egyptian Revival	EGYPT
703	Roman Tuscan Mode	RO TUSC
704	Octagon House	OCTAGON
705	High Victorian Gothic	HI GOTH
706	High Victorian Italianate	VICITAL
707	American Mansard	MANSARD
707	Second Empire	2nd EMP
708	Stick Style	STICK
708	Carpenter Gothic	C GOTH
709	Eastlake	EAST L
710	Shingle Style	SHINGLE
711	Romanesque	ROMAN
712	Queen Anne	Q ANNE
713	Brownstone	BROWN S
713	Brick Row House	BR ROW
713	Eastern Townhouse	E TOWN
714	Western Row House	WEST ROW
714	Western Townhouse	W TOWN
715	Monterey	MONTEREY
716	Western Stick	W STICK
717	Mission Style	MISSION
800	EARLY 20th CENTURY AMERICAN	EARLY 20 C
801	Prairie House	PRAIRIE
802	Bungalow	BUNGALOW
803	Pueblo	PUEBLO
803	Adobe	ADOBE
804	International Style	INTERNAT
805	California Bungalow	CAL BUNG
900	POST WORLD WAR II AMERICAN	POST WW2
901	California Ranch	C RANCH
902	Northwestern	NORTH W
902	Puget Sound	P SOUND
903	Functional Modern	FUN MOD
903	Contemporary	CONTEMP
904	Solar House	SOLAR
905	"A" Frame	A FRAME
906	Mobile Home	MOBILE
907	Plastic House	PLASTIC

CHAPTER 8
CONSTRUCTION*

While many home builders are quite reputable, some builders long ago discovered that they could save thousands of dollars during the construction of a house and most of the buying public would never discover it until long after the builder had left the scene. By using cheaper materials and shoddy construction techniques, the builder reduces cost and this, in turn, either increases the builder's profit (or reduces losses) or allows the builder to reduce the price of the house so it appears to be a "bargain."

The ultimate loser is not the builder but the consumer who lives in the house and finds for each dollar the builder saved, he or she is faced with many dollars of continual maintenance costs. Dollars are not the only loss the consumer suffers, however. There are some problems which develop as a result of poor construction that can never be corrected. A wet basement or defective framing system are two such examples. Even when the deficiencies can be corrected, however, how is the homeowner to be compensated for the loss of time and the inconvenience and annoyance that occurs?

What constitutes good construction is not universally agreed upon by builders, architects, lenders and the government. Perhaps the best set of standards, however, are those known as the "Minimum Property Standards" (MPS) established by the Federal Housing Administration of the U.S. Department of Housing and Urban Development. We have been referring to those standards as "FHA-MPS" or FHA standards.

In many cases builders are carefully supervised. For example, many houses are built for specific owners who supervise the construction themselves, sometimes with the help of an architect. Such houses are "custom-built homes." Many other houses are initially financed with

* Portions of this chapter are based on HOUSES–The Illustrated Guide to Construction, Design and Systems by Henry S. Harrison, © 1976 by REALTORS NATIONAL MARKETING INSTITUTE®.

FHA guaranteed mortgages. Both the FHA and the lender will then supervise the construction of these houses to ensure that they meet with the FHA-MPS.

Other houses are financed with conventional mortgages from a variety of lending institutions. These institutions vary in their ability and desire to establish quality standards and in making the necessary inspections to see they are being met. Those lenders who do require that the houses they mortgage are of good quality and then insist that builders meet their standards have made a major contribution towards improving the housing stock in our country. Building inspectors play a major role in ensuring that houses are built at least to the minimum requirements of the local building code.

The purpose of this chapter is to help educate you, the consumer, who will have to pay up to $5 for each dollar a builder saves, not to mention your time, inconvenience and annoyance. We hope that, armed with the information in this chapter and with the help of professionals, you will be able to spot a shoddily-built house from a house that is well constructed. Once you can tell the difference, you can choose which you want and insist that you get what you are willing to pay for.[1]

GROUNDS AND SITE IMPROVEMENTS

Let's start our house inspection on the outside. When you buy a home you get, in addition to the actual house, all the site improvements and appurtenant structures (see Glossary-Index).

LANDSCAPING

The first impression you get of a house is heavily influenced by the landscaping. As a house gets older, in fact, the gardens and landscaping tend to become more profuse and more a factor in the house's saleability. This is one of the many advantages of a used or older house.

All of the landscaping is part of the real estate. If the seller wishes to keep some plants he or she will have to contract with the buyer for this right. There have been many unhappy scenes when buyers have arrived at a house they purchased only to find shrubs and flowerbeds missing or in the process of being removed.

If you are buying the house from a builder you have two possibilities for ensuring your satisfaction with the landscaping. One is to get an allowance from the builder to finish the landscaping yourself. The other is to have a written contract with the builder that spells out who is responsible for establishing the lawn and planting the shrubs. For example, if the builder fails to provide enough topsoil, the lawn may erode.

---

[1] For more detailed information on house construction see Harrison, *HOUSES*.

Then, unless you have a well-drawn written agreement, you will have to pay to re-establish the lawn.

Inspect the grounds carefully. Is the yard level or are there sunken sections that will have to be filled? A sunken section may be a sign of a broken storm drain, sanitary sewer line or broken drain tile. These conditions will continue to get worse and may lead to costly repairs.

Next, look at the trees. Have any of them been damaged in the construction process or any other way? Has the ground level at the base of a tree been raised or lowered? Just a small change of the ground level at a tree's base will often damage or kill it. And it is quite expensive to have trees repaired or to have dead trees removed and replaced.

Next, check on the condition of the driveway and sidewalks. If the driveway is paved and in poor condition, you will soon be faced with an expensive repair job. Cracked sidewalks are dangerous and should be repaired immediately.

POOLS AND TENNIS COURTS

Does the house have a swimming pool? An above-ground pool in most areas is considered to be personal property and is not normally included as part of the sale. If it is indeed the intention of the current owner to remove the pool, there should be provision made to repair the damage to the lawn where the pool was. And what about the fences, patio and other improvements around the pool? How will they be effected if the pool is removed?

If the above-ground pool is to be part of your purchase, you should have it inspected to determine that everything is in good working order.

An inground swimming pool is an expensive item that adds considerable value to a house. However, in many areas the value added is not equal to the cost. Again, a professional inspection should be made of the pool and all the equipment needed to make it usable. Pool owners know that even when everything is in good repair, it is an expensive, time consuming proposition to keep a pool safe, and in usable working order.

Tennis courts are also a major amenity to a house. Again, since you are probably paying a considerable price for them their condition should be carefully checked. Bad drainage is often a problem that is difficult to correct. Most experienced tennis players can judge the condition of the court surfaces and the state of repair of the surrounding fences.

The exterior inspection should also include the exterior lights and outlets. All the outlets should be weatherproof. (This is covered in more detail in Chapter 9.)

DRAINAGE

In many areas storm water drainage is an important consideration. The land should always slope away from the house. This is a very common deficiency which, depending upon the topography of the lot, may or may not be easy to correct. There should be at least a six-inch drop within six feet of the house. Without this minimum slope a wet basement may develop and the foundation may sink and then crack. This will cause a whole series of problems throughout the house.

A further check of the drainage should be made to determine how the storm water drains off the lot. It should flow away from the house. While you are checking you should look to see if your neighbor's storm water is draining onto your lot and into your foundation. If the neighboring lot naturally drains onto your lot, there probably is nothing you can do about it except to divert the water away from your house. However, if during your neighbors' building and grading they changed the flow of the storm water, you may legally be able to have them restore the flow to its original drainage point.

Sometimes drainage is accomplished by running the water into a dry well. This is a deep hole filled with gravel used to collect water running off the house. A dry well should be located away from the foundation walls (15 feet is the minimum safe distance).

Retaining walls are designed to hold back the earth where the lot slopes so steeply that damage would occur from the sliding earth. They can be expensive to build and usually should be at least a foot thick. They should be set on a footing that goes into the ground below the frost line (see Glossary-Index). When the wall is incorrectly constructed pressure will build up behind it and it will tilt forward until, eventually, it falls over and has to be replaced.

Some lots have fences and walls on their boundary lines or inside the lot for a variety of purposes. You should determine from the current owner who owns these fences and walls and who is responsible for keeping them repaired.

For a complete Grounds and Site Improvements checklist, see Checklist 20, page C-43.

SUBSTRUCTURES

No matter what type of foundation is selected, an excavation is dug for the footings, which is the perimetric base of concrete. The hole should be at least six inches to natural, undisturbed soil in order to provide adequate bearing except where bearing is on a stable rock formation and below the prevailing frost line.

FOOTINGS AND FOUNDATION WALLS

The purpose of the footing is to provide support for the dwelling without excessive differential or overall settlement or movement. A footing is laid by pouring the concrete into wooden forms set at a level below the

FIGURE 45
FOOTING AND FOUNDATION

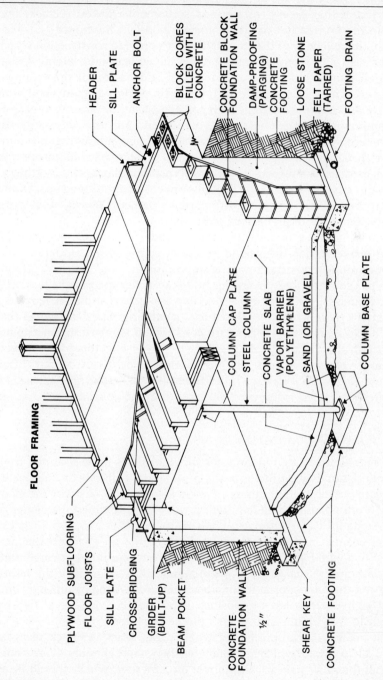

HEADER

SILL PLATE

ANCHOR BOLT

BLOCK CORES FILLED WITH CONCRETE

CONCRETE BLOCK FOUNDATION WALL

DAMP-PROOFING (PARGING)

CONCRETE FOOTING

LOOSE STONE

FELT PAPER (TARRED)

FOOTING DRAIN

COLUMN CAP PLATE

STEEL COLUMN

CONCRETE SLAB

VAPOR BARRIER (POLYETHYLENE)

SAND (OR GRAVEL)

COLUMN BASE PLATE

FLOOR FRAMING

PLYWOOD SUB-FLOORING

FLOOR JOISTS

SILL PLATE

CROSS-BRIDGING

GIRDER (BUILT-UP)

BEAM POCKET

CONCRETE FOUNDATION WALL

½"

SHEAR KEY

CONCRETE FOOTING

frost line and on undisturbed earth. It should be noted that all sub-structures will settle to a certain extent unless they are located on solid bedrock and that excess shifting and settlement will cause cracks and leaks in the foundation wall and uneven floors in the house.

Since the objective of the foundation is to provide construction which assures safe and adequate support for all vertical and lateral design loads, all foundation walls are poured or laid on top of the footings. Block walls must be properly laid and well mortared, then filled with concrete and made watertight with cement plaster or other waterproofing compounds. Cinder blocks are porous and are thus inferior to cement blocks for a solid foundation. Brick and tile, although good foundation materials, are costly and require substantial skill for proper laying, as does stone, which was once very popular in the Northeast.

The three basic forms of foundations are basements, crawl spaces and slab-on-ground. Houses built with partial basements usually were done so to save money unless a rock ledge existed.

For basementless houses, the finish grade is a major factor in the choice between slab-on-ground or crawl space as a foundation. For slab-on-ground construction, it is important that the finished ground grade fall sharply away from the house in order to prevent flooding.

Crawl spaces, which provide flooding protection and also provide a convenient place to run heating ducts, plumbing pipes and wires that must be accessible for repairs, are constructed similarly to basements except that the distance from the floor to the joists is three to four feet. The floor can be concrete, as in a basement, or it can be dirt, often covered with a vapor barrier. In northern regions, crawl spaces must be insulated or heated to prevent pipe freezing and cold floors.

MAIN BEARING BEAM AND COLUMNS

Since most houses are too large for the floor joists to be spanned from one foundation wall to the opposite foundation wall, one or more bearing beams resting on columns or piers are used to support the floor joists. If only one beam is required, it runs roughly down the center of the basement or crawl space.

Steel beams, because of their high strength, can span greater distances than wood beams of the same size. They should be covered with metal lath and plaster so they will maintain their strength if the house burns and they are subject to high temperatures. Wood beams may be a six by eight-inch to ten by ten-inch solid member or several two by six-inch to two by ten-inch planks placed together.

Most beams are supported by wood posts, brick or block piers or metal Lally columns which are concrete-filled steel cylinders. It is important that the post, pier or column rest on a footing, which should be at least two feet square and one foot thick. Steel columns require both caps and base plates.

WET OR DAMP BASEMENT

Dampness is the main problem with basements. It damages wall and floor coverings, furniture, clothing and other possessions. It also poses a health hazard—especially when the basement is used for sleeping. Some of the causes of basement dampness which can be thwarted by the careful builder are poor foundation wall construction, excess ground water not properly carried away by ground tiles, poorly fitted windows or hatch, a poorly vented clothes dryer, gutters and downspouts spilling water too near the foundation wall and a rising water table in the ground.

A basement that is wet or damp only part of the year can usually be detected any time by careful inspection. All the walls should be checked for a powder-white mineral deposit a few inches off the floor. Only the most diligent cleaning will remove all such deposits after a basement has been flooded.

Stains along the lower edge of the walls and columns and on the furnace and hot water heater are indications of excessive dampness, as is mildew odor.

The causes of a wet and damp basement are numerous. Some are easily corrected and others are almost impossible to correct. In areas where the soil drainage is poor or the water table is near the surface of the ground, it is necessary to have well constructed footing and foundation drains to maintain a dry basement. They should be installed when the house is constructed since it is a major expense to do so afterwards. The same is true of a vapor barrier under the basement floor, which is very easy to put down during construction but impossible afterwards.

Cracks in the floor and walls may be patched with various widely marketed compounds. A more drastic step is to dig down and repair the wall from the outside.

What appears at first to be a major water problem might be traced to a leak in a window or the hatch door. A simple caulking job will stop the water from coming in. Water will leak in through a window at the bottom of a well that does not drain properly in a heavy rain storm. Extending the drain line or deepening the dry well solves this problem.

If there is an edge of the roof line without a gutter, water may be running off and collecting next to the foundation wall. The water that is collected by the gutter and flows into the leaders must be diverted away from the foundation wall. The leader should run into a sewer drain, dry well or splash pan—in that order of preference.

Dampness and mildew may also be caused by moisture condensing on the walls, ceiling and pipes. Proper ventilation eliminates this problem.

For a complete Substructures checklist, see Checklist 21, page C-45.

FRAMING AND EXTERIOR WALLS

FRAMING

Nine out of ten houses in this country are of wood frame construction. Many of them are covered with wood siding; others may be covered with wood shingles, composition shingles or siding, brick veneer or stucco. Regardless of the type of exterior covering, these houses are in the general classification of wood frame construction. There are three different basic wood frame constructions: Western platform, balloon and plank and beam.

Balloon frame construction is used primarily for multi-story masonry veneer houses. It represents a very small percentage of single-family houses. Plank and beam construction was used in Colonial houses and has again become popular for contemporary houses where the planks and beams are used as exposed, finished materials.

Platform frame construction is the way the vast majority of American houses are built. The subfloor extends to the outside edges of the building and provides a platform upon which exterior walls and interior partitions are erected.

Wall framing should be strong and stiff enough to support the vertical loads from floors and roof. Moreover, the walls should be able to resist the lateral loads resulting from winds and, in some areas, from earthquakes.

Studs, which in exterior walls are placed with the wide faces perpendicular to the direction of the wall, should be at least a mininum two by four inches for one and two-story buildings. In one-story buildings studs may be spaced 24 inches, on center, unless otherwise limited by the wall covering. In all cases an arrangement of multiple studs is used at the corners to provide for ready attachment of exterior and interior surface materials.

Where doors or windows are to be located, provision is made by a header of adequate size, the ends of which may be supported either on studs or by framing anchors when the span or opening does not exceed three feet in width.

DEFECTIVE HOUSE FRAMING

Once a house is a few years old, signs of defective framing can be detected visually. One sign is bulging exterior walls, which are best seen by standing at each corner of the house and looking along the wall.

Window sills that are not level are a sign of settling, defective framing or original sloppy carpentry. Sticking windows may be a sign of settling or defective framing.

FIGURE 46
WESTERN PLATFORM FRAMING

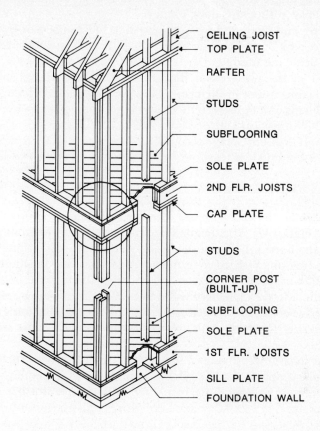

CEILING JOIST
TOP PLATE
RAFTER
STUDS
SUBFLOORING
SOLE PLATE
2ND FLR. JOISTS
CAP PLATE
STUDS
CORNER POST
(BUILT-UP)
SUBFLOORING
SOLE PLATE
1ST FLR. JOISTS
SILL PLATE
FOUNDATION WALL

A sure sign of trouble is a large crack developing on the outside of the house between the chimney and the exterior wall. Other tip-offs to defective framing are cracks running outward at an angle from the upper corners of window and door frames.

Sagging and sloping floors may be detected visually or by putting a marble on the floor and watching to see if it rolls away. This may be a sign of defective framing.

Cracks in the walls other than those discussed above should be a cause of concern but in themselves are not conclusive evidence of framing problems. All houses settle unless built upon solid rock. Rare is the house that does not develop some wall and ceiling cracks. They should be of most concern when accompanied by some of the other signs of defective framing.

SHEATHING

Exterior walls should be braced by a layer of material known as sheathing (See Figure 47). The diagonal method of placing sheathing is preferable to the horizontal because additional strength and stiffness may be provided by one by four-inch members set into the outside face of the studs at an angle of 45 degrees and nailed to the top and bottom plates and studs. Moreover, where wood sheathing boards are applied diagonally, let-in braces are not necessary. In either case, sheathing should be nailed to sills, headers, studs, plates or continuous headers and to gable end rafters.

Wood sheathing provides a solid nailing base. Plywood makes an excellent sheathing material as does fiberboard and gypsum. New products combine the sheathing, insulation and exterior finish.

SHEATHING PAPER

Weathertight walls are provided by covering the sheathing on the outside with sheathing paper which may be either asphalt-saturated felt weighing not less than 15 pounds per 108 square feet or any other impregnated paper having equivalent water-repellent properties.

EXTERIOR WALL COVERINGS

There are a wide variety of siding and other exterior coverings which are applied over wood framing. Often a house has more than one type of siding on it.

If bevel siding or square-inch boards are used, they should be applied horizontally and lapped one inch with nails driven just above the lap to permit possible movement due to change in moisture conditions. Where shingles are installed in double courses (double layers) the butt of the exposed shingle extends about one-quarter inch below the undercourse or layer in order to produce a shadow line.

Shingles should be nailed with corrosion-resistant nails of sufficient length to penetrate the sheathing, using two nails for shingles up to eight inches wide and three nails for wider shingles.

Stucco is still popular in dry climates where it can be applied directly to the surface of a solid masonry wall. However, the application of stucco to a wood frame wall is generally more involved than that of other finishes.

A masonry veneer wall is really a frame wall with some variety of masonry siding, most commonly clay bricks, concrete bricks, split blocks or stone. In houses with masonry veneer walls, all of the structural functions of the walls are performed by the framing and not by the one-unit thick masonry which is tied to the frame wall.

A variety of other types of siding materials are available. These include aluminum, stone, hardboard, gypsum board, fiberglass and metals.

MASONRY CONSTRUCTION

Only a small percentage of our houses are truly masonry construction as opposed to frame construction with masonry veneer. Solid masonry walls, if well constructed, are very durable and easily maintained. However, they should be insulated and they do require a larger foundation than a wood frame wall does.

A hollow masonry wall is built of two units that are separated into an inside and outside wall by between two to four inches of air space and bonded together with metal ties or joint reinforcement.

Masonry bonded walls are similar to cavity walls except that the two layers of masonry known as wythes are joined by masonry header courses instead of by metal ties. Although they are economical to construct, their insulation qualities are inferior to cavity walls and they are, therefore, used mainly in the Southwest.

For a complete Framing and Exterior Wall checklist, see Checklist 22, page C-47.

INSULATION AND VENTILATION

The topic of our times is energy conservation, and it appears this problem will continue to gain importance. Insulation is the most effective way to reduce fuel consumption in a home. We have been using inorganic fibrous insulation, "mineral wool," for over 100 years but it really did not become popular until the 1920's and 1930's.

Many pre-World War II houses were built without any insulation. As building materials became lighter the need for insulation increased. Today any home built without adequate insulation regardless of the climate is a substandard product.

The two primary benefits of insulation are fuel economy and occupant comfort. Its secondary benefits are the reduction of sound transmission and the reduction of fire danger. Insulation keeps the heat inside when it is cold outside and the heat out when it is hot outside. Therefore, good insulation is important in most climates.

SAVINGS

When examining the economic benefits of insulation, the first question that arises is, how much can be saved by the proper insulation of a house? The answer depends upon many factors but mainly upon how weatherproof the windows and doors have been made and upon the quality both of the ceiling insulation and ventilation and of the wall insulation. The calculation of the heat losses and gains in terms of insulation is a subject best left to heating and cooling experts. However, local electric companies will supply complete information on how the losses and gains can be calculated.

Here are some rules of thumb for heating and cooling savings obtained by adding various types of weatherproofing and insulation to a frame, one-story building:

Insulation Description	Fuel Cost Savings
Weatherstripping all doors and windows	3–5%
Storm windows and doors on all openings	10–20%
Minimum attic or ceiling insulation	5–10%
Maximum attic or ceiling insulation	15–20%
Minimum wall insulation	5–15%
Maximum wall insulation	10–20%

The total difference between fuel costs for an uninsulated house and for an otherwise identical one with storm windows and doors and good insulation in the walls and ceiling can be over 50 percent.

"R" RATINGS

The standard measurement for the effectiveness of insulation is its "R" value (resistance to heat flow). The higher the "R" value the better the insulation. Thus, most brand name insulation products are marked with their "R" values.

Over-ceiling or under-roof insulation should have an "R" rating from R-19 in mild climates where there is no air conditioning and gas or oil heat to R-38 or better in colder climates or hot climates or where there is electric heat or air conditioning.

Exterior wall insulation requires an R-19 rating for hot or cold climates or electric heat or air conditioning, down to R-11 for mild climates, no air conditioning and gas and oil heat.

Floor insulation, if a house is built over a crawl area, should be at least R-11 and preferably R-13 in mild climates and R-19 to R-22 in colder climates. When the house is built on a slab, only edge floor insulation is required. And when the house is built over a basement, no floor insulation is needed at all.

"COLD WALL" EFFECT

When examining the occupant comfort benefits of insulation the first to consider is reduction of the "cold wall" effect. The human body feels uncomfortable when it is losing heat too fast. A room also feels uncomfortable when it is losing heat too fast. Even if a room itself feels warm body heat will radiate to a nearby cold surface (wall, floor, ceiling) and produce a chilled feeling. In the summer, reverse conditions are in effect when excessively warm surfaces make it difficult for the body to maintain its normal temperature.

To compensate for the discomfort produced by heat radiation, most people will set the thermostat higher in the winter and lower in the summer, thereby increasing the fuel cost. But insulation helps to make a house comfortable without increased fuel costs because it helps make room-to-room and floor-to-ceiling air temperature more uniform. Moreover, it reduces drafts from convection currents which are generated by interior surface-air temperature differences.

"SUPER INSULATION"

A good deal has been written about the so-called "super insulated house." This is a special type of construction that uses two by six-inch wall studs instead of the conventional two by four-inch stud. This permits extra insulation in the walls that would not otherwise be possible. These houses often have insulated glass in the windows and high quality weather stripping. There is no question that all this extra insulation will increase the fuel savings. However, there is a question as to whether the insulation is cost effective at the current cost of fuel. Also, some problems have arisen about these houses being so airtight that they do not ventilate properly.

COST EFFECTIVENESS

The subject of cost effectiveness will become more prominent as the pressure to insulate and use solar energy is increased by the government and other fuel conservationists.

If it costs $3,000 to insulate a house which would result in an annual fuel cost savings of $800 and if mortgage money costs 12 percent, it would take about five years to save the cost of the insulation. This would be considered to be cost effective. The general rule is that you should be able to recover the cost of the improvement in less than 10 years.

WINDOWS

A substantial amount of heat is lost through the windows. It has been estimated that the typical window, when closed, lets out as much heat as a four-inch diameter hole in the wall would let out.

One way to cut down the heat loss is with better insulation. Two pieces of single or double-strength glass may be hermetically sealed together with an air space between them. This is known as insulating glass. It is often used in electrically heated houses.

Glass that is tinted or bronzed reflects heat and has some insulation qualities. Tinted glass reduces the ability to see inside the house from the exterior.

The purpose of weather stripping on windows is to provide a seal to prevent air and dust leakage. A common kind of weather stripping used today is the spring tension type of bronze, aluminum, rigid vinyl, stainless or galvanized steel or rigid plastic steel. Other types are woven felt, compression sash guides and compression bulbs.

Storm windows and screens reduce heat loss and transmission. In cold climates they save sufficient fuel to justify their expense and inconvenience, which vary with the house construction, climate and habits of the people in the house.

Storm doors, screen doors and combination storm and screen doors are often hung outside the regular door to provide additional insulation in the winter and ventilation in the summer.

VENTILATION

Ideally a dwelling should provide natural ventilation in areas such as attics and basementless spaces in order to minimize decay and deterioration of the house and to reduce attic heat in the summer. Thus, FHA makes the following recommendations:

1. Eight mesh per inch screening should be used to cover all exterior openings.
2. At least four foundation wall ventilators should be provided in basementless spaces or crawl spaces unless one side of such space is completely open to the basement.
3. Cross ventilation should be provided in an attic and in spaces between roofs and top floor ceilings by venting. All openings should be designed to prevent the entrance of rain or snow.

For a complete Insulation and Ventilation checklist, see Checklist 23, page C-49.

ROOFS, FLASHING, GUTTERS AND DOWNSPOUTS

ROOFS

The roof is so important that buying a house is known colloquially to some as "putting a roof over our heads." The roof of the house is subject to intensive wear and tear from the elements. The roof will have to be repaired and replaced from time to time. None of the existing roofing materials will last anywhere near the typical life of the house.

The Underwriters' Laboratory (U.L.) tests and rates most of the roofing being produced today for fire resistance, wind resistance, quantity of saturant and efficiency of saturation, thickness and distribution of coating asphalts, adhesion and distribution of granules, weight count, size, coloration and other characteristics of finished products before and after packing.

In high wind areas, a minimum of U.L. Class C wind resistant roofing should be used. More fire protection, and usually longer trouble-free life, is obtained from wind resistant Class B and Class A shingles. In low wind areas, wind resistant shingles are not necessary, but a minimum of Class C should be used to provide fire protection and satisfactory life. Classes B and A are still better quality.

ROOFING MATERIALS

Shingles are sold by weight per square. The higher the weight the longer the shingle will last and the more it will cost. A heavy shingle weighs more than 30 pounds per square. Since labor is a big factor in roofing cost, it usually pays to buy heavyweight shingles since the total cost in the long run will be less.

The roof must be constructed first so that it will support its own weight plus that of loads from snow, ice and wind.

FLASHING

Whenever a roof is complicated by an intersection of the joining of two different roof slopes, adjoining walls or projections through the surface by chimneys or pipes, or other protrusions, the joint must be flashed. Flashing is usually accomplished by first nailing metal strips across or under the point, then applying a waterproofing compound or cement and finally applying the roofing material over the edges to permanently hold it in place.

ROOF COVERING

Shingles and shakes made of wood, asphalt, asbestos, cement, slate or tile are used for the majority of house roofs. However, metal roofs, clay tile and built-up or membrane roofs can also be found.

The difference between a shingle and a shake is that a shingle is sawed and a shake is split. A shake may have a sawed back and still be called a shake.

The handsplit wood shingle or shake was one of the first roof covering materials used in this country, dating back to early colonial days. What made them so durable was western red cedar wood which is highly resistant to rot and decay. Most of the wood shingles and shakes made today in this country are western red cedar.

When applied to roofs, shingles have a life expectancy that decreases as the slope of the roof decreases and the grade of the shingle decreases. A premium shingle on a normal house roof with a 45 degree slope should last 20 years in most parts of the country.

Other good roofing materials are slate, shingle tile, and interlocking tiles known as French Tile, Spanish Tile, Mission Tile, Roman Tile and Greek Tile. Composition roll roofing, like that used on commercial and industrial buildings is also suitable for houses with flat roofs.

DEFECTIVE ROOFING

Water may leak through the roof for a variety of reasons. Asphalt shingle roofs may leak in a high wind if light grade shingles are used.

As these shingles get older they curl, tear and become pierced with holes. Wood shingles may curl, split, become loose and broken and fall off the roof while asbestos shingles may crack and break. Metal roofs can rust, become bent and pierced with holes. Roll and built-up roofs may become loose, torn, patched and worn through.

GUTTERS AND DOWNSPOUTS

Gutters and downspouts provide means for controlled water disposal from roofs to prevent damage to the property or to prevent unsightly appearance of walls when roof overhangs are not provided. If gutters are not provided, a diverter or other means must be used to prevent water from roofs from draining on uncovered entrance platforms or steps.

Gutters or eavetroughs catch the rain water as it reaches the edge of the roof and carry it to the downspouts or leaders. In northern climates it is important to install gutters below the slope line so that snow and ice can slide clear.

Metal gutters are attached to the house with various types of metal hangers and are the most common type now being made. Aluminum, copper, galvanized iron and other metals are used in the construction of these gutters.

Wood gutters are still used but mostly in the Northeast. They are attached to the house with noncorroding screws bedded in elastic roofer's cement to prevent leakage. Built-in gutters are made of metal and set into the deeply notched rafter a short distance up the roof from the eaves. Pole gutters consist of a wooden strip nailed perpendicularly to the roof and covered with sheet metal.

Downspouts or leaders are vertical pipes that carry the water from

FIGURE 47
EXTERIOR WALLS

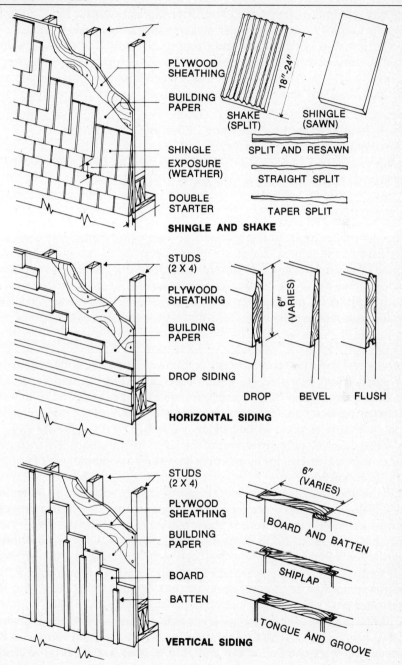

PLYWOOD SHEATHING

BUILDING PAPER

SHAKE (SPLIT)

SHINGLE (SAWN)

18"-24"

SPLIT AND RESAWN

SHINGLE

EXPOSURE (WEATHER)

STRAIGHT SPLIT

DOUBLE STARTER

TAPER SPLIT

SHINGLE AND SHAKE

STUDS (2 X 4)

PLYWOOD SHEATHING

BUILDING PAPER

6" (VARIES)

DROP SIDING

DROP   BEVEL   FLUSH

HORIZONTAL SIDING

STUDS (2 X 4)

PLYWOOD SHEATHING

BUILDING PAPER

6" (VARIES)

BOARD AND BATTEN

BOARD

BATTEN

SHIPLAP

TONGUE AND GROOVE

VERTICAL SIDING

the gutter to the ground and sometimes into sewers, dry wells, drain tiles or splash pans. Their most common shapes are rectangular, corrugated rectangular, corrugated round and plain round. They must be large enough to carry the water away as fast as they receive it.

The junction of the gutter and downspout should be covered with a basket strainer to hold back leaves and twigs, especially if the gutter is connected to a storm or sanitary sewer which might become clogged and difficult to clean out.

For a complete checklist on Roofs, Flashing, Gutters and Downspouts, see Checklist 24, page C-51.

INTERIOR FLOORS, WALLS, CEILINGS AND STAIRS

FLOOR FRAMING

The floor framing is an integral part of the overall framing system. Regardless of the general framing method used for the rest of the house, floor framing is relatively simple and done the same way in most houses. Basically, floors consist of subflooring resting on joists (floor beams) stiffened by bridging; the joists are carried by girders, walls or load bearing partitions.

SUBFLOORING

Plywood is the most common material now being used for subflooring. When properly installed the grain of the outer plies should be at right angles to the joists. The plywood panels should be staggered so that the division between adjacent panels comes over different joists. Installed this way, it is as good as boards or planks.

Wood boards with a minimum thickness of three-quarter inch and maximum width of eight inches may be installed diagonally to or at right angles to joists.

Plank and beam floor systems are usually made with two by six or two by eight-inch tongue and grooved or splined planks spanning between beams generally spaced four to eight feet on center. The planks serve as the subfloor and working platform and transmit the floor loads to fewer but larger members than in wood joist floor systems.

Panelized floor systems are increasing in popularity. Panels are either premanufactured in the mill or on the job site and set in place over the joists.

Bridging is used to stiffen the joists and prevent them from deflecting sideways. Strips of wood or bands of metal are fastened crosswise between the joists and nailed top and bottom to form the bridging. There should be a line of bridging for each six to eight feet of unsupported length of joist.

FLOOR COVERINGS

Carpeting, which can be installed over either finished flooring or sub-flooring, is rapidly gaining in popularity. It is now being used in virtually every room in the house, including bathrooms and kitchens.

Ceramic tile is another popular floor covering. It can be set in plaster. Over the subflooring a waterproof building paper is laid and then wire mesh. Ceramic tile can also be attached with special adhesive to a smooth concrete floor or to a subfloor covered with a special adhesive or special underlayment material.

Concrete slabs may be used for floor covering with no further treatment or they can be painted with special concrete paint or covered with other flooring covering.

Resilient tiles such as vinyl or vinyl asbestos are glued down with special adhesives according to the individual manufacturer's recommendation for the particular tile.

Terrazzo flooring is made of colored marble chips mixed into cement. After being laid, it is ground down to a very smooth surface.

Wood block flooring may be installed over an underlayment or directly to most subfloorings. Wood strip flooring may be installed directly over the joists or over subflooring. The boards over wood flooring are nailed at right angles to the subflooring except when the subflooring is plywood or is laid diagonally. It is best to put a layer of 15-point asphalt impregnated felt or other suitable building paper on top of the subflooring in order to prevent drafts, dust and moisture from coming up through the strips.

Flooring must be kept dry at all times before and during installation. It is often kiln-dried to a low moisture content of six to eight percent and must be kept that way. Flooring that is moist when laid shrinks in the dry winter, leaving ugly joints. After the flooring is laid it is scraped, sanded and varnished.

Among other popular floor coverings are linoleum, asphalt tile, rubber tile and cork tile.

WEAK AND DEFECTIVE FLOORS

The most common cause of sagging floors is floor joists that are either too small or lack support because of inadequate bridging.

Floors that have been exposed to water may warp and bulge upwards. Wide cracks between the floorboards are a sign of poor workmanship or shrinkage caused by wood that was improperly dried or not stored correctly at the time of installation. Fortunately, rough, stained, discolored, blemished, burned or gouged floors can usually be fixed by refinishing.

INTERIOR WALLS AND CEILINGS

Interior walls which support weight from above are called load bearing and must be stronger than non-load bearing walls that are used only as partitions. Frame interior walls are made of studs and covered with a variety of wall coverings. Load bearing, masonry walls should be six inches thick when supporting one floor and eight inches thick when supporting more than one floor.

WALL AND CEILING FINISHES

Plaster walls are constructed by applying up to three coats of plaster over either metal lath, wire lath, wire fabric, gypsum lath, wood lath or fiberboard lath which has been attached to the studs or furring strips.

A well constructed plaster wall provides a high degree of soundproofing. Its main disadvantages, however, are high cost and susceptibility to cracking.

As long as cracked plaster is tight to the wall it may be sufficient to just patch and redecorate a crack.

Bulging plaster on the ceiling is dangerous and should be repaired. When this is suspected, the defect can often be detected by pressing a broom handle against the ceiling and feeling if there is any give in the plaster.

Gypsum drywalls are constructed by nailing, gluing or screwing sheets of gypsum boards directly to the studs or masonry or to furring strips attached to the masonry wall.

Moreover, in the construction of gypsum drywalls, all exterior corners should be protected with metal corner beads, angles or wood moulding to prevent damage and all joints in wall board surfaces intended to receive paint or wallpaper finishes should be taped and cemented.

Other popular interior wall materials are plywood, hardboard, fiberboard and wood paneling. Ceramic and plastic tile are often used on portions of bathroom walls. They may be installed by setting them in a cement plaster base (known as a mud job) or attached to the walls with special adhesives.

CRACKED, LOOSE OR LEAKING TILES

The principal area where tile problems occur is around the tub, especially when there is a shower that splashes water on the tile wall. Defective grout will allow the water to seep behind the tile and loosen the glue. New waterproof adhesives help eliminate this. Tiles set in plaster also are less likely to present problems.

The wallboard itself may become damaged by moisture. Special waterproof wallboards have now been developed to cut down this problem.

STAIRS

The objective of the well planned stairway is to provide safe ascent and descent and a design and arrangement which assures adequate headroom and space for moving furniture and equipment. A handrail can be attached to the wall with brackets or supported by posts called balusters. A simple test for adequate design is to check the stairs on all of the

FIGURE 48
STAIRS

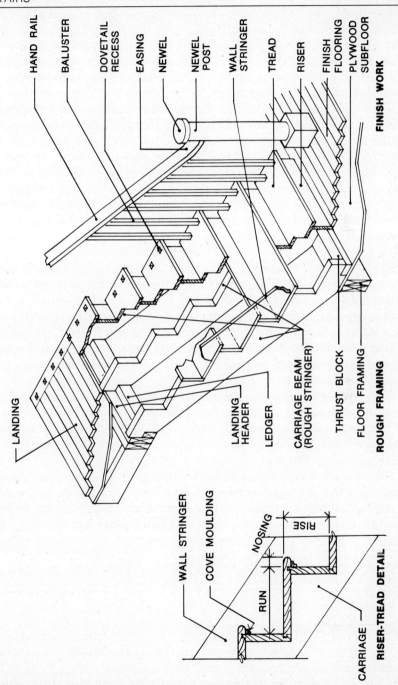

HAND RAIL
BALUSTER
DOVETAIL RECESS
EASING
NEWEL
NEWEL POST
WALL STRINGER
TREAD
RISER
FINISH FLOORING
PLYWOOD SUBFLOOR

FINISH WORK

LANDING
LANDING HEADER
LEDGER
CARRIAGE BEAM (ROUGH STRINGER)
THRUST BLOCK
FLOOR FRAMING

ROUGH FRAMING

WALL STRINGER
COVE MOULDING
NOSING
RISE
RUN
CARRIAGE

RISER-TREAD DETAIL

following features: headroom, width clear of handrail, run, rise, winders, landings, handrail and railings (See Figure 48).

INTERIOR STAIRS

The first feature which must be taken into consideration with interior stairs is headroom. For main stairs there should be a minimum of six feet, eight inches of headroom and for basement and service stairs a minimum of six feet, four inches.

The maximum riser height for interior stairs is eight and one-quarter inches. Landings of no less than two feet, six inches should be provided at the top of any run of stairs having a door which swings toward the stair. A continuous handrail should be installed on at least one side of each flight of stairs exceeding three risers. Stairs which are open on both sides, including basement stairs, should have a continuous handrail on one side and a railing on the open portion on the other side. Railings should also be installed around the open sides of all other interior stairwells including those in attics.

EXTERIOR STAIRS

All exterior stairs, with the exception of those running to the basement of the house, require: (1) that the width be that of the walk but that it be no less than three feet, (2) that the run be no more than 11 inches, (3) that the rise be no more than seven and one-half inches and that all rise-heights within a flight be uniform and (4) that a continuous handrail be installed on all open sides of stair flights to a platform more than four risers or 30 inches above finish grade.

Unprotected exterior stairs to the basement require the following: (1) that the headroom be at least six feet, four inches, (2) that the width clear of handrail be at least two feet, six inches, (3) that the run be no more than seven and one-half inches and (4) that a handrail be installed on at least one side if the stairs exceed four risers.

For protected exterior stairs to the basement the following are required: (1) that the headroom be at least six feet, two inches, (2) that the run be at least eight inches plus a one and one-half-inch nosing and (3) that the rise be no more than eight and one-quarter inches.

For a complete checklist on Interior Floors, Walls, Ceilings and Stairs, see Checklist 25, page C-53.

FIREPLACES, CHIMNEYS AND VENTS

FIREPLACES

The fireplace has never lost its popularity with Americans. Even when fuel saving was not a big issue fireplaces were sought by many people who used them primarily for decorative purposes. Now that energy conservation is a matter of prime concern they are being justified on that basis. What the real reason for their acceptance is really does not matter very much. They continue to be popular and home buyers in large numbers are willing to pay for them.

A fireplace usually is constructed of masonry. There are many fireplace designs and variations, of which the simplest and most common is the single opening with a damper and hearth. Other designs, however, feature two, three or four openings.

The opening of the fireplace should be wider than it is high, but it should not be very deep because the shallower the fireplace, the more heat is reflected into the room. The inside walls should go back at an angle so that the rear inside wall is at least one and one-half feet narrower than the front opening because square inside corners interfere with the air flow and cause smoking and poor combustion. The rear inside wall should slope forward to the back of the damper.

A damper (see Figure 49) is a desirable feature. It should be at least eight inches above the top, but it should not be set directly on top of the fireplace opening because such a position would, at times, allow smoke to escape into the room. Another desirable feature is an ash dump connecting to an ash pit with an ash-cleanout door.

Inside, out of sight in a well constructed fireplace (See Figure 49) there is the smoke shelf, smoke chamber and flue.

The inner hearth (really the back hearth under the fire), together with the cheeks and back of the fireplace, must be built of heat-resistant materials in order to withstand the intense heat of the fire. Thus, fire brick and fire clay are the most common materials used. A front hearth extending at least 16 inches from the front of the fireplace and at least eight inches beyond each side is needed as a precaution against flying sparks.

CHIMNEYS AND VENTS

Chimneys and vents should be constructed and installed to be structurally safe, durable, smoketight and capable of withstanding action of flue gases. The efficiency of any heating system (except electric) depends upon the chimney or vent. Defective chimneys and vents may constitute serious fire hazards.

Whatever its construction, the chimney is the heaviest portion of the house and it must be supported by its own concrete footings. These footings must be so designed that they will not let the chimney settle faster than the rest of the building.

The masonry chimney walls should be eight inches thick when they are exposed to the exterior of the house. "Masonry and factory-built chimneys should extend at least two feet above any part of a roof, roof ridge or parapet wall within 10 feet of the chimney," according to FHA standards.

FIGURE 49
MASONRY CHIMNEY

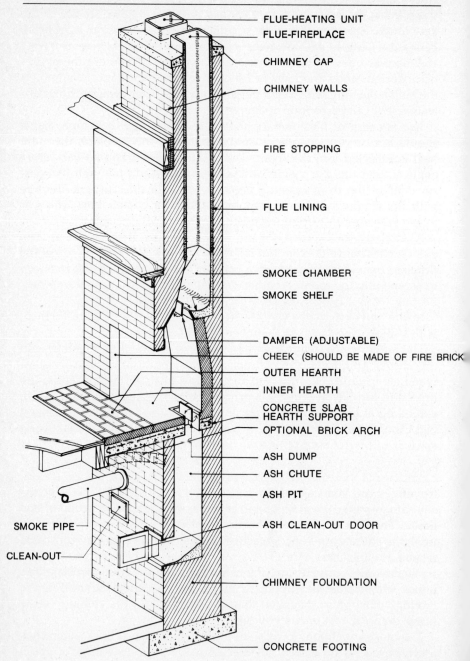

- FLUE-HEATING UNIT
- FLUE-FIREPLACE
- CHIMNEY CAP
- CHIMNEY WALLS
- FIRE STOPPING
- FLUE LINING
- SMOKE CHAMBER
- SMOKE SHELF
- DAMPER (ADJUSTABLE)
- CHEEK (SHOULD BE MADE OF FIRE BRICK
- OUTER HEARTH
- INNER HEARTH
- CONCRETE SLAB HEARTH SUPPORT
- OPTIONAL BRICK ARCH
- ASH DUMP
- ASH CHUTE
- ASH PIT
- ASH CLEAN-OUT DOOR
- CHIMNEY FOUNDATION
- CONCRETE FOOTING

SMOKE PIPE

CLEAN-OUT

The furnace and hot water heater are connected to the chimney by a smoke pipe through a metal or terra cotta collar built into the brickwork. For fire safety, the smoke pipe should be at least 10 inches below the floor joists and the joists further protected with plaster or a shield of metal or asbestos. "The smoke pipe should not exceed 10 feet in length or 75 percent of the vertical height of the chimney, whichever is less," according to FHA standards.

The heart of the chimney is the vertical open shaft through which the smoke and gas pass from the fire to the outside air. The size of the flue required for best combustion efficiency depends upon the size of the fireplace or furnace, its design and the type of fuel being used.

The flue should extend out of the top of the chimney wall a few inches. The top of the wall is capped with concrete, metal, stone or other noncombustible, waterproof material sloped from the flue to the outside edge. The cap should be at least two inches thick at the outside edge.

Another type of chimney is made and assembled in a factory. Many prefabricated units consist of a flue liner encased in a concrete wall. The units should be Underwriters Laboratories-approved and should be the proper size and design for the fireplace or other appliance involved.

For a complete checklist on Fireplaces, Chimneys and Vents, see Checklist 26, page C-55.

TERMITES AND OTHER VERMIN

Termites, known more specifically as subterranean termites, are becoming more and more a threat to our wood homes. This was not always so, especially in northern United States. Were it always so, many of our fine historic homes would no longer be standing today as they were not constructed to be termite-resistant. From time to time the government has published maps showing in which parts of the country termites are considered to be a problem. Each edition of these maps shows that the termite danger line is moving further north.

The subterranean termite is an insect which attacks in colonies and derives its nourishment from cellulose materials such as wood, fabrics, paper and fiber board. To obtain nourishment, the termite may attack wood structures above the ground by means of shelter tubes attached to foundation walls, piers and other construction members in contact with the ground. However, only under conditions which permit the insect to establish and maintain contact with soil moisture is a colony able to penetrate and consume wood. This requirement indicates that a barrier separating wood from earth, supplemented by inspection, is a practical and effective method for preventing damage by termites.

Protection of wood structures to provide maximum life involves three methods of control which can be handled by proper design and construction. One or more of the following methods may be employed: (1) controlling the moisture content of wood, (2) providing effective termite barriers, (3) using naturally durable or treated wood. It is possible by careful planning and attention to construction details to produce a frame house that will resist damage by subterranean termites. Control of moisture content of wood is a practical and effective method for prevention of decay.

TERMITE BARRIERS

Termite barriers are provided by any building material or component which can be made impenetrable to termites and which drives the insects into the open where their activities can be detected and eliminated. When there are adequate separation clearances as just described, termite barriers should not be needed except in very heavily infested areas.

The following are the five types of termite barriers:

1. Preservative-treated lumber for all floor framing up to and including the subfloor.
2. Properly installed termite shields.
3. Chemical soil treatment.
4. Poured concrete foundations.
5. Poured, reinforced concrete caps, at least four inches thick, on unit masonry foundations.

Slab-on-ground construction requires special consideration in areas where the termite hazard is a significant problem. Concrete slabs vary in their susceptibility to penetration by termites; thus, they cannot be considered to provide adequate protection unless the slab and supporting foundation are poured integrally to avoid cracks or holes through which termites may enter.

Where other types of slab construction are used, termites may penetrate through joints between the slab and wall. They may also enter through expansion joints or openings made for plumbing or conduit. Thus, it is necessary at these points to provide a barrier either by the use of termite shields, coal tar pitch or chemical soil treatment.

Masonry veneer in contact with the ground may provide access for termites in infested areas. For this reason, the veneer should be kept at least eight inches above the finished grade unless termite shields are installed in an approved manner or the soil on the exterior has received a chemical treatment.

Naturally durable or treated wood should be used when the member is so located that it cannot be maintained at a safe moisture content or where climatic or site conditions are such that construction practices alone are not sufficient for control of termites. It should be used where wood is embedded in the ground, where it is resting on concrete which is in direct contact with earth or where it is not possible to maintain

FIGURE 50

DIFFERENCES BETWEEN WINGED ADULT ANTS AND TERMITES

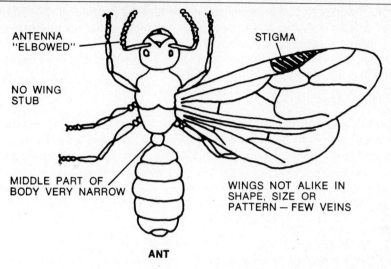

ANTENNA "ELBOWED"

STIGMA

NO WING STUB

MIDDLE PART OF BODY VERY NARROW

WINGS NOT ALIKE IN SHAPE, SIZE OR PATTERN — FEW VEINS

ANT

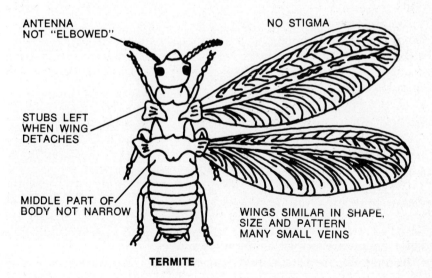

ANTENNA NOT "ELBOWED"

NO STIGMA

STUBS LEFT WHEN WING DETACHES

MIDDLE PART OF BODY NOT NARROW

WINGS SIMILAR IN SHAPE, SIZE AND PATTERN MANY SMALL VEINS

TERMITE

recommended separations between wood and earth. Termite resistant species are redwood, bald cypress and eastern red cedar.

The best way to check for termites is to hire a professional. The FHA, VA and other lending institutions require professional termite inspections in many areas of the country.

Termites work slowly. If they are caught in the early stages of infestation they may be stopped at a cost of a few hundred dollars. Damage done in the more advanced stages of infestation may cost thousands of dollars to repair.

Maintenance inspections of the house, at least annually in the spring, will detect problems at an early stage. Such inspections should concentrate on three specific areas: (1) foundation, including crawl spaces; (2) attic spaces and roof and (3) exterior surfaces, joints and architectural details. When termite shelter tubes are discovered, they should be destroyed and the ground below should be poisoned. When such evidence of termites is discovered, it is best to call a professional exterminator.

VERMIN

Rats, mice and a variety of other rodents and animals like the same type of food and shelter as humans. Often when such rodents move into a house, they will remain there happily until expelled.

Vermin may transmit diseases, destroy property and are a source of annoyance. To control vermin a house should be made as rodent-proof as possible. Food and water sources should be made inaccessible. Many poisons are available for household use. For extreme problems an exterminator will kill off the existing population and help prevent future infestations.

In addition to termites a partial list of insects which often invade our homes includes: flies, mosquitoes, cockroaches, fleas, ticks, moths, millipedes and centipedes, crickets, earwigs, ground beetles, ants, carpenter ants, spiders, scorpions, mites, wasps, bees, hornets, yellow jackets, bedbugs, lice and silverfish. Besides being a nuisance, insects may transmit diseases and destroy property. The best long run methods of control are to close up or screen any holes through which insects may enter and to eliminate sources of food and water. Household poisons will produce temporary relief but an exterminator may be needed.

For a complete checklist on Termites and Other Vermin, see Checklist 27, page C-57.

MISCELLANEOUS CONSTRUCTION DETAILS

In this section we will cover the balance of the items that should be considered during the house inspection and evaluation. Included will be moulding; doors, windows and screens; TV reception; cabinets and counters; and painting and decorating.

MOULDING

One of the distinguishing differences between older houses and newer ones is the use of interior moulding. In older houses architects often designed custom moulding that was made at mills with special machines that cut, planed and sanded the lumber into the desired shapes. Today many owners of these houses strip off layers of paint and dirt and restore the mouldings to their original beauty.

The use of interior moulding in a modern house may be limited to simple casing around the doors and windows, baseboards and ceiling moulding although all of these may not be present. In more elaborate houses and in houses that are in the architectural style of a certain period, extensive or elaborate moulding may be used. The elaboration may be increased by using two or three pieces of moulding together.

DOORS, WINDOWS AND SCREENS

There are seven basic types of doors: batten doors, sliding glass doors, folding doors, flush solid doors, flush solid core doors, flush hollow core doors and stile and rail doors.

Doors can be installed so that they either swing, slide or fold open and shut. Their intended location and use must be considered in selecting which method should be employed.

For a door to function properly and appear unblemished it must be handled and stored correctly before installation.

To ensure proper hanging, the door frame should be square and plumb and doors should fit with a total clearance of about three-sixteenths inch in both directions. Too little clearance will cause the door to stick in humid weather and excessive clearance permits the weather and sound to pass through. Inside doors usually require two hinges and outside doors three hinges.

Windows serve three basic functions of lighting, insulation and ventilation.

The sash window came into popularity about the last quarter of the seventeenth century.

Double-hung sash windows and casement windows are the two most common styles found in houses. In new construction the horizontal sliding window and the clerestory (also clearstory) window, a window placed high in the wall or in the ceiling, is also gaining popularity. There are a variety of other window styles, each with its own advantages and disadvantages.

While checking windows, some with missing locks and window lifts or counter balance weights may be discovered. It may also be difficult to reach over the kitchen sink to open that window if it is the double-hung type. Dust streaks or water stains around the window trim can be evidence of leakage.

A special look should be taken at the windows in children's rooms. Are they high enough to be safe yet low enough to allow escape in the event of a fire or other emergency?

TELEVISION RECEPTION

Good television reception is very important to many families. In areas where there is good reception from a variety of channels it is taken for granted. However, there are areas in the country that are not served by cable and where there is only limited reception. In many of these areas an expensive TV antenna installation is often required for satisfactory reception. Whether these antennas are part of the real estate or removable personal property varies from area to area.

If you are not familiar with the area in which you are moving you should check into the matter of television reception. The quality of reception could well be a factor your family would consider important in selecting a house. If there is a substantial TV antenna on the house, the sales contract should indicate to whom it will belong after the sale.

CABINETS AND COUNTERS

A major national survey showed that the lack of sufficient storage cabinets and counter space was one of the major complaints Americans had about their houses. Today most cabinets and counters are standard, millmade products that are purchased by the builder completely ready to be installed.

Cabinets and counters are an important part of the kitchen, bathrooms and lavatory, laundry room and recreation room. Built-in cabinets are often found in bedrooms, dens and other rooms in more expensive houses. Specific kitchen cabinet requirements are discussed in the kitchen portion of Chapter 6.

Cabinets and counters should be checked for adequacy, quality of construction and style. For example, you are going to have a problem if all your furniture is contemporary and all the cabinets are Mediterranean style.

A wide selection of counter top material is available. The most common ones, in descending order of cost, are:

- Stainless steel
- Ceramic tile set in mortar
- Ceramic tile attached with adhesive to wood
- Hardwood-laminated
- Melamine-laminated (Formica) with molded edge
- Melamine-laminated (Formica) with stainless steel or cut Melamine edge
- Vinyl

- Laminated polyester
- Linoleum (the most popular material prior to World War II)
- Tempered hardboard

PAINTING AND DECORATING

When you purchase your home you may have to repaint and decorate all or part of it either because you don't like the color and style of the decoration, or because the surface needs to be repainted or decorated.

A good outside paint job typically may last five years. However, this may vary depending upon the climate, quality of the original paint, how the surface was prepared and how the paint was applied, what exposure the paint has to the sun and wind and what the quality of the air is.

All exterior paints should be standard commercial brands with a history of satisfactory use under conditions equal to or similar to the conditions present in the area concerned.

Application of paint should be in strict accordance with manufacturers' directions. Ready-mixed paint should not be thinned, except as permitted in the application instructions. Exterior painting should be done only in favorable weather. All surfaces should be free of dew or frost and must be dry to the touch except with certain masonry paints formulated for application to wet surfaces. Painting should not be done when the temperature is below 40 degrees. All surfaces to be finished should be clean and free of foreign material such as dirt, grease, asphalt or rust.

Application should be made in a professional manner to provide a smooth surface. Additional coats may be required if the finish surface does not provide acceptable coverage or hiding. Certain pigments provide excellent hiding ability even when thinly applied. With paints of this type, care must be taken to obtain adequate coverage if the coating is to offer reasonable durability.

For a checklist on Miscellaneous Construction Details, see Checklist 28, page C-59.

CHAPTER 9
MECHANICAL SYSTEMS*

For those few who have spent time in houses without a complete set of mechanical systems you need no reminder of how important these systems are to the way most of us are accustomed to living. They are essential in order for a house to provide both shelter and comfort. It is essential that they be properly selected for the house, correctly installed and constantly kept in efficient working order.

It is not expected or necessary that a homeowner or home buyer be an engineer or mechanic in order to enjoy homeownership. However, it is very helpful to have some basic knowledge about mechanical systems. We cannot help but feel sorry for those who have spent hours in the dark awaiting the arrival of the electrician only to find a new fuse solves the problem, or who have spent hours in the cold because one did not know how to throw the reset switch on the oil burner motor.

We have divided the mechanical systems into six categories: heating, cooling, plumbing, hot water, electrical and miscellaneous.

HEATING SYSTEMS

Central heating is an expected feature of most American homes. But it was not always so. The central heating and hot water systems of today are generally under 100 years old.

Central heating and hot water systems can be classified by dividing them into the kinds of fuels or the type of transfer medium used to carry the heat from the ignited fuel to the rooms in the house.

PRINCIPLES OF HEATING

In order to understand the various heating systems and how they work, it is first necessary to know a little about heat itself and what makes people feel warm or cold.

* Portions of this chapter are based on *HOUSES—The Illustrated Guide to Construction, Design and Systems* by Henry S. Harrison, © 1976 by REALTORS NATIONAL MARKETING INSTITUTE®.

The body itself has its own heating system, providing enough heat for human survival in a wide range of temperatures, which explains how the human race survived so long without much heat. Maximum comfort, however, is obtainable in a very narrow range of temperatures and only when the heat loss given off by the body by radiation, convection and evaporation is in balance. When it is too slow a person feels hot and when it is too fast he feels cool.

Radiation is the transfer of heat by direct rays from the body to cooler surrounding objects, such as cold windows, walls and floors. A person putting a hand next to a cold wall will feel a chill as the rays leave the hand.

Convection is the transfer of heat by the circulation of air around the body. The movement of the air by wind or a fan or a draft speeds up the heat loss and chills the body. Evaporation is a minor source of heat loss.

The ideal heating system should supply that amount of heat which will keep the body heat loss in balance. It must also prevent drafts, warm the floors and walls and provide steady temperatures from room to room and floor to ceiling.

HOT AIR SYSTEMS

Gravity systems are found primarily in older houses. Cold air is heated in a furnace that looks like a giant octopus (see Figure 51). Because hot air rises, it goes up unaided in a series of ducts and into the rooms being heated through wall, floor or ceiling registers. When it cools, the air descends through other ducts or hallways by the force of gravity. This system is characterized by the distribution of hot, dirty, dry air unevenly through the house. With some rare exceptions, such a furnace should be replaced with a modern forced air system.

Another type of gravity air system is a floor furnace. These are used in small houses usually under 1,000 square feet, especially in moderate climates. The furnace is suspended below the floor and the hot air rises from the furnace through a flush grille in the floor. There usually are no ducts.

Space heaters are rarely satisfactory except in mild climates, cottages or for supplementary heat beyond the main heating system.

Modern warm (or hot air) heating systems utilize some type of pressure blower to push the heated air through ducts. One common duct system is called an "extended plenum system" (see Figure 52). The air is heated in the furnace and forced, by a fan, through a large duct called a plenum (usually under the first floor) to smaller ducts that are connected to registers in the areas to be heated. The air then finds its way back to the furnace by traveling under doors which are set high enough off the rug or floor to allow the air to pass out through return ducts to the furnace.

Two common air distribution systems that are used when the house is

FIGURE 51
GRAVITY HOT AIR SYSTEM

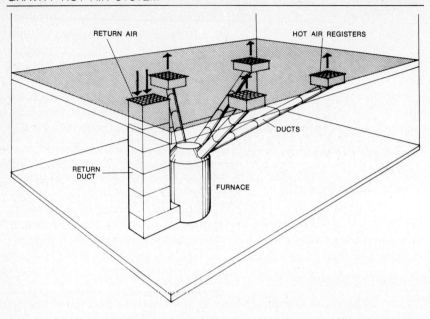

FIGURE 52
EXTENDED PLENUM SYSTEM

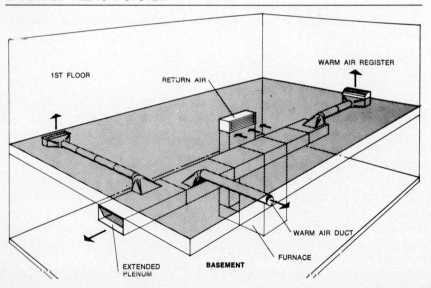

FIGURE 53
PERIMETER RADIAL DUCT WARM AIR SYSTEM

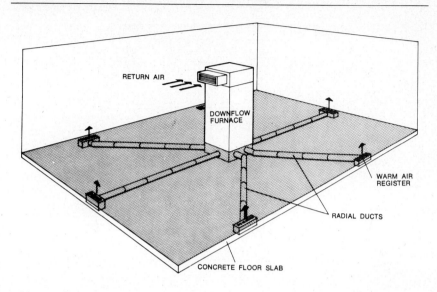

FIGURE 54
PERIMETER LOOP WARM AIR SYSTEM

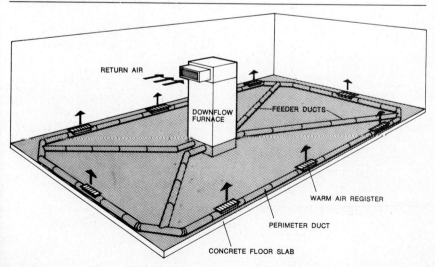

FIGURE 55
AIR REGISTERS

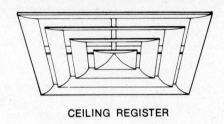

CEILING REGISTER

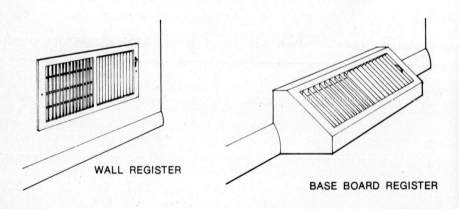

WALL REGISTER

BASE BOARD REGISTER

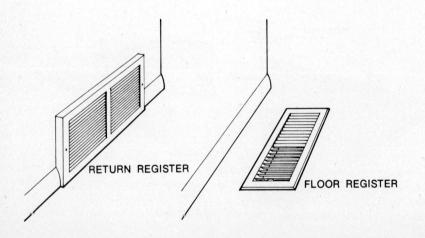

RETURN REGISTER

FLOOR REGISTER

built on a concrete slab are the perimeter radial duct system (Figure 53) and the perimeter loop system (Figure 54). Again, the air is heated in the furnace and forced by a fan through the ducts and out through the air registers into the areas to be heated. The cooled air again either finds its way back to the furnace by going under the doors or is returned through cold air ducts.

In all these systems air registers are connected to the ends of the ducts. They have slats or fins which help distribute the air evenly into the areas being heated. Some have a way of being opened or closed to provide a means of controlling the amount of air being released into the room.

Since heated air rises, the best place for the registers (Figure 55) is either in the floor or low down on the wall. The best place for the return duct is also low down and on the opposite side of the room from the warm air registers.

A sometimes advertised advantage of a warm air system is that the ducts can also be used for the air conditioning. This is usually not really an advantage as air conditioning registers work best when they are high up on the walls or in the ceiling. Also, air conditioning usually requires larger ducts than most heating systems have.

HOT WATER HEATING SYSTEMS

In a hot water (hydronic) system, water is heated in a boiler of cast iron or steel. It is then pumped (except in older gravity systems) by one or more circulators, each controlled by a thermostat, through finger-size tubes into baseboard panels, radiators or tubes embedded in the walls, ceiling or concrete slab. Water is an excellent heating medium, retaining heat longer than any other common medium.

In a one-pipe series connected system (Figure 56) the radiators, baseboard panels or convectors are connected so that the pipe runs through each unit. The main advantage of this system is its low cost. The major disadvantage is that because the water must run through each unit there are no individual control valves. Also, the units at the end of the loop are not as hot as the first units on the loops.

A better, single pipe system (Figure 57) connects each unit separately to the loop with an individual take-off pipe and shutoff valve. This allows individual regulating of each unit as well as control of the loop, as in the series connected system. Special fittings are required to keep the water running in the proper direction and to induce flow into the radiators.

The best system is a two-pipe reverse return system (Figure 58) where one pipe delivers the hot water and another returns it to the furnace. To take maximum advantage of a two-pipe system, it must be set up so that the first radiator to receive the warm water is the last radiator on the return line. This is called a reverse flow system.

FIGURE 56
ONE-PIPE SERIES CONNECTED HOT WATER SYSTEM

This system may be identified by looking up at the part of the basement ceiling that is directly under the first floor radiators. In a one-pipe series connected hot water system, one wide-diameter pipe will be seen going in and out of each radiator. There will be no small-diameter feeder pipes.

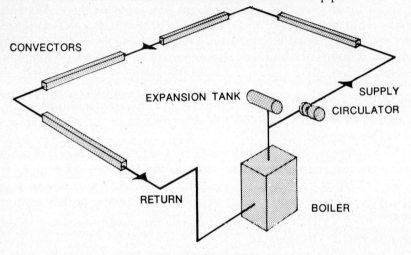

FIGURE 57
SINGLE PIPE INDIVIDUAL TAKE-OFF HOT WATER SYSTEM

Looking up at the area of the basement ceiling that is directly under the first floor radiators, one wide-diameter pipe will be seen under each radiator. Each of these pipes will be connected to its radiator by two smaller feeder pipes.

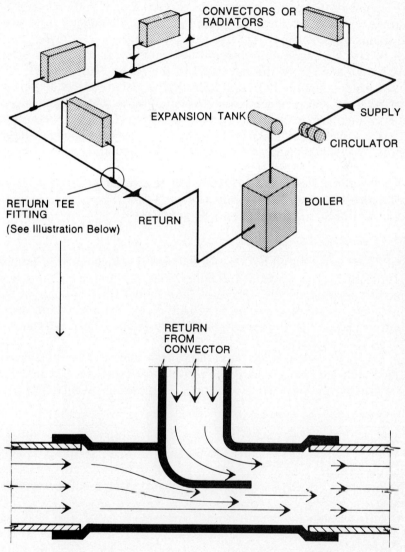

A hot water system generally uses radiators, baseboard panels or convectors (Figures 59, 60, 61 and 62) to distribute the heat into the room. These three units depend upon both convection (air being warmed as it passes over the heated metal and then circulating into the room) and radiation (heat waves being transferred directly from the heated metal to the object being heated by radiant energy). There are also combination systems in which the heat is brought to the radiator by warm water. A fan in the radiator blows air over the radiator fins, heating rooms by convection.

A radiant heating system depends solely upon the direct transfer of heat by radiation from the hot metal to the object being heated. The heated water is pumped through coils of pipe that are embedded in the floor, walls or ceiling or some combination of these. This system is particularly adaptable to slab construction where the coils are embedded in the slab. A major advantage is the absence of visible radiators or baseboards. A disadvantage is slow response to changing weather or other conditions affecting the temperature of the room.

A hot water system can be expanded to perform other functions from melting ice and snow on the sidewalks and/or driveway to heating an indoor or outdoor swimming pool or greenhouse.

STEAM HEATING SYSTEM

Steam heat is produced by a furnace which is a boiler with a firebox underneath it. The water in the boiler boils, making steam which is forced by its pressure through pipes into the radiators throughout the house. In a single pipe system the steam cools, turns back into water and runs back to the furnace to repeat the cycle. In a two-pipe system it returns via a separate pipe.

A two-pipe system tends to be less noisy than a one-pipe system. Noise is a disadvantage inherent to all steam systems as is the difficulty in controlling the heat when only small amounts are needed.

ELECTRIC HEATING SYSTEM

When electricity is used in the same way as oil, gas or coal to heat the air in a hot air furnace or the water in a hot water furnace, it can be thought of as just another fuel. What makes it unique in house heating is its use with resistance elements which produce heat at the immediate area to be heated.

Electric resistance elements, which convert electricity into heat, are embedded in the floors, walls and ceilings to provide radiant heat. The advantages claimed for electric radiant heat are the lack of visible radiators or grilles and the comfort obtainable without the necessity to heat the room air hot enough to drive out the moisture. Its acceptance by the public is not universal and substantial experimentation is still being con-

FIGURE 58
TWO-PIPE REVERSE RETURN HOT WATER SYSTEM

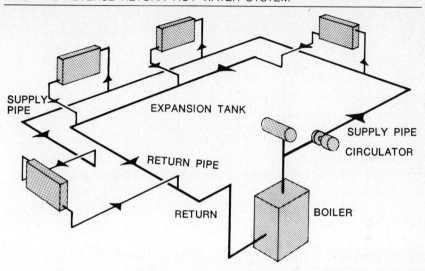

FIGURE 59
TWO-PIPE STEAM SYSTEM—CAST IRON RADIATOR

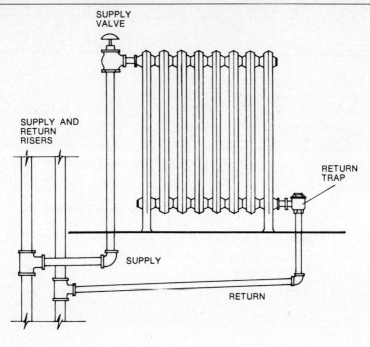

FIGURE 60
BASEBOARD CONVECTOR

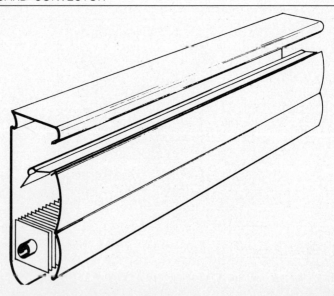

FIGURE 61
TWO-PIPE HOT WATER SYSTEM—CAST IRON RADIATOR

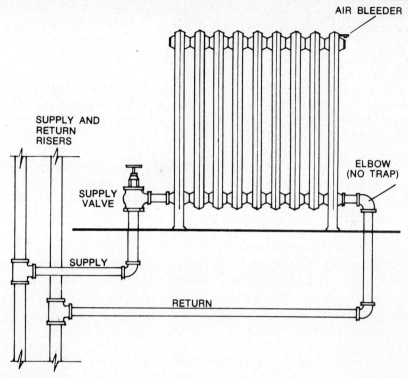

AIR BLEEDER

SUPPLY AND
RETURN
RISERS

ELBOW
(NO TRAP)

SUPPLY
VALVE

SUPPLY

RETURN

FIGURE 62
ONE-PIPE STEAM SYSTEM—CAST IRON RADIATOR

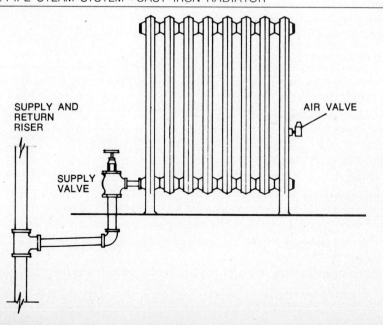

SUPPLY AND
RETURN
RISER

AIR VALVE

SUPPLY
VALVE

ducted by the manufacturers and others. Electric heat also provides the advantage of individual temperature control for each room.

Electric heating panels, also with individual resistance elements, are often used for auxiliary heat in bathrooms, additions to the original house and summer homes.

HEAT CONTROLS

As heating costs rise it becomes increasingly important to conserve energy. One way this can be done is to control the use of heat. It is a waste of energy to heat unused areas of the home. When the temperature is reduced in these unused areas and at night, significant energy can be saved.

Different heating systems allow various levels of control, ranging from some electric systems that control each room individually to steam, hydronic and air systems with only one control zone for the entire house, usually with a thermostat. It is best to place the thermostat two to four feet from the floor. Common mistakes are to place it too high or to put a lamp, radio or TV near it.

A thermostat is a control device that turns off the heat when it rises above a preselected temperature. However, it can only detect the temperature at one spot. When it controls more than one room, the room in which the thermostat is located must be kept warm in order to provide heat for other rooms supplied by the same distribution system. This is wasteful.

More sophisticated thermostats have a device in them called an anticipator, which shuts off the heating shortly before the desired temperature is reached. Because the system does not cool off instantly, the room will be brought to the desired temperature. Thermostats that automatically lower the heat during the sleeping hours are also available. In many houses this will result in fuel savings.

SOLAR HEATING

One can hardly pick up a newspaper or magazine today without finding an article on solar energy. Our federal government has committed itself strongly to the development of solar energy. You can get the latest available information from the government by writing to the National Solar Heating and Cooling Information Center, Post Office Box 1607, Rockville, Maryland 20850.

There are a wide variety of solar heating systems available today and it is expected that many more will be available in the near future. The goal of all these systems is to collect the radiant energy released by the sun and use it to heat and cool the house and its domestic hot water.

The most common systems work as follows (see Figure 63 for an illustration):

1. Solar collectors, usually placed in the attic or on the roof, absorb

heat radiated from the sun. These collectors will work both when the sun directly shines on them and also, but less effectively, when clouds block the sun's rays.

2. The heated fluid in the collectors, which is often water mixed with antifreeze, is either pumped or flows by the force of gravity into storage tanks. On a bright, sunny day this solution may get as hot as 250 degrees. The tanks typically store from 500 to 1,000 gallons. These tanks are often called heat exchangers. Sometimes instead of one tank there is a series of smaller tanks and the water is moved from one to another as it gets hotter.

Another system has the collectors heat air which is blown into large storage tanks that are filled with rocks or other material that absorbs the heat from the air until it is needed.

3. When the house requires heat, water from the heating system is pumped into coils in the storage tank where it absorbs heat much the way it would be heated if the coils were in a furnace. If the heating system is a warm air system then air is blown into the storage tank where it is heated when it comes into contact with the hot stones or other storage material.

4. The heated water or air is then utilized much the way warm water or air is utilized in a conventional system.

Most solar systems cannot provide all of the heat that will be required. What percentage of the needed heat they will provide depends upon the climate, type of system and the construction of the house. Often houses that use solar energy will be carefully insulated and weather stripped to reduce heat loss as much as possible.

Typically, even the best solar systems produce only about 75 percent of the required heat in most climates. In order to produce the additional needed heat, a supplemental heating system is required. This may be anything from a few electric resistance heaters to a complete additional heating system. Heat pumps are also used as supplemental heating systems.

The efficiency of the systems can be improved with controls that regulate the flow of fluids within the system. The system should be built so that it will prevent the water from freezing. This can be accomplished by draining the collectors when there is insufficient sunlight to prevent the water in the collectors from freezing.

There are a variety of ways a house can be designed to take advantage of the heating capacity of the sun without mechanical assistance. This is known as "passive" solar energy. Some of these techniques are described in Chapter 16.

SUMMARY

No matter what heating system is used, it should be checked out by a prospective purchaser. Poor heating is a major complaint homeowners

FIGURE 63
SPACE HEATING SYSTEM IN A SOLAR HOUSE

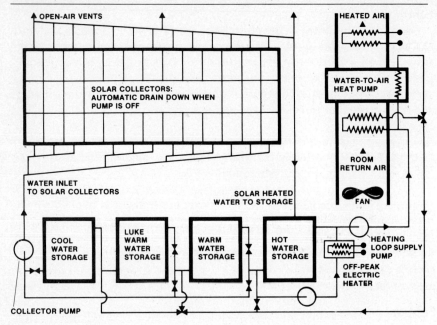

Collector type: Flat plate
Location: Main roof
Circulating fluid: Water
Freeze protection: Drain down
Manufacturer: Sunworks

Source: Energy House, an 1832-square foot solar powered, energy efficient house; a cooperative effort of Rochester (New York) Institute of Technology, Rochester Gas and Electric Corporation and Rochester Home Builders' Association.

have about their houses. The major causes of poor heating are insufficient insulation and an inadequate or poorly functioning heating system.

The condition of the furnace is often reflected in its appearance. An old furnace encased in asbestos probably is getting ready to give trouble. An adequate-sized, clean furnace without rust may require minor repairs but usually has plenty of good life left in it.

A free or nominally priced inspection of the heating system is often available from the fuel suppliers in the area.

For a complete checklist on Heating Systems, see Checklist 29, page C-61.

COOLING SYSTEMS

Prior to World War II little was done to mechanically cool houses except to move the air around with fans. Today many houses have central air conditioning systems and the trend in most areas seems to be towards greater use of these systems.

FANS

Fans are still an accepted method of cooling. The air inside the house may be cooler than the outside air yet may feel warmer because of the lack of air movement. A simple room fan (especially when the temperature and humidity are not too high) will often make the room seem much cooler. This is because moving air increases the rate of evaporation of body moisture and increases the body's cooling efficiency. The fan in a warm air heating system may be used to move the air and to bring cooler basement air up into the house. (Again, this works best when the temperature and humidity are not too high.)

An attic ventilation fan cools in several ways. During the day it removes the hot air from the attic, which when left in place soon seeps down into the house, substantially raising the overall interior temperature. For best results the attic fan should be large enough to remove air equal to the volume of the house every minute. For example, a house that is 10,000 cubic feet should have an attic fan rated to remove 10,000 cubic feet of air per minute.

In many areas of the country the outside air temperature drops sharply during the night. The attic fan is used to replace the hot daytime air with cool night air. In some areas of the country a timing device is needed to turn off the fan to prevent the house from overcooling. If the house is well insulated and kept closed during the following day, the inside air may remain substantially cooler than the hot outside air.

Window exhaust fans work on the same principle as attic fans. They are especially effective in changing cool night air for hot daytime air in bedrooms and living areas.

EVAPORATION COOLING

In some areas of the West the humidity is low most of the time, even in periods of high heat. In these places, a simple system of blowing air across wet excelsior or some other water-absorbing material will cool the air substantially. What happens is that the water evaporates and, in the process, cools the air. Package units are manufactured for home installation in windows. They are simple machines and are less expensive than conventional air conditioning.

AIR CONDITIONING PRINCIPLES

With the exception of fans and evaporation cooling, most domestic air conditioning uses either electric power compressor-cycle equipment or gas absorption-cycle equipment. These are the same systems used in household refrigerators. The basic law of physics that applies to both types is that when a liquid is changed to a vapor or gas, heat is absorbed and when the vapor is compressed back into a liquid, the heat it previously absorbed is given off.

In an electric system the refrigerant that is changed back and forth from gas to liquid is usually Freon.

In a gas power absorption cycle system, ammonia is often used as the refrigerant, with water as the absorbent, or water is used as the refrigerant and a lithium bromide solution as the absorbent.

ELECTRIC ROOM AIR CONDITIONING UNITS

Millions of room compressor-cycle air conditioning units are manufactured and sold in this country each year. They now provide an economical solution to summer heat.

Widely available are low cost 4,000 and 5,000 B.T.U. units that can be carried home from the store and easily installed. These units run on 110 volts and use so little electricity that they can be plugged into a regular wall outlet in most homes with modern wiring. They will nicely cool a small room in many climates.

Larger room air conditioners range upward in size from the popular 8,000 to 12,000 B.T.U.s all the way to as high as 35,000 B.T.U.s. These units generally require 220 volts and should be installed on their own separate electric lines.

DUCTED CENTRAL AIR CONDITIONING SYSTEMS

These systems can be custom-made or can be prewired, precharged factory-assembled packages that are connected at the home site. The condenser portion is set outside the house on the ground or on the roof. It is connected by pipe to the evaporator air-handling unit that is inside the house. The air-handling unit, consisting of the evaporator and a fan, is located inside the house and is connected to a system of ducts that distribute the cool air throughout the areas of the house to be cooled.

A hydronic heating system can also be combined with a cooling system. A water chiller is coupled to the boiler to supply cold water to a special type of convector that has been placed in each room as a replacement for the old style radiator. Conversion of old style hydronic systems to combination systems is often so costly that it is less expensive to install a separate new set of air conditioning ducts.

**For a complete Air Conditioning checklist,
see Checklist 30, page C-63.**

PLUMBING

In a typical single-family house the plumbing system is like an iceberg—only a small part of it is visible.

The best way to cut through the mystery that exists in the minds of so many when it comes to plumbing is to discuss it in its various parts.

Technically, parts of the heating, hot water and air conditioning systems are also plumbing. However, for ease of understanding they were discussed earlier in this chapter.

WATER SUPPLY

When a public water supply is available it should be used. An attempt to save money by using a well when this is not necessary is an economy made at the possible expense of family health.

In the absence of available public water the next best supply is a well which is dug on the lot and water from it pumped into the house. There are some houses that obtain water from rivers, streams, lakes and even rain water collected from the roof and stored in tanks. None of these latter systems are considered to be satisfactory water supplies, however, since they do not provide a sufficient quantity of dependably pure water.

Water supplied by public water systems is usually piped in the streets in water mains. A copper pipe of at least three-fourths-inch diameter taps into this line and runs underground into the house. Instead of copper, one to one and one-quarter-inch galvanized iron pipe may also be used. There should be a cutoff valve at the street edge to shut off the water in an emergency. It is usually found in a hole covered with a steel or iron plate. Another cutoff valve for the same purpose should be located where the pipe enters the house. The pipe should not be run where it is likely to be disturbed, such as under the driveway.

A well should be capable of delivering a sustained flow of five gallons per minute. The water quality should meet the chemical and bacteriological requirements of the health authority having jurisdiction. Generally, except in arctic conditions, the well should be located outside the building foundation at a minimum depth of 20 feet. It should be located at least 100 feet from an absorption field or seepage pit and 50 feet from a septic tank.

An artesian well is one drilled through impermeable strata, deep enough to reach water that is capable of rising to the surface by internal hydrostatic pressure. It still requires a pump to develop sufficient pressure for household use. The only way to be sure a well meets these important standards is to have it tested professionally.

There are two basic types of well pumps, the submergible pump located inside the well and the basement pump. The pump capacity should not exceed the flow rate of the well or the pump will drain the well and bring up dirt. At least a 42-gallon storage tank is needed to provide a smooth flow of water.

WATER PIPES

Pipes should carry water throughout the house to the various fixtures without leaking, making noise, reducing the pressure or imparting any color or taste to the water.

Brass has been used for piping for many years, but it is now expensive. Older brass pipes tend to crystallize and become coated on the inside in areas where the water is corrosive.

Galvanized steel pipes are easily attacked by corrosive water. Galvanized wrought iron is similar to steel but is more resistant to corrosion.

Copper comes as rigid pipe and flexible tubing. In many areas it is the only acceptable material. Joints are usually made by soldering copper joints to both pipe ends. Lead used to be a popular material. It is still used for the pipe from the water main to the house in some areas but it is rarely used inside the house.

Plastics are the newest material used for pipes. The manufacturers claim and many builders agree that plastic is as good as any other material and may indeed be better. It is gaining acceptance although it still is not permitted in many cities.

WATER SOFTENERS

In many areas of the country large amounts of calcium, magnesium, sulphates, bicarbonates, iron or sulphur are often found in the water. These minerals react unfavorably with soap, forming a curd-like substance difficult to rinse from clothes, hair and skin. The bicarbonates, when heated, form a crust inside pipes and cooking utensils and a ring in the bathtub. Iron will stain clothing and sulphur makes the water taste and smell bad.

The simplest water softener is a manual single tank that is connected to the water line. Inside the tank is a mineral called zeolite which will exchange the offensive minerals in the water for sodium chloride (common salt). The zeolite must be poured into the tank. In a typical area with normal water use, salt must be added and the zeolite flushed out about twice a week. Those not willing to perform that task can obtain a two-tank automatic unit that will add the salt and flush the zeolite automatically. Of course, salt still has to be fed into the second tank every month or so. The zeolite is best at removing the calcium and magnesium. If the amount of iron, sulphur and other minerals is still very high, a third tank with special filters and chemicals may be needed for their complete removal.

PLUMBING FIXTURES

The parts of the plumbing system that compare to the above-water portion of an iceberg are the fixtures. Bathroom fixtures consist of lavatories, wash basins, bathtubs, showers, toilets (also known as water closets in the plumbing trade) and, occasionally, bidets.

Kitchen fixtures consist of sinks, laundry sinks, dishwashers and garbage disposals. In other areas of the house additional laundry tubs, sinks, bar sinks, outside sill cocks and other fixtures are found.

BATHTUBS

The bathtub is the most expensive fixture in the bathroom and builders are often tempted to economize with it. Four different materials are generally used for tub construction.

By far the most common type of tub is made of cast iron coated with enamel. The cheaper grades have regular enamel and the better grades acid-resisting enamel. Unfortunately, it is very difficult to tell by looking what type of enamel has been used, except that most colored tubs are the acid-resistant type. In general, a cast iron tub is better than a steel tub.

Other satisfactory tubs are made of ceramic tile and steel covered with vitreous enamel. Fiberglass is gaining in popularity and well may be the product of the future for bathtubs. It is light and often is cast in one piece in conjunction with the wall, thus making the tub easy to clean and waterproof at the edge joining the wall. The finish, however, is not quite as hard as vitreous enamel and is more susceptible to scratches.

The most common tub size is five feet long and 14 to 15 inches deep. Even a few inches difference in depth, however, makes a big difference in comfort, as does six extra inches in length. There is a big comfort difference between a standard five-foot, 14-inch deep tub and a five and one-half-foot, 16-inch deep tub. The cost difference is about $100.

Sunken tubs are status symbols which appeal to some. Their prestige must be weighed against their hazardous nature and the back-breaking chore of bathing children in them.

The imprint of the name of the national manufacturer stamped on

FIGURE 64
BATHROOM FIXTURE SIZES

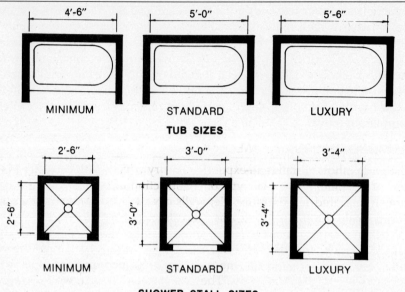

MINIMUM   STANDARD   LUXURY

TUB SIZES

MINIMUM   STANDARD   LUXURY

SHOWER STALL SIZES

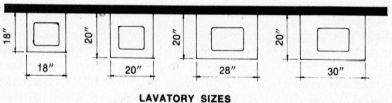

LAVATORY SIZES

each fixture should be checked because a fixture without a name stamped on it often is the lowest grade or a second. Most good grade fixtures have solid handles with grooves for fingers. Poor grade faucets are zinc or aluminum castings and often have cross-shaped handles.

TUB-SHOWER COMBINATIONS

By far the most popular shower arrangement is to have the shower located over the end of the tub. This arrangement costs little more than the tub alone to install. A shower rod with a double shower curtain is all most families need to keep the bathroom dry.

SHOWERS AND STALL SHOWERS

A separate shower stall is an expensive luxury which many people feel is still worthwhile. A popular type of construction includes a floor pan of concrete covered with ceramic tile, walls covered with ceramic tiles and a glass door. Anything but a one-piece floor pan will eventually leak, and other wall coverings rarely work.

A less expensive prefabricated steel model is also commonly used. Here the floor pan is also a one-piece concrete pan and the walls are painted steel or galvanized iron. The door is usually open, with a rod for a curtain. These units are quite satisfactory although not very luxurious in appearance.

The newest product is a one-piece fiberglass stall. These are attractive, come in many shapes, often eliminate the need for a shower curtain and are reported to be quite satisfactory. Cleaning the ceramic tile and steel models is difficult and time-consuming, but the fiberglass model cleans easily.

Leaking usually takes place through the walls, at the joint between the wall and floor pan and around the seam at the edge of the floor pan and drain. In new houses it is impossible to tell by inspection if the shower will leak, so a good builder's guarantee is important. In older houses inspection of the ceiling under the shower usually will show telltale marks of any leaking. New painting or papering in this area may be suspect as it may have been done to hide leak marks. Ceramic tile walls are most susceptible to leaking, but this problem is less likely with steel and is unlikely with fiberglass. Ceramic tile showers and steel showers both may leak at the wall pan joint. This is unlikely with fiberglass. All types of stall showers may leak at the pan-drain joint.

WASH BASINS

The most satisfactory way to install a wash basin is to set in into a vanity counter. This provides the much needed space alongside the basin on which to stand beauty aids, shaving equipment and the baby's things.

Basins are made of the same materials as tubs and these materials have the same advantages and disadvantages as when they are used for tubs. The most common satisfactory material is cast iron covered with acid resistant vitreous enamel. The product of the future is a fiberglass basin molded together with the vanity counter top as one piece.

The size of the basin is important. For a bathroom, an 18-inch wide basin is minimum standard. Larger sizes range from 20 to 28 to 30 inches in luxury models. Fifteen inches is a minimum satisfactory depth, but 18 to 20 inches is better. One should look under the basin for the imprint of a national manufacturer because if there is no name the fixture may be a second or the lowest grade.

TOILETS

The design and quality of the toilet is more important than other plumbing fixtures because the toilet is a sophisticated mechanism. Most residential toilets consist of a bowl and tank which stores sufficient water to create a proper flushing action.

The quality of a toilet is judged by its performance in the following areas: self-cleaning properties, free rapid flushing action, quiet during flushing action and ease of cleaning around exterior.

There are four basic types of toilets, practically all of which are now made of vitreous china. (See Figure 65 for illustrations.)

The washdown bowl type is an inferior product that is used only to save money. It can be recognized by its almost round shape and its straight line profile in front.

The majority of toilets currently made are the reverse trap bowl type. Its self-cleaning characteristics and flushing action are quite satisfactory but moderately noisy. The reverse trap bowl toilet is only slightly more expensive than a washdown and a much better buy.

An improved version of the reverse trap toilet is a siphon jet. It covers a larger surface of the bowl with water. The trapway is larger and thus less subject to clogging and noise during the flushing action.

A still better siphon jet is the wall-hung model which makes for easy cleaning around the toilet area. Unfortunately, this toilet costs substantially more to install and is usually found only in custom built homes.

The most luxurious toilets are the one-piece, low profile siphon action toilets. They provide almost silent flushing action, almost no dry interior bowl surface and therefore excellent self-cleaning action.

One may easily test each toilet in a house. Just throw in a piece of crumpled facial tissue, toilet paper or cigarette butt and flush the toilet. The water should flow swiftly over all the interior wall, thereby performing a self-cleaning action and the noise should not be excessive. Watch how quickly and surely the paper goes down. Watch and listen to the refilling action to determine if it is quick and quiet.

FIGURE 65
TOILET TYPES

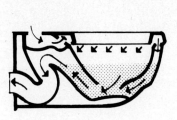

WALL-HUNG SIPHON JET

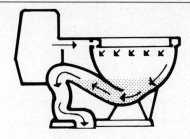

LOW PROFILE SIPHON ACTION

WASHDOWN

REVERSE TRAP

SIPHON JET

BIDETS

Bidets are a standard fixture in continental baths. In America they are rare but slowly gaining in popularity. They are usually installed by people of European background and those who travel to Europe often, or more likely as a status symbol or conversation piece.

BATHROOM FITTINGS

Fittings include faucets, spigots, shower heads, pop-up drains—the working parts of the plumbing system. These will require repair and replacement many times during the life of a house.

A faucet controls the flow of water into the fixture and often is also designed to mix hot and cold water. The most common type of arrangement is two separate valves, one each for the hot and cold water.

A better arrangement is a single control valve feeding through one spout. The temperature of the water is controlled by moving a knob or lever to the right or left. Water volume is controlled by moving the same knob or lever in and out or backward and forward.

A pressure balancing valve is most commonly found controlling a shower head. The water volume is usually preset and the user selects only the temperature by turning the valve handle. A pressure sensing device adjusts the flow of hot or cold water to compensate for pressure changes, thus keeping the temperature even and safeguarding against scalding.

The ultimate is a thermostatic control valve that automatically senses the water temperature and adjusts the flow to maintain the preselected desired temperatures. This type of valve gives more precise temperature control than the pressure balancing valve and it usually also permits control of the water volume as well.

Most manufacturers make three grades of fittings. One way to spot the low grade is by the cross shape or inexpensive looking handles. The best buy is the middle grade which usually has attractive rounded handles with contours for the fingers. Luxury grade fixtures have elaborate handles and platings of such exotic materials as gold or brass.

A quality shower head swivels in any direction, has an adjustable spray control handle and is self-cleaning. All showers should have an "automatic diverter control" that switches the flow of water back to the tub faucet after each shower so that the next user will not accidentally get wet or scalded.

KITCHEN FIXTURES

Most kitchen sinks are installed in some type of counter top. The sink may be either a single or a double type, the latter with a drain board on one or both sides.

Kitchen sinks may be made of acid-resistant enamel, cast iron, enameled steel, stainless steel or Monel metal. Most modern kitchen sinks have a combination faucet with a swing spout. A separate spray attachment on a flexible tube is also very common.

The drain should have a removable crumb cup or better, a combination crumb cup and stopper. Also available is an attachment for a kitchen sink that provides boiling water or ice cold water instantly.

Though technically part of the plumbing system, a dishwasher is really a household appliance like the stove, refrigerator and washing machine. The best place for a dishwasher is under a kitchen counter near the sink.

Waste disposal devices are installed under the kitchen sink, connected to the drain. When filled with garbage and flooded with running water, their fast rotary action breaks up the garbage into particles small enough to go down the drain to the sewer or septic tank.

There is still much to be said for a laundry tub in the basement or laundry room even if there is an automatic washing machine and clothes dryer. It can be used for soaking clothes without tying up the washing machine. It also provides a good place to wash household articles, plants, paint brushes and other supplies.

OUTSIDE SILL COCK

An outside sill cock (or bib cock) is a water faucet on the outside of the house with a screw nose to which a hose can be connected. FHA Minimum Property Standards require a minimum of two per house. They should be located on opposite ends of the house. In areas subject to freezing these faucets should be the frostproof type and have individual shutoff valves inside the house so they can be drained and turned off for the winter months.

DRAINAGE SYSTEM

The drainage system starts at each fixture with a curved pipe called a trap. A popular misconception is that the principal purpose of the trap is to catch objects that fall down the drain. The real purpose is to provide a water seal to prevent the seepage of sewer gas into the house.

Drainage lines that run horizontally are called branches and those that run vertically, stacks. The pipes that receive the discharge from the toilets are called soil lines and those that receive the rest of the discharge, waste lines. Vent pipes from each stack to the roof prevent the sewer gas from building up pressure in the system.

Pipes for drainage systems are often made of cast iron, copper, plastic, tile, brass, lead or fiber. Special fittings are often used, especially on the cast iron pipes, that aid the flow of the sewage.

The biggest difference between waste pipes and water pipes is the lack of pressure in the waste pipe system. The water pipe must be strong enough to contain the water pressure; it should not have to depend upon gravity to make the water flow to the fixture. Since there is no pressure in a waste drain line, the pipes must be slanted so that the waste will flow from each fixture through the main lines into the sewer or sewage disposal system. Generally, drain lines are much larger than water pipes.

SEPTIC TANKS AND CESSPOOLS

National government surveys indicate that about one-half of all septic systems malfunction at least yearly. During these periods of malfunction untreated sewage flows into the ground and surrounding waterways causing a serious health hazard. Many septic tanks, unknown to their owners, are malfunctioning all or most of the time.

A typical septic system (see Figure 66) consists of a large concrete tank with a capacity of 900 gallons (about eight by four by four feet) buried in the ground. One end accepts the waste material from the house drain line. Once inside the tank, the waste tends to separate into three parts. The solid waste materials (only about one percent of the total volume) sink to the bottom. The grease (also less than one percent of the total volume) rises to the top. The rest is liquid. Bacteria in the tank decompose the solid wastes and grease and a relatively clear liquid flows from the opposite end through the drain line either into a distribution box that directs the liquid into a network of buried perforated pipes called a leaching field or into a seepage pit. From here the liquid runs off into the ground to be absorbed.

Here are some of the things that can go wrong (and usually do):

1. The tank may be too small for the size of the family using the system and the bacteria do not have sufficient time to decompose the wastes.
2. The tank may crack and undecomposed waste escapes into the ground.
3. Bacteria in the tank are killed by antibiotics discharged with human wastes.
4. The bacteria are killed by detergents and other chemicals discharged into the tank or by sudden changes in temperature.
5. The leaching fields become clogged with paper and undecomposed wastes.
6. The soil does not have the capacity to absorb the waste.
7. The water table rises and floods the leaching field.

A cesspool is similar to a septic system except that instead of a tank there is a covered cistern of stone, brick or concrete. The liquid seeps out through the walls directly into the ground rather than into a leaching field or seepage pit. It is even more likely to malfunction for any or all of the above reasons.

FIGURE 66
SEPTIC TANK AND ABSORPTION FIELD SYSTEM

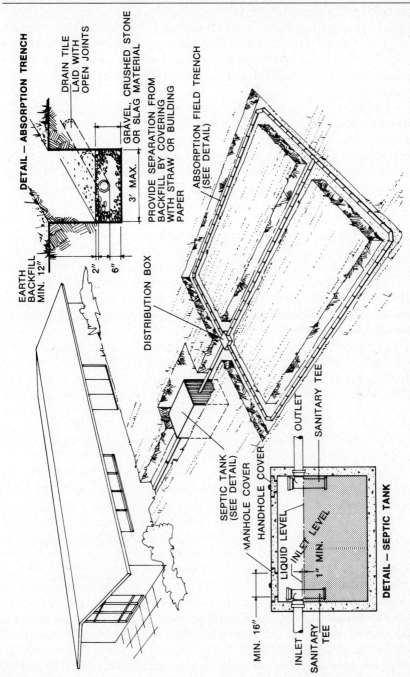

DETAIL — ABSORPTION TRENCH

DRAIN TILE LAID WITH OPEN JOINTS

GRAVEL, CRUSHED STONE OR SLAG MATERIAL

PROVIDE SEPARATION FROM BACKFILL BY COVERING WITH STRAW OR BUILDING PAPER

3' MAX.

EARTH BACKFILL MIN. 12"

2"

6"

ABSORPTION FIELD TRENCH (SEE DETAIL)

DISTRIBUTION BOX

SEPTIC TANK (SEE DETAIL)

MANHOLE COVER

HANDHOLE COVER

OUTLET

SANITARY TEE

LIQUID LEVEL

INLET LEVEL

1" MIN.

MIN. 16"

INLET

SANITARY TEE

DETAIL — SEPTIC TANK

When you buy a house with a septic system or cesspool it should be professionally tested. Often the local health department will make the test free or at a nominal charge.

Septic system problems may sometimes be corrected by simply pumping out the tank. It is important to learn the location of the clean-out hole when you buy a home with a septic system. Often it is buried at an unmarked location. This will save a lot of unnecessary digging and searching.

Sometimes new leaching fields are required. Unfortunately, there are situations when the soil absorption rate is poor or the water table is close to the surface and little can be done to make the system function properly. If there are odors in the yard or unusual green spots in the lawn you can count on there being serious problems.

SEWERS

Because septic systems and cesspools work so poorly it is much better for a house to be connected to a municipal sewer system. When there is a municipal sewer system available, the waste disposal lines should be connected to it and the use of the septic system or cesspool discontinued. This is required if the house is going to be financed with a government-insured mortgage. There is little merit to the arguments of some that they wish to continue to use their septic systems and cesspools when municipal sewers are available.

DEFECTIVE PLUMBING AND NOISES IN THE PLUMBING SYSTEM

Plumbing suffers from the two major problems of leaking and clogging with rust and mineral deposits. Leaking can be detected by visual inspection. Old style iron or steel pipes are much more likely to develop leaks than corrosion-resistant copper and bronze. Iron and steel pipes can be detected with a small magnet which will be attracted to an iron or steel pipe but not to copper or bronze pipe.

Insufficient water pressure can be caused either by clogged pipes, an undersized water main from the street, low water pressure in the street main or problems in the well or plumbing system. Water pressure can be tested by turning on full all faucets in the bathroom on the highest floor and then flushing the toilet. A substantial reduction of flow in the faucets is a sign of trouble and the system should be checked by a plumber to determine the cause and the cost to correct it.

Stains in the bathtub and lavatories are a sign of rusting pipes or unsoftened hard water. If hard water is suspected, a sample can be professionally tested by a firm selling water softeners. Such a firm can also recommend what equipment will be needed and tell how much it will cost to provide soft water.

Leaks under sinks may be only from a loose washer but may also be caused by a cracked fixture.

A high-pitched whistling sound when the toilet is flushed is caused by the valve in the toilet closing too slowly. A simple adjustment by a plumber will eliminate the noise. A sucking sound when the water runs out of a fixture is often made by a siphoning action in the trap caused by improper venting of the waste stack. If unclogging the vent doesn't work, only a major change in the vent system will eliminate the noise.

A hammering noise in the water pipes when the water is turned off is caused by a buildup of pressure in the pipe. In high pressure areas, air chambers, which are pipes filled with air, are installed at the fixtures connected to the water line. They provide a cushion of air which lets the pressure build up more gently. Pressure buildup is a serious problem which, if gone uncorrected, will result in broken or leaking pipes. It may be possible for a plumber to install one or two large air chambers in the system or a variety of other mechanical devices designed to correct the trouble.

The sound of running water is caused by undersized pipes and pipes that run in walls that are not sound-insulated. Wrapping the pipe with a noise insulation material may help. If the noise is very objectionable the pipe may have to be replaced with a larger one.

For a complete Plumbing checklist, see Checklist 31, page C-65.

DOMESTIC HOT WATER SYSTEMS

Dishwashing, clothes washing, showers, baths and personal hygiene all require substantial amounts of hot water. A house without the ability to supply this need is almost always deficient. Hot water usually is either made by the furnace or a separate hot water tank.

HOT WATER FROM THE FURNACE

Hot water may be made in a hot water or steam furnace by the installation of a coil in the boiler. A storage tank may, optionally, be added to the system. This type of system, called a "summer-winter hook-up" in some parts of the country, provides a steady, small supply of hot water which may be exhausted by too much use at one time. The recovery rate is fast, however, and hot water will shortly replenish itself when exhausted. Another disadvantage is the need to run the furnace all year.

ELECTRIC HOT WATER HEATERS

There are two basic types of electric hot water heaters. The "quick recovery" type has one or two heating elements which turn on as the water is used and bring the water temperature in the tank up, starting immediately after it is lowered. In some areas, an "off peak" system is used. The tank produces most of the hot water during the night when the electric rates are low and makes hot water during the day only when the night-produced supply has been exhausted.

One and two-element "quick recovery" tanks range in size from 30 gallons, suitable only for one or two people who use a limited amount of hot water, to the more popular 66 and 82-gallon sizes. Most of the "off peak" tanks are the 82-gallon size.

GAS HOT WATER HEATERS

Gas hot water tanks range in size from 30 to 82 gallons. Gas produces a faster recovery rate than electricity, so a slightly smaller tank than would be required for electric heat can be used. However, the cost per gallon of gas hot water tanks of similar quality is higher, so the difference becomes academic. A 30 or 40-gallon tank is suitable only for one or two people whose use of hot water is limited. The more popular sizes are the 52 and 82-gallon sizes.

OIL HOT WATER HEATERS

The recovery rate of an oil hot water heater is very fast, compared to gas or electricity. Because of this, a 30-gallon tank will provide enough hot water for the needs of most families. The operating cost in most areas is less than gas or electricity. What limits the popularity of oil hot water heaters is their initial high cost and high installation expense. This is especially true if there is not a flue and oil storage tank already available.

SOLAR HOT WATER HEATERS

One of the things one observes when visiting Israel is that almost every building has on its roof a solar collector that is part of the domestic hot water heating system. In that country, these systems are well beyond the experimental stages of development.

A typical hot water system consists of one or two solar collectors, usually part of the roof or mounted onto the roof of the house. The collectors are connected by transfer pipes filled with water (often mixed with antifreeze) to a storage tank. The fluid in the transfer pipes travels in a loop through the collector panels to the storage tank and back to the collector panels again and again. The water either flows only from the force of gravity or is aided by an electric pump. (See Figure 67.)

As the water flows through the storage tank (often called a heat exchanger) the heat in the transfer pipes is absorbed by the water in the storage tank. There often is an expansion tank connected to the transfer pipes to compensate for pressure differences which develop when the water in the transfer pipes changes temperature. The water in the storage tank (usually 80 gallons or larger in size) can become quite hot, sometimes reaching close to the boiling point.

The rest of the solar hot water system is similar to a traditional electric

FIGURE 67
DOMESTIC HOT WATER SYSTEM IN A SOLAR HOUSE

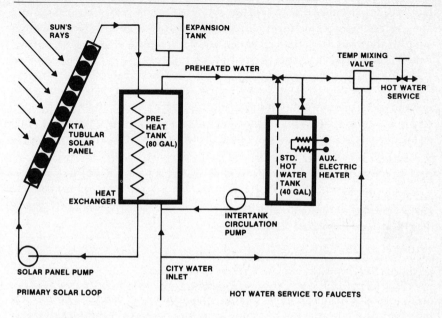

Source: Energy House, an 1832 square-foot solar powered, energy efficient house; a cooperative effort of Rochester (New York) Institute of Technology, Rochester Gas and Electric Corporation and Rochester Home Builders' Association.

system. Water is pumped from the heat exchanger into a conventional hot water tank (usually the quick recovery kind). If the water is hot enough it is circulated into the household plumbing system hot water lines. If it is too hot it is mixed with cold water by a temperature mixing valve. If the water is not sufficiently hot, the heating element in the hot water tank boosts it to the desired temperature.

The length of the pipe from the source of hot water to the fixture should be less than 15 feet. Longer pipes cause a great deal of heat loss and the inconvenience of having to let the water run for a while before it becomes warm. This can be partially corrected by insulating the hot water pipe. Also, it is possible to install a return system from the fixture to the hot water source, which provides a continuous circulation of water from the heater to the fixture and back to the heater.

For a complete Domestic Hot Water checklist, see Checklist 32, page C-67.

FUELS

Our country's number one problem is energy conservation. The cost to heat and cool a home has become a major expense in the typical home-owner's budget.

However, the cost to heat and cool homes of approximately the same size may vary tremendously from home to home in the same climate. This difference may be caused by the design, type of construction, insulation, weather stripping, the efficiency of the heating and domestic hot water system, the habits of the home occupants and the type of fuel being used.

Unfortunately, often the existing heating and domestic hot water system does not use the fuel that is most economical in the area in which the home is located. The choice of what fuel to use is rarely made by the family who is going to pay the fuel bills. To complicate the matter further, the house may have used the most economical fuel when it was built; but since then relative costs of fuels may have changed in the area and what was once the most economical fuel no longer is.

It rarely pays to tear out an existing, working heating or domestic hot water system and replace it. Sometimes it does, however, pay to convert the system to the most economical fuel available.

All other things being equal, the prudent home buyer should select a home that uses the most economical fuel available. If this fuel is not the one you are getting, then you must decide if the other advantages of the home outweigh this disadvantage. There are some other advantages and disadvantages besides price of different kinds of fuel which will be covered here. However, the most important difference is how much it will cost to produce adequate heating, cooling and domestic hot water for you and your family.

In spite of claims to the contrary, natural gas, liquid petroleum (L.P.), gas, fuel oil and electricity are all about equally safe and clean. Coke and coal are definitely dirtier. Except when these are used, the extent of safety and cleanliness is governed by the condition of the heating system itself. With the exception of a few isolated areas of the country, coal and coke are rarely used in new systems for residential heating. In general, systems using them as fuel are fast becoming obsolete.

FUEL OIL

Oil is still the least expensive fuel in the Northeast and Northwest sections of the country and is competitive in some other sections. It may be stored in the basement of the house in one or two free-standing tanks not more than 275 gallons in size (larger tanks and more than two tanks in a basement are considered unsafe). Outside tanks buried in the ground commonly have 550 or 1,000-gallon capacities. Many oil companies offer automatic delivery, regulated by a system of measuring the degree days of heat required, that virtually ensures a continuous supply with a reserve in the event of interrupted supply. The larger the storage tank the less the per-gallon cost of the oil. New kinds of burners have increased the potential efficiency, but they are more complex than gas burners, require more maintenance and have a shorter life expectancy. Oil tanks require maintenance and periodic replacement and take up living space in the basement.

The price of oil tends to fluctuate substantially throughout the season. World politics and new laws requiring the use of only low-sulphur fuel in many areas have raised the price.

NATURAL GAS

Natural gas offers the convenience of continuous delivery via pipeline without the necessity of storage tanks. Many suppliers offer lower rates if the hot water heater and cooking ranges are also gas. A gas furnace and burner is less complex than an oil furnace and burner. It requires less maintenance and has a longer life expectancy. It needs no on-site storage, but in the event of a supply interruption there is no reserve supply. In most areas of the country (the major exceptions being the Northeast and Northwest) gas is the most economical fuel.

Recently shortages of natural gas have developed in parts of the country. As a result, new homes have been built that have been forced to use more expensive alternate fuels. The consumer should buy these houses at a discount, all other things being equal.

LIQUID PETROLEUM GAS

L.P. (liquid petroleum) gas is used in rural areas. It requires on-premises storage tanks and is usually more expensive than natural pipeline gas. In other respects it is similar to natural gas.

ELECTRICITY

Electricity appears to be the fuel of the future. It requires no on-premises fuel storage and can be used like coal, gas or oil to heat air in a hot air furnace or water in a hot water furnace or water heater. When used with resistance units at the area to be heated, it is unique. This system is the least expensive to install, since it requires no furnace, no furnace room, no ducts, no flue and no plumbing.

It does require, however, a much larger electric service into the house and wiring to each unit. When used in colder climates, special care in construction is required to eliminate air leaks and provide sufficient insulation. It has the disadvantage of no emergency on-site supply. Electric resistance heating systems and heat pump systems are unquestionably the most versatile, convenient and controllable systems. To date, in spite of advertising to the contrary, electric heat costs remain high except in certain lower-cost power areas.

SOLAR ENERGY

Hopefully the 1980s will go down in history as the decade in which solar energy became a practical fuel for heating homes. Almost daily the newspapers carry another release about another experimental solar heating system.

By and large, solar energy is still experimental. The cost is usually not competitive with that of conventional fuels. One problem is that the efficiency of the system tends to fall off rapidly as the system ages. The government predicts that by 2000, 20 percent of our energy will be solar. See Chapter 16 for further information on solar energy.

COMPARISON OF FUEL COSTS

It is possible for a typical consumer who is not a mathematical genius to do all the calculations needed to decide what is the most economical fuel in your area.[1] If you are fortunate, you will be able to find some impartial, reliable person or agency that has already done calculations and reached a valid conclusion based on current costs. The figures supplied by many fuel companies, their institutes, public relations departments and advertising departments are not always objective or 100 percent accurate. Furthermore, information supplied by the government (especially about solar energy) also often appears to be nonobjective.

---

[1] Henry S. Harrison, *Houses—The Illustrated Guide to Construction, Design and Systems* (Chicago: REALTORS NATIONAL MARKETING INSTITUTE®, 1976) Ch. 7.

Since it is impossible to compare directly the cost of one fuel against the cost of another, it becomes necessary to first find some common denominator to use as a unit of comparison. Heat is measured in units called calories or therms. These units are so small, however, they are hard to use. A bigger unit, called a British Thermal Unit, the B.T.U., was developed. This is the amount of heat it takes to raise the temperature of one pound of water one degree Fahrenheit, still a very small amount of heat. In home heating the cost per million B.T.U.s is the standard measurement used.

The way to compare the relative costs of fuels is to figure out how much it will cost to make a million B.T.U.s of heat with each kind of fuel in your area.

Don't be confused by the claims that it requires less energy to heat or cool various houses because of the kind of fuel used. For example, an "all electric" house may be advertised to require less energy because it has very good insulation. It is true it will use less energy but not because of the fuel, but rather because of the insulation. This house would also use less fuel if heated with gas or oil.

For a checklist on Fuels, see Checklist 33, page C-69.

ELECTRIC SYSTEM

It was just over 100 years ago that Thomas Edison created the first practical light bulb and then went on to develop a complete electric system. Today's home depends heavily upon electricity for lighting, running all or part of the heating and cooling systems, pumping water if there is a well and for the many appliances that are an important part of most Americans' lives.

ELECTRIC SERVICE ENTRANCE

The home wiring system starts with the service entrance which brings the power from the street through an electric meter to a distribution panel. The service entrance may be designed to bring in 30, 60, 100, 150, 200, 300 or 400 amperes of electricity into the house. The amount of electricity that an appliance or light uses is measured in watts. A watt is the number of amperes consumed times the voltage of the service.

A 30-ampere service will provide electricity for a total usage at one time of 6,900 watts. This amount of service is still found in many older, one-family houses. The panel box (usually black) most often has four fuses in it. It will provide enough electricity for lighting and very limited appliance use. However a 30-ampere service is obsolete and should be replaced.

A 60-ampere service was the standard for many years for small to

FIGURE 68
ELECTRIC SERVICE ENTRANCE

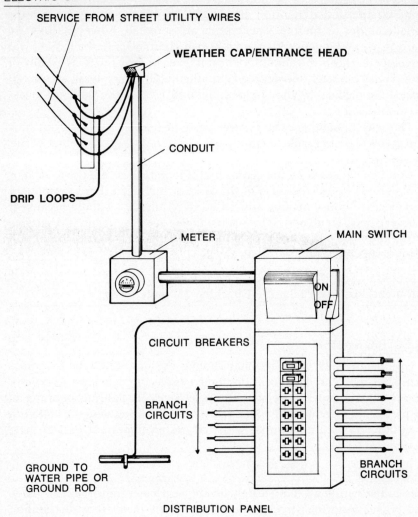

Here is the usual relationship between ampere service, number of circuit breakers and maximum number of watts:

Size of Service	No. of Branch Circuits (fuses or circuit breakers)	Maximum No. of Watts
30 ampere	4	6,900
60 ampere	6 to 8	13,800
100 ampere	12 to 16	23,000
150 or more amperes	20 or more	30,000 or more

medium houses, serving a demand of not more than 13,800 watts at one time. A builder installing a 60-ampere service today, however, is probably trying to save money and should be judged accordingly. Many homeowners with 60-ampere services are converting to larger services. A 60-ampere service panel box usually has only six to eight fuses or circuit breakers.

It is easy to understand why 30 and 60-ampere services are not adequate by looking at this list of appliances and the power they consume:

- Electric range up to 3,000 watts per burner
- Toaster 1,000 to 1,500 watts
- Clothes dryer 4,000 to 5,000 watts
- Water heater 3,000 to 5,000 watts
- Air conditioners 2,000 to 12,000 watts
- Hair dryer 750 to 1,200 watts

A 100-ampere service is the standard today for most small and medium sized houses without electric heat or central air conditioning. It provides 23,000 watts of power. A typical panel box will have 12 to 16 fuses or circuit breakers. There may also be some small separate distribution boxes for the major appliances. A house with less than a 100-ampere service is or soon will be obsolete.

In larger houses and where electric heat, central air conditioning or a large number of appliances are used 150 to 400-ampere services are needed.

Most homes today are served by a three-wire, 220 to 240-volt service. The electricity is brought from the transformer at the street into the house through three wires. Two wires each carry 110 to 120 volts and the third is a ground wire. The wires are strung through the air overhead and connected to a service head, then run through a piece of conduit pipe down the wall to the electric meter (which may be inside or outside the house) into a distribution panel box. An alternate method is to bring the wires in from the street through underground conduit pipe. The use of underground wires is increasing as public resistance to the unsightly overhead wires increases.

DISTRIBUTION PANEL AND PROTECTIVE DEVICES

The distribution box must provide a switch that will cut off all electric service to the house when the switch is manually pulled. It also must contain either a fuse or a circuit breaker that will disconnect the entire system automatically if the system is overloaded.

Fuses and circuit breakers are the two types of devices used to cut off the electricity automatically. A fuse is nothing more than a piece of wire that will melt when more than the prescribed amount of electricity flows through it, thus making a gap in the wire system across which the electricity cannot flow.

Circuit breakers are a special type of automatic switch that will turn themselves off when excess electricity passes through them. They may be turned back on manually and will again turn themselves off if the problem that originally tripped them off has not been corrected.

The distribution box also divides the incoming electric service into separate branch circuits that lead to the various areas throughout the house.

Each individual circuit is protected by a fuse or a circuit breaker. If an overload or short circuit occurs on the circuit, it will automatically shut off without tripping the main fuse or circuit breaker and shutting off the service for the whole house.

CIRCUITS AND WIRING

In the panel box the electric power is divided into separate branches known as circuits. Each circuit will serve a separate area of the house or an individual appliance. General circuits run to each area of the house. Connected to them are the permanently installed lighting fixtures and receptacle outlets, into which are plugged lamps and appliances. Each general circuit is protected with a 15-ampere fuse or circuit breaker and should serve 360 to 500 square feet of floor area. A 1,500-square foot house could meet the minimum standards with three general circuits but should have five for convenience and expansion.

Special circuits for small appliances are protected with 20-ampere fuses. They provide 2,400 watts of power and there should be at least two special circuits in each house.

Large appliances such as clothes dryers, water heaters, ranges, dish-washers, freezers and large window air conditioners require large amounts of watts and often 220 to 240 volts and special three-wire cir-cuits using larger wire. These circuits are protected with 30 to 60-ampere fuses or circuit breakers.

The old system of wiring a house was to run two insulated wires parallel to each other from the panel box to the outlets and fixtures. The wires were run a few inches apart and attached to the house with white porcelain insulators called knobs. When the wire passed through a wall or joist, it went through white porcelain tubes, hence the name, knob and tube wiring. This system is obsolete and often must be replaced, often at a major expense.

Today, nonmetallic cable is the next cheapest system available. Each wire, in addition to its own insulation, is wrapped with a paper tape and then encased in a heavy fabric and treated to be water and fire resistant. A similar cable has a thermoplastic insulation and jacket. The cables are attached to the joists and studs with staples. These cables are prohibited in many major cities.

Armored cable (or B.X. cable) consists of insulated wires wrapped in heavy paper and encased in a flexible, galvanized steel covering wound

FIGURE 69
TYPES OF WIRE

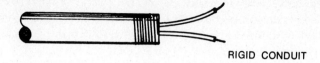

RIGID CONDUIT

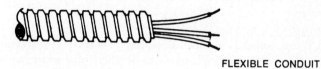

FLEXIBLE CONDUIT

ARMORED (BX) CABLE

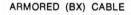

NONMETALLIC CABLE

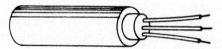

SURFACE RACEWAY

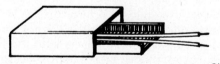

KNOB AND TUBE

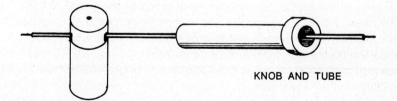

in a spiral fashion. This system has wide acceptance. Surface raceways made of metal or plastic are sometimes used in houses, mostly for repairs and in solid core walls and partitions.

Flexible steel conduit is constructed similarly to B.X. cable except that it is installed without the wire. Wires are drawn through the conduit after installation.

Rigid steel pipe, which looks like water pipe, is still the most preferred and expensive method and meets the most rigid codes. Like the flexible conduit, the wires are pulled through after it is installed. Most outdoor installations are rigid conduit, although vinyl insulated wire has been developed that can be buried in the ground.

Telephones and doorbells use low voltage wiring which does not present a safety hazard and therefore can be run loose throughout the walls and along the joists. Intercommunication and music systems are also becoming very popular. These systems also use low voltage, hazard-free wiring. Music at will throughout the house, answering the door without opening it, talking from room to room are all possible with this equipment.

The increase in crime has brought an increase in houses wired with burglar alarm systems. Some houses also have fire warning systems.

OUTLETS

The duplex receptacle was, until 1960, the most common type of household outlet used. It accepts a two-prong plug, the type most often found on lamps and small appliances. In 1960 the National Electric Code required that all receptacles be the grounding type designed to also accept a three-prong plug. Many small appliances are wired with a third ground wire that is attached to the frame or metal housing of the appliance. The third slot in a grounded outlet is connected to a water pipe or other grounding metal. Grounding of an appliance by using a three-prong plug and receptacle reduces its shock hazard.

There are special waterproof receptacles with caps for outside use, clock outlets, TV outlets, locking outlets and a variety of other special purpose outlets. The receptacle for a 220 to 240 volt line is designed to accept only special plugs. A standard two or three-prong plug cannot be plugged into it. It is also so designed to accept only plugs for appliances using only the exact number of amperes it will supply.

Outlets should be conveniently located throughout the house. This requires that outlets be installed in all habitable rooms so that no point along the floor line is more than six feet from an outlet. In rooms without permanent light fixtures at least three outlets should be provided regardless of the room size; two outlets should be installed over kitchen counters and one should be installed next to the mirror in the bathroom.

FIGURE 70
MINIMUM CONVENIENCE OUTLETS

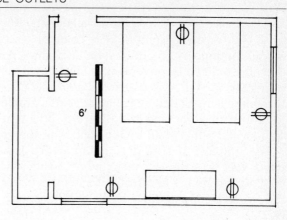

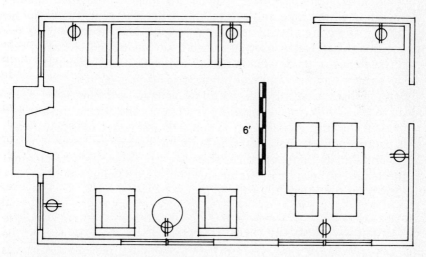

Notice that no point on usable wall space is further than six feet from an outlet.
(Recommendations for minimum number of outlets are FHA Minimum Property Standards.)

SWITCHES

Wall switches are used to control permanently installed light fixtures and may also be used to control wall outlets. Rooms without permanent light fixtures are becoming very common as ceiling fixtures in some rooms continue to go out of style and lamps gain in popularity. However, it would be inconvenient to have to walk into a dark room to turn on a lamp. A wall switch near the door that controls the wall outlet into which the lamp is plugged eliminates this problem. It is also convenient to control fans, garbage disposals and some other small appliances by a wall switch rather than by the switch on the appliance itself.

The simplest and most common switch is a two-way snap switch which has two copper contact points inside. When the switch is up in the "on" position it lets the electricity pass to the fixture or outlet. When the switch is flipped down to the "off" position, the electricity is turned off.

Three-way switches are used to control a fixture or outlet from two different places. With this wiring and switching arrangement, the fixture or outlet is turned from "off" to "on" or "on" to "off" when the position of either switch is changed; therefore the up position is not necessarily the "on" position or the down position the "off" position.

Some other, more expensive switches are those with lighted handles (some glow all the time and others only when the switch is in the off position). There are also switches that turn on and off when a door is opened or closed (often used in closets), key controlled switches, pull chain switches, outside weatherproof switches, touch switches, time delay switches and a variety of other specialized switches.

Some houses are controlled by a low voltage switching system. Instead of the switch directly opening and closing the circuit, it controls a relay which in turn operates the switch. The advantage of this system is that control panels, located throughout the house, can control many lights and outlets from one place. These control panels are often located at the main entrance or in the master bedroom. Dimmer switches are used to vary the intensity of the light.

For a complete Electricity checklist, see Checklist 34, page C-71.

MISCELLANEOUS SYSTEMS AND EQUIPMENT

As our technology increases more and more mechanical systems and special equipment will be installed in our homes. Some of the items now found in homes that have not already been covered elsewhere in this book are heat pumps, humidifiers, intercommunication and sound systems, burglar and fire alarms, automatic doors, elevators and stair lifts,

FIGURE 71
HEAT PUMP

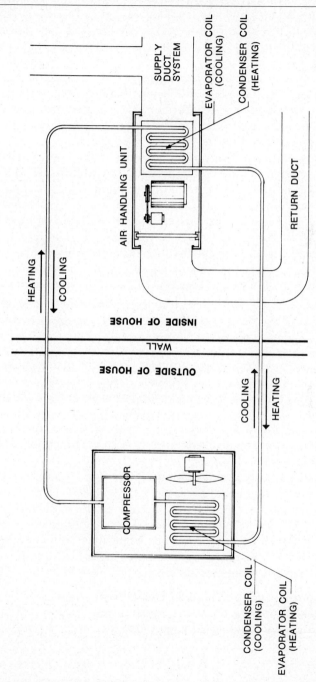

incinerators, laundry chutes, central vacuum cleaners, saunas, special tubs, exercise equipment, computer controls, plus a long list of special hobby items and unique custom features.

It is beyond the scope of this book to describe all these special items except humidifiers and heat pumps.

HUMIDIFIERS

Dry air in the winter can be a problem with all types of heating systems, contrary to the popular misconception that it is a warm air heating deficiency. The major controlling factor is the construction of the house. Moisture is generated by the activities of daily living, such as cooking and bathing, and is drawn out of the house in the winter to the dry air outside through leaks and cracks. A tight, very well-insulated house will retain sufficient moisture for comfortable living, which is about 25 to 30 percent relative humidity.

A dry air problem can be corrected by the addition of a humidifying device to a hot air heating system or with portable humidifying devices. Often a small vaporizer in the bedroom at night will solve the problem.

Occasionally, in a super-insulated, electrically heated house the reverse problem will develop, resulting in wet walls and windows. In this case, an exhaust fan connected to a humidistat control will effectively control the humidity.

HEAT PUMPS

The heat pump electric system provides both heating and cooling from a central system. It is actually a reversible refrigeration unit. In the winter it takes heat from the outside air, ground or well water and distributes it in the house. Its efficiency decreases when it is very cold outside and it must be supplemented with resistance heating. In the summer the system cools by extracting heat from the inside of the house like a typical air conditioning unit.

This modern heating and cooling system (see Figure 71) still constitutes a small percentage of systems being installed. Heat pumps work best in moderate climates. They have received a lot of publicity and have tended to be oversold in some areas. Like air conditioners, they have a compressor which tends to wear out when they are over about seven years old. If the house you are looking at has a heat pump we recommend you have it professionally inspected.

For a checklist on Miscellaneous Systems and Equipment, see Checklist 35, page C-73.

Rate	5 years
6	19.33
6 1/4	19.45
6 1/2	19.57
6 3/4	19.68

CHAPTER 10
NEGOTIATING

While not quite in the realm of the supernatural, there is a certain air of mystery and romance attached to buying a house. If you react as most people we know your pulse rate will increase by 25 percent from the time you spot the house you want until the time your offer is finally accepted or rejected. In addition, you will be constantly fearful throughout this period that someone else will want the house and make a higher offer.

You will be able to think of little else during the negotiating period. The problem is compounded many times if you are negotiating directly with the seller rather than through a real estate broker.

WHAT'S IT WORTH (TO YOU)?

The first step in the negotiating process is for you to find out what the house is worth and whether you are ready, willing and able to pay that price. We discuss in other chapters how to obtain help from appraisers, real estate brokers and salespeople and lenders in determining what the house is worth on the market. You, of course, can be the only one to determine what it is worth to *you.*

It is human instinct to want to buy the property for as little money as possible. Nobody wants to "overpay" for a house. Many people proudly tell how they got a "bargain" on their homes, but the fact is that most houses are sold at prices that are close to their value. Furthermore, it really makes little difference in the long run if you pay $1,000 more or less for a house. Even the most skilled appraisers admit they rarely can estimate the value of a house within a thousand dollars.

Suppose your "dream house" has an asking price of $67,900. You decide the house is worth $65,000 so you make a $61,000 offer to "see what will happen." After some time and several offers and counteroffers you have raised your offer to $65,000 and the seller has "come down" to $65,500. Your pulse races still faster, as your heart which wants the house and your psyche which does not want to overpay both pour adrenalin into your system. Almost inevitably at this point the salesperson might let you know that some potential buyer is about to make an offer. Now the decision is up to you. If you fail to act another buyer may get your house.

STOP!

1. Ask yourself, if I concluded that the house is worth $65,000 why all of a sudden is somebody offering more?
2. Ask yourself, suppose I pay an extra $500—what does it really mean?
3. Tell your psyche to get off your back. How does it know you are overpaying. Why does your psyche think it can estimate within one percent? Tell your psyche you will tell your friends the house was really worth $66,900 if that will make it happy.
4. Figure out if you can afford the additional $500.

If your $65,000 offer was based on a 75 percent, 30-year, 12 percent monthly payment mortgage, you would have been offering to put $16,250 down and make monthly payments on a $48,750 mortgage of $501.45 per month.

Now if you raise your offer to $65,500 you will have to make a down payment of $16,375 ($125 more) and monthly payments of 505.31 ($3.86 per month more).

WHAT SHOULD YOU DO?

You have to decide how you feel about your heart, your psyche, the $125 additional down payment and the $3.86 per month additional payment.

If you decide you really don't want to increase your offer you should withdraw your offer and wait. You might let it be known that you are now considering another house. Then set forth the reasons why you don't want to pay more and tell the real estate agent you are willing to resubmit the same offer together with your reasons for not raising it. You might suggest some short deadline so you will be free to proceed to negotiate for the other house you are considering. When the buyer and seller are this close together, a skillful real estate practitioner will be able to bring them together to make the final sale.

PROFESSIONAL NEGOTIATING

Fortunately, there has been an almost imperceptible but very real change in the process of buying and selling a house. Where once it was relegated to a battle of wits between buyer and seller, a ritual of haggling, that tradition now seems destined to take its place among family folklore. Of course there will always be vestiges of "trading" with its attendant excitement, but house buying will never again be quite the way it was. Where once negotiating was considered a fine art, a new school considers it a science. The reason? Simple. Enter the real estate broker or salesperson.

The real estate professional is highly trained in selling houses, including presenting offers and helping buyers and sellers reach agreement. The broker's or salesperson's objectives are to obtain a signed contract of sale which properly expresses the agreement of the parties and to complete the sale as swiftly and efficiently as possible. To this end, the broker or salesperson will negotiate with a combination of experience and training, science and sophistication. Discretion and judgment are the tools of the real estate practitioner's trade. He or she acts as a virtuoso and an amateur psychologist. Skill, training and diplomacy are the hallmarks of the successful real estate practitioner.

You must remember throughout the process that legally the real estate agent represents the seller. While he or she owes a duty of honesty and fair dealing to you, the buyer, the agent owes a fiduciary duty to the seller. The real estate practitioner cannot, except under the rarest of circumstances, be a "dual" agent.

THE NEGOTIATING PROCESS

To explore what you can do to improve your negotiating position, let's start again and go step by step through the process of looking for a home.

SELECTING A REAL ESTATE AGENT

The first step is to select one or more real estate agents to work with you to help you find the home you are seeking. We have discussed in Chapter 3 the difference between a REALTOR® and a non-REALTOR® broker or sales agent, and we have recommended ways of selecting a REALTOR® to serve you.

In the first meeting with a broker you will make your needs known, based upon the size of your family, personal desires and, of greatest import, price. By all means, represent yourself correctly from square one. Don't try to impress brokers with even the slightest exaggeration of your financial status. You wouldn't fool them for very long anyhow. (This includes the other side of the coin, crying "poor mouth.") Surely you would not want them to misrepresent the truth in any way. Mutual candor saves a lot of time and is one of the niceties of a relationship.

Once you have determined how much you can afford to pay for a house (see Chapter 1), and what you want, the broker can show you properties which he or she feels will suit your requirements.

When you find a house you feel you want the next step is to make your initial offer.
STOP!
Before you make any offer you must be satisfied you know approxi-

mately how much the house is worth. The asking price may be greatly overstated and you could make a serious mistake by offering too much for the house even if the initial offer is well below the asking price. We have covered elsewhere how value is estimated (see Chapter 12).

THE OFFER

The majority of real estate brokers use a standard form variously known as "Contract of Sale," "Bond for Deed," "Purchase Agreement," "Deposit Receipt" and other names depending upon geographical location. (See Chapter 14, Sales Contracts.)

The real purpose of the written offer, which consists of the offer and acceptance, is to bind the buyer and seller to their agreement. The offer safeguards buyer and seller in very specific terms. Time is then provided to (1) verify that the title is free and clear or contains nonobjectionable encumbrances, (2) allow for any inspections or appraisals that are needed and (3) allow for obtaining a commitment for any needed financing.

The broker really does not draw up a sales contract but instead fills in some kind of "binder." This is really a contract to enter into a contract. Since it usually does not cover all of the conditions of the sale, it can lead to problems and often a second round of negotiations. However, millions of sales have been made with the use of binders. When binders are used it is even more important to spell out exactly how the deposit is going to be treated and under what circumstances it will be forfeited to the seller and when it will be returned to the seller.

When all parties have signed the binder it is turned over to an attorney who then draws up a formal sales contract which again all the parties then sign. Chapter 14 goes over in detail what you should have in a sales contract.

When you are satisfied that the written offer correctly expresses your offer and all the conditions you wish it to contain you should sign at least four copies.

- One copy is for you to keep.
- One copy is for the broker.
- One copy is for the seller to keep.
- One copy is for the seller to sign and return to you.

Additional signed copies may also be needed for financing and other purposes according to the custom of your area.

Important! You should always get, *immediately,* a copy of any document which you sign.

CASH DEPOSIT

This is the customary point in the sales transaction where a cash deposit, sometimes termed "earnest money," is paid by the buyer. It is a down payment, usually up to ten percent of the purchase price, to show good faith. In most cases, the bigger the deposit, the greater the chance of the sale going through.

The written offer must clearly spell out who is going to hold the deposit. It should also spell out when it will be turned over to the seller and when and under what conditions it will be returned to the buyer.

PRESENTING THE OFFER

After you sign a sales contract or binder and have given the broker or salesperson a deposit your offer will be presented.

There are some things that you can do to help get the offer accepted:

1. Prepare a list of improvements and repairs that you feel will be needed together with their estimated cost to be shown to the seller.
2. Tell the broker or salesperson about other houses you are considering and how their prices compare with the house on which you are making an offer.
3. Submit any appraisal report you have that supports your offered price.
4. Allow a reasonable but short period of time for the seller's consideration of the offer so you will be free to make other offers.
5. Don't ever, even in the strictest of confidence, suggest you will go higher if your offer is refused.

It is now up to the broker or salesperson to present your offer.

He or she will consider all the variables. Are there structural or site problems which are justifications for a lower offer? If you found drawbacks or weaknesses, the salesperson will diplomatically suggest to the seller that while you're pleased overall, you do recognize areas which need improvement. Were you doing this yourself, it might be taken as a personal attack and negotiations would break down if not cease altogether. The salesperson or broker will make your offer and explain it objectively and dispassionately. When cool heads prevail, many an offer which comes in considerably under the asking price will be accepted. Or a counteroffer may be elicited, but that is also progress.

NON-PRICE NEGOTIATING POINTS

There is another point that should be kept in mind during the negotiations. It is often not just the price that is the problem. Here are some other possible concessions you might offer to make instead of raising the offering price:

1. Increase the deposit.
2. Change the mortgage contingency (amount, term, interest, etc.).
3. Offer a larger down payment.
4. Change the proposed closing date.

5. Offer free or reduced rent for occupancy by the seller after the closing.
6. Offer to buy some of the furniture and other furnishings.
7. Offer to assume unpaid taxes, insurance premiums or other expenses.
8. Find out what else the sellers might want that would induce them to accept your offer.

COUNTEROFFER

At the counteroffer stage, negotiating requires a lot of patience and common sense on the part of both the buyer and the seller. The salesperson will assist and guide by pointing out logically just where the "give and take" is and how each of you benefits. That is the direction in which the salesperson or broker will probably move in this final phase.

The next step will be to reduce the difference between your offer and the counteroffer by calculating what the actual increase in down payment and the number of dollars per month of mortgage payment would be. This is not a bad thing to do. And, if the salesperson hasn't already mentioned it (which would be some kind of a phenomenon) he or she will point out that even as you hesitate, the house could be sold to someone else. But then you already knew all that.

Sooner or later either your offer will be accepted, or you will come to the conclusion you are not willing to pay what the seller wants, or the house will be sold to somebody else. If either of the latter happens, you will have to start all over again. If your offer is accepted and only a binder was signed, then a formal sales contract must be drawn up by an attorney. Usually some additional items will have to be negotiated that were not covered by the binder.

In some areas it is the practice to record the contract. This makes it less likely that the seller will sell to another buyer for a higher price, or for any other reason. It also ensures that the buyer will get the house for the price agreed upon.

At this point, if you haven't already done so it is recommended that you consider obtaining the services of your own attorney.

The sale has now been negotiated. You must now obtain financing (see Chapter 11). You might also have to have a survey, title search and various inspections done (see Chapters 3). And you will need special kinds of insurance (see Chapter 13). Much of this will have to be taken care of before the closing of the transaction (see Chapter 15) where full payment is made, the deed is delivered and everything is finally signed and sealed by buyer and seller.

For a complete checklist on Negotiating see Checklist 36, page C-75.

CHAPTER 11
FINANCING

When purchasing a house there are several financing options available, the most common of which we will cover in detail in this chapter. However, before any loan can be arranged you must first prepare for your cash commitment—the down payment.

THE DOWN PAYMENT

The down payment you can afford, together with the amount of mortgage money you can borrow, will determine the maximum you can pay for a home. The down payment should not be so large as to exhaust the cash resources needed for other family expenditures, and the mortgage payment must not exceed an amount you can comfortably handle each month.

Although most people manage to save (or inherit) enough money for a down payment, it is possible to buy a home with no money. Some people qualify for special Veterans Administration loans of 100 percent of the cost of the home. Others can obtain a loan to be used as a down payment. Technically, this may not be a mortgage but for all practical purposes, as far as its effect on the family budget is concerned, it is like having another mortgage.

There are two other ways to buy a house with little or no down payment. One is to arrange to build a home and do a significant portion of the work yourself. This is sometimes known as "sweat equity." The newest way is the homesteading program which allows for the purchase, at a nominal amount, of a house in the inner-city which can then be renovated with borrowed money or grants given under a variety of special programs.

Most families, however, either have or start some type of savings program in order to accumulate the down payment.

The amount of money that should be put down on the purchase of a home is a decision every buyer must make. This is a complicated decision to which there is no pat or easy answer. Generally the greater the amount of the down payment the better mortgage terms you are going to be able to negotiate and the smaller the mortgage payments are going to be. However, money that is not put into the down payment provides a reserve for other expenditures connected with the purchase of a home or for other investments and business enterprises. Also, a mortgage, especially a long-term one at a fixed rate of interest, may be payable in the future with dollars that are much less valuable than the dollars loaned at the time of the purchase of the house. (This has been true based on past history, but there is no guarantee that history will repeat itself).

The final down payment decision is one only you can make, considering all these factors including the family's feelings about security, investments, travel, luxuries, education and the future of the economy.

The balance of the purchase price usually is money borrowed from a lender—the mortgage.

SOURCES OF MORTGAGES

Mortgage money can come from a variety of sources. The list below shows common sources of mortgages. In 1975 savings and loan associations supplied about half of the mortgage money, followed far behind by commercial banks, federally supported agencies, mutual savings banks and life insurance companies, in that order. All the other sources together supply only about five percent of the funds.

Loan Sources

Savings and loan associations
Commercial banks
Federal agencies
Life insurance companies
Mutual savings banks
Purchase money mortgages
Second mortgages
Mortgage bankers

A GOOD PLACE TO START

A good place to start looking for a mortgage is at the lending institution that currently holds the mortgage. If the mortgage is at an interest rate below current rates, the lender should be anxious to have the house sold and the old, low rate mortgage paid off. If the mortgage is assumable, the bank should be made aware of the pending sale.

If a larger mortgage is needed, ask the lender to make some concessions in the form of lower interest, lower down payment or longer mortgage term.

Lenders are businesspeople. If you can show them how to increase their effective yield, they should be willing to go along with your proposed concessions.

Here is an example of how you might suggest an interest concession by the lender:

- There is an unpaid balance of $45,000 on an old, 8 percent mortgage. The effective yield is 8 percent.
- The current interest rate is 14 percent. You need a $55,000 mortgage. You offer 12 percent interest. This means the lender would have to put $10,000 cash into the new mortgage at 12 percent that could have been loaned elsewhere at 14 percent.

Here is how you demonstrate that the lender is much better off doing this than using the $10,000 as part of someone else's 14 percent mortgage:

Old Mortgage: $45,000 @ 8% = $3,600 Interest[1]
    New Rate: 10,000 @ 14% = 1,400
    _____   _____
Total Portfolio: $55,000 $5,000 Interest

The effective yield to lender ($5,000 ÷ $55,000) is 9.1 percent as compared to your offer of 12 percent.

SAVINGS AND LOAN ASSOCIATIONS (S & Ls)

There are now about 11,000 savings and loan associations (headquarters and branch offices) throughout the country. They receive about one-third of all the savings deposits and supply about half of all the home mortgage loans.

Savings and loan associations can be either federally or state chartered. All federally chartered S & Ls are regulated by the Federal Home Loan Bank (FHLB). Many state chartered S & Ls voluntarily also are subject to FHLB supervision. This makes them eligible to borrow from the FHLB when they need funds to pay off accounts being withdrawn by depositors or to make additional mortgages.

Almost all S & Ls also belong to the Federal Savings and Loan Insurance Corporation (FSLIC). This is a federally created insurance company that insures deposits made by the public up to $100,000 per account.

S & Ls can loan up to 95 percent (higher for some VA and FHA guaranteed mortgages) of the appraised value of a home for a period up to 30 years. Most S & Ls require insurance (FHA, VA, private mortgage insur-

---

[1] To simplify this example, we have assumed annual payments. If the payments are monthly, there would be an insignificant difference.

ance, etc.) on the high loan-to-value-ratio loans. S & Ls also make loans on mobile homes and loans for home improvements.

COMMERCIAL BANKS

Home mortgages traditionally have been a secondary activity of commercial banks. These banks are primarily interested in making short-term loans for commercial purposes. However, because of the sheer size of the commercial bank industry they still are a major source of home mortgages.

Commercial banks usually make conventional mortgage loans up to 80 percent of the home's appraised value for periods up to 30 years. They make privately insured mortgages for up to 95 percent of the property value and FHA and VA insured mortgages for any loan-to-value-ratio permitted by the specific program. Commercial banks are excellent sources for construction mortgages. They often sell their mortgages to other lenders in what is known as the secondary mortgage market.

FEDERALLY SUPPORTED AGENCIES AND CORPORATIONS

Three government agencies and corporations together are the major purchasers of mortgages from primary lenders. As such, they are part of the secondary mortgage market.

Agency	Initials	Trade Name
1. Federal Home Loan Mortgage Corporation	FHLMC	Freddie Mac
2. Federal National Mortgage Association	FNMA	Fannie Mae
3. Government National Mortgage Association	GNMA	Ginnie Mae

These agencies sell securities in the open security market and raise large sums of money from the proceeds of these sales. They use this money to buy mortgages from primary lenders such as savings and loans and sometimes mortgage bankers. The consumer does not deal directly with any of these agencies. He or she usually does not know when the mortgage has been purchased by one of these agencies because the primary lender continues to service the loan. It continues to collect the payment and handle any correspondence or other problems directly with the borrower.

The secondary mortgage market has made more money available for home mortgages than would have been available if all the funds had to come from consumer deposits in savings and loans and banks.

INSURANCE COMPANIES

Life insurance companies and, to a smaller extent, casualty insurance companies used to be major sources of home mortgages. In recent years they have been withdrawing from small home loans and shifting to large mortgages on multifamily and commercial properties. They prefer the ease of handling and the higher interest rates on these large loans.

Those insurance companies that have stayed in the home loan business have mostly done so in the capacity of purchasers in the secondary mortgage market. Some have mortgage bankers who assemble groups of home mortgages together and sell them to the insurance company in a block. The mortgage banker then continues to collect payments and service individual loans.

MUTUAL SAVINGS BANKS (MSBs)

From the viewpoint of a borrower there is not much difference between a mutual savings bank and a savings and loan association. These institutions are few in number (less than 500) and most of them are located in New England and the Middle Atlantic States. MSBs invest about 75 percent of their assets in home mortgages. Although they are few in number, they account for almost 10 percent of the nation's home mortgages. All mutual savings banks are state chartered but their deposits are federally insured.

Most MSBs can make conventional mortgages up to 95 percent (higher for some VA and FHA insured mortgages) of the appraised value of a home when they are insured and 80 percent (in some states 90 percent) when they are uninsured, for periods up to 30 years.

PURCHASE MONEY MORTGAGES

Sellers who do not need large amounts of cash upon selling are in an excellent position to enhance the salability of their homes. Such sellers can give a purchase money mortgage to the buyer which will give them the needed income while at the same time supplying the buyer with needed financing.

People who retire and plan to move into either a rental unit or a less expensive house or in with another member of the family are often in a position to offer purchase money mortgages. In many of these situations and in other situations as well, while the sellers do not need large amounts of cash, what they do need is steady future income which a purchase money mortgage can provide. When a reasonable down payment is made and a buyer who has been screened for credit worthiness, the possibility of a foreclosure is very low. There often is less risk holding a good first mortgage then there is in other comparable investments. The rate of interest the seller will receive is often very favorable when compared to other alternative investments. Also the receipt of regular monthly payments is often very desirable.

Sellers often need to be educated on the desirability of this type of investment. Often they must overcome fears that go back to the Depression of the 1930s. Here is where a real estate broker or salesperson who is knowledgeable and enjoys the confidence of the seller can be very helpful.

The buyer should consult with the broker or salesperson to propose a mortgage that will most likely be acceptable to the buyer. This proposed mortgage then should be incorporated into the offer. The salesperson then will be in a good position to educate the seller on the advantages of an offer which includes holding a purchase money mortgage.

SECOND MORTGAGES

Sometimes a seller is willing to hold a second mortgage, which is typically an additional loan imposed on top of the first mortgage taken out when the borrower needs additional money.[2] For the seller a second mortgage may make possible the sale of the home at a price that would not otherwise be possible. It also provides a good investment with regular payments that will suit the seller's future need for income rather than a nonexistent need for immediate cash. A good second mortgage compares favorably with other alternative investments. Again it may be necessary to educate the seller about the advantages of holding a second mortgage on the house he or she is selling. Many sellers do not understand second mortgages and have unfounded fears based on rumors and other misinformation.

It is quite common for second mortgages to be for shorter periods of time than the first mortgage. Often payments are based on a long-term mortgage payment schedule in order to keep them at a level the buyer can afford. Such a mortgage may contain a provision that allows it to be paid off in full after a specified number of years. This is called a "balloon payment."

The main advantage to the buyer or the seller holding a purchase money second mortgage is the need for a lower down payment.

Another advantage is that the needed first mortgage will be less, which may result in a lower interest rate, longer term or availability from sources that would not give a larger mortgage.

MORTGAGE BANKERS

Mortgage bankers have for many years been significant sources of residential mortgages. Mortgage bankers assemble a group of individual mortgages and sell them. Usually they continue to service the mortgage. Most are private firms that have mainly but not exclusively concentrated their residential business on government insured or backed mortgages. A substantial portion of their business is the origination and services of FHA and VA insured mortgages. They also originate conventional mort-

[2] John W. Reilly, *The Language of Real Estate* (Chicago: Real Estate Education Company, 1977).

gages and sell them to insurance companies, pension funds and the Federal Home Loan Mortgage Corporation.

OTHER SOURCES

All the other sources of mortgages only account for about five percent of total mortgages. However, even this small percentage is a very large dollar figure.

Some of these sources are pension funds, credit unions, rich relatives, sellers, real estate agents, foundations, private individuals and corporations (See section on private first and second mortgages later in this chapter.)

DOCUMENTATION OF MORTGAGES

Because mortgages involve large sums of money and often extend over many years, it is necessary that they be carefully documented so that the agreement between the borrower and the lender can be enforced should either default on their obligations. Of course the obligation of the lender is primarily to loan the money and the obligation of the borrower is primarily to make the loan repayments. Therefore it would seem that it is more for the protection of the lender than the borrower that careful documentation is needed. But this is not completely true because the borrower must be protected from overly harsh actions by the lender in the event the borrower is unable to make every payment on schedule. There has to be a careful balance between the rights of the borrower and the need of the lender to be protected.

Real estate loans are generally secured against the real estate itself, and hence against one of the basic needs of life—shelter. Because of the importance given by our society to rights surrounding property ownership, laws pertaining to real estate are among the oldest and most complex. What this means to the home buyer is that the documents involved with real estate loans can be expected to be long and, to the layman's eye, very confusing.

What the home buyer should understand is that the greater part of the documents simply recite existing state and federal law as it affects the rights and obligations of borrower and lender. Especially in the case of mortgages issued by federally regulated lending institutions these documents are stipulated by federal regulation. Therefore there will be little if any difference among lending institutions, nor will the lenders have the flexibility to alter their mortgage papers to meet the objections of a borrower or borrower's attorney. But at the same time these papers are widely accepted as being equitable to all concerned.

In mortgages, land contracts and other loans arranged between the buyer and other sources such as nonfederally regulated banks, credit unions, fraternal organizations, private trusts and, most importantly, the seller there are many ways in which the loan documents can be drawn. There is a far greater possibility of variations of the rights and obligations of both parties in these situations, especially in those loans between private parties. No agreement should be entered into in these cases without professional legal cousel.

A state that has foreclosure legislation most favorable to the borrower may attract few funds from outside the state. Those states that give the greatest protection to the lender, with short periods for foreclosure, tend to attract more funds from around the country. It is to the advantage of prospective borrowers to have a sufficient amount of available mortgage money in the state as this will be reflected in lower interest rates, better terms and greater ease in obtaining a mortgage.

A typical mortgage consists of at least two documents. The first is the mortgage deed (sometimes called deed of trust) document that pledges the property as collateral for the loan. Where the title actually vests during the period of the loan varies depending upon the type of document and the laws of the area in which the property is located.

Nobody should sign a mortgage (or other similar document) without the advice of an attorney. These are complex documents and must be carefully drawn up to protect the interests of all parties.

MORTGAGE CLAUSES

There are some clauses in a typical mortgage with which the borrower should be familiar since they go beyond the obligation of the borrower just to make timely payments.

The insurance clause is a requirement that the borrower provide insurance on the property during the term of the mortgage. The insurance required may be a homeowner's policy or fire and extended coverage insurance, and/or liability insurance. The clause often stipulates a required amount of insurance and requires that the lender be named in the insurance policies. New federal regulations now also require flood insurance and sometimes earthquake insurance in areas where these hazards are known to exist.

There is usually also a covenant that the borrower will not remove or demolish any improvements without permission of the lender.

Another clause spells out how the property taxes will be paid. Some mortgages require that the taxes be paid in monthly installments along with the regular mortgage payment. These payments may be held in escrow (with or without interest depending on the law of the individual state) to pay the taxes when due. Other mortgages just require that the borrower pay the taxes when due and gives the lender the right, if they remain unpaid, to pay them and then add the amount paid to the mortgage.

There is usually a clause requiring that the borrower keep the property in good repair at all times.

The prepayment clause spells out when the borrower may make prepayments on the mortgage. Some mortgages allow prepayment at any time. Others spell out a penalty if a prepayment is made and still others do not permit any prepayment at all.

The acceleration clause stipulates that if the borrower fails to keep up any of the provisions of the mortgage or fails to make timely payments, the entire debt will become payable.

The nonassumption clause, often called the "due-on-sale" clause, gives the lender the right to prohibit the borrower from allowing anyone to assume his mortgage upon sale of the secured real estate. Specifically, it gives the lending institution the right to call due ("accelerate") the mortgage in the event that the mortgage is either assumed or the home is conveyed with a second mortgage, land contract or other means to a new owner.

This clause has only been used in recent years and is not uniformly enforced by all lenders. In addition, FHA mortgages do not contain this provision, and it has only limited application in VA mortgages. Therefore it is advisable, prior to arranging mortgage financing and prior to commiting yourself to buy or sell through an assumption of a mortgage, to be thoroughly familiar with the policies of the lending institution involved, *at the time such a transaction is contemplated*. In cases where the lender chooses not to enforce this clause, the assumable mortgage can become an attractive selling, and of course buying, feature.

PROMISSORY NOTE

Nearly all mortgages include a second document which is a promissory note or bond. The signing of this note makes the borrower personally obligated to repay the loan. In the event that payments are not made as agreed and the property is foreclosed by the lender and then sold, the borrower may still be personally liable if the proceeds of the sale are not sufficient to pay off the entire unpaid balance of the loan, plus the expenses of the foreclosure action and foreclosure sale. Often these expenses can be very large. In some areas the lender can try to attach (put a lien on) other property of the borrower or garnishee wages.

METHODS OF FINANCING

CONVENTIONAL LOANS

In spite of all the special programs and insurance plans that are now available, the majority of all the mortgages made by all lenders are still conventional loans. These loans, the simplest kind of mortgage to obtain, are made by the lending institution to the borrower without the guarantee or insurance of the FHA or VA.

The prospective borrower makes an application to the lender for the desired mortgage usually after a sales contract or binder has been signed by both the buyer and the seller and the sale is bound with a deposit.

FIGURE 72
SAMPLE MORTGAGE APPLICATION

RESIDENTIAL LOAN APPLICATION

MORTGAGE APPLIED FOR	☐ Conventional ☐ FHA ☐ VA ☐	Amount $	Interest Rate %	No. of Months	Monthly Payment Principal & Interest $	Escrow/Impounds (to be collected monthly) ☐ Taxes ☐ Hazard Ins. ☐ Mtg. Ins. ☐
Prepayment Option						

SUBJECT PROPERTY

Property Street Address		City		County	State	Zip	No. Units
Legal Description (Attach description if necessary)						Year Built	

Purpose of Loan: ☐ Purchase ☐ Construction-Permanent ☐ Construction ☐ Refinance ☐ Other (Explain)

Complete this line if Construction-Permanent or Construction Loan ☞	Lot Value Data Year Acquired $	Original Cost $	Present Value (a) $	Cost of Imps. (b) $	Total (a + b) $	ENTER TOTAL AS PURCHASE PRICE IN DETAILS OF PURCHASE.

Complete this line if a Refinance Loan | Purpose of Refinance | Describe Improvements [ ] made [ ] to be made

Year Acquired	Original Cost $	Amt. Existing Liens $				Cost: $

Title Will Be Held In What Name(s)	Manner In Which Title Will Be Held

Source of Down Payment and Settlement Charges

This application is designed to be completed by the borrower(s) with the lender's assistance. The Co-Borrower Section and all other Co-Borrower questions must be completed and the appropriate box(es) checked if ☐ another person will be jointly obligated with the Borrower on the loan, or ☐ the Borrower is relying on income from alimony, child support or separate maintenance or on the income or assets of another person as a basis for repayment of the loan, or ☐ the Borrower is married and resides, or the property is located, in a community property state.

BORROWER				**CO-BORROWER**		
Name		Age	School Yrs	Name	Age	School Yrs
Present Address No. Years ____ ☐ Own ☐ Rent				Present Address No. Years ____ ☐ Own ☐ Rent		
Street				Street		
City/State/Zip				City/State/Zip		
Former address if less than 2 years at present address				Former address if less than 2 years at present address		
Street				Street		
City/State/Zip				City/State/Zip		
Years at former address ☐ Own ☐ Rent				Years at former address ☐ Own ☐ Rent		
Marital Status ☐ Married ☐ Separated ☐ Unmarried (incl. single, divorced, widowed)	DEPENDENTS OTHER THAN LISTED BY CO-BORROWER NO. AGES			Marital Status ☐ Married ☐ Separated ☐ Unmarried (incl. single, divorced, widowed)	DEPENDENTS OTHER THAN LISTED BY BORROWER NO. AGES	
Name and Address of Employer	Years employed in this line of work or profession? ____ years Years on this job ____ ☐ Self Employed*			Name and Address of Employer	Years employed in this line of work or profession? ____ years Years on this job ____ ☐ Self Employed*	
Position/Title	Type of Business			Position/Title	Type of Business	
Social Security Number***	Home Phone	Business Phone		Social Security Number*** Home Phone	Business Phone	

GROSS MONTHLY INCOME				**MONTHLY HOUSING EXPENSE****			**DETAILS OF PURCHASE**	
Item	Borrower	Co-Borrower	Total		PRESENT	PROPOSED	Do Not Complete If Refinance	
Base Empl. Income	$	$	$	Rent $			a. Purchase Price	
Overtime				First Mortgage (P&I)	$	$	b. Total Closing Costs (Est.)	
Bonuses				Other Financing (P&I)			c. Prepaid Escrows (Est.)	
Commissions				Hazard Insurance			d. Total (a + b + c)	$
Dividends/Interest				Real Estate Taxes			e. Amount This Mortgage	( )
Net Rental Income				Mortgage Insurance			f. Other Financing	( )
Other† (Before completing, see notice under Describe Other Income below.)				Homeowner Assn. Dues			g. Other Equity	( )
				Other:			h. Amount of Cash Deposit	( )
				Total Monthly Pmt.	$	$	i. Closing Costs Paid by Seller	( )
Total	$	$	$	Utilities			j. Cash Reqd. For Closing (Est.)	$
				Total	$	$		

DESCRIBE OTHER INCOME

⬦ B—Borrower C—Co-Borrower	NOTICE:† Alimony, child support, or separate maintenance income need not be revealed if the Borrower or Co-Borrower does not choose to have it considered as a basis for repaying this loan.	Monthly Amount $

IF EMPLOYED IN CURRENT POSITION FOR LESS THAN TWO YEARS COMPLETE THE FOLLOWING

B/C	Previous Employer/School	City/State	Type of Business	Position/Title	Dates From/To	Monthly Income
						$

THESE QUESTIONS APPLY TO BOTH BORROWER AND CO-BORROWER

If a "yes" answer is given to a question in this column, explain on an attached sheet.	Borrower Yes or No	Co-Borrower Yes or No	If applicable, explain Other Financing or Other Equity (provide addendum if more space is needed).
Have you any outstanding judgments? In the last 7 years, have you been declared bankrupt?			
Have you had property foreclosed upon or given title or deed in lieu thereof?			
Are you a co-maker or endorser on a note?			
Are you a party in a law suit?			
Are you obligated to pay alimony, child support, or separate maintenance?			
Is any part of the down payment borrowed?			

*FHLMC/FNMA require business credit report, signed Federal Income Tax returns for last two years, and, if available, audited Profit and Loss Statements plus balance sheet for same period.
**All Present Monthly Housing Expenses of Borrower and Co-Borrower should be listed on a combined basis.
***Neither FHLMC nor FNMA requires this information.

FHLMC 65 Rev. 8/78

FNMA 1003 Rev. 8/78

FIGURE 72
SAMPLE MORTGAGE APPLICATION (continued)

This Statement and any applicable supporting schedules may be completed jointly by both married and unmarried co-borrowers if their assets and liabilities are sufficiently joined so that the Statement can be meaningfully and fairly presented on a combined basis; otherwise separate Statements and Schedules are required (FHLMC 65A/FNMA 1003A). If the co-borrower section was completed about a spouse, this statement and supporting schedules must be completed about that spouse also.

☐ Completed Jointly   ☐ Not Completed Jointly

ASSETS		LIABILITIES AND PLEDGED ASSETS			
		Indicate by (*) those liabilities or pledged assets which will be satisfied upon sale of real estate owned or upon refinancing of subject property			
Description	Cash or Market Value	Creditors' Name, Address and Account Number	Acct. Name If Not Borrower's	Mo. Pmt. and Mos. left to pay	Unpaid Balance
Cash Deposit Toward Purchase Held By	$	Installment Debts (include "revolving" charge accts)		$ Pmt./Mos.	$
				/	
Checking and Savings Accounts (Show Names of Institutions/Acct. Nos.)				/	
				/	
				/	
Stocks and Bonds (No./Description)				/	
				/	
				/	
Life Insurance Net Cash Value Face Amount ($		Other Debts Including Stock Pledges		/	
SUBTOTAL LIQUID ASSETS	$				
Real Estate Owned (Enter Market Value from Schedule of Real Estate Owned)		Real Estate Loans		/	
Vested Interest in Retirement Fund					
Net Worth of Business Owned (ATTACH FINANCIAL STATEMENT)					
Automobiles (Make and Year)		Automobile Loans			
				/	
Furniture and Personal Property		Alimony, Child Support and Separate Maintenance Payments Owed To			
Other Assets (Itemize)				/	
		TOTAL MONTHLY PAYMENTS		$	
TOTAL ASSETS	A $	NET WORTH (A minus B) $		TOTAL LIABILITIES	B $

STATEMENT OF ASSETS AND LIABILITIES

SCHEDULE OF REAL ESTATE OWNED (If Additional Properties Owned Attach Separate Schedule)

Address of Property (Indicate S if Sold, PS if Pending Sale or R if Rental being held for income)	Type of Property	Present Market Value	Amount of Mortgages & Liens	Gross Rental Income	Mortgage Payments	Taxes, Ins. Maintenance and Misc.	Net Rental Income
		$	$	$	$	$	$
TOTALS →		$	$	$	$	$	$

LIST PREVIOUS CREDIT REFERENCES

B—Borrower C—Co-Borrower	Creditor's Name and Address	Account Number	Purpose	Highest Balance	Date Paid
				$	

List any additional names under which credit has previously been received _____

AGREEMENT: The undersigned applies for the loan indicated in this application to be secured by a first mortgage or deed of trust on the property described herein, and represents that the property will not be used for any illegal or restricted purpose, and that all statements made in this application are true and are made for the purpose of obtaining the loan. Verification may be obtained from any source named in this application. The original or a copy of this application will be retained by the lender, even if the loan is not granted. The undersigned ☐ intend or ☐ do not intend to occupy the property as their primary residence.

I/we fully understand that it is a federal crime punishable by fine or imprisonment, or both, to knowingly make any false statements concerning any of the above facts as applicable under the provisions of Title 18, United States Code, Section 1014.

_____ Date _____   _____ Date _____
Borrower's Signature   Co-Borrower's Signature

INFORMATION FOR GOVERNMENT MONITORING PURPOSES

If this loan is for purchase or construction of a home, the following information is requested by the Federal Government to monitor this lender's compliance with Equal Credit Opportunity and Fair Housing Laws. The law provides that a lender may neither discriminate on the basis of this information nor on whether or not it is furnished. Furnishing this information is optional. If you do not wish to furnish the following information, please initial below.

BORROWER: I do not wish to furnish this information (initials) _____   **CO-BORROWER:** I do not wish to furnish this information (initials) _____

BORROWER		CO-BORROWER	
RACE/ NATIONAL ORIGIN	☐ American Indian, Alaskan Native ☐ Asian, Pacific Islander ☐ Black ☐ Hispanic ☐ White ☐ Other (specify) _____	RACE/ NATIONAL ORIGIN	☐ American Indian, Alaskan Native ☐ Asian, Pacific Island ☐ Black ☐ Hispanic ☐ White ☐ Other (specify) _____
SEX	☐ Female ☐ Male	SEX	☐ Female ☐ Male

FOR LENDER'S USE ONLY

(FNMA REQUIREMENT ONLY) This application was taken by ☐ face to face interview ☐ by mail ☐ by telephone

_____   _____
(Interviewer)   Name of Employer of Interviewer

FHLMC 65 Rev. 8/78 Forms and Worms 315 Whitney Ave., New Haven, CT. 06511   **REVERSE**   FNMA 1003 Rev. 8/78

Often the borrower makes more than one application or verbal inquiry as part of the process of shopping for the best mortgage available based on the amount of the mortgage, interest rate, special conditions and term.

The formal application will ask for information about the borrower and his or her family, including present employment and employment history, income, outstanding debts and details about the house to be purchased, including the purchase price and the down payment.

As soon as the application is completed it is screened by the lender to determine if the applicant qualifies for the mortgage. If it passes this initial test the lender then proceeds this way:

1. A credit report is obtained about the potential borrower from an outside credit bureau, and information about income and sources of the down payment are verified.
2. An appraisal of the property is undertaken, either by the lender's own appraisal department or an outside appraiser.
3. When the credit report, verifications and appraisal are obtained they are assembled, together with the application, and presented to the lending institution's loan committee which will decide whether or not to lend the money requested. The committee will base this decision on its judgment as to the applicant's ability to repay the loan on schedule, the value of the property and the availability of funds for the loan.
4. If the application is approved the lender will make a committment to the applicant, usually in writing, setting forth the exact amount of the proposed mortgage together with the interest rate, term and other special conditions that may apply to the loan.
5. After the committment is accepted the formal process of conveying title to the property is begun by ordering a title search from an attorney, title company or abstract company, depending upon the local custom. This process is often initiated by the real estate broker representing the seller.

The actual closing and transfer of title are covered in Chapter 15.

FHA-INSURED MORTGAGES

The Federal Housing Administration, more than 40 years old, is now part of the Department of Housing and Urban Development (HUD). The way it primarily operates is to insure mortgages made by conventional lenders. The program is financed by insurance premiums in the form of additional interest that is added to the mortgage payment paid by the borrower. This insurance payment is typically equivalent to one-half percent interest.

There are a variety of FHA-insured programs and they continue to change. For many years FHA-insured mortgages were a significant portion of the single-family mortgage market. The FHA established standards of construction and design for new houses and other properties it insured. These standards were a major factor in improving the overall quality of housing in this country.

With the advent of private mortgage insurance companies that compete with the FHA for single family house mortgages the FHA shifted its emphasis to other areas.

The Housing and Community Development Act of 1977 has made FHA-insured mortgages desirable for houses located in our cities. Some of the provisions of this act are to reduce the required down payment (three percent of the first $25,000 and five percent of the balance of the purchase price). The maximum loan for a single-family house that now can be insured is $60,000. Under this program it might be possible to buy a $55,000 house with only a $2,250 down payment.

Mobile homes and home improvement loans are also covered liberally under this new program.

There are problems involved in getting an FHA-insured mortgage. Many lenders just don't want to be involved with the red tape, paper work and extra time that, in spite of continual streamlining efforts by the FHA, still seem to be associated with their programs.

Private mortgage bankers have gotten into the FHA mortgage field by developing the expertise to process the loans for the profit they can make selling the completed loan to a traditional lender. Most mortgage bankers are reputable business people who are performing a needed service. However, they are not "bankers" in the traditional meaning of the word and are not subject to the very strict regulations that banks are subject to. Therefore, one should check on the reputation of a mortgage banker just as you would any other business person.

Another problem with FHA-insured (and VA-insured) mortgages is that the maximum interest the lender may charge is controlled by the government. Often in periods of rising interest rates this is lower than the prevailing rates. Under these circumstances lenders will not make the loans unless there is some way to compensate them for the low interest rate. They often make up the difference by charging discount points, commonly known simply as "points".

A point is one percent of the amount of the mortgage. Points are paid to the lender at the beginning of the mortgage. Technically, the point is paid by the seller to the lender. However, often it is the buyer who really pays when a shrewd seller increases the price of the house sufficiently to cover the cost of any points that will have to be paid.

For example, a house is sold for $65,000 and financed with a $45,000 FHA-insured mortgage and the lender charges two points for the loan. The seller will have to pay a one-time fee of $900 to the lender at the beginning of the loan.

Points are subject to negotiation. When you find that the lender is going to charge points for the mortgage, you should check with other lenders to see if they, too, will charge the same points. Often there is a difference even within the same community on the point charging policy of various lenders. This can be one of the most important factors to consider in shopping for a mortgage.

VA-GUARANTEED MORTGAGES

The Veteran's Administration (VA) guarantees the payment of loans made to eligible veterans. The VA guarantee is like mortgage insurance although there are some important technical differences. The advantages to the borrower are longer terms, lower interest rates, lower down payments and the fact that the loan can be assumed with certain restrictions by a new owner if the home is sold. Second mortgages are not allowed.

The advantage to the lender is that the VA guarantees up to 60 percent or $17,500 (whichever is less) of the loan without charge to the borrower.

The VA requires that the property be appraised by a VA approved appraiser on VA approved forms. The VA will approve the loan even if the purchase price exceeds the VA appraisal, providing the borrower is willing to pay more and put in additional cash to make up the difference.

Veterans should contact the local VA office or write to the Veteran's Administration, Washington, D. C. 20420, to determine if they are eligible for a VA-guaranteed mortgage.

FARMER'S HOME ADMINISTRATION LOANS

The Farmer's Home Administration (FmHA) is a government agency that loans money for the purchase of homes (new or used) in rural areas. A rural area is defined as being outside of a standard metropolitan city and in a community with fewer than 20,000 people.

FmHA loans are available only to borrowers who are unable to obtain conventional mortgages. One type of loan the FmHA makes is to borrowers who have an adjusted family income of $10,000 or less. These loans have interest credits that reduce the interest rate to as low as one percent. Another type is for borrowers whose income is more than $10,000 and less than $15,600. Loans to borrowers in this category are at eight percent interest.

Under this program a typical loan is for a house up to about $35,000 in value. The loan can be up to 100 percent of the appraised value and for terms up to 33 years.

A unique feature of this program is that there is an annual review of the loan. If the income of the borrower has increased the interest rate may be adjusted and if the borrower is able, he or she is required to obtain a conventional mortgage. Like many government programs this program is continually subject to change.

Current information about the program may be obtained from any local FHA or Farm Home Administration Office or from the Farmer's Home Administration, Department of Agriculture, Washington, D.C. 20250.

PRIVATELY INSURED MORTGAGES

There are large and small national private insurance companies (the largest is the Mortgage Guarantee Insurance Company—MGIC) which insure conventional mortgages similar to the way the FHA and the VA insure mortgages. These companies are in direct competition with the FHA.

The borrower pays a premium (usually one-half percent) of the amount of the mortgage to the insurance company. The insurance company, in return, guarantees 20 to 25 percent of the initial loan, thereby substantially reducing the lender's risk. Lenders usually will make loans with lower down payments when they are insured. Often the borrower is not required to maintain the insurance through the entire period of the loan. The insurance coverage is usually not needed after a period of five to ten years because the loan-to-value ratio is at that point sufficiently large.

Private mortgage insurance seems to be gaining in popularity. It gives lenders more flexibility in their lending policies by expanding their market for conventional mortgages to a big segment of the market that could not afford the larger down payments required for uninsured conventional mortgages.

Mortgages through private insurance companies can be processed easier and faster because procedures are very streamlined. There is still substantial bureaucratic red tape and delay associated with the VA and FHA. Another advantage of privately insured mortgages is that the primary lending institutions can more easily sell them in the secondary mortgage market.

FEDERAL LAND BANK MORTGAGES

There are 12 Federal Land Banks which have about 625 Federal Land Bank Associations throughout the country. They are all part of a federal agency called the Credit Administration which was established by Congress in 1933. A recent government report shows that 23.5 percent of all the construction of farm buildings and the purchase of farm land is financed with Federal Land Bank mortgages.

Each Land Bank Association is owned cooperatively by the borrowers, who must become members in order to obtain a loan. Five percent of the proceeds of each loan must be used to buy shares of the association.

Loans are based on a percentage of "normal value" which is usually less than "market value." Therefore most Federal Land Bank Mortgages require substantial down payments.

Because timber value can also be included as part of "value," these mortgages are especially attractive for vacation homes in the woods.

You can get a free packet of information on how to obtain a Federal Land Bank Loan and the address of the Land Bank Association nearest to you by writing to Information Division, Farm Credit Administration Washington, D.C. 20578

STATE INSURED MORTGAGES

Some states are now going into the mortgage business in order to encourage industrial development. Some also have programs that are designed to encourage purchases and improvements of inner-city homes. These programs are constantly changing and vary considerably from state to state. Information about state loan programs can be obtained either from local lenders or by writing to your state treasurer.

MUNICIPAL MORTGAGES

Some communities have issued bonds and raised substantial sums of money. This money is loaned to individual property owners within the community. In most cases the terms of these municipal mortgages are far more favorable to the borrower than mortgages from other sources.

SUBSIDIZED HOME OWNERSHIP

The 1968 Housing Act aids low-income families in purchasing homes by making available low or no down payment mortgages and by subsidizing the mortgage payments. This program has never gotten much beyond the experimental stages but it is still available and does offer a potential source of funds to those who would otherwise not be able to afford their own homes.

LAND CONTRACT (Also, contract sale, purchase money mortgage, installment sale)

The land contract is a procedure in which no outside mortgage is used. Instead, the buyer gives the seller an agreed-upon down payment and then makes payments until the purchase price is paid off. The seller retains an interest in the property until it is paid off although the exact interest the seller retains in the property varies from area to area. Each contract is a result of individual negotiation.

Usually this financing method is used when a low down payment is needed as an inducement to make the sale and the buyer is willing to pay a higher price in consideration of the low down payment.

As a borrower it is important to understand all the provisions of the contract, especially what happens when a payment is late, what alterations and improvements, if any, can be made to the property and who is responsible for fire and other damage. Usually it is best for the buyer to maintain the insurance policies. These contracts should always be written by an attorney.

TRUST DEEDS

Trust deeds are really a special form of mortgage. The unique feature is the use of three parties: the lender is the beneficiary, the borrower is the trustor, and the person who enforces the terms of the agreement is the trustee. The trustee has only sufficient title to carry out the terms of the trust deed once there is a default. The trustor has the right to use the property and is responsible for its upkeep and expenses. The main advantage of a trust deed is that it provides for a quick resale in the event the borrower does not make timely payments.

PRIVATE FIRST AND SECOND MORTGAGES

There are a variety of other mortgage sources besides lending institutions, the seller and government agencies and corporations. Together, all these other sources account for only about five percent of the mortgages but this is still a large number of mortgages.

Pension funds primarily are interested in large mortgages on commercial properties. However, some do buy blocks of mortgages that have been assembled for the mortgage bankers or primary lenders. Pension funds usually do not directly collect the payments or service home mortgages.

Credit unions are increasing their activity in the home mortgage field. Recent legislation makes it easier for them to sell their mortgages in the secondary mortgage market, and this should further increase their ability to make mortgage funds available for their members.

Corporations, private individuals, real estate agents and relatives are all potential sources of mortgage loans. The interest rates and terms of these mortgages often reflect other considerations such as the relationship among the parties and other profit made as a result of the transaction.

Family resources often play an important role in the purchase of a first home. Although the parents' or other relatives' willingness to lend and the purchasers' willingness to borrow will vary widely from family to family according to financial ability and personal inclination, families have often seen the loan or gift of a down payment as an important part of the investment of family assets. It is advisable in these cases to have these arrangements discussed with an attorney or estate planner. Family gifts can have significant subsequent tax and estate consequences, and it is a good idea to avoid unforeseen future problems.

NEW LOAN INSTRUMENTS

Prior to the Depression most home mortgages required only interest payments. A typical mortgage of $15,000 (this would be a big mortgage in those days) at five percent interest (high interest then) would require that the borrower only make annual payments of $750 or semiannual payments of $375. Mortgages were rarely paid by monthly payments. The mortgage would normally not be paid off even when the home was sold as the new owner would just assume the payments.

After the middle 1930s the monthly amortizing mortgage became the standard mortgage instrument. The theory was that the property depreciated and the lender recovered the principal of the loan approximately at the anticipated rate of depreciation. Since World War II our almost continuous inflation has meant that borrowers build up equity in their homes at a much faster rate than any decrease in value. A problem with this type of mortgage is that the interest rate is fixed. In periods when interest rates are increasing the lending institutions find themselves with fixed-interest loans that produce, as income, less interest than they must pay their customers in order to attract money into their institutions.

As a result some new types of mortgages have recently been developed. You should be familiar with these new mortgages and decide if any of them seem to be better for you than the traditional monthly payment amortizing mortgage which still is by far the most common financing arrangement. Not all of these new mortgages will be available or legal in your area. You may have to search to find the one you want.

VARIABLE RATE MORTGAGE (VRM)

Distinguishing Characteristics: After some specified period of time the interest rate can be adjusted to reflect the then-current rates.

- Advantages to Borrower: Initial interest rate is often lower than regular rate. Loan terms are often more liberal. Often contain no prepayment penalty and are assumable by new owner when the house is sold.
- Advantages to Lender: Interest rate is adjustable so lender is not forced to hold loans that produce interest below current rates.

GRADUATED PAYMENT MORTGAGE

Distinguishing Characteristics: The monthly payment of interest and amortization is lower during the initial term of the loan (usually five to ten years) than during the remainder of the loan.

- Advantages to Borrower: Payments are low when income is low. As income and inflation increase it presumably will be easier to make larger payments. Since less income is needed to make the initial payments, the borrower will qualify for a larger loan based on income.
- Advantages to Lender: Allows lender to make larger loans and serve a bigger market.

FLEXIBLE PAYMENT MORTGAGE

Distinguishing Characteristics: Similar to the graduated payment mortgage except that initial payments include no amortization payments, only interest.

- Advantages to Buyer: Same as Graduated Payment Mortgage.
- Advantages to Lender: Same as Graduated Payment Mortgage.

FLEXIBLE LOAN INSURANCE PROGRAM

Distinguishing Characteristics: The seller agrees to place part of the down payment into a savings account which is pledged to secure the loan. Thus, the seller guarantees part of the risk of the mortgage. In a way the sellers assume the same risks they would have if they had given a second mortgage. Like the Graduated Payment Mortgage the payments usually are lower in the initial period of the mortgage and the amount of mortgage may be higher because the borrower can qualify for a larger mortgage based on income.

- Advantages to Buyer: Same as Graduated Payment Mortgage.
- Advantages to Lender: Same as Graduated Payment Mortgage.

DEFERRED INTEREST MORTGAGE

Distinguishing Characteristics: The initial payments are even lower than the Graduated Payment and Flexible Payment mortgages since not only is the amortization not paid but all or some of the interest payments are deferred to the future.

- Advantages to Buyer: Same as Graduated Payment Mortgage.
- Advantages to Lender: Same as Graduated Payment Mortgage.

ROLL-OVER MORTGAGE

Distinguishing Characteristics: This is a variation of the Variable Rate Mortgage. The mortgage is for some fixed period of time, usually five years or more. At the end of that time the lender and borrower renegotiate a new mortgage at a new interest rate. If they cannot agree on a new rate, then the loan is paid off without any penalties.

- Advantages to Buyer: Initial rate is often lower than regular rate. Often contains no prepayment penalty and may be assumable. Borrower does not have to automatically accept new interest rate.
- Advantages to Lender: Same as Variable Rate Mortgage.

REVERSE ANNUITY MORTGAGE

Distinguishing Characteristics: This very new concept allows the lender to make regular payments to the borrower, therefore increasing the amount of the mortgage on a regular monthly basis. The loan is usually repayable upon death of the borrower or sale of the property.

- Advantages to Buyer: This is a way that retired people can convert the often substantial equity in their homes into an income stream which they need to maintain their homes and to pay living expenses. It is a way of borrowing that in effect reduces one's estate.
- Advantages to Lender: Opens up new mortgage markets and allows lenders to serve more customers. The substantial equity in the borrower's home makes these loans low-risk.

EQUITY SHARING

This is a variation of what commercial property owners call a joint venture. The home buyer splits the ownership of the house with a second party who does not live in the house. It may be a relative, employer, friend, the real estate broker, the seller or almost anyone interested in making a real estate investment. The second investor often puts up some of the down payment and may contribute money towards the monthly payments. It is quite common in equity sharing transactions that the resident-owner receives the right to buy out the investor-owner at an agreed-upon price at some time in the future. In Palo Alto, California, Stanford University recently inaugurated such a program to help young professors purchase homes after the University found that steep home prices in the area were hindering its attempts to recruit faculty.[3]

SWING LOANS

Often, especially when market conditions are slow, a property owner who is moving from one house to another finds it is necessary to buy the new house before selling the first one. When the seller is counting on the proceeds of the sale of the first house to produce funds for the down payment on the second he or she must make alternate arrangements to obtain these funds. One way to do this is to borrow the money from a lending institution.

Typically, swing loans are not secured by a mortgage if the lender feels the borrower is credit-worthy. The lender relies on the borrower's equity in the first home to be used for repayment of the loan when the first house is eventually sold. The loan gets it name based on the fact that the loan "swings" on the equity in the first house.

APPRAISALS AND FINANCING

An appraisal is required for almost all home purchases by the mortgage lender. The amount of mortgage that you are going to be offered by a lender is going to be determined by your ability to pay, your credit rating and the appraisal on the house you intend to purchase. For example, suppose you have made an offer on a one-story house in the amount of $65,000 which has been accepted by the seller. You have

---

[3] *Wall Street Journal*, May 1, 1980.

FIGURE 73

MONTHLY PAYMENT FACTORS (PER $1,000 OF MORTGAGE)*

Interest Rate	Term of Mortgage					
	5 years	10 years	15 years	20 years	25 years	30 years
6	19.33	11.10	8.44	7.16	6.44	6.00
6 1/4	19.45	11.23	8.57	7.31	6.60	6.16
6 1/2	19.57	11.35	8.71	7.46	6.75	6.32
6 3/4	19.68	11.48	8.85	7.60	6.91	6.49
7	19.80	11.61	8.99	7.75	7.07	6.65
7 1/4	19.92	11.74	9.13	7.90	7.23	6.82
7 1/2	20.04	11.87	9.27	8.06	7.39	6.99
7 3/4	20.16	12.00	9.41	8.21	7.55	7.16
8	20.28	12.13	9.56	8.36	7.72	7.34
8 1/4	20.40	12.27	9.70	8.52	7.88	7.51
8 1/2	20.52	12.40	9.85	8.68	8.05	7.69
8 3/4	20.64	12.53	9.99	8.84	8.22	7.87
9	20.76	12.67	10.14	9.00	8.39	8.05
9 1/4	20.88	12.80	10.29	9.16	8.56	8.23
9 1/2	21.00	12.94	10.44	9.32	8.74	8.41
9 3/4	21.12	13.08	10.59	9.49	8.91	8.59
10	21.25	13.22	10.75	9.65	9.09	8.78
10 1/4	21.37	13.35	10.90	9.82	9.26	8.96
10 1/2	21.49	13.49	11.05	9.98	9.44	9.15
10 3/4	21.62	13.63	11.21	10.15	9.62	9.33
11	21.74	13.78	11.37	10.32	9.80	9.52
11 1/4	21.87	13.92	11.52	10.49	9.98	9.71
11 1/2	21.99	14.06	11.68	10.66	10.16	9.90
11 3/4	22.12	14.20	11.84	10.84	10.35	10.09
12	22.24	14.35	12.00	11.01	10.53	10.29
12 1/4	22.37	14.49	12.16	11.19	10.72	10.48
12 1/2	22.50	14.64	12.33	11.36	10.90	10.67
12 3/4	22.63	14.78	12.49	11.54	11.09	10.87
13	22.75	14.93	12.65	11.72	11.28	11.06
13 1/4	22.88	15.08	12.82	11.89	11.47	11.26
13 1/2	23.01	15.23	12.98	12.07	11.66	11.45
13 3/4	23.14	15.38	13.15	12.25	11.85	11.65
14	23.27	15.53	13.32	12.44	12.04	11.85
14 1/4	23.40	15.68	13.49	12.62	12.23	12.05
14 1/2	23.53	15.83	13.66	12.80	12.42	12.25
14 3/4	23.66	15.90	13.83	12.90	12.61	12.44
15	23.79	16.13	14.00	13.17	12.81	12.64
15 1/4	23.92	16.29	14.17	13.35	13.00	12.84
15 1/2	24.05	16.44	14.34	13.54	13.20	13.05
15 3/4	24.19	16.60	14.51	13.73	13.39	13.25
16	24.32	16.75	14.69	13.91	13.59	13.45
16 1/4	24.45	16.91	14.86	14.10	13.79	13.65
16 1/2	24.58	17.06	15.04	14.29	13.98	13.85
16 3/4	24.72	17.22	15.21	14.48	14.18	14.05
17	24.85	17.38	15.39	14.67	14.38	14.26
17 1/4	24.99	17.54	15.57	14.86	14.58	14.46
17 1/2	25.12	17.70	15.75	15.05	14.78	14.66
17 3/4	25.26	17.86	15.92	15.24	14.97	14.87

* To determine amount of monthly payment multiply the factor shown times each $1,000 of mortgage. For example, the monthly on a $50,000, 25 year, 10 percent mortgage would be 9.09 × 50 = $454.50.

approximately $15,000 cash available so you decide to apply for a conventional mortgage to a lender whose policy it is to loan 80 percent of the purchase price or appraisal, whichever is less.

It is your intention to obtain a $52,000 mortgage which will leave you $2,000 for closing costs, moving costs and some new furniture.

The bank appraiser inspects the house, and you are later informed that the appraisal came in at $62,000. This means that the lender will only give you $49,600 and you are going to need $15,400 cash. It appears you will have to use all your cash just to buy the house and you still will be short $400 plus the closing and moving costs.

At this point, there are several choices you may make. First of all, you may have additional sources of cash available and you really don't care if the down payment is a little more than you expected. In this case you may accept the mortgage that is offered.

A second possibility is that you will go to another lender which hopefully will come in with a higher appraisal. If the new appraisal comes in at a higher figure all you probably have lost is the cost of the first appraisal, if you had agreed to pay for it. If this second appraisal is low too you may begin to wonder if you paid too much for the house. Lending institution appraisers tend to be conservative people so don't be too surprised if their appraisals are slightly below your purchase price.

Another possibility is that the lender will still give you the amount of mortgage that you want if you will agree to purchase private mortgage insurance. Since this insurance often costs one-half percent of the full amount of the mortgage, for the example above it would cost about $225 extra per year to get the additional $2,400 you wanted.

What many buyers do not realize is that there may be something you can do about the original low appraisal. First ask to see the appraisal. Many lenders are reluctant to show you their appraisals; but if you persist it is quite likely you can obtain it. New federal laws and banking regulations are being interpreted as making it mandatory that many lenders show their appraisals to applicants when specifically requested to do so, especially when the borrower has paid for the appraisal.

When the person you are dealing with at the lending institution will not show you your appraisal, do not hesitate to go over his or her head, even if you must go to the institution's president or chairman of the board. These people are often sensitive to pressure from the public. You may even be able to get help from the State Banking Commission, Department of Consumer Affairs or similar state agency. If you have an attorney, the attorney can help you contact the appropriate lending institution and state officials.

Once you have gotten the appraisal, check it for accuracy. A hastily made appraisal will often be full of errors. If you find a substantial number of errors you should request that another appraisal be made or the original one corrected. Often these corrections will result in a value change that will be in your favor.

It is often a good idea to select your own independent fee appraiser to appraise the house. The best time to engage this service is before you sign the binder or sales contract (unless it contains a provision which permits you to obtain an appraisal and void the contract if you are not satisifed with the results).

PROFESSIONALISM

Unfortunately there is a great deal of difference in the abilities of appraisers. Many states do not even require that they be licensed. In those states anyone can declare himself or herself to be a real estate appraiser and many people do who have little or no training. Even in those states with licensing laws the fact that an appraiser is licensed only assures the public that he or she will have a bare minimum of knowledge, experience and training.

Many appraisers who work for lenders are well qualified and their market value estimates are based on sound research and years of experience. Unfortunately, others are poorly trained, have little experience and often do not take the time to inspect the house properly or do the necessary market research.

A good way to find a qualified appraiser is to check the professional designations the appraiser has. The American Institute of Real Estate Appraisers awards the RM (Residential Member) and MAI (Member Appraisal Institute) designations to those who have satisfactorily demonstrated, through examination, demonstration appraisals and experience, that they are adequately qualified. AIREA has the reputation of having maintained rigid standards in its designation-awarding program.

Another professional organization that is nationally recognized and also has high standards for the awarding of its designations is the Society of Real Estate Appraisers. It awards three designations, the SRA (Senior Residential Appraiser), SRPA (Senior Real Property Appraiser) and SREA (Senior Real Estate Analyst).

There are a variety of other national and regional appraisal organizations that also award professional designations. Requirements of these organizations range from strict education and experience requirements to only the payment of a fee. The alphabet soup of designations does not always help the public select a competent appraiser unless the public is well informed. (More about appraisal designations and appraisals in general in Chapter 12.)

The best way to select an appraiser is to seek the advice of someone you have confidence in who is familiar with an appraiser's services and will give you an informed opinion and recommendation.

ADDITIONAL WAYS TO HELP YOURSELF FINANCE YOUR HOME

If, after reading this chapter and attempting to come up with the needed down payment and acceptable financing, you are still unsuccessful, you should consider the following list of 42 possible ways to solve your problem.[4]

1. Borrow the cash value in life insurance;
2. Sell negotiable securities such as stocks or bonds;
3. Obtain an advance on your own or your spouse's future wages;
4. Borrow money from your union;
5. Obtain loans or gifts from your relatives;
6. Obtain future bonuses that might be due;
7. Get secondary loans secured by other real property;
8. Refinance other property you own;
9. Get a blanket mortgage that includes other property you own;
10. Get an unsecured personal loan from the bank or banks you currently do business with;
11. Obtain personal loans using personal assets as collateral such as jewelry; equipment; stamp, coin and other hobby collections; cameras, etc.
12. Obtain a loan by assigning future rents on other property you or your family owns;
13. Get a passbook loan;
14. Obtain a business loan;
15. Refinance your automobile;
16. Sell some of your assets to generate cash;
17. Have the builder or seller take a purchase money mortgage;
18. Accumulate the down payment between the date of original purchase and the date of final closing;
19. Develop "sweat" equity by doing some of the work on the house yourself;
20. Use co-mortgagor or co-grantor to help qualify for maximum mortgage;
21. Pledge or assign securities (stocks and bonds) as collateral;
22. Offer the lender compensating balances from some account you control;
23. Have salesperson or broker loan all or part of the commission to you;
24. Use a contract of sale or contract of deed;
25. If your spouse is not working, have him or her take temporary employment;
26. Finance the personal items included in the sale separately from the home purchase;
27. Use private insurance plans for conventional loans;
28. Use income tax refunds;
29. Use Christmas, Chanukah and other club funds;
30. Use special financing your company has for transferees;

---

[4] Based on "What To Do When They Can't Get a Mortgage," *real estate today*®, February, 1975.

31. Exercise your stock options and sell the stock or borrow money using the stock as collateral;
32. Obtain loans by pledging dividends from stocks or other securities;
33. Use letters of credit from banks or individuals;
34. Get an FHA-insured mortgage;
35. Get a Veteran's Administration-insured mortgage;
36. Get a savings and loan association mortgage;
37. Get an insurance company mortgage;
38. Get a savings bank mortgage;
39. Get a mortgage from other private lending source;
40. Get a commercial bank loan;
41. Try the Home Farm Bank Association—for rural areas;
42. Negotiate a lease with an option to purchase.

For a complete checklist on Financing, see Checklist 37, page C-77.

CHAPTER 12
APPRAISERS AND APPRAISING

As a home buyer and/or homeowner you naturally are vitally concerned with the value of your home. At the very outset, you need to know the house's value in order to pay a fair price for it. An appraisal will give you this information. Next, the insititution that lends you money for a mortgage must know the property's value in order to determine how much money it is willing to lend you, based on the value of your property as security. The lending institution will authorize its own appraisal for this purpose.

A substantial portion of the revenue of the community in which your home is located will come from "ad valorem" property taxes. These are assessed based on the value of the home, determined by an assessment which is another kind of appraisal. And the amount of insurance you carry on your house should be based on the "insurable value." If you have a loss from fire or other insurable peril (see Chapter 13) the amount you receive will be based on an appraisal of the damage. Likewise, in the event of the death of an owner, the estate taxes will be levied based on the value of the home at the time of the death of the owner.

Each of the above can be classified as an appraisal, which is defined as the process of making a supported estimate of value of a property based on research. A professional who estimates property value is an appraiser. (A person estimating value for property tax purposes is called an assessor.)

There are many technical definitions of an appraisal. One very useful one states that an appraisal is a "supported estimate of defined value (usually in writing) rendered by an impartial person skilled in the analysis and valuation of real estate." A well-made appraisal is prepared by following a prescribed appraisal process outlined in Figure 74. This is an orderly, step-by-step process which, when skillfully followed by a trained appraiser, will lead to a valid estimate of a property's value.

USING AN APPRAISER IN BUYING A HOUSE

Many people use appraisers to help them determine if the price they are planning to pay for a home is the true market value of the property, although there is no legal requirement that an appraisal be performed. One good way to be certain an appraisal is performed, if you as the buyer wish it, is to have the sales contract contain a clause that makes the sale conditional upon an appraisal of the house being made which indicates that the proposed selling price is the market value (further in this chapter, we will define market value). In most communities there are independent, well-trained and experienced "fee appraisers" who can be employed by a home buyer to make an estimate of the value of the home he or she is planning to purchase.

Many home buyers mistakenly believe that the lender's appraisal will protect them from overpaying for a house. In reality this is seldom true. The appraiser who is employed by a lending institution is primarily interested in the value of the house as mortgage security. Another problem with this, depending on the lender's appraiser, is that there usually is no way for the borrower to know what the qualifications of the lender's appraiser are unless he or she looks into the appraiser's professional experience and affiliations (see below).

In some states appraisers are licensed which gives some indication that they have adequate qualifications to make a valid appraisal. However, in many states no license is required so anyone can advertise his or her services as an appraiser. As with any professional, the best way to select an appraiser is based on the recommendation of someone knowledgeable in the field and in your community, such as your REALTOR®, lender, attorney, accountant or insurance agent.

PROFESSIONAL ORGANIZATIONS

One excellent indication of the qualifications of an appraiser are the designations he or she has received from recognized appraisal organizations. There are two major national appraisal organizations: The American Institute of Real Estate Appraisers (AIREA) was founded in 1932 and is an affiliate of the NATIONAL ASSOCIATION OF REALTORS®; the Society of Real Estate Appraisers (SREA) was originally part of the Savings and Loan League but is now an independent organization.

AIREA awards two designations to its members. The RM (Residential Member) recognizes appraisers who are qualified to make residential appraisals.

The MAI (Member Appraisal Institute) designation recognizes appraisers who are qualified to appraise a variety of properties, including residential properties of all sizes. To receive the designation an individual must have been recommended by the local AIREA chapter and must satisfy strict educational and experience requirements. Candidates

FIGURE 74
THE APPRAISAL PROCESS FOR THE
SINGLE-FAMILY RESIDENCE

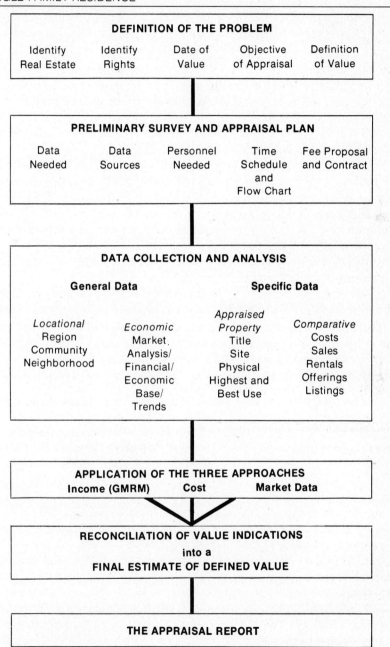

DEFINITION OF THE PROBLEM

| Identify Real Estate | Identify Rights | Date of Value | Objective of Appraisal | Definition of Value |

PRELIMINARY SURVEY AND APPRAISAL PLAN

| Data Needed | Data Sources | Personnel Needed | Time Schedule and Flow Chart | Fee Proposal and Contract |

DATA COLLECTION AND ANALYSIS

General Data   **Specific Data**

| *Locational* Region Community Neighborhood | *Economic* Market Analysis/ Financial/ Economic Base/ Trends | *Appraised Property* Title Site Physical Highest and Best Use | *Comparative* Costs Sales Rentals Offerings Listings |

APPLICATION OF THE THREE APPROACHES
Income (GMRM)   **Cost**   **Market Data**

RECONCILIATION OF VALUE INDICATIONS
into a
FINAL ESTIMATE OF DEFINED VALUE

THE APPRAISAL REPORT

for designations are required to establish their ability and expertise by submitting demonstration appraisal reports.

The Society of Real Estate Appraisers (SREA) awards the SRA (Senior Residential Appraiser) designation which is roughly equivalent to the RM designation of AIREA, and the SRPA (Senior Real Property Appraiser) designation which recognizes an appraiser's ability to appraise a variety of types of properties. SREA also awards the SREA (Senior Real Estate Analyst) designation.

There are other national and regional appraisal organizations, some made up of only real estate appraisers and others which accept affiliated professionals and other types of appraisers. Such groups are the American Society of Farm Managers and Rural Appraisers, the Association of Federal Appraisers, the American Society of Appraisers and the National Association of Independent Fee Appraisers.

WHAT IS A GOOD APPRAISAL?

To judge what a good appraisal is it is helpful to know some of the terminology and the required minimum contents of an appraisal. AIREA requires that a written appraisal contain, at a minimum, the following (an appraiser may make a verbal appraisal provided the appraiser's files contain this same information):

1. The objective of the appraisal and the definition of value. The objective of most appraisals is to estimate market value (other objectives might be to estimate insurable value, assessed value, salvage value, etc.) Market Value has been defined as:

"The most probable price in terms of money which a property should bring in a competitive and open market under all conditions requisite to a fair sale, the buyer and seller each acting prudently, knowledgeably and assuming the price is not affected by undue stimulus. Implicit in this definition is the consummation of a sale as of a specified date and the passing of title form seller to buyer under conditions whereby:

1. Buyer and seller are typically motivated.
2. Both parties are well informed or well advised and each is acting in what they consider their own best interest.
3. A reasonable time is allowed for exposure in the open market.
4. Payment is made in cash or its equivalent.
5. Financing, if any, is on terms generally available in the community at the specified date and typical for the type of property in its locale.
6. The price represents a normal consideration for the property sold unaffected by special financing amounts or terms, services, fees, costs or credits incurred in the transaction."[1]

[1] Byrl N. Boyce, *Real Estate Appraisal Terminology*, 2nd Ed. (Chicago: American Institute of Real Estate Appraisers and Society of Real Estate Appraisers, 1980).

2. Every appraisal must be as of a specific date. The market and the condition of the property can change substantially even in short periods of time.

3. The certification and signature of the appraiser. The appraiser should certify, with a written signature, that he or she has not presently, or in the contemplated future, an interest in the property (unless it is disclosed in the report); that the assignment was not taken with the fee conditional upon a predetermined value being estimated and that the appraisal was made in accordance with the professional standards of the Institute or other similar organization.

4. A statement of any qualifying conditions which the value estimated is subject to. An example of such a qualifying condition is that the appraiser assumes the mechanical systems are in good working order and need no major repairs.

5. An adequate description and specific facts about the identification and description of the property and its ownership. The location, site and improvements all should be adequately described in the report.

6. The factual data the appraiser used to reach a value judgment and an analysis and interpretation of this data. This is what is meant by a supported estimate of value as opposed to just an opinion of value that is not supported with facts and reasoning.

7. The data should be processed through one or more of the three traditional approaches to value (Market Data Approach, Cost Approach, Income Approach).

MARKET DATA APPROACH

In most appraisals the best method of estimating the market value of a house is the Market Data Approach. Using this approach the appraiser follows these five steps:[2]

1. Finds comparable sales, listings and offerings.[3]
2. Verifies each sale including selling price, terms, motivation, the relationship of the principles involved, etc.
3. Analyzes each comparable property and compares it to the property being appraised as to time of sale, location, physical characteristics and conditions of sale.
4. Makes the necessary adjustments to compensate for the disimilarities noted between the comparables and the property being appraised.

---

[2] George F. Bloom and Henry S. Harrison, *Appraising the Single Family Residence* (Chicago: American Institute of Real Estate Appraisers, 1978).

[3] Comparable properties or sites are commonly referred to as "comps."

The adjustments are derived by comparing comparables with each other whenever possible.
5. Derives an indicated value for the house being appraised by comparison with the adjusted selling prices of the comparables.

COST APPROACH

The Cost Approach is another way the appraiser can estimate the value of a property. This approach should rarely be used alone in the appraisal of a single-family residence but rather as a way to support the value estimated by the Market Data Approach. The appraiser follows these five steps to arrive at a value via the Cost Approach:

1. Estimates the value of the site as if vacant and available to be put to its highest and best use.
2. Estimates the current cost of reproducing (or replacing) the existing improvements.
3. Estimates the accrued depreciation from all causes.
4. Deducts the accrued depreciation to arrive at an indicated value of the improvements.
5. Adds the site value developed in Step 1 for a total indicated value for the property.

In the Cost Approach terms are often used that have unique meanings to appraisers. Here are the meanings of some of these:

Reproduction Cost: The cost of reproducing the improvements being appraised as of the date of the appraisal.

Depreciation: The difference between the value of the land, plus the reproduction cost of all the improvements and the value of the property on the date of the appraisal. Stated another way, the difference between what it would cost to build the improvements on the data of the appraisal and what they are worth on that same data.

Depreciation can be classified into three categories:

1. Physical deterioration—wear and tear and disintegration.
2. Functional obsolescence—a lack of desirability in layout, design, material and style, and subsequent loss of utility or an overimprovement.
3. Economic obsolescence—the negative effect on value from factors external to the property.

One term that has been causing a lot of problems for appraisers is "Remaining Economic Life." This is the period of time from the date of the appraisal to the end of the house's economic life. It is that length of time the house will contribute value to the property. Or, approached a different way, it is the period of time during which the value of the house and the value of the lot are in excess of the value of the lot without a house upon it.

Some lending institutions will limit the term of a mortgage so it will not exceed the estimated remaining economic life. Unfortunately, this usually increases the monthly payments, and all things being considered, this rarely increases the lender's security. It rarely makes a mortgage more secure to be paid off in, say, 25 years rather than 30 years. The amount of additional amortization in the early years of the mortgage is not significantly increased. (See Figure 75).

INCOME APPROACH

The value of single-family residences can also be estimated by using the Income Approach in a special way known as the Gross Monthly Rent Multiplier method. The theory behind this approach is that there is a relationship between the unfurnished monthly rental of a house and its value.

When sufficient data is available, the appraiser follows these steps to estimate a value via the Income Approach:

1. Develops an applicable multiplier.
   a. Finds houses that have recently sold in the neighborhood that are comparable and were rented at the time of sale.
   b. Divides the sale price of each comparable house by the monthly rental to derive a monthly rent multiplier, known as a Gross Monthly Rent Multiplier (GMRM).
   c. Reconciles the multipliers developed in Step b to obtain a single multiplier or range of multipliers applicable to the appraised property. This is not an average; it is a judgment of comparability and applicability.
2. Estimates economic rent for the residence being appraised.
   a. Finds comparable rentals in the neighborhood.
   b. Analyzes each comparable rental and compares its features with those of the appraised property.
   c. Estimates the adjustments required to obtain an indicated rental for the property being appraised.
   d. Considers each comparable carefully, with emphasis on the need for adjustments, and formulates an opinion of the market (economic) rent of the appraised house based upon the actual rents of the comparables.
3. Estimates the value of the residence being appraised by multiplying the estimated market rent by the estimated monthly multiplier (or range of multipliers) to obtain an indicated value of the property being appraised via the Income Approach.

FIGURE 75

EFFECT OF SHORTENING THE MORTGAGE TERM

Illustration of the effect of shortening the term of a typical mortgage of $50,000 at 10 percent interest:

Initial Amount	$50,000	$50,000
Interest Rate	12%	12%
Term	25 yrs	30 yrs
Monthly Payment	$526.50	$514.50
Balance at end of one year	$49,662	$49,818
Balance at end of five years	$47,826	$48,831

HOW TO OBTAIN THE BEST APPRAISAL

YOUR OWN APPRAISAL

When the purpose of the appraisal is to estimate the value of the property you are buying, you will of course have the right to select whatever appraiser you wish. The quality of the appraisal will depend upon the appraiser, so professional affiliations and reputation are quite important.

If you elect to have your own appraisal done, review the final appraisal report and decide if it appears to be an adequate job. Pay particular attention to what comparable sales have been used. Many REALTORS® will supply a buyer with recent comparable sales as part of the process he or she uses to educate the buyer about the value of the house and what is a fair offer. If the comparable sales you are aware of have not been used in the appraisal report, ask that the appraiser consider these sales too since they might change the appraiser's opinion about the value of the property.

LENDING INSTITUTION APPRAISALS

A recent development in residential appraising has substantially improved the quality of many lending institution appraisals. Lenders often sell their mortgages to quasi-governmental organizations in order to raise additional money with which to make more mortgages. The two largest buyers of the mortgages are the Federal Home Loan Mortgage Corporation (known as the mortgage corporation or Freddie Mac) and the Federal National Mortgage Association (FNMA, known as Fannie Mae). Both of these organizations require that the appraisal of any house used as the security on a mortgage they are buying be done on a standard form in a manner acceptable to them.

There are different forms for different classes of residences. The one used for single-family residences in fee simple ownership is known as a Residential Appraisal Report (FHLMC Form #70—FNMA Form #1004). This form is rapidly becoming the standard form used by many appraisers for their single-family residential appraisals. It has been accepted by both the American Institute of Real Estate Appraisers and the Society of Real Estate Appraisers.

As a borrower there are also some steps you can take to assure the lender will use a qualified appraiser.

First, before you sign you loan application, ask who will do the appraisal and if you may have a say in the selection of the appraiser. If you are not satisfied with the qualifications of the proposed appraiser you should ask that a qualified one be used. If the lender will not comply with your request, consider using another lender.

Second, ask if you will have an opportunity to review the finished appraisal prior to a final decision being made about your loan. Again, if the answer is no, you may elect to change lenders.

Third, try to go to the property with the appraiser. It is only human nature to do a more careful job when somebody is watching.

OTHER TYPES OF APPRAISALS

Since this is a book on advice about how to buy a house it is beyond the scope of the book to discuss other types of appraisals in very much detail. However, we would like to pass on some advice to you.

Look into the appraisal made by the assessor that is the basis upon which your property taxes are based. In most areas you have a right to see this appraisal. If you find mistakes in the appraisal point them out to the assessor and ask that they be corrected. If the mistake has resulted in an excess assesment, you should, of course, ask for a refund of the excess taxes you have paid.

Periodically, many communities have a revaluation. Often these are done by large, national firms who specialize in mass appraisal work. It is important that you review this appraisal and check it for errors. If you feel your assessment is too high, make an appeal. It is usually relatively easy to do so. Studies show that a very high percentage of people who appeal their assessments get a reduction which results in a tax savings.

For a complete checklist on Appraisals, see Checklist 38, page C-79.

CHAPTER 13
INSURANCE

A home is a major investment that can be damaged or destroyed by a variety of perils such as fire, storms, earthquake and floods. The same is true of your possessions. In addition, homeownership exposes you and your family to potential claims arising out of bodily injuries and property damage caused by your house or your family and its pets.

Should you have to be out of the house temporarily because the house is damaged, the additional living expenses you incur can be substantial. There are a variety of other perils that may damage or destroy your home and its possessions and a variety of other exposures to loss that you should consider protecting yourself against, including the ability to make mortgage payments should the family income be disrupted.

RISKS

Here is a summary of the most common potential exposures to financial loss you risk as a homeowner.

1. *Damage to your home* caused by a variety of perils:
   fire and lightning
   windstorm or hail
   explosion
   riot or civil commotion
   falling aircraft
   vehicles
   smoke
   vandalism and malicious mischief
   theft
   breakage of glass
   water damage from leaking pipes, overflowing fixtures, leaks in the

roofs and walls, ground water, backing-up sewers, discharge from
heating system and appliances
earthquake
landslides, volcanic eruption
theft
falling objects
weight of ice, snow or sleet
collapse of the house
electrical damage
flooding

2. *Damage to your possessions* caused by the same variety of perils your home is exposed to.

3. *Additional living expense* caused by the need to move out of your house when it is damaged by any of the discussed perils.

4. Loss of your property because the *title to it turns out to be defective.*

5. Loss of the property because the mortgage payments cannot be made due to the *death or disability of the family wage earner.*

6. Damage to the property caused by *mechanical and structural defects.*

7. Loss of money as a result of liability claims for *injury caused by members of your family and pets to other people and their property.*

8. Miscellaneous losses caused by the damage or destruction of your detached garages, pool houses, storage sheds, barns, seasonal dwellings you own in the same state or other states, personal property away from your premises, watercraft and their trailers, grave markers, trees, shrubs, lawns and plants, cost to remove debris after your home is damaged, loss caused by need to replace items at today's higher replacement cost, charges of the fire department (in some communities) to put out your fire, loss of your credit cards, glass breakage, medical expenses of guests injured on your premises for which you are not legally liable, damage you do to property of others for which you are not legally liable.

There are a variety of different insurance policies available that will protect you against such losses. You need to consider these policies and select those that will provide the protection you need. If you have unlimited money to pay insurance premiums you probably could buy 100 percent coverage. Since your funds probably are limited you must pick and choose in order to stay within your budget. Generally you can reduce your insurance costs by:

1. Deciding not to insure against some of the potential losses and electing to pay these losses yourself in the event they occur.

2. Electing to pay part of some potential losses yourself. This is done by selecting options available in many policies that provide for your participation in loss payments.

BUYING INSURANCE

There are two basic sources from which to buy insurance. One way is directly from the insurance company. The other way is from an independent insurance agent who represents many companies.

Companies that sell insurance directly to the consumer market the insurance either by mail or at retail locations where the customer places an order with a company employee who represents only that company. Some companies also employ insurance agents who sell only their own insurance policies.

The advantage of buying insurance directly from an insurance company is that it is a convenient, impersonal transaction that may at times be less expensive than buying similar insurance sold through independent agents.

The major disadvantage is that you are dealing with a company employee who is primarily looking out for the company's best interests and the short run profit of selling you a policy. This employee usually has little to gain from your long-run satisfaction, and rarely has anything to do with claims.

The other way is to buy your insurance from an independent insurance agent who represents many companies and selects the company which he or she feels is best suited for your needs. Good independent insurance agents build a close relationship with their customers. Their success depends on the long-run satisfaction of their customers. They are anxious to have their customers renew their insurance year after year and to have the customer recommend them to their relatives and friends.

Many insurance customers build a relationship with an independent insurance agent that is similar to their relationship with their accountant, lawyer, physician and REALTOR®. One significant difference is that an independent agent also becomes involved in the claims settlement process. It is a complex process, and it is good to have the help of someone who will protect your interests, knows what is covered by your policy and knows how you can present your claim in a way that you get all that you have coming to you.

Many independent insurance agents claim that the insurance they sell is no more expensive than that which is sold directly by the company. They claim that someone has to be paid to service the customer and that it costs no more for their services than for the services of an insurance company employee. They point out that if you have any problems trying to buy a policy because of accidents, losses, location or age of people being insured, an independent agent who profits from all your insurance will work harder to solve your problem than a company employee who is just interested in selling a specific policy. Independent agents

246 HOME BUYING—THE COMPLETE ILLUSTRATED GUIDE

also claim that because they give large amounts of profitable business to the insurance companies that often the companies will write or retain policies for them that they would not otherwise write or keep if it were not for this supporting business.

SELECTING THE PROTECTION YOU NEED AND CAN AFFORD

Fortunately the insurance industry has made the coverage you need obtainable by developing a series of insurance policies that package together many different coverages. Together these policies can provide you with the coverages you need.

After you have selected the source or sources from which you will purchase your insurance you should consider with these sources each of the following alternative insurance policies. You must decide which policies you want and then make a series of decisions about each policy that will custom-tailor it to provide exactly the coverages you need.

Here is a list of the insurance policies for homeowners you should consider:

1. Homeowner's Policy (special similar policies are available for condominium and cooperative owners)
2. Flood Insurance
3. Title Insurance
4. Mortgage Life Insurance
5. Income Protection Disability Insurance
6. Home Warranty Insurance

In the balance of this chapter we will discuss each of these policies and how you can go about tailoring them to provide the coverages you need and can comfortably afford.

HOMEOWNER'S INSURANCE

The information that is provided in this section is typical of many homeowner policies being offered in most states. But it is important that you know exactly what you are covered for in your policy.

A package policy known as a homeowner's policy is now available in all 50 states. In most states this policy provides coverage for:

- Dwelling
- Related private structures such as detached garages, pool houses, storage sheds, barns, etc.
- Seasonal (secondary) dwelling in the same state or some other state
- Personal property of the homeowner and family on the premises
- Personal property of the homeowner and family away from the premises anywhere in the world

- Personal property at a new place of residence (usually for 30 days)
- Scheduled personal articles based on a list supplied by the insured
- Watercraft and their trailers
- Loss of use (living expense insurance)
- Grave markers
- Trees, shrubs, lawns and plants
- Debris removal
- Replacement cost of buildings
- Fire department service charge (in some communities)
- Credit card forgery and counterfeit money

Coverage usually can be added for glass breakage and appurtenant structures rented to others. Usually the policy also includes premises and personal liability coverages, medical payments to others and coverage for damage to property of others.

LIMITS OF COVERAGE

Each of the items listed above has a limit to the amount of coverage that is provided. Sometimes these limits can be increased or decreased by the payment of additional (or reduced) premiums.

It is easy just to accept a policy from an agent and put it away without checking the coverage until after a loss occurs. Then, too late, it is discovered that the limit of coverage is too low but could have easily been set at an adequate amount prior to the loss.

Some of the basic limits of a homeowner's policy relate to the amount of coverage that is selected for the dwelling. The appurtenant structures are usually covered for 10 percent of the dwelling limit; unscheduled personal property for 50 percent of the dwelling coverage, with 10 percent of this amount, but not less than $1,000, applying to unscheduled personal property away from the premises and additional living expenses up to 10 percent of the dwelling coverage.

An important provision of many homeowner's policies is that when sufficient coverage is taken out on a property, damage to the dwelling will be paid for on a replacement cost basis rather than its actual cash value (which includes depreciation) up to a specified amount. This means, for example, if you have to repaint a fire-damaged room that had a five-year-old paint job, you would receive the cost of a new paint job even though the one that was damaged was old and almost ready to be redone.

In order to receive this important benefit the amount of insurance on the dwelling must equal at least 80 precent of the replacement cost of the dwelling. This does not include the value of the site, site improvements, detached buildings, architects' fees, below-ground pipes and certain other specified items.

You need to determine (with help if necessary) what the current replacement cost of the house is. This often bears little relationship to the value of the property because included in the property value is the site and site improvements, other buildings and improvements on the site such as courts, pools, fences, etc. The sale price or value takes into consideration how much the improvements have depreciated. None of these factors relate to replacement cost, so using the sale price or value of the property as a guide to replacement cost may produce a figure that is way off. The following people and publications can help you estimate the replacement cost of your home.

- Appraiser
- Local contractor
- Real estate agent
- Insurance agent
- Representative of the insurance company
- National cost service publications which regularly issue data on construction and building component costs.[1]

Other limits are unrelated to the basic dwelling coverage. They may be selected by the insured. The amounts offered for no additional premium are often low and the insured should consider raising these limits to reflect personal needs.

The personal liability protection pays, on behalf of the insured and his or her family, all sums which they are legally obligated to pay as damages because of bodily injury or property damage caused by the insured premises or the activities of the insured and the insured's family. (The primary exclusions are automobile and business-related occurrences.) Medical expenses for injury of people other than the insured and the insured's family are often covered regardless who is actually liable. There is also coverage that usually applies to property damage caused by the insured's dwelling or family.

A variety of other limits of coverage are built into the typical homeowner's policy. Loss of use is usually limited to 10 to 40 percent of the dwelling coverage depending upon the policy form. Coverage of any one tree, shrub or plant is very limited. Some policies provide coverage for part of any fire department service charge. Credit cards, forgery and counterfeit money are covered for limited amounts. Glass coverage is very limited.

There are substantial limitations on the coverage of personal property besides the usual 50 percent of dwelling coverage on the premises and 10 percent of $1,000, whichever is greater, away from the premises. Un-

---

[1] Examples: *Boeckh Building Valuation Manual*, Milwaukee; *Building Construction Cost Data*, Duxbury, MA; *Dodge Building Cost Calculator and Valuation Guide*, New York; *Marshall Valuation Service*, Los Angeles; *Residential Cost Handbook*, Los Angeles.

scheduled jewelry and furs are limited in most states. Silverware is often limited. Money, bullion, gold, silver platinum, manuscripts, deeds, and passports usually have special limits or coverage. Watercraft and their trailers are also limited.

Many of these basic limits of coverage can be raised to higher amounts for an additional premium. Most homeowner's insurance buyers raise the personal liability limits to at least $100,000 and schedule many articles of personal property, especially items of jewelry, so they will be covered for their actual value.

Homeowner's insurance policies protect the items covered against a variety of perils. There are three different types of policies that vary depending on which perils they cover. They range from the standard form with its limited list of perils, to the broad form with a more extended list, to the most comprehensive coverage known as an "all risk" policy. It is also possible to buy a policy that provides "all risk" coverage for the real estate and broad form coverage for the personal property.

BASIC FORM

The most limited form is known as the basic form (often called a Form HO-1 homeowner policy). It provides coverage for direct damage or loss of covered items caused by:

- Fire and lightning
- Wind storm or hail
- Explosion
- Riot or civil commotion
- Aircraft
- Vehicles
- Smoke
- Vandalism or malicious mischief
- Theft
- Breakage of glass (or safety glazing material)

BROAD FORM

A more inclusive form of homeowner's policy is known as the broad form (often called a Form HO-2 homeowner's policy). It provides coverage for direct damage to or loss caused by any of the perils previously described that are covered by the basic form, *plus* damage or loss caused by:

- Falling objects (must damage roof or wall first)
- Weight of ice, snow or sleet
- Collapse of a building or any part of a building
- Accidental discharge or overflow of water or steam from within a

plumbing, heating or air conditioning system or from within a household appliance

- Sudden and accidental tearing apart, cracking, burning or bulging of a steam or hot water heating system, an air conditioning system or an appliance for heating water
- Freezing of a plumbing, heating or air conditioning system or of a household appliance, subject to a "reasonable care" condition during vacancy, unoccupancy or construction
- Sudden, accidental damage from artificially generated electrical current except loss to tubes, transistors or similar electronic components

ALL RISK FORM

The most inclusive form of homeowner's insurance is known as the "all risk" form. All risk provides for coverage for damage or loss caused by *any peril* including all those covered by the basic and broad forms except those which are specifically *excluded* in the policy.

Perils usually *excluded* from coverage under the "all risk" portion policy are:

- Freezing or leakage when the property has been left vacant unless "reasonable care" has been taken to prevent the loss
- Damage to a fence, paving, patio, swimming pool, foundation, retaining wall, bulkhead, pier, wharf or dock caused by freezing, thawing, pressure or weight of water or ice, whether driven by wind or not
- Loss from theft from the building or any materials or supplies used in its construction until the dwelling is completed and occupied
- When the dwelling is vacant for over 30 consecutive days before a loss there is no coverage for vandalism and malicious mischief or the breakage of glass and other safety glazing materials
- Continuous or repeated seepage or leakage of water or steam over a period of time from within a plumbing, heating or air conditioning system, or from within a household appliance
- Other exclusions: wear and tear; marring; deterioration; inherent vice; latent defect; mechanical breakdown; rust; mold; wet or dry rot; contamination; smog; smoke from agricultural smudging or industrial operations; settling, cracking, shrinking, bulging or expansion of pavements, patios, foundations, walls, floors, roofs or ceilings; damage by birds, vermin, rodents, insects or domestic animals; loss from flood and earthquake. (Earthquake may be covered with an additional endorsement and flood with a special policy. Both perils are covered in more detail later in this chapter.)

It is hard from this list to understand just what is covered by an all risk policy that is not covered by a policy that names the perils as the standard form or broad form homeowner's policies do. Following is a list of examples of items that have been covered by an all risk policy that would not have been covered by a named-peril policy.[2]

- Loss caused by acid: Acid used to unclog drain backed up and severely damaged the porcelain lining on a cast iron tub.
- Losses caused by animals: A circus elephant went on a rampage; a deer jumped through a window.
- Damage done by appliance: A washing machine was not balanced properly and damaged a nearby water heater.
- Damage caused by bleeding: A guest had a violent hemorrhage.
- Damage caused by children: Two boys went on a spree with a hammer.
- Dropped objects: storm windows, logs, sliding mirror, scale, object dropped into toilet—all real examples of covered claims from dropped objects.
- Heat damage: Faulty thermostat caused excessive heat which did extensive damage.
- Damage by lawn mower: Blades damaged outside portion of heating and air conditioning equipment.
- Oil damage: Oil from fuel delivery escaped into house.
- Paint damage: Spray paint can used in dark by mistake instead of bug bomb.
- Other examples are scorching, smoke and soot, tar damage, underground property damage, vehicle damage.

Water damage is probably the most important coverage of an all risk policy. A frequently covered damage is to interior walls and ceilings when snow and ice on a roof alternately thaw and freeze, blocking the drains and then getting inside the house. Other often-covered water damage is caused by a lawn sprinkler or rain and snow driven through an open window or louvers.

An all risk policy is the best policy insurance companies sell. It usually costs considerably more than a named-peril policy and often requires a higher deductible. Insurance companies usually apply more rigid underwriting standards and pay their agents a lower commission for these policies. (An old saying among insurance agents contends that the best policies to buy are the ones the companies do not want to sell.)

CONDOMINIUM INSURANCE

The insurance industry has developed a special policy for owners of individual condominium units. This policy is actually quite similar to a

---

[2]*Rough Notes Monthly Policy, Forms and Manual Analysis* (Indianapolis: Rough Notes Co., Inc., 1978).

tenant's policy in that it does not cover most of the dwelling, which is covered separately by the master condominium policy issued in the name of all the unit owners through their condominium association.

The typical condominium policy covers personal property against the same broad perils as listed in a regular broad peril homeowner's policy. It also covers improvements made to the real estate by the condominium owner against loss or damage caused by these same broad perils, and it covers additional living expense.

The policy is similar to a homeowner's policy except in the following ways which are unique problems associated with the condominium form of ownership:

- There is usually coverage for glass and safety glazing materials which belong to the unit owner.
- There is often $1,000 coverage for additions, alterations, fixtures, improvements and installations which are part of the building within the unfinished interior surfaces of the perimeter walls, floors and ceilings of the insured's condominium unit.

A special optional coverage that is often available for an extra premium is "Loss Assessment Coverage" which reimburses the insured for any assessment levied by the condominium association for uninsured loss to collectively owned condominium property. This coverage is only for the same perils covered by the unit owner's policy. There is also similar condominium owner coverage available for assessments levied as a result of earthquake damage to the collectively owned property.

MODIFIED FORM POLICY

Another specially developed policy is the modified form (often called a Form HO-8 homeowner's policy). It is designed to provide coverage where either the homeowner or the insurance company did not want any replacement cost coverage. There are often other reduced coverages such as a $1,000 overall theft protection limit and a special $250 deductible. This form of insurance should only be purchased when it is not possible to obtain a regular homeowner's policy or when insurance must be obtained at a minimum cost.

"REPLACEMENT" COST

A unique feature of a homeowner insurance policy is that it will pay the "replacement cost" of damaged items rather than the "actual cash value," provided sufficient insurance is carried by the homeowner.

Here is an example of how this provision works: Suppose you had a small fire in your kitchen and the damage was to the range and paint job. The 10-year-old range would now be $350 to replace. The five-year-old paint job would now cost $400 to do again. The policy has a $50 deductible. If the loss were adjusted on an "actual cash value," an adjuster might claim that both the range and paint job were 50 percent depreciated and offer $325 as a settlement ($350 range, less 50 percent depreciation equals $175, plus $400 less 50 percent depreciation, minus the $50 deductible).

The replacement cost provision of the homeowner policy provides that if the amount of coverage on the dwelling is at least 80 percent of its replacement cost, then losses will be adjusted on a replacement cost basis. In the above example, the insured would receive $350 for the range and $400 for the paint, less the $50 deductible, or $700.

This is a valuable additional benefit and it usually pays for the homeowner to carry sufficient insurance to meet the 80 percent requirement.

DESIGNING A HOMEOWNER POLICY TO FIT YOUR NEEDS

An ideal homeowner policy should be designed to be custom-tailored to fit the needs of each homeowner. Here are the steps you should take to custom-design a policy to fit your family's needs:

1. Decide how much the basic dwelling coverage should be. In order to receive all of the policy benefits (the most important being replacement cost reimbursement for losses up to a specified amount), this coverage must be set at 80 percent of the replacement cost of the dwelling (not including the site, improvements and uninsurable portions of the dwelling).

2. Select which policy form you want: standard, broad, all risk, modified or condominium. You can mix an "all risk" on the real estate with a broad perils on the personal property.

3. Decide if the automatic limit for the unscheduled personal property on the premises (usually 50 percent of the dwelling coverage) is correct for your belongings. Increase or decrease the limit as appropriate.

4. Decide what is adequate liability coverage. The basic limit is rarely sufficient. Most families require at least a $100,000 liability limit.

5. Make up a schedule of jewelry, furs and other items you wish insured that exceed the value limitations in the policy.

6. Decide what overall deductible you wish. The higher the deductible the lower the premium. Most people select a deductible that is too low.

7. Decide what other extensions of coverages and increased limits you wish. Here are some you should consider:
   - Theft from unattended automobile
   - Office, school or studio occupancy liability
   - Secondary locations coverage
   - Physicians, surgeons, dentists and veterinarians away from premises coverage

- Earthquake or volcanic eruption coverage
- Continuous renewal
- Coverage on appurtenant structures rented to others
- Increased limits for other appurtenant structures
- Additional amount of unscheduled personal property in a secondary residence
- Increased limits for credit card, forgery and counterfeit money
- Scheduled personal property endorsement (used to cover jewelry, furs, camera equipment, musical instruments, silverware, golfing equipment, fine arts, stamp and coin collection or any other valuable collection)
- Unscheduled jewelry, watches and furs increased limits
- Increased limits for money and securities
- Increased limit for unscheduled personal property away from the premises
- Scheduled glass coverage
- Additional residence premises—rented to other
- Business pursuits
- Farmer's comprehensive liability
- Incidental farming personal liability
- Watercraft coverage for boat over 25 horsepower or otherwise not covered in basic policy
- Personal injury coverage for liability arising out of: false arrest, detention or imprisonment or malicious prosecution, libel, slander, defamation of character, invasion of privacy, wrongful eviction or wrongful entry
- Snowmobile coverage
- Automatic inflation coverage increases policy on a regular basis at a predetermined amount to keep up with inflation

8. Special coverages often added to the condominium form of policy:
   - Alterations and additions coverage from broad perils to all risk and increase of limits to above $1,000
   - Coverage during rental of the premises to others without limitation as to time
   - Coverage for appurtenant private structures solely owned by the insured on the condominium premises
   - Coverage to indemnify the insured for assessments by the condominium association for uninsured loss to collectively owned condominium property
   - Glass breakage of insured additions and alterations

EARTHQUAKE COVERAGE

Coverage against damage caused by earthquake and earthslide, perils that are excluded in the usual homeowner insurance policy, can be obtained either as a separate policy or as an endorsement to a homeowner's policy.

In California, where there is a constant threat of earthquake, a surprising number of homeowners still do not have this kind of protection. The possibility of damage by earthquake is less in other states but it is almost universally agreed by geologists that no state is 100 percent free from this potential hazard.

The premium for this coverage is based on the potential hazard in your area and the type of construction of your house. When the hazard is low, the premium is as low as three cents per $100 of coverage. In these low-hazard states $50,000 coverage would cost only $15. Some insurance agents do not want to bother writing earthquake insurance, so you may have to ask for it.

FLOOD INSURANCE

Hardly a year goes by without major floods and millions of dollars of damage to American homes, but homeowner insurance policies *do not* provide coverage for loss and damage caused by flooding. In 1968 the National Flood Insurance Act made flood insurance available at reasonable cost to millions of property owners who previously could not obtain flood protection.

A "flood" is defined in a typical flood insurance policy as a general and temporary condition of partial or complete inundation of normally dry land areas from:

1. The overflow of inland or tidal waters.
2. The unusual and rapid accumulation of runoff of surface waters from any source.
3. Mud slides which are caused or precipitated by accumulation of water on or under the ground.

The homeowner insurance policies previously described in this chapter all contain broad exclusions of coverage for a variety of water damage losses including flood, surface water, waves, tidal water or tidal waves, overflow of streams or other bodies of water, or spray from any of the foregoing—all whether driven by wind or not. They also exclude loss from water which backs up through sewers and drains and water below the surface of the ground, including that which exerts pressure on or flows, seeps or leaks through sidewalks, driveways, foundations, walls, basements or other floors, or through doors, windows, or any other opening in sidewalks, driveways, foundations, walls or floors. It is crystal clear that flood coverage is not contained in the typical homeowner's policy.

A flood insurance policy insures the house, garage, other ancillary buildings and the contents of these buildings against all direct loss by flood. The policy is also extended to provide coverage for 30 days to any place to which any of the property must be moved for protection from the flood, *but not elsewhere.*

The coverage of a flood insurance policy is limited to the actual cash value of the property at the time of loss, or the cost to repair or replace the property with material of like kind and quality within a reasonable time after loss, whichever is less.

A special feature of flood insurance for single-family dwellings only is that the policy will pay replacement cost when the amount of insurance in force is equal to at least 80 percent of the replacement cost of the house at the time of the loss or was the maximum amount of insurance available at the time of issue or renewal.

A flat deductible of $200 is usually applied separately to loss of the house and loss of its contents even when caused by the same flood. What this mean is that if you carry sufficient insurance (80 percent of the replacement cost) you will receive "new for old." For example, if your house would cost $40,000 to replace today (exclusive of the site, site improvements and certain underground parts of the house) and you carried $35,000 insurance you would meet the 80 percent requirement. Then if your 10-year-old wallpaper with a depreciated value of $250 was damaged, you would be paid its replacement cost of $600 (minus $200 deductible applied only once to the building loss). However, if you carried only $30,000 of insurance, it would not meet the 80 percent requirement.

In the above example you would be paid $250, the depreciated or actual cash value of the wallpaper (again, minus $200 deductible applied only once to the building loss). In the event the cost of repair or replacement is more than $1,000 or more than five percent of the whole amount of the insurance applicable to the building structure, repair or replacement will be conditional on your actually making the repair or replacement.

Flood insurance policies also cover damage done during hurricanes by the inland movement of water from the oceans or the Mississippi River.

Some of the items *not covered* by a flood insurance policy are accounts, bills, currency, deeds, evidences of debt, money, securities, bullion, manuscripts or other valuable papers or records, stamps or coins. There are "all risk" type floater policies available for most of these items which do provide flood coverage. Other items which are also usually excluded and are more difficult to insure are fences, outdoor swimming pools, bulkheads, wharves, piers, bridges, docks or other open structures located on or partially over water or property in or on them.

ELIGIBILITY FOR FLOOD INSURANCE

Unfortunately, flood insurance is not available to everyone. To be eligible for the insurance the property must be located in a community which has been designated as eligible by the Federal Insurance Administrator of the U.S. Department of Housing and Urban Development. A community must apply to become eligible for coverage. Usually a community first applies to become eligible under the "Emergency Program."

Under this program, the community agrees to some general efforts to reduce flood losses. It usually does this guided only by preliminary flood control data. In communities that qualify for the Emergency Program, only a limited amount of subsidized insurance is available and the rate is the same for all structures regardless of their flood risk.

Currently the amount of coverage available and its cost in communities that have qualified for the Emergency Program is:

- Single-family dwelling: $35,000 of insurance @ $25 per $100 coverage
- Other residential structures: $100,000 of insurance @ $25 per $100 coverage
- Contents, residential: $10,000 of insurance @ $35 per $100 coverage

You may learn if your property is eligible for coverage by contacting your local insurance agent (who may or may not be familiar with the plan) or by writing the National Flood Insurance Program, P.O. Box 34294, Bethesda, Maryland, 20034.

Communities may also qualify for coverage under the Regular Program. Under this program full limits of flood insurance coverage become available for structures and personal property within their borders. When communities have taken the necessary steps to be part of the Regular Program, a detailed map is prepared called a Flood Insurance Rate map which shows flood elevations and outlines risk zones.

In Regular Program communities, single family residences can be covered for $35,000 at $25 per $100 plus an additional second layer of coverage of up to $150,000 at rates that vary according to the location of the property. Contents in residences in addition to $10,000 of coverage at $35 per $100 may be covered for an additional $50,000 at rates that vary according to the location of the property. Other residential structures may be covered for up to $200,000. These limits and rates vary for Hawaii, Alaska, U.S. Virgin Islands and Guam.

TITLE INSURANCE

TITLE DIFFICULTIES

Real estate, traditionally, has been considered a special kind of valuable possession. It has such great value and is so important to both its owners and the entire community that special, very strict and complicated laws have evolved to control its ownership and the manner in which title is transferred from one owner to another.

A variety of other people, besides the owner, may have some rights in a piece of property even though their names are not shown on the deed. Some examples of other parties who possibly may have some rights in the property you are about to buy are:

- Mortgagors who have not fully been paid off
- Tenants who have valid, unexpired leases (verbal or written)
- Parties with mining, oil or air rights, in some states
- A mechanic such as a plumber, electrician, carpenter, etc., who has done work on the property and who has not been paid in full
- Creditors involved in a bankruptcy action
- Holders of judgments from other lawsuits
- Parties to suits involving the real estate or its owners
- Husbands and wives of the owner or a former spouse may have a special interest known as dower interest.
- The taxing authority, which may be the community, state, federal government, local homeowner's association, sewer authority or any other body having the legal right to levy taxes against the property, may have rights due to unpaid taxes.
- There may be rights of way for roads, power lines and pipe lines, tracks, communication lines or a variety of other possible rights of way or easements.
- Heirs of former owners often have rights to the property of a deceased relative. Wills are complicated documents that often are contested years later by dissatisfied heirs who claim they were unintentionally or illegally omitted.

Aside from other people having an interest in the house you are buying, there are additional problems that may affect the quality of the title to the property you are receiving from the person you believe to be the sole and current owner.

Another complicated matter is the mental competency of former owners who have sold the property. People who are insane or legally incompetent cannot sell their property without court permission or unless they have signed away their dower rights. In addition, any sale made by a minor may be invalid or not binding on the minor unless it has been made by a guardian or conservator approved by the court.

It is always a problem for corporations to sell property, since the sale usually must be properly authorized by their respective boards of directors. It is difficult to determine if the authorization has been made in compliance with a corporation's charter or bylaws. Sales by corporations are further complicated when challenged by stockholders or if the corporation goes out of business, is sold, goes into receivership or bankruptcy or is dissolved.

Another problem that complicates title transfer is name changes and confusion caused by similar names and misspelled names. Documents giving people rights in a property may be lost because of these name variants. And sometimes a person who has been declared legally dead returns to claim his or her property.

In many states a deed is not valid until it is signed, sealed and delivered. There have been cases where the deed has been delivered without the consent of the signer or where the signer has died before the documents were delivered. Both of these events may make the sale invalid.

Sometimes the wrong people sign the deeds. Children with the same names as their parents sign to sell property that really is not theirs. Second wives have been known to sign deeds when the property really belonged to former wives.

Finally, there is human error. A whole variety of mistakes is possible such as improperly prepared documents, failure to obtain all the needed signatures, a poor title search that fails to show up documents that affect the quality of title, or documents that were lost, misfiled or misindexed so that nobody would have found them no matter how diligently the title was searched.

TITLE SEARCH

After reading all these potential causes of title problems, you may conclude that it is difficult, if not impossible, to get a good title to the home you are buying.

A good title search will uncover most of these problems. Also, many sellers are willing to issue a warranty deed by which they guarantee the quality of the title they are selling. In some areas the attorney who does the closing will issue a "certificate of title" which guarantees that the title is good. (These attorneys usually carry errors and omissions insurance to protect them from losses that incur as a result of their mistakes.)

If you get a good title search from a qualified source, a warranty deed and a certificate of title from the closing attorney, you are likely to get a good title.

Based on the number of claims paid by title insurance companies and companies that insure closing attorneys for errors and omissions, the odds are quite favorable that your title will be good. However, there are many title problems, and the potential loss is very great in the unlikely event you have received a defective title.

USING TITLE INSURANCE AS PROTECTION

Many lenders and many buyers feel that they are not prepared to gamble with the title of property they own no matter what the odds are and therefore protect themselves by insuring the quality of the title with title insurance.

Title insurance is a form of insurance that protects owners and lenders against the risk that the title to a property they own or have an interest in is defective. Like other forms of insurance, title insurance is sold by insurance companies, but they are usually companies which specialize in this form of insurance.

Normally a title insurance policy is written at the time the home is purchased. It may protect just the lender or it may protect both the lender and the owner. Unlike most other forms of insurance, you pay for it only once (not annually) and it is good for as long as you own the property. The premium is quite reasonable (usually well under one per-cent of the value of the property being insured).

A major advantage of title insurance is the peace of mind that results from knowing that many years after you have purchased your home, you will be able to sell it without any trouble or extra unexpected ex-pense. With no insurance, when you go to sell a property years after you have purchased it and a title defect is discovered, you will have to hire an attorney, at your expense, who will attempt to clear the title. The seller, closing attorney and others involved may no longer be around. You may encounter substantial delays and expenses before you are able (if ever) to sell the property. This may happen at a time when you nei-ther have the money nor can afford the delay or wish to be subject to the stress of this unexpected problem.

If you have title insurance and a title defect develops, all you have to do is notify the title insurance company. It will step in and take care of the whole matter, hiring an attorney at its expense. The company will pay any costs incurred to clear up the title, and these costs may be quite large. If it is unable to clear the title, the company will pay you for the loss you sustain up to the limit of your policy.

MORTGAGE LIFE INSURANCE

Insurance agents know that the best time to sell life insurance to people is when some event in their lives makes them especially aware of how dependent their family is upon their income-producing ability. Buying a house is one of these times, as often a new commitment is made to make substantial regular payments. If the payments are not made there is the threat that the family's home will be taken away.

You must answer the question of how much money your family will need to live in the way you wish them to live and where this money will come from. One of the decisions you should make is whether they will keep or sell the house. If you decide they should keep it, the mortgage, taxes, insurance and other running costs will have to be paid. If you have mortgage life insurance the mortgage payments will be eliminated. Under these circumstances you may decide that mortgage insurance fits into your estate planning and should be purchased.

What is especially appealing about a mortgage life insurance policy is its low cost as compared to almost any other type of life insurance, especially if the insured person is young. Unfortunately, however, this is a very simplistic solution to the overall problem of estate planning. A real solution can only be obtained by careful planning, usually with the help of a trained estate planner who might be a life insurance agent, accountant, attorney or bank trust officer.

The most common type of mortgage life insurance policy is a reducing term insurance policy. A typical policy is written initially for an amount approximately the same as the mortgage. Each year as the unpaid balance of the mortgage decreases, the amount of insurance also reduces. However, usually the premium remains the same so actually the cost of the insurance increases each year, as you are buying less insurance each year for the same premium.

Whereas homeowner insurance is written on standard forms, each life insurance company generally issues its own policies. Therefore, there are hundreds (or maybe thousands) of different policies, each one with different clauses, benefits, conditions, premiums, etc. It is difficult for the consumer to understand the fine differences between policies.

CHOOSING A MORTGAGE LIFE POLICY

Fortunately, there are several things the consumer can do to obtain a satisfactory policy at a fair price.

First of all, buy from a reputable agent and insist your policy come from a good company. If the agent recommends a policy from a company you are not familiar with, you can obtain information about the company by writing to your state insurance commissioner. Another way is to look it up in the "Best" directory.[3] This is an objective service that rates life insurance companies by their financial strength and their reputation for giving good service.

Secondly, it is important to know that the least expensive form of mortgage insurance is a policy that is just a simple reducing term insurance policy. That is, it is a policy whose face value (the death benefit) reduces each year approximately at the same rate as the mortgage balance decreases. The premium is based on the initial amount of insurance, the rate of reduction, the age of the insured and any additional frills that are included.

EXTRAS

It is the additional frills that run the cost of life insurance up. Since the insurance companies and the insurance agents make their minimum profit and commission on a pure reducing term insurance policy (mortgage insurance) there is a natural tendency to promote some of the more profitable frills. We are not saying that there is anything wrong with the many extra coverages that are offered. We only caution that they are

---

[3] *Best's Insurance Reports* (Morristown, NJ: A.M. Best Co., 1980).

designed to do things other than pay off the mortgage in the event of the death of the insured, which is the purpose of mortgage insurance.

Some of the usual extras that are sold with mortgage term insurance are:

- *Accidential Death Protection* (also known as double or triple indemnity). This coverage pays double or triple the face value of the policy if the insured is killed or dismembered by accidental means.
- *Waiver of Premium* is a provision in the policy that provides for the payment of the insurance premium if the insured becomes unable to work because of illness or accident.
- *Guaranteed Convertability* is a provision that allows the policy to be converted into other nonreducing forms of insurance.
- *Cash Value* is the basic difference between term insurance and whole life insurance, permanent insurance, endowments and hundreds of other life insurance policies. Cash values are created by payment of an extra premium that is not needed to pay for the cost of the term insurance portion of the policy. This extra premium is invested by the insurance companies in mortgages and other investments. The return on these investments (less the insurance company's operating cost and profits and the agents' commissions) is used to build up a reserve that is similar to savings in the insured's account.

Another point of confusion is the difference between mutual life insurance companies and stock life insurance companies. In theory a mutual life insurance company is owned by the policyholders rather than the stockholders as is a stock insurance company. The mutual insurance companies imply that the profits that would have gone to the stockholders are distributed to their policyholders.

This difference between mutual insurance companies and stock insurance companies has been greatly exaggerated. The fact is that the bulk of the dividends distributed by mutual insurance companies comes from extra premiums they charge their policyholders. They then invest those extra premiums and distribute the earnings. The policyholders mostly get back in the form of dividends their own money plus interest. The amount of profit a typical stock company makes is nowhere near the dividend distribution of most mutual insurance companies.

Mortgage life insurance is a good idea for many families. Careful consideration is important before selecting many of the fringes that are often offered by agents who sell these policies.

INCOME PROTECTION DISABILITY INSURANCE

The mortgage payment and other living expenses must be made even when the family income producers cannot work because of illness or injury. Savings, loans, employment benefits and other financial sources can be used to carry a family through a nonincome producing period. However, some families elect to buy an insurance policy known as income protection or disability insurance (or other similar name) to help make the payments. As with life insurance, each insurance company writes its own policy with its own benefits, special clauses and premium rates.

This is one of the most difficult of all insurance policies to buy; special care must be taken in the selection of an agent and insurance company. In addition, there is a lot of subjective judgment needed to settle a claim fairly, so the reputation of the insurance company for fair claim settlement is very important. A knowledgeable insurance agent is the best source of this information.

The basic concept of these policies is very simple. When the income producer is out of work because of illness or accident, the policy pays a weekly or monthly payment until the insured goes back to work. In most states this payment is limited to 75 percent of the normal income.

When buying this type of policy you must make the following decisions:

1. Amount of weekly (or monthly) benefit needed
2. Acceptable waiting period before benefits begin, for:
   - accidental injury
   - illness
3. Anticipated length of benefit period, for:
   - accidental injury
   - illness
4. Needed benefits for partial disability, for:
   - accidental injury
   - illness

A good policy is quite expensive. The best way to reduce the cost is to accept substantial waiting periods before the benefits begin.

A significant difference among insurance policies and companies is how they define what total disability is. A poor definition, for example, requires that the injured person be confined to home, be visited regularly by a physician, and be unable to work in any way. A liberal definition would be the inability to work at a job or profession suitable for the insured based on previous education and training. These clauses become very important in the adjustment of claims where the policy has long-term benefit periods and the insured has a stroke, heart attack, nervous breakdown, cancer or other illness that interferes with the ability to work.

Many professional insurance agents feel this type of insurance is more important than mortgage life insurance.

HOME WARRANTY INSURANCE

A home buyer can obtain an insurance policy that will insure the home against structural and mechanical defects. These policies have been around for years but it is only recently that their popularity has begun to increase rapidly and they have become widely available. The coverage comes in a variety of forms and each company's policy is different. Also, the type of policy that is offered on a new house is often different from the coverage offered on used houses.

Usually the policy is purchased by the home seller or builder, but a recent development is the greater availability of those policies to home buyers. They can be obtained as part of a home inspection package (see Chapter 3), when purchased by a home buyer.

The National Association of Home Builders endorses insurance programs for their member builders. Programs are also being made available by some of the national real estate franchise companies.

A home warranty policy runs for a period of one to ten years. Of course, the home buyer should seek as long a policy as possible.

The coverages provided by a policy varies but usually includes two parts:[4]

1. Structural Failures
   - The structural soundness of the exterior and interior walls, including floors and ceilings
   - The structural soundness of the foundation and basement
   - The roof: structural soundness and absence of water penetration
2. Mechanical System Failures
   - The central heating system
   - The interior plumbing system, including the hot water heater
   - The electrical system
   - The central air conditioning system
   - Appliances such as ovens, ranges, dishwashers and water softeners
   - Septic tanks and wells

All policies do not offer all of these coverages and they can be full of fine print that substantially reduces the coverages they appear to be giving. The policies that have been approved by the National Association of Home Builders provide good protection. However, even these are not all alike and some provide substantially more coverage than others. For example, policies that are issued without an inspection may be much more limited than one issued based on an inspection, yet they both may

---

[4] *Home Inspection—A Guide to Concept and Implementation* (Chicago: NATIONAL ASSOCIATION OF REALTORS® 1978).

be endorsed. A buyer is usually much better off getting the broader policy that requires an inspection.

Some policies also have a provision that provides reimbursement for costs and expenses incurred in securing alternative living quarters in the event a covered defect renders the property uninhabitable.

For a complete Insurance checklist, see Checklist 39, page C-81.

CHAPTER 14
SALES CONTRACTS

During the period of negotiation, some type of written agreement must be prepared that will express the agreement reached by the buyer and the seller. It almost always must be in writing because almost every state has adopted a set of laws called a "Statute of Frauds" which requires that a contract creating or transferring an interest in real estate must be in writing to be enforceable. Oral alterations to real estate contracts are also not enforceable.

Buyers must be very careful to get everything they agree to in writing and not to rely on verbal promises. Often a seller will agree verbally to include certain items in the sale or to provide some financing if the buyer is unable to obtain a needed mortgage. If the sellers change their minds and back out on any oral promises (even if there were witnesses who heard the sellers make the promises) the buyers would still be obligated to live up to their part of the written agreement.

VALIDITY OF CONTRACTS

Every contract for the purchase of real estate should contain certain items, the omission of which can make the contract voidable. Exactly what makes a contract voidable is a complex legal matter. Just because a contract is sloppy or poorly drawn does not automatically mean that one or both parties can enjoy a "free way out".

Below are seven items that a well-drawn sales contract should contain. If the contract does not contain these seven basic items, we recommend you consult an attorney to be certain the contract you are signing will not be voidable.

1. **A Description of the Property.** This description must be clear enough and sufficiently complete to ensure that there is no confusion about what is being bought and/or sold.

2. **Agreement to Purchase.** This is a positive statement that the buyers agree to purchase the property from the owners.
3. **Agreement to Sell.** This is a positive statement that the owners agree to sell the property to the purchasers.
4. **Signature of the Parties.** The agreement must be signed by all the owners of the property or people authorized to sign for them and the buyer or buyers or people authorized to sign for them. The parties who sign the contract must be legally competent.
5. **Consideration and Conditions of Payment.** The agreement must specify the purchase price and how it will be paid and whether the agreement is conditional upon the buyers obtaining financing.
6. **Conveyance Statement.** This is a statement concerning what kind of title will be transferred from the sellers to the buyers and what kind of document will be used to transfer the title.
7. **Closing.** There must be a statement as to when and where the closing will take place.

EARNEST MONEY RECEIPT (offer and acceptance, binder, deposit receipt, etc.)

Since a real estate transaction cannot be based on oral promises of the parties, it is necessary to sign a written agreement. Under some circumstances a very short contract is extremely effective. Much depends upon the complexity of the transaction.

When you make an offer and tender a deposit you must decide if you are prepared to go through with the sale no matter what happens. You might want to reserve the right to make further inquiry about the property or make the transaction conditional upon certain future events taking place such as your being able to obtain needed financing or having the house inspected by experts and the results of these inspections turning out to your satisfaction.

To the extent that your initial offer to purchase contains reservations requiring mutual agreement to certain essential terms beyond the minimum seven essential contract terms, it really ceases to be binding. What you have signed is an "agreement to agree" which courts will not enforce.

It is human nature to want to avoid long, detailed contracts, and there is no question that the short form contract has a legitimate place in some real estate transactions. Unfortunately, as a general rule, a short contract usually fails to provide the buyer with the protection that is needed. Many matters are often left unresolved. Sometimes unresolved matters are settled and then a more formal sales contract is signed. Sometimes these matters are left unsettled until the closing (which is a poor time for negotiations), or after the closing in a lawsuit based on some important misunderstanding or misrepresentation.

Before any early contract or agreement is signed, you, the buyer, should review the sales contract checklist (page C-83), asking yourself how each of the items covered is going to be resolved and in your judgment whether the item should be covered in the contract, receipt or binder. Keep in mind that any oral agreements will not be enforceable.

THE CONTRACT

What will happen at the closing will probably depend a great deal upon what is in your sales contract.

The sales contract is the foundation upon which the closing is built and the essence of the entire transaction. Standard sales contracts are generally prepared either by attorneys who work with real estate boards, companies that print forms or bar associations who work with Boards of REALTORS®. The only people who can legally prepare a contract are attorneys. Real estate brokers can use these standard contracts. They fill in the appropriate blanks and make minor additions, deletions and alterations as needed. However, they cannot draw or prepare contracts of sales.

Theoretically, if the sales contract is complete and well prepared there will be nothing to be negotiated at the closing. The closing will just be a mechanical process. However, when items of importance are left unagreed upon and are not covered in the sales contract they have to be negotiated at the closing. This is a poor time for negotiation since everyone is tense and there is a lot of pressure. Also, there are many people involved at the closing all of whom will put their two cents in, trying to settle any remaining problems.

The standard contracts that real estate brokers fill in vary from area to area, but they all should cover the same basic elements.

It is recommended that you review the following list of 37 items and decide if they should be included in your sales contract to provide you with the maximum protection you will need for the purchase you are considering. It is unlikely that all of these items will apply to your purchase, for each sale is unique. It is also possible that your transaction will have special conditions which will have to be written into the sales contract to cover the special agreements made by you and the seller.

On the following pages is a discussion of each of these 37 items. We have purposely omitted examples of a contract since contracts are legal documents that should be drawn by attorneys. The language of these provisions often varies from area to area. Often there are local customs and laws that make specific wording necessary for each area.

1. Correct name of the buyer(s) and seller(s)
2. Description of the property
3. Deposits

4. Personal property to be included in sale
5. Purchase price
6. Information about the closing
7. Who will pay the closing costs
8. Mortgage clause
9. Condition of property at closing
10. Reinspection prior to closing
11. Sellers' promise to care for property until the closing
12. Sellers' representations about the history of the property
13. Requirement for marketable title
14. Payment of conveyance taxes
15. Payment of real estate taxes
16. Liens, easements, grants, rights of way and deed restrictions
17. Ordinances, zoning regulations, municipal regulations, public or private laws, building and health codes, environmental regulations, coastal wetlands, inland wetlands, and flood plain regulations
18. Mechanics' liens
19. Survey
20. Real estate practitioners involved in the transaction
21. Adjustment of other taxes
22. Other adjustments
23. Assignability of contract
24. Binding on heirs and successors
25. Contract superseding other agreements
26. Contract constituting the entire agreement
27. Default by the buyer
28. Default by the seller
29. Insurance requirements and risk of loss by fire and other insurable perils
30. Occupancy after the closing by seller
31. Occupancy before the closing by buyer
32. "Degenderizing" the agreement
33. Addenda-attaching clause
34. Agreement surviving closing clause
35. Date of the contract and when void if not signed by all parties
36. Signatures
37. Date of signatures

When the contract is for a house that is to be built rather than for an existing house, a special contract is needed. Building a custom house is covered in Chapter 17.

1. Correct Name of the Buyer(s) and Seller(s). The buyer wants to be certain that the person who signs the contract to sell either owns the property or is authorized to sign on behalf of whomever does have title.

Signing to sell a house that one does not own certainly opens the signer to a potential lawsuit, but you want to buy a house, not a legal action. The minimum step you should take to protect yourself is to ask the signer of the contract if he or she is the only owner of record. If others also have an interest in the title (the most common "others" are spouses and parents), they should sign the sales contract too. A better idea is to check where titles are recorded in your area to see who really is the owner of record. This is one of many services your attorney can perform for you if he or she is retained prior to the closing.

If you plan to take title in some name other than your own, either the proposed owner should also sign the contract or the contract should contain a provision permitting you to assign your interest without permission from the seller (See Item 23).

2. Description of the Property. The description of the property must be accurate enough so there can be no confusion as to what is being purchased. Sometimes just the name of the community, the street and lot number is sufficient. Other times a complete deed description is needed. If the seller is not including all of the property owned contiguous to the piece being sold, special care must be taken to describe what is being sold and what is being retained by the seller.

3. Deposits. Usually a deposit is put down when the offer is first made. The contract should specify the amount of the deposit, who will hold it and under what circumstances it will be turned over to the seller or returned to the buyer. It should also spell out what happens when there is a dispute over the deposit. Will it be settled by a court action or by binding arbitration or some other means? Sometimes the deposit is made in parts. When an additional deposit is called for it should be clear when it is due.

4. Personal Property. There should be a clear understanding between the seller and the buyer as to what items of personal property will be included in the sale. What constitutes personal property varies from area to area. Moreover, typical buyers and sellers are not experts on the applicable laws. Therefore, a careful inspection of the house should be made jointly by the buyer and seller; any item that might be personal property should be discussed and an agreement reached as to whether it will be included or whether the seller intends to remove it from the premises.

Many real estate professionals can relate tales of bitter arguments either at the closing or when the buyer took possession that resulted from a misunderstanding about what stayed as part of the sale. For example, in one transaction, the buyer inspected the premises both prior to the closing and after the sellers had moved out. The buyer was shocked to find that the outdoor cement block barbecue had been disassembled and removed when the sellers moved. The sellers claimed it was a present from their children and they never intended to include it in the sale. The matter never was resolved and the sale did not go through.

Here is a list of items that can cause problems. Whether they are considered real estate or personal property may vary from area to area, and it is not very important. What is important is that the buyer and seller agree whether they are to be included or excluded from the sale:

- Screens
- Storm windows and doors
- TV antenna
- Draperies, curtains, blinds and rods
- Carpeting and rugs
- Shades and awnings
- Hot water heater
- Window air conditioners and humidifiers
- Heating equipment
- Special light fixtures
- Inter-communication and music systems
- Garage door openers
- Shrubbery and plants
- Appliances

5. Purchase Price. It almost goes without saying that the contract should state the purchase price, which is usually in terms of money. However, sometimes there are other considerations such as some item of personal property or other parcels of real estate that are part or all of the consideration being paid by the buyer for the property. If all of the purchase price is not going to be paid by the time of closing then how it will be paid should be carefully spelled out in the contract. For example, there might be a transaction in which, in addition to the money consideration, the buyer includes a valuable sailboat. To complicate the transaction further the transaction may close in May and the buyer may not be required to deliver the boat until the end of the sailing season in October. Obviously, such a sales contract has to contain special provisions to cover this unusual transaction and method of payment.

6. Information About the Closing. Each area of the country has its own traditions and customs of handling a real estate closing (called a settlement in many places). The location of the closing should be stated in the contract. Common places are at the lending institution, attorney's office, broker's office or at the title company office.

There should also be a statement as to when the closing will be held.

Sometimes a precise date is stated. Other common wording is "on or before" a certain date. Sometimes it is particularly important to either the buyer or seller when the closing actually takes place. When this is so, the contract should state that "time is of the essence" and what penalty either party will suffer if they cause the closing to be delayed.

Someone always has to search the title. Again, who does this varies from area to area. In some areas (but not many) the buyer selects who will do the search. In most areas the lender, title company, closing attorney or real estate broker makes this determination. It really makes little difference to the buyer who does the search as long as it is expedited, it is competitive in price and it is done in a manner satisfactory to whomever is going to issue the title insurance policy or certificate of title.

No matter where the closing takes place it is now subject to the conditions and requirements of the Real Estate Settlement Procedures Act. This law and its relation to real estate closings is covered extensively in Chapter 15.

As explained in Chapter 13 in the section on title insurance, it is strongly recommended that the buyer of a home obtain title insurance.

7. Who Will Pay the Closing Costs. The costs of the closing are actually not one cost but a collection of costs, some paid by the buyer and some by the seller. Many printed contracts contain a provision that the closing costs be divided as is customary in the community in which the property is located. This does not preclude the negotiation of some other arrangement. Some of the costs of a real estate closing are the search of title, title insurance or certificate of title, drawing the deed, preparing the mortgage(s), attorney's fees for holding a closing, and recording of the documents. When a seller is particularly anxious to sell he or she may agree to pay all the closing costs as an inducement to the buyer. This may be especially helpful if the buyer has a limited amount of cash available.

8. Mortgage Clause. The contract should spell out the amount of the mortgage the buyer will need to complete the transaction, the interest rate and the term. How long the buyer will have to obtain the mortgage and what effort the buyer must make to obtain the mortgage should also be a part of this clause. The clause should also state the buyer's obligation to notify the seller when the needed mortgage commitment is obtained or if the buyer is unable to obtain the needed mortgage. (See Chapter 11 on financing.)

9. Condition of Property at Closing. This important buyer protection clause has been left out of many contracts we have seen. It should spell out what condition the property must be in at the time of the closing. Often the property is required to be in the same condition as it was when the sales contract was signed except for normal wear and tear. Sometimes the seller agrees to make repairs, modernizations and/or renovations prior to the closing. Such work should be carefully described (often on an addendum sheet) so there will be no misunderstanding. There should be a statement that the buyer has inspected the premises and agreed to take them "as is" or a statement about what representations about the condition of the improvements and mechanical systems have been made by the seller.

In many cases people sign sales contracts agreeing to take the property "as is" although, had they asked, the seller would have been willing to make representations about the improvements and mechanical systems. When the seller insists that the property be accepted in "as is" condition the buyer should consider the implications of this condition and if it is acceptable. Under these circumstances obtaining professional inspections becomes even more important.

10. Reinspection Prior to Closing. The contract should give the buyer the right to reinspect the property immediately prior to the closing to determine if it has been adequately maintained from the time of the signing of the sales contract and that everything that has been included in the sale still remains on the premises. Before the closing is the correct time to straighten out any problems about the condition of the property and what is to be included—not after the closing when the seller has your money and may be off to places unknown. Of course this is also the time to check to see if all promises, repairs, modernizations and renovations have been made as agreed.

11. Sellers Promise To Care for the Property until the Closing. The longer the time between the signing of the sales contract and the closing, the more important to the buyer this provision becomes. It is unwise for the buyers to assume that the sellers will continue to care for the property the same way after the sales contract is signed as they did in the past. Many sellers start to let things go immediately upon signing the contract after taking extra special care of the property prior to its being sold.

As a buyer you want to receive the house in as good or better condition than it was when you signed the sales contract except for normal wear and tear. This means the seller is going to have to be required to continue to maintain the property, including the watering and caring for the lawn and shrubs. It seems to be human nature to let these items go especially once a sales contract has been signed.

It also should be required in the contract that the sellers deliver the premises including the basement, attic and grounds in broom-clean condition and that they will not leave any rubbish or personal property anywhere on the premises or grounds.

12. Sellers' Representations About the History of the Property. Sellers should be required to make a truthful representation about the history of the property as they know it to be. The old concept, "caveat emptor," let the buyer beware, has outlived its usefulness.

For example, the sellers know if there has been any accumulation of surface or subsurface water in the basement and, if there has been, what they have done to try and eliminate the problem. How is a buyer of a home in August supposed to know about water problems that exist in March unless the seller tells them about the past problems? The only way is to obtain an accurate history of the house you are planning to buy.

The buyers should find out if the house has been damaged by fire or other perils while it was owned by the sellers and if it was, how the damage was repaired.

Septic systems often do not function correctly. Again, a history of problems and how they were corrected will help the buyers estimate possible future problems.

The sellers should reveal what problems, if any, there have been with the well, well pump and water softening system, including the pipes. The sellers should relate any problem getting adequate water and if to the best of their knowledge the quality and quantity of the water meet all the local health department standards.

Sometimes there are leased fixtures on the premises such as a domestic hot water tank or water softening equipment. These should be specified in the contract together with a statement that everything else (fixtures) are owned and paid for.

The seller should state whether they have any knowledge of any termites, carpenter ants, rats, mice or other vermin and if and when an exterminator has been called in.

Many properties are sold without a survey. In this case, the sellers should represent to the best of their knowledge all of the improvements that are located on the premises including the appurtenances, systems, driveways and walks, fences and walls, septic system and leeching fields, wells and pipes. The sellers should also represent that to the best of their knowledge there are none of the above or anything else belonging to anyone else within the boundaries of the property. If there are, these should be noted in the contract. There should also be a representation that the well, well pipes and utility connections serve no other premises.

You may expect strong opposition when you ask for these representations. You will have to decide how important they are to you. The sellers' attorney may advise the sellers not to make any representations and sell the property only "as is." Then the sellers may have to make a difficult decision if they are faced with the possibility of losing the sale unless the information is given out.

13. Requirement for Marketable Title. As a buyer you want to get a good title to the property, and the contract should state that this is what you will get. A good and marketable title means an ownership that is readily saleable to a future buyer at market value. For a title to be marketable, it must be determined that the seller is the true owner of the property and that he or she is capable of selling it. This means that the chain, or history, of the ownership must run to the grantor. The sellers may not be able to sell the property if they are minors, incompetent or improperly authorized (this is especially true if the owner is a partnership, corporation, trust, foundation, estate or governmental body).

The legal description in the document that conveys the title must be accurate and complete.

It is difficult to spell out in a sales contract exactly what a marketable title is. One problem is that this varies from area to area. It has become common practice to insert in the sales contract a provision that states that "marketable title is that which is defined by the standard of title of the Bar Association of the state in which the property is located" and that the property will be conveyed by a deed in a form that is insurable by a standard title insurance policy (See Chapter 13).

Most sellers of single-family homes convey a fee simple title subject sometimes to some easements for local utilities such as telephone wires or sewer lines. If the title is going to be other than an uncomplicated conveyance of fee simple by a warranty deed, you should consult an attorney to be sure you get a title that will be saleable when you decide to sell your home. There are other forms of title which also are acceptable. Again, an attorney will help you be certain the title you receive is satisfactory. (See Item 16 in this list for more information about good title.)

14. Payment of Conveyance Taxes. In many areas when a property is conveyed from one owner to another the local or state government collects a conveyance tax. The contract should specify that this tax will be paid and who will pay it.

15. Payment of Real Estate Taxes. In most areas real estate taxes (called ad valorem taxes) are levied once a year. They may be payable annually, semiannually, quarterly, monthly or some other way. It is a requirement of many mortgages that in addition to the regular monthly mortgage payment to the lender that an additional sum be paid that is held in escrow by the lender and used to make tax payments. In some communities taxes are paid in advance while in others they are paid in arrears. The seller owes the taxes on the home until the date of the closing (unless some other date is mutually agreed upon). The buyer starts to owe taxes from the date he or she takes title to the property.

There should be a clause in the sales contract that requires that all tax payments due by the date of the closing are to be paid including any penalties and interest due for late payments. It should also provide that the seller will be given a credit for any taxes paid for beyond the date of the closing and that the buyer will be given a credit if the tax payments made by the seller do not pay all of the taxes due up to the date of the closing. This tax adjustment process is known as prorating the taxes.

16. Liens, Easements, Grants, Rights of Way and Deed Restrictions. Ideally, the property should be free and clear of all encumbrances. However, this is rarely the case. Usually there will be a variety of encumbrances listed in the deed or recorded separately. If they will not interfere with the use of the property or the future sale of the property at market value, then the buyer should accept title to the property. If, however, the encumbrances will interfere, either now or in the future, with the use of the property or its resale at market value, the buyer may elect either not to accept the encumbered title or ask for a price reduction.

When it is discovered that the current owners, because of some past inadequate title search or legal opinion do not have clear or marketable title to the property, consult with your attorney to determine if the problem can be solved within a time period that is acceptable to you. Based on this opinion you can decide to wait or refuse to go through with the sale. Depending upon what your sales contract says you may just get your money back or you may be entitled to be paid damages because the seller could not live up to his or her part of the contract.

Often it is discovered that there are liens against the property because the owner has not paid all debts others think are due to them. Typical liens are a result of a mortgage, tax, special assessment, mechanic's and/or supplier's lien, vendee's and vendor's liens, surety bail bond, attachment, judgment (state and federal), descendant's debts, etc. It is often possible to clear these liens either before or at the closing by paying them off or substituting some other property as security. Mechanics' liens present special problems and are covered by a separate item in most contracts. It is up to the closing attorney, title insurance company or other person responsible for the closing or settlement to supervise the removal of any liens that are to be released.

Many properties are subject to easements; usually they will not be removed at the closing. An easement is a right somebody or something has to use your property either temporarily or permanently. Some common easements are roads, rights of way, utility lines, pipelines, sewer lines, driveways of others, party walls, advertising signs, etc. Again, a judgment must be made as to the effect of the easements on the buyer's right to use the property and to sell it at full market value in the future. If either of these rights are impaired the buyer has the option of not completing the sale or seeking a price reduction. It is prudent for a seller to list in the sales contract any known unusual easements such as a high voltage power line or high pressure gas line and thereby obtain the buyer's consent to them.

Deed restrictions are restrictions on the use of the property that were established by a former owner for the purpose of protecting other nearby properties. It is very common for a developer to put a set of uniform deed restrictions in all of the deeds of a development or subdivision. A typical deed restriction in a residential development restricts the use of all the sites to single-family dwellings, specifically prohibiting multiple-family, commercial or industrial use of the land. Even if the zoning regulation permitted some or all of these other uses, the deed restriction would still prohibit them. Other common deed restrictions on residential lots control the size and design of the improvements, location on the lot of the improvement, restrictions about the construction of fences and walls and restrictions limiting the keeping of animals to household pets. The list of deed restrictions is almost endless; a property owner can restrict the use of the land subject only to a few limitations. The restriction, however, must be legal and in the public interest. Therefore, any restriction based on discrimination is not enforceable.

Deed restrictions may run for a specified number of years or for an indefinite period of time. It is possible to have them removed if one owner acquires all the properties the restrictions apply to, by mutual agreement of the affected property owners, or by the courts when they can be shown the restrictions have outlived their usefulness because of substantial changes in the neighborhood. Also, the courts will sometimes rule that if there is a wide lack of enforcement of the restrictions over a period of time, the restrictions have in essence been abandoned and are no longer enforceable.

The best way to handle existing deed restrictions is to spell them out in the contract. Like the other encumbrances, if they are not spelled out, a judgment has to be made as to whether they affect the usability and future marketability of the property.

17. Ordinances, Zoning Regulations, Municipal Regulations, Public and Private Laws, Building and Health Codes, Environmental Regulations, Coastal Wetlands, Inland Wetlands and Flood Plain Regulations. The government (federal, state and local) has what is known as "police power" to regulate the use of property in order to protect the public health, welfare, safety and morals. Police power is the basis for planning and zoning regulations, building codes (including electric and plumbing codes), health codes, subdivision regulations, environmental regulations, coastal wetlands and inland wetland regulations.

When you purchase a property you get it subject to all these regulations. There should be a statement in the contract to this effect. There should also be a representation by the seller that there are no known violations of any of them unless they are stated in the contract.

18. Mechanics' Liens. A mechanic's lien is a special claim by such people as contractors, subcontractors, workmen, material suppliers, architects and others who perform work on real estate. Special state statutes give these people the right to place a lien on a property they have worked on if they are not paid for their labor and materials. These laws are quite complex. The main problem as far as a buyer is concerned is that there is often a substantial period of time between when the work is performed and when a lien can be placed on the property. What this means is that it is possible that somebody who worked on the property prior to its being sold and who was not paid could place a lien on the property after title was transferred to a new owner. For all practical purposes the new owners would be responsible for the unpaid bills unless the former owner paid them.

Every sales contract should contain a special provision requiring the seller to deliver to the buyer an affidavit that no one has rendered services or delivered materials to the premises during the past 60 days (or whatever the period is for recording mechanics' liens is in the state the property is located) who has not been paid in full. If such debts exist they must be paid before or at the closing or the sale price must be adjusted to reflect the debt.

Unfortunately even an affidavit is not absolute protection for the buyer as it may be false and the seller may be unwilling or unable to be held accountable when a lien is filed even though the seller provided an affidavit. The only absolute protection the buyer has is a title insurance policy that does not contain a mechanic's lien exception (see Chapter 13).

19. Survey. A survey is a map of the property made by a licensed surveyor that shows the boundaries of the property, the location of any improvements on the property and sometimes the topographical features of the property. It specifically identifies the property and brings to light any encroachments onto or from the property.

Many lenders require that there be a survey on any property they accept as mortgage loan security. However, many homes continue to be sold without a survey. A buyer should obtain a survey of every property purchased. Also, the title insurance policy can be structured to ensure the accuracy of the survey (see Chapter 13).

The contract should contain a provision about surveys. If there is already an old survey, there should be a statement whether it will be updated, who will order the work done and who will pay for it. If there is no known survey, the contract should state if one will be required, who will order it and who will pay for it.

When there is an old survey that will not be updated the seller should supply the buyer with an affidavit at the closing that no structural changes have been made outside the dwelling since the date of the survey or, if there have been changes, what they were.

20. Real Estate Practitioners Involved in the Transaction. The contract should contain a representation by the buyer and seller stating what real estate brokers or salespeople, if any, were involved in the transaction, who will pay them, how much they will be paid and when they will be paid. If there were no such people involved in the transaction, there should be a representation by the buyer and seller to that effect.

21. Adjustment of Other Taxes. There should be a provision that, besides real estate taxes, other taxes on personal property and any other tax on the property that is customarily adjusted in your area will be adjusted at the time of the closing.

22. Other Adjustments. There should be a provision that specifies what other costs of items included in the sale will be adjusted at the closing. Often, the buyer, as part of the negotiation process, can get some or all of the items included without adjustment if he or she asks. Many printed contracts contain a provision that calls for adjustment of those items that are customarily adjusted in the area. From the buyer's point of view it is best not to use this stock clause but rather to list the items that will be adjusted and to keep the list as short as possible. Some common items that are adjusted are:

- Homeowners association dues
- Fuel oil
- Mortgage interest (when a mortgage is assumed)
- Insurance premiums (when a policy is taken over)
- Sewer, water, electric and gas charges

23. Assignability of Contract. Many printed sales contracts contain a standard provision that the contract may not be assigned by either party without permission of the other party.

Normally, a seller would not assign his or her interest in a contract unless it develops that he or she is not the true owner (sometimes other members of the family turn out to have some ownership interest so the assignment is needed to obtain clear title to the policy). However, the buyer could elect, for tax or personal reasons, to sell the property to another person, corporation, foundation or trust.

It is not at all uncommon, especially in a rising market, for the buyer to assign his or her interest in a sales contract to another party, usually at a higher price than he or she has contracted to buy it for. By doing this the buyer can make a guaranteed profit without taking title to the property.

The assignability of the contract should be negotiated, and the buyer and seller should agree who has the right to assign and if they will need the consent of the other party. The assignment provision of the contract should then be written to reflect the agreement reached by the buyer and seller.

24. Binding on Heirs and Successors. Many printed sales contracts contain a standard provison that the contract is binding upon the heirs and successors of the buyer and seller.

This provision should be negotiated by the buyer and seller. A contract that would force a widow or widower to purchase a house he or she did not need or could not afford may not reflect what the parties actually wish to have happen. Both the buyer and seller may have tax or personal reasons why they do not wish the contract to be binding on their successors or heirs.

25. Contract Superseding Other Agreements. The contract should contain a provision that the agreement supersedes any and all prior understandings and agreements between the buyer and seller.

Often as part of the negotiation process there are several contracts drawn and signed by one or the other, but not both parties. These may reflect offers, concessions and agreements proposed by one party or the other and never totally agreed upon by both parties. The problem comes about when an item that was agreed upon by both parties in the negotiation process is not included in the final sales contract. One party then claims it should have been part of the final agreement and the other claims that further negotiation eliminated agreement. By putting a provision in the contract that all previous agreements are set aside unless they are included in the final sales contract, the problem is avoided.

26. Contract Constituting the Entire Agreement. The contract should contain a statement that it constitutes the entire agreement between the buyer and seller or should specify the other agreement or agreements to which it is subject. A typical problem arises when a supplemental agreement is prepared as part of an earlier sales contract that is never signed by both parties. Unless such an agreement is specifically mentioned in the final sales contract it cannot later be claimed to have been part of that agreement.

27. Default by the Buyer. The sales agreement must carefully spell out what will happen if the buyer fails to go through with the sale. For example, the contract may provide that if the buyer defaults all earnest money is returned to the buyer and the contract is terminated. It may provide that if the buyer defaults all earnest money is kept by the seller and that the contract is terminated. Or it may provide that the seller should tender a deed and, if the buyer still refuses to go through with the sale, the seller has the right to sue the buyer for the purchase price and possibly damages. How severe a penalty will be extracted from the buyer in the event of a default by the buyer is a matter to be negotiated.

28. Default by the Seller. The contract might provide that if the seller is unable or unwilling to go through with the sale all earnest money (and possibly closing expenses) will be returned to the buyer and the contract will be terminated.

If the contract does not contain a clause specifically prohibiting it, the buyer may elect to sue the seller either for specific performance (forcing the seller to go through with the sale) or damages (based on the difference in the market value of the property and the contract sale price). Even though the seller has acted in good faith an unanticipated flaw in the title or other unsolvable problem at the closing may cause the buyer to sue for damages unless alternative remedies are provided.

29. Insurance Requirements and Risk of Loss by Fire and Other Insurable Perils. Most sales contracts have a provision that the seller assumes all risk of loss to the property until the closing. In many areas the risk of loss shifts to the buyer when the sales contract is signed unless the contract contains a clause saying the risk remains that of the seller.

It is good practice to include a clause in the contract that requires the seller to insure the property with a homeowner's insurance policy to 80 percent of the house's replacement cost, together with earthquake and flood coverage (if the property is in a flood zone) and adequate liability coverage. In the event of a loss the buyer should have the option either of having the property repaired or accepting the damaged property in its damaged condition and, in addition, receiving the insurance proceeds. Sometimes the clause provides that if the loss is over a certain amount of money then the buyer may elect to cancel the sale.

Also covered in the insurance clause should be what happens if the seller fails to make the necessary repairs or when the seller's cost to repair the property is less than the insurance received. Usually the seller must turn over to the buyer any insurance claim money not used to repair the premises.

The seller usually pays for the insurance from the signing of the sales contract until the closing but this is a matter which may be negotiated. The contract should spell out the results of the negotiation.

30. Occupancy After the Closing by the Seller. Some sales contracts contain a provision allowing the seller to occupy the dwelling after the date of the closing rather than requiring that the seller deliver occupancy and possession of the premises and all keys to the buyer at the time of the closing.

When occupancy is permitted after the closing there should be a provision that states how much the seller will pay for the use and occupancy during the agreed-upon period of time. Often the rate of charge is increased substantially for any period of time that exceeds the final occupancy period. There may also be a provison that spells out the absolute last day occupancy by the seller will be permitted.

31. Occupancy Before the Closing by the Buyer. Some sales contracts contain a provision allowing the buyer to occupy the dwelling before the closing. Generally it is not a good idea to put this clause in a sales contract. In essence, what is really being created is a lease, and a lease is a complex document with many provisions to cover all of the situations unique to the landlord/tenant relationship.

If the tenant is going to occupy the premises prior to the closing it is a good idea to have a lease drawn up and signed by both the buyer (tenant) and seller (landlord) covering all terms and conditions of the occupancy.

32. "Degenderizing" the Contract. If the contract uses the masculine gender there should be a clause that states that the use of the masculine gender refers also to the feminine gender and the use of the singular refers to the plural, and vice versa, whenever the context so requires.

33. Addenda-Attaching Clause. Often additional pages called addenda are attached to the sales contract and made part of the contract. The contract should contain a clause stating that the additional terms and provisions appearing on the addenda pages attached to the sales contract are specifically made a part of the contract.

34. Agreement Surviving Closing Clause. The sales contract should contain a provision stating that the sales contract containing the terms, conditions, promises and representations of the buyer and seller will survive (carry over after) the closing.

35. Date of the Contract. There should be a provision in the contract that spells out what the date of the contract is. This is needed since often the buyer and seller sign the contract on different dates. This clause can spell out that the effective date of the contract is either when the buyer or the seller signs the contract. It is also quite common for this clause to state that if all parties have not signed the contract within a specified number of days after the date the buyer or seller have signed the contract, the contract is void.

The purpose of this provision is to prevent one party from holding the contract signed by the other party for any long period of time without signing the contract and making it a binding agreement.

36. Signatures. The contract should have a place for the signatures of all the buyers and sellers and witnesses and notaries (if this is customary on real estate sales contracts in the area).

37. Date of Signatures. There should be a place on the contract to indicate on what date the buyer and seller each signed the sales contract.

OTHER ITEMS TO CONSIDER

MAKING THE CONTRACT CONDITIONAL UPON APPRAISAL AND INSPECTIONS

Although such provisions are common in commercial and industrial sales contracts and are not usual in residential sales, it is possible for the sales contract to contain a clause making the sale conditional upon the buyer obtaining certain appraisals and/or inspections. In industrial and commercial transactions, the high cost of the property usually justifies the extra expense for inspections. In the case of residential property, it is up to the principals in the transaction to decide if the added expense is warranted and in line with the value of the property.

Any provision making the sale conditional on inspections or appraisals essentially makes the contract less of a contract and more of an option.

Inspection and/or appraisal provisions make the sale conditional upon the buyer obtaining:

- An appraisal of the property, including a provision that the appraiser's opinion must be that the contract price is not in excess of the appraiser's opinion of the value of the property and that if it is, the buyer has the option of terminating the contract and receiving the deposit back.
- Inspections by whatever inspectors the buyer deems necessary, such as home inspector, architect, contractor, termite inspector, septic system inspector, well expert, electrician, heating system inspector, roofer, insurance agent, lender, relatives and friends.

Such clauses may state that if each specified inspection is not satisfactory or if the inspector recommends immediate work be done on the house, the buyer will notify the seller of the results of the inspection(s). If the deficiencies are of such a nature that they cannot be corrected, the buyer would have the option of terminating the contract and receiving the full deposit back. Or the buyer could offer to accept the property with the deficiencies at a reduced price. The seller would then have to decide whether to accept the reduced price or to terminate the contract and refund the buyer's deposit in full. If the deficiences are correctable, the provision can provide that the buyer must notify the seller of the deficiencies and offer him or her the opportunity to have them corrected. If the seller agrees to correct the deficiencies then the buyer would be obligated to close the transaction.

However, if the seller refuses to correct the problems, the buyer may elect to terminate the agreement and receive back the deposit, or the buyer may offer the seller a reduced price for the property with the uncorrected deficiencies. At that point the seller would have to decide whether or not to accept the reduced price.

If the seller refuses either to accept a reduced price or to repair the deficiencies, the ball is then passed back to the buyer who must decide whether to accept the property with the deficiencies or to terminate the agreement.

In order for an appraisal or inspection provision to be fair, the contract should specify how much time is to be allowed for the inspections to be carried out and for the seller to make indicated repairs if he or she chooses to do so. The contract should also not be so worded as to require the seller to do anything he or she does not wish to do, but rather should give the seller the choice of doing indicated repair work or face the possibility of the termination of contract.

With all of these contingencies, it is easy to see why an appraisal or inspection clause tends to make the contract an option instead of a binding contract. If both principals are pleased with the intent and results of such a provision, however, a desirable conclusion can be reached.

HOME WARRANTY

Many sellers arrange for their houses to be covered by a home warranty insurance policy covering the structure and mechanical systems. The sales contract should describe any such policy and make provisions for its transfer to the buyer. The contract should specify who will pay for the policy at which point in the transaction.

When there is no existing home warranty insurance policy the buyer may want a provision to be added to the contract making the contract conditional upon the buyer's being able to obtain such a policy. Again, in this case the contract would become an option.

INSTALLMENT LAND CONTRACT

In some areas an *installment land contract,* also known as a land contract or real estate contract or bond for deed, is the agreement used for the purchase of real estate. This agreement calls for payments to be made over an extended period of time. The unique feature of this agreement is that title remains with the seller.

Typically, an installment land contract is used when a buyer is unable to provide a down payment large enough to induce the seller to go to the expense of transferring title. Its most common use is for the sale of a vacant lot. The seller often reasons that if title is transferred on a small down payment, the cost to transfer title and the possible cost to regain clear title if the buyer defaults on payments may exceed the down payment and what installment payments have been made by the buyer. On the other hand, the seller reasons that he or she would like to make the sale to the prospective buyer, hoping the buyer will live up to the terms of the contract.

The solution is an installment land contract which calls for whatever down payment the buyer can afford plus payments (usually regular monthly payments) over a specified period of time (one to five years being typical). Most installment land contracts call for the payment of interest on the unpaid balance of the purchase price. When each payment is made it is allocated between interest and principal reduction.

A typical installment land contract provides that title remains in the name of the seller and no deed is prepared until a specified number of timely payments have been made by the buyer. At some specified time the buyer obtains title to the property and may receive a deed and give the seller a purchase money mortgage, or the buyer may pay off the balance due from his or her own improved financial resources or by obtaining a mortgage from a lending institution or some other source.

A common clause in an installment land contract is that in the event of a default in payment by the buyer the contract is cancelled and all the money paid by the buyer is deemed to be rent.

The installment land contract is primarily designed to protect the seller. However, it does provide a mechanism for buyers to obtain property they might not otherwise be able to obtain.

A buyer entering into such an arrangement should be certain that the seller will be able to produce an acceptable deed at the agreed-upon time. A common way to provide for this is either to be certain that the seller is someone of substance and permanence in the community or to insist upon assurance that the seller has good title. This usually requires that a title search be made. The buyer can also request that a deed be drawn and held in escrow (by a mutually agreed-upon third party) until the specified time for delivery. When this is done the buyer is guaranteed that if he or she makes all of the agreed-upon payments a good title to the property will be received, even in the event of death or other unforeseen happenings to the seller.

RENT WITH OPTION TO BUY

Another type of agreement for the purchase of real estate is an *option*. This is an agreement whereby the seller agrees to sell a property at a stipulated price to a potential buyer at a specified future time. Usually the potential buyers pays some type of consideration (either substantial or nominal) to the seller for this future right. Often options are coupled together with leases. A well-drawn option should contain all the terms of a sale.

From the buyers' point of view an option-to-buy agreement is especially advantageous in a situation involving a job transfer. In essence, in a transfer situation or not, an option gives the buyers a chance to "try out" the house before they commit themselves to buy.

For a complete checklist on Sales Contracts, see Checklist 40, page C-83.

CHAPTER 15
THE CLOSING

Assume now that you have bought the house you want. You are figuratively and literally on the "threshold" as the time of closing or settlement arrives. A contract or binder has been signed. You now must get ready for what should be one of the highlights of your life—the day the property officially becomes yours. Variously called "the closing," "the settlement," or "passing papers," depending on the geographical location, this ceremony in essence means that ownership of the property transfers from the seller to you, the buyer. It is the culmination of the home buying process—an exciting time when the title to the property and the property itself finally become yours.

SALES CONTRACT

What will happen at the closing will probably depend upon what is in your sales contract. The contract is the foundation upon which the closing is built. As pointed out in the previous chapter, this is a formal document. Sometimes it is a form document filled out by the broker or salesperson. It may be just a simple earnest money receipt, binder or offer and acceptance.

However, when the sales contract is complete and well prepared nothing will have to be negotiated at the closing. The closing will simply be a mechanical process. When items of importance have not been covered in the contract, they will have to be negotiated at the closing. This is a poor time for negotiation as everyone is tense and there is a lot of pressure. Also, there are many people involved, all of whom will put their two cents in trying to settle any remaining problems.

Under the best of circumstances, in a convivial atmosphere of good faith and satisfaction, the closing transaction is still a complicated, time-consuming procedure. There must be payment in full, the deed must be delivered and all other details must be completed at this time.

RESPA

For the protection of the consumer (you), the Real Estate Settlement Procedures Act (RESPA) became law in June, 1975, and was revised in 1976. RESPA covers most mortgage loans used to finance the purchase of houses, condominiums, co-ops and other residential units. RESPA was *not* designed to set the prices of closing (settlement) services. Instead, it provides you with information that can take the mystery out of the closing process, so that you can shop for settlement services and make informed decisions.

Before you get to the closing, get the booklet, "Settlement Costs and You," a Department of Housing and Urban Development (HUD) Guide for Home Buyers. (Actually, the lender is *required* by RESPA to give you a copy of this booklet).[1]

Studying this guide early can be a revelation, and one which could have considerable impact on your decision making. It describes the settlement process and nature of the various charges, and suggests questions you might ask lenders, attorneys and others to clarify what services they will provide for the charges quoted. It also contains information on your rights and remedies available under RESPA, and alerts you to unfair or illegal practices.

To repeat, when you submit or the lender prepares your written application for a mortgage, the lender is *legally required* under RESPA to give you a copy of this booklet. If the lender does not give it to you in person on that specific day, the booklet must be put it in the mail to you no later than three business days after your application is filed.

The lender must also, under the same terms, provide you with good faith estimates of closing service charges you are likely to incur.

Your lending institution (bank, savings and loan association, credit union, etc.) is permitted to follow the practice of designating specific settlement service providers. The lender may designate or have available a list of those attorneys and others it approves to be used for legal services in preparing the mortgage, title exam services, title insurance or the conduct of the settlement (closing).

Under RESPA, as part of the good faith estimates, a statement is required in which the lender sets forth:

1. The name, address and telephone number of each provider designated. This must include a statement of the specific services each designated firm is to provide for you, as well as an estimate of the amount the lender anticipates you will have to pay for the service, based on the lender's experience as to what the designated provider usually charges. If the services or charges are not clear to you, ask

---

[1] Should you wish a free copy before you approach the finality of a closing, write Consumer Information Center, Pueblo, Colorado, 81009.

further questions. (Ask lots of questions, until you are thoroughly satisfied.)

2. Whether each designated individual or firm has a business relationship with the lender. A conflict of interest may exist; let no one be naive about that! For example, take the situation where the provider of a settlement service must choose between your interests and those of the lender. Where legal services are involved, it is wise always to employ your own attorney to ensure that your interests are properly protected. It is equally wise to contact other firms to determine whether their costs are competitive.

If all has gone well up to this point, your first logical step in the closing process is to review your sales contract. You should be completely knowledgeable about it so that when you sit down at the closing a few days hence, you will know precisely what each stipulation is.

A good way to review the sales contract is to use Checklist 40 on sales contracts at the back of this book. Each time you develop a "no" answer on the checklist you should consider if you are satisfied with that particular situation.

For example, the house you are buying may be heated by a system that uses oil as fuel. If you note in the closing statement that no provision is made for a fuel oil adjustment, remind your attorney that you did not make an arrangement for fuel oil adjustment. Your attorney should be prepared to determine if the seller is going to include the oil in the tank free or if he or she expects an adjustment. Also, will the seller come to the closing with information about how much oil is in the tank? You may take the position that you expected the oil to be included and therefore this may be an item that will have to be negotiated at the closing.

A complete review of your sales contract as outlined above will provide you with a list of all the potential items you will have to negotiate at the closing. As we have stated previously, a well-drawn sales contract will result in few, if any, items to be negotiated at the closing while a short form or poorly negotiated contract may require substantial negotiation to resolve all outstanding items.

SETTLEMENT COSTS

A variety of costs will have to be paid by either the buyer or seller either before or at the closing. These include:

1. Commissions
2. Escrow fee
3. Title examination
4. Title insurance
5. Legal fees
6. Loan related charges and fees

7. Prepaid property taxes and other adjustable expenses
8. Mortgage interest from closing date to first regular payment period
9. Other charges and commissions.
10. Escrow for future taxes, insurance and other payments

COMMISSIONS

Often the services of a REALTOR® or salesperson are used to bring about the transaction. Usually he or she is paid by the seller a commission that is a percentage of the sale price. The real estate agent acts as agent for the seller. This is true, even when a broker other than the listing broker locates the house for the buyer, or the buyer contacts a broker who has listed the property for sale. This is so even when the selling broker is dealing with the buyer and then locates a property listed with another broker. In this case by custom these real estate practitioners become sub-agents of the listing agent and the listing agent pays a portion of his or her commission to the sub-agent for services in facilitating the sale. But in each case, the real estate broker owes a fiduciary duty to the seller.

There are some exceptions however; a buyer should be aware that under some circumstances he or she can become liable for a payment of a commission. For example, the buyer may contact a broker to help look for a house. A house may be located which is owned by someone who is willing to sell but who does not wish to pay a commission. Another possibility is that the broker who has the listed house for sale does not wish to employ another broker as sub-agent.

In both of these circumstances it is possible, depending upon the arrangements between you as a buyer and the broker, that you may have to pay the broker for his or her services. If you do not wish to pay a broker, you should make this clear at the outset. Since they usually expect to be paid by the seller anyway you should not run into any resistance because of your clarification. If there is any doubt about who is going to pay any broker involved in the transaction, the time to get the matter straightened out is before you sign the sales contract.

ESCROW FEES

In some areas an escrow agent is used to close the transaction. If the sales contract is silent on the subject the agent's fee will be paid by either the buyer or the seller or split between them in a manner that is customary in the area where the property is located. As pointed out in Chapters 10 and 14, you, as a buyer, do not have to be bound by local customs. If you can get the seller to agree to pay all or part of the escrow fee and your sales contract contains this agreement, this is what will happen.

If you are going to be responsible for all or part of the escrow fee you should request that the lender supply you with a list of recommended escrow agents in the area. You might try asking the lender which of them is the least expensive. Many lenders, when directly asked, will supply you with the information. Others will either tell you they do not know or will refuse to give you the information even if they do know.

Under these circumstances you will have to shop around if you want to save money on the escrow fees. If escrow agents know you are shopping around they might quote you a fee at the low end of the range where they might be tempted to charge you a higher fee if you did not ask about fees until it was too late to go elsewhere.

TITLE EXAMINATION

Title assurance charges include the cost for a title search and examination of the results of the search by whomever is going to issue either a certificate of title or a title insurance policy. Someone will have to make a title history abstract or bring an existing abstract up to date. One potential way to save some money is by asking the seller who did the title search when the current owner purchased the house. Since that title searcher will only have to bring the existing abstract up to date he or she may be willing to work for less than somebody else who has to make a new abstract. However, the only way to be sure you are getting the lowest price is to shop around.

Again, who pays for the title search will depend upon the custom of the area in which the house is located if the sales contract is silent on the subject or according to what has been negotiated between the buyer and the seller if the result of the negotiation is specified in the contract.

TITLE INSURANCE

You may elect, either because it is a requirement of the lender or just for your own protection and peace of mind, to buy a title insurance policy (see the section on title insurance in Chapter 13).

Title insurance is usually paid for with a one-time premium charge that may range from $2 to $4 per $1,000 of value insured. Some title insurance policies cover just the lender's interest in the property. Others also cover the owner's interest as well. You must decide whether you want your ownership protected too. The small difference in cost between a title insurance policy that just protects the mortgagor's interest and one that also protects the owner's interest in the property is usually well worth it.

Again, shopping around will often produce a substantial range of fees. The attorney who sells a title insurance policy may receive a fee of 50 percent or more which is supposed to pay for all or some of the title search and whatever other legal services are involved. If, as part of the closing the attorney is already being paid for these same services, he or she may offer a credit either against the cost of the services or the title insurance premium to avoid being paid twice for the same services rendered.

Sometimes there is also a difference in the premium different title insurance companies charge for identical policies. Only by shopping around will you be able to locate the source with the lowest charges.

LEGAL FEES

Attorneys can provide a variety of services in the process of buying and selling a home. The buyer may use an attorney to help negotiate. Depending upon how the negotiation proceeds this may take only a few hours or may take many hours extended over a period of weeks or months.

When an attorney is hired to represent the buyer during the negotiations, the buyer should make a fee arrangement with the attorney for services. The arrangement may be some agreed-upon amount per hour or it may be a fixed fee.

Checking over or drawing the sales contract is another common service the attorney may perform. Again, an agreed-upon fixed fee or hourly rate should be established prior to the work being done. The same attorney may also perform some or all of the functions previously discussed concerning escrow fees, title examination and title insurance.

There should be a clear understanding about whether the attorney will represent just you and be paid only by you or, at the closing, also represent the seller and the mortgagor. It is customary in some areas that one attorney represent all the parties (buyers, sellers, lenders, title insurance company) at the closing. This sometimes takes the wisdom of Solomon on the part of the attorney when he or she discovers the various parties have opposite interests relating to some unresolved item at the closing. If an attorney decides to represent two or more parties to a transaction it should be permitted only if all the parties agree in advance and decide exactly how the attorney will be paid.

Other functions often performed by an attorney at the closing are the preparation of the deed, mortgage instruments and closing statement. What functions are performed by attorneys and what functions are performed by others varies considerably from area to area and even within the same area according to the wishes of the buyers, sellers and lenders.

LOAN-RELATED CHARGES AND FEES

There is often a substantial difference in the effective cost of a mortgage loan between one available lender and another in the same area. The most obvious is the interest rate on the mortgage. Although this is very important, a lender with a higher rate of interest might wisely be selected if some other terms of the loan were more favorable. For example, it might be worthwhile to pay a little more interest if the term of the mortgage was longer, the rate of interest fixed over the period of the mortgage rather than subject to readjustment at some future day, the down payment lower, prepayment penalties less or other origination costs lower. The whole subject of selecting mortgages is covered in Chapter 11.

Here is a list of some of the fees and other charges that often are charged by the lenders to either the buyers or the sellers. Not all lenders charge all these different fees and charges, but only by asking in advance what a lender does normally do are you going to get the lowest possible charge.

1. Lender's appraisal for mortgage, VA appraisal, FHA appraisal
2. Inspection of property by lender, VA, FHA
3. Settlement costs
4. Preparing the mortgage note and mortgage deed
5. Preparing other loan papers
6. Lender's attorney's fee to review papers
7. Photographs required by lender
8. Lender's charge for overhead, clerical costs, postage, stationery, etc.
9. Amortization schedules
10. Passbooks or payment books
11. Membership in lender's organization (such as a credit union, a mutual savings bank or a mutual savings and loan)
12. Escrow fee or charges
13. Notary fees
14. Commitment fees of the Federal National Mortgage Association and fee for the preparation and recording of an assignment of the mortgage to this association or any other purchaser of the mortgage in the secondary mortgage market
15. Trustee's fees or charges
16. Loan application
17. Loan processing fee
18. Recording fees for mortgage instruments
19. Credit reports
20. Hazard insurance required by lender
21. Flood and/or earthquake insurance required by lender
22. Survey required by lender
23. Title examination by representative of lender
24. Title insurance required by lender
25. Interest from the date of the closing to the first payment period
26. Points charged by lender to the buyer and/or seller
27. Late payment charges
28. Prepayment penalties

According to RESPA you are entitled to a list of these charges the day before the closing. Usually, however, by then it is too late to do anything about them except round up the needed money to make the payments. So the time to find out about all of the charges is when you make your initial mortgage application. Show the list above to the representative at the lending institution and ask which of these charges the lender makes and how much they will be.

In the process of shopping around for a lender you may find substantial differences in the mortgages you are offered. Generally there are three basic differences that must be weighed one against the other in order to judge which mortgage is the best for you—interest rate, loan cost, mortgage term. Obviously if one lender is best in all three categories the choice is easy. However, what often happens is that one lender has a lower interest rate, but higher costs and possibly a different mortgage term. Also, you cannot make the judgment solely on initial cost but must also consider for example prepayment penalty charges.

Here is one rule of thumb which you can use to calculate the combined effect of the interest rate on your loan and the one-time settlement charges (paid by you) such as "points" (a point is one percent of the original mortgage amount). While not perfectly accurate, it is usually close enough for meaningful comparisons between lenders. The rule is that one-time settlement charges equaling one percent of the loan amount increase the interest charge by one-eighth of one percent. The one-eighth factor corresponds to a pay-back period of approximately 15 years. If you intend instead to hold the property for only five years and to pay off the loan at that time, the factor increases to one-quarter.

Here is an example of the rule. Suppose you wish to borrow $40,000. Lender A will make the loan at 11.5 percent interest, but charges a two percent origination fee, a $250 application fee, and requires that you use a lawyer for title work, selected by the lender at a fee of $400.

Lender B will make the loan at 12 percent interest, but has no additional requirements or charges. As part of that 12 percent interest, however, Lender B will not charge an application fee and will absorb the lawyer's fee. What are the actual charges for each case?

Begin by relating all of Lender A's one-time charges to percentages of the $40,000. loan amount:

2 percent origination fee = 2   percent of loan amount
$250 application fee   = 0.5 percent of loan amount
$400 lawyer's fee   = 1   percent of loan amount
Total   3.5 percent of loan amount

Since each one percent of the loan amount in charges is the equivalent of one-eighth percent increase in interest, the effective interest rate from Lender A is the quoted or "contract" interest rate, 11.5 percent plus .44 percent (3.5 times one-eighth), or a total of 11.94 percent interest. Since Lender B has offered a 12 percent interest rate, Lender A has made a more attractive offer. Of course, it is more attractive only if you have sufficient cash to pay Lender A's one-time charges and still cover your down payment, moving expenses, and other settlement costs.

This is simply a method to compare diverse costs on an equal basis. The calculation should be sensitive to your assumption about the period

FIGURE 76
SETTLEMENT COSTS WORKSHEET

Use this worksheet to compare the charges of various lenders and providers of settlement services.

	PROVIDER 1	PROVIDER 2	PROVIDER 3
800. ITEMS PAYABLE IN CONNECTION WITH LOAN			
801. Loan Origination Fee %			
802. Loan Discount %			
803. Appraisal Fee to			
804. Credit Report to			
805. Lender's Inspection Fee			
806. Mortgage Insurance Application Fee to			
807. Assumption Fee			
808.			
809.			
810.			
811.			
900. ITEMS REQUIRED BY LENDER TO BE PAID IN ADVANCE			
901. Interest from to @ $ /day			
902. Mortgage Insurance Premium for months to			
903. Hazard Insurance Premium for years to			
904. years to			
905.			
1000. RESERVES DEPOSITED WITH LENDER			
1001. Hazard insurance months @ $ per month			
1002. Mortgage insurance months @ $ per month			
1003. City property taxes months @ $ per month			
1004. County property taxes months @ $ per month			
1005. Annual assessments months @ $ per month			
1006. months @ $ per month			
1007. months @ $ per month			
1008. months @ $ per month			

(Form Continues on Next Page)

FIGURE 76
SETTLEMENT COSTS WORKSHEET (continued)

1100. TITLE CHARGES

1101. Settlement or closing fee	to
1102. Abstract or title search	to
1103. Title examination	to
1104. Title insurance binder	to
1105. Document preparation	to
1106. Notary fees	to
1107. Attorney's fees	to
(includes above items numbers:)	
1108. Title insurance	to
(includes above items numbers:)	
1109. Lender's coverage	$
1110. Owner's coverage	$
1111.	
1112.	
1113.	

1200. GOVERNMENT RECORDING AND TRANSFER CHARGES

1201. Recording fees: Deed $	:Mortgage $	:Releases $	
1202. City/county tax/stamps: Deed $	:Mortgage $		
1203. State tax/stamps:	Deed $	:Mortgage $	
1204.			
1205.			

1300. ADDITIONAL SETTLEMENT CHARGES

1301. Survey	to
1302. Pest inspection	to
1303.	
1304.	
1305.	

1400. TOTAL SETTLEMENT CHARGES (enter on lines 103, Section J and 502, Section K)

of time you plan to own the house before paying off the mortgage. As indicated above, the factor increases to one-fourth if you expect to sell and pay off the mortgage in five years. Applying this new factor to the above illustration, the effective interest rate for Lender A would be 11.5 percent plus .87 (3.5 × 1/4) for a total of 12.37 percent interest. In this case, A's offer is no longer more attractive than Lender B's which was 12 percent.

In doing these calculations you should also be careful as to which one-time fees you place into the calculation. For example, if Lender B did not include in the charge a legal fee but told you that you had to secure legal services in order to obtain the loan, you would have to add to Lender B's interest rate the legal fee that you had to incur.

You can use this method to compare the effective interest rates of any number of lenders as you shop for a loan. If the lenders have provided Truth-in-Lending disclosures (see section later in this chapter), these are an even better comparative tool. You should question lenders carefully to make sure you have learned all the charges they intend to make. The good faith estimate you receive when you make a loan application is a good checklist for this information, but it is not precise. Thus, you should ask the lender how the charges and fees are computed.

The booklet, "Settlement Costs and You" has a worksheet designed to help you compare the settlement costs of lenders (see Figure 76).

PREPAID PROPERTY TAXES AND OTHER ADJUSTABLE EXPENSES

Most sales contracts provide that the buyer will pay to the seller, in addition to the price of the house, payments for certain items specified in the sales contract. Typical items include:

1. Prepaid taxes
2. Prepaid fuel
3. Prepaid association dues
4. Prepaid mortgage interest (when an existing mortgage is assumed)
5. Prepaid insurance premiums (when an insurance policy is taken over)
6. Prepaid sewer, water, electric and gas charges

If, on the other hand, any of these items is due and its payment is in arrears (overdue), the buyer may elect to make the payment and receive a credit towards the purchase price from the seller.

Again, it is worthwhile repeating that the custom in your area does not bind you. Often you can negotiate with the seller and eliminate those adjustments which result in your needing extra cash at the closing. Whatever you negotiate that is different from the custom of the area should be specified in the sales contract.

MORTGAGE INTEREST FROM CLOSING DATE TO FIRST REGULAR MORTGAGE PAYMENT PERIOD

Many lenders set up their mortgages so the first payment is due between one and two months after the date of the closing. If the regular mortgage payment includes one month's interest payable in arrears and it is going to be one and one-half months until it is due then at the closing one-half month's interest will be collected and turned over to the lender. In other words, any interest due because the first regular payment is insufficient to cover the interest from the date of the closing to when the first mortgage payment is due is collected at the closing by the lender.

OTHER CHARGES AND COMMISSIONS

A mortgage is taxed in many states and the tax is due at the time it is recorded. Also, there is often a special fee collected to record the mortgage. The total typical mortgage and bond or note taxes can be as high as $5 per $1,000 of mortgage debt (one-half of one percent).

Many states require stamps, fees, or a surtax on deed. This is a carry-over from the old Federal Tax Stamp that was charged at the rate of 55 cents per $1,000 sale price above any assumed mortgage. Although this tax is no longer charged by the federal government, many states have replaced it with a similar charge of their own.

If all or part of the property is rented, the seller should pay to the buyer all rents or deposits that cover periods beyond the date of the closing.

Also, when someone helped you get a mortgage they may charge you a commission or finder's fee for this service, payable at the closing.

ESCROW FOR FUTURE TAXES, INSURANCE AND OTHER PAYMENTS

Many lenders require that, in addition to the regular monthly mortgage payment, the borrower deposit with the lender sufficient money to pay property taxes, hazard insurance and sometimes various other payments. This money is held by the lender either in an interest-bearing or non-interest-bearing escrow account until it is needed.

ESCROW CLOSING

Settlement practices differ from state to state. In some parts of the country, a settlement may be conducted by an escrow agent, which may be a lender, a real estate agent, a title company representative, an attorney or an escrow company. After entering into a contract of sale, the parties sign an escrow agreement which requires them to deposit specified documents and funds with the agent. Unlike other types of closings, the parties do not meet around a table to sign and exchange documents. The agent may request a title report and policy, draft a deed or other documents, obtain rent statements, pay off existing loans, adjust taxes, rents and insurance between the buyer and seller, compute interest on loans, and acquire hazard insurance. All this may be authorized in the escrow agreement. If all the papers and monies are deposited with the agent within the agreed time, the escrow is then "closed."

The escrow agent then records the appropriate documents and gives each party the documents and money each is entitled to receive, including the completed Uniform Settlement Statement (see Figure 77). If one party has failed to fulfill the agreement, the escrow is not closed and legal complications may follow.

PROTECTION AGAINST UNFAIR PRACTICES

A principal conclusion of Congress in RESPA is that consumers need protection from ". . . . unnecessarily high settlement charges caused by certain abusive practices that have developed in some areas of the country." The potential problems discussed below may not be applicable to most loan settlements, and most professionals in the settlement business will give you good service. Nevertheless, you may save yourself money and worry by keeping the following considerations in mind.

KICKBACKS

Kickbacks and referrals of business for gain are often tied together. RESPA prohibits anyone from giving or taking a fee, kickback or anything of value under an agreement that business will be referred to a specific person or organization. It is also illegal to charge or accept a fee or part of a fee where no service has actually been performed. This requirement does not prevent agents for lenders and title companies, attorneys, or others actually performing a service in connection with the mortgage loan or settlement transaction from receiving compensation for their work. It also does not prohibit payments pursuant to cooperative brokerage, such as a multiple listing service and referral arrangements between real estate agents.

The prohibition is aimed primarily at eliminating the kind of arrangement in which one party agrees to return part of the fee in order to obtain business from the referring party. The danger is that some settlement fees can be inflated to cover payments to this additional party, resulting in a higher total cost to you. There are criminal penalties of both fine and imprisonment for any violation of these provisions of law. There are also provisions for you to recover three times the amount of the kickback, rebate, or referral fee involved through a private lawsuit. In any successful action to enforce your rights, the court may also award you court costs together with a fee for your attorney.

TITLE INSURANCE

Under the law, the seller may not require, as a condition of sale, that title insurance be purchased by the buyer from any particular title company. A violation of this will make the seller liable to you in an amount equal to three times all charges made for the title insurance.

FAIR CREDIT REPORTING

There are credit reporting agencies around the nation which are in the business of compiling credit reports on citizens covering data such as how you pay your bills and if you have been sued, arrested, filed for bankruptcy, etc. In addition, this file may include your neighbors' and friends' views of your character, general reputation, or manner of living. This latter information is referred to as an "investigative consumer report."

The Fair Credit Reporting Act does not give the right to inspect or physically handle your actual report at the credit reporting agency, nor to receive an exact copy of the report. But you are entitled to a summary of the report, showing the nature, substance and sources of the information it contains.

If the terms of your financing have been adversely affected by the credit report, you have the right to inspect the summary of that report free of charge (there may otherwise be a small fee). The accuracy of the report can also be challenged and corrections required. For more detailed information on your credit report rights contact the Federal Trade Commission (FTC) in Washington, or the nearest FTC regional office.[2]

FILING COMPLAINTS

As with any consumer problems, the place to start if you have a complaint is back at the source of the problem (the lender, settlement agent, broker, etc.). If that initial effort brings no satisfaction and you think you have suffered damages through violations of the Real Estate Settlement Procedures Act, you may be entitled to bring a civil action in the U. S. District Court for the district in which the property involved is located, or in any other court of competent jurisdiction. This is a matter best determined by your attorney. Any suit you file under RESPA must be brought within one year from the date of the occurrence of the alleged violation. You may have legal remedies under other state or Federal laws in addition to RESPA.

You should note that RESPA provides for specific legal sanctions only under the provisions which prohibit kickbacks and unearned fees and which prohibit the seller from requiring the buyer to use a particular title

---

[2] The FTC Buyer's Guide No. 7: *Fair Credit Reporting Act* is a good summary of this Act.

FIGURE 77
UNIFORM SETTLEMENT STATEMENT

A. U.S. DEPARTMENT OF HOUSING AND URBAN DEVELOPMENT SETTLEMENT STATEMENT	B. TYPE OF LOAN	
	1. ☐ FHA 2. ☐ FMHA 3. ☐ CONV. UNINS.	
	4. ☐ VA 5. ☐ CONV. INS.	
	6. FILE NUMBER:	7. LOAN NUMBER:
	8. MORT. INS. CASE NO.:	

C. NOTE: This form is furnished to give you a statement of actual settlement costs. Amounts paid to and by the settlement agent are shown. Items marked "(p.o.c.)" were paid outside the closing; they are shown here for informational purposes and are not included in the totals.

D. NAME OF BORROWER:	E. NAME OF SELLER:	F. NAME OF LENDER:

G. PROPERTY LOCATION:	H. SETTLEMENT AGENT:	I. SETTLEMENT DATE:
	PLACE OF SETTLEMENT:	

J. SUMMARY OF BORROWER'S TRANSACTION:		K. SUMMARY OF SELLER'S TRANSACTION:	
100. **GROSS AMOUNT DUE FROM BORROWER**		400. **GROSS AMOUNT DUE TO SELLER**	
101. Contract sales price		401. Contract sales price	
102. Personal property		402. Personal property	
103. Settlement charges to borrower (line 1400)		403.	
104.		404.	
105.		405.	
Adjustments for items paid by seller in advance		Adjustments for items paid by seller in advance	
106. City/town taxes to		406. City/town taxes to	
107. County taxes to		407. County taxes to	
108. Assessments to		408. Assessments to	
109.		409.	
110.		410.	
111.		411.	
112.		412.	
120. **GROSS AMOUNT DUE FROM BORROWER**		420. **GROSS AMOUNT DUE TO SELLER**	
200. **AMOUNTS PAID BY OR IN BEHALF OF BORROWER**		500. **REDUCTIONS IN AMOUNT DUE TO SELLER**	
201. Deposit or earnest money		501. Excess deposit (see Instructions)	
202. Principal amount of new loan(s)		502. Settlement charges to seller (line 1400)	
203. Existing loan(s) taken subject to		503. Existing loan(s) taken subject to	
204.		504. Payoff of first mortgage loan	
205.		505. Payoff of second mortgage loan	
206.		506.	
207.		507.	
208.		508.	
209.		509.	
Adjustments for items unpaid by seller		Adjustments for items unpaid by seller	
210. City/town taxes to		510. City/town taxes to	
211. County taxes to		511. County taxes to	
212. Assessments to		512. Assessments to	
213.		513.	
214.		514.	
215.		515.	
216.		516.	
217.		517.	
218.		518.	
219.		519.	
220. **TOTAL PAID BY/FOR BORROWER**		520. **TOTAL REDUCTION AMOUNT DUE SELLER**	
300. **CASH AT SETTLEMENT FROM OR TO BORROWER**		600. **CASH AT SETTLEMENT TO OR FROM SELLER**	
301. Gross amount due from borrower (line 120)		601. Gross amount due to seller (line 420)	
302. Less amounts paid by/for borrower (line 220)	( )	602. Less reduction amount due seller (line 520)	( )
303. **CASH (☐ FROM) (☐ TO) BORROWER**		603. **CASH (☐ TO) (☐ FROM) SELLER**	

FIGURE 77
UNIFORM SETTLEMENT STATEMENT (continued)

		PAID FROM BORROWER'S FUNDS AT SETTLEMENT	PAID FROM SELLER'S FUNDS AT SETTLEMENT
L. SETTLEMENT CHARGES			
700.	**TOTAL SALES/BROKER'S COMMISSION based on price** $ @ %		
	Division of commission (line 700) as follows:		
701.	$ to		
702.	$ to		
703.	Commission paid at Settlement		
704.			
800.	**ITEMS PAYABLE IN CONNECTION WITH LOAN**		
801.	Loan Origination Fee %		
802.	Loan Discount %		
803.	Appraisal Fee to		
804.	Credit Report to		
805.	Lender's Inspection Fee		
806.	Mortgage Insurance Application Fee to		
807.	Assumption Fee		
808.			
809.			
810.			
811.			
900.	**ITEMS REQUIRED BY LENDER TO BE PAID IN ADVANCE**		
901.	Interest from to @ $ /day		
902.	Mortgage Insurance Premium for mo. to		
903.	Hazard Insurance Premium for yrs. to		
904.	yrs. to		
905.			
1000.	**RESERVES DEPOSITED WITH LENDER FOR**		
1001.	Hazard insurance mo. @ $ /mo.		
1002.	Mortgage insurance mo. @ $ /mo.		
1003.	City property taxes mo. @ $ /mo.		
1004.	County property taxes mo. @ $ /mo.		
1005.	Annual assessments mo. @ $ /mo.		
1006.	mo. @ $ /mo.		
1007.	mo. @ $ /mo.		
1008.	mo. @ $ /mo.		
1100.	**TITLE CHARGES**		
1101.	Settlement or closing fee to		
1102.	Abstract or title search to		
1103.	Title examination to		
1104.	Title insurance binder to		
1105.	Document preparation to		
1106.	Notary fees to		
1107.	Attorney's fees to		
	(includes above items No.:)		
1108.	Title insurance to		
	(includes above items No.:)		
1109.	Lender's coverage $		
1110.	Owner's coverage $		
1111.			
1112.			
1113.			
1200.	**GOVERNMENT RECORDING AND TRANSFER CHARGES**		
1201.	Recording fees: Deed $; Mortgage $; Releases $		
1202.	City/county tax/stamps: Deed $; Mortgage $		
1203.	State tax/stamps: Deed $; Mortgage $		
1204.			
1205.			
1300.	**ADDITIONAL SETTLEMENT CHARGES**		
1301.	Survey to		
1302.	Pest inspection to		
1303.			
1304.			
1305.			
1400.	**TOTAL SETTLEMENT CHARGES** (enter on lines 103 and 502, Sections J and K)		

insurer. If you feel you should recover damages for violations of any other provision of RESPA, you should consult your lawyer.

Most settlement service providers, particularly lenders, are supervised by some governmental agency at the local, state and/or federal level. Others are subject to the control of self-policing associations. If you feel a provider of settlement services has violated RESPA, you can address your complaint to the agency or association which has supervisory responsibility over the provider. The supervisory agency for the lending institution should be noted on the back cover of the booklet, "Settlement Costs and You." If the lender has given you this information elsewhere, the lender is not required to provide it here.

For the names of agencies supervising other settlement providers, you will have to check with local and state consumer agencies. You are also encouraged to forward a copy of complaints regarding RESPA violations to the HUD Office of Consumer Affairs and Regulatory Functions which has the primary responsibility for administering the RESPA program.[3] Your complaints may lay the foundation for future legislative or administrative actions to correct such problems.

UNIFORM SETTLEMENT STATEMENT

Until RESPA required the use of a standard closing statement form for residential closings, whoever conducted the closing was free to choose from several forms. There was a tremendous variety of forms in use. It was not uncommon for even the various attorneys involved in a closing or an experienced real estate broker to have great difficulty in following the mathematical calculations used by the person conducting the closing. The home buyer stood little chance of understanding what was happening in time to make any protest of what might appear to be an excess charge or a mathematical error.

Now any home buyer who wishes can learn exactly how the uniform statement is filled out and how all the mathematical calculations are made. You can then follow the closing step by step to be certain you are paying for those items in the amounts you previously agreed on and that you receive credit for everything you have coming to you.

If you are planning to check the calculations on the settlement you should exercise your right to obtain the preliminary figures the day before the closing.

As we mentioned earlier, the Real Estate Settlement Procedures Act provides *disclosure of settlement costs one day before closing and delivery*. One business day before settlement, you have the right to inspect the form,

---

[3] Send copies of complaints and inquiries to: Assistant Secretary for Consumer Affairs and Regulatory Functions; Attention: RESPA Office; U. S. Department of Housing and Urban Development; 451 7th St. S. W.; Rm 4100; Washington, D.C. 20410.

called the Uniform Settlement Statement (see Figure 77), on which are itemized the services provided to you and fees charged to you. This form (developed by the U.S. Department of Housing and Urban Development) is filled out by the person who will conduct the settlement meeting. Be sure you have the name, address, and telephone number of the settlement agent if you wish to inspect this form or if you have any questions.

Even if the settlement agent does not have all costs available the day before closing, he or she is obligated to show you, upon request, what is available.

The Uniform Settlement Statement must be delivered or mailed to you (while another statement goes to the seller) at or before settlement. If, however, you waive your right to delivery of the completed statement at settlement, it will then be mailed at the earliest practicable date.

In parts of the country where the settlement agent does not require a meeting, or in cases where you or your agent do not attend the settlement, the statement will be mailed as soon as practicable after settlement, and no advance inspection is required.

The Uniform Settlement Statement is not used in situations where:

1. There are no settlement fees charged to the buyer (because the seller has assumed all settlement-related expenses), or
2. The total amount the borrower is required to pay for all charges imposed at settlement is determined by a fixed amount and the borrower is informed of this fixed amount at the time of loan application. In the latter case, the lender is required to provide the borrower, within three business days of application, a list of services rendered.

TRUTH-IN-LENDING

The lender is required to provide you a Truth-in-Lending statement by the time of loan consummation, which discloses the annual percentage rate or effective interest rate which you will pay on your mortgage loan. This rate may be higher than the contract interest rate because the latter includes only interest, while the annual percentage rate or effective rate includes discount points, fees and financing charges and certain other charges. The Truth-in-Lending statement will also disclose any additional charges for prepayment should you pay off the remaining balance of the mortgage before it is due.

Lenders are not required to provide you a Truth-in-Lending disclosure at the time of loan application, when the good faith estimate of settlement costs and the informational booklet are given to you. However, since the annual percentage rate the lender will be charging you is an important item of information which you can use as you shop for services, you may want to request it at the time of application.

CLOSING DAY

On settlement or closing day, the property officially becomes yours. Methods and practices of this ceremony differ from state to state. In some areas settlement may be conducted by an escrow agent who may be the lender (banker), the real estate broker, attorney or title company representative. Regardless of who the "officer" is, you, the buyer should have *your* lawyer attend the closing with you. Some brokers prefer to have both the buyer and seller together at the closing, although this is not really necessary. The necessary papers may be signed in advance by either one, while the other signs at the settlement.

The closing often takes place in the offices of the lending institution which is financing the buyer's mortgage, or it may be in the lawyer's office (yours or the lender's, whichever is agreed upon). In any case it should be a place where *all* documents pertinent to the exchange of property are gathered and coordinated by the person in charge.

A final closing statement will be made at this time. The buyer will be asked to sign a promissory note or bond, promising to repay the money borrowed to purchase the house, and an instrument of security commonly known as the mortgage in favor of the lender, which puts the property up as security for the loan. This is in essence a double transaction encompassing a sale and the financing of it.

Next, the seller is asked to execute a deed to convey to the buyer title to the property. When everything is in order, the buyer will pay the balance of the down payment and the buyer's share of closing costs, previously reckoned on the closing statement.

After the closing, the deed and mortgage will be recorded in the local property repository (variously titled in different areas of the country—it may be the "Hall of Records," "Town Hall," etc.) Upon recording, the deed will be mailed to the buyer and the mortgage (security instrument) to the lender. The mortgage will remain on record as a lien against your newly acquired property until you have paid it off in full.

At closing, you will take possession of receipts for any payments, a copy of the property survey with boundaries shown (where required), your buyer's closing statement and, if you have built or bought a new house, the builder's warranty, appliance and systems guarantees.

The closing statement will show what you paid on the down payment and other settlement costs and will list the amounts already paid.

You legally become the owner of your home when the deed is "delivered" to you and you accept it. This is just a formality as you will give it right back to whomever is going to have it recorded.

Finally, together with all your papers you should receive the keys to the premises unless you have arranged for the seller to keep possession after the closing. You are now the proud owner of your new home.

For a complete Closing checklist, see Checklist 41, page C-89.

PART FOUR
FURTHER CONSIDERATIONS

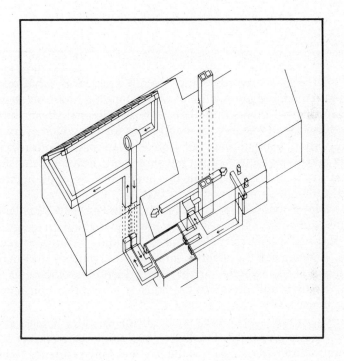

CHAPTER 16

SPECIAL KINDS OF RESIDENCES AND FORMS OF OWNERSHIP

When one hears the words "single family residence" what often first flashes into the mind is a picture of a free-standing house on its own lot, with a fee simple ownership. This is the traditional dream house, so often referred to in our literature and news media, which every American supposedly wants to own as soon as he or she can afford to do so.

A true picture of the American housing scene, however, shows that in addition to many homes that fit this traditional description, there are millions of single-family residences that are quite different.

This chapter focuses on special forms of ownership such as condominiums, cooperatives, time sharing, and houses built on leased land. It also discusses special purpose houses including resort and recreation houses, housing for the elderly, farm houses, ranches and mansions. Information is also included about Planned Unit Developments, mobile homes, modular and prefabricated houses, log cabins, houseboats and historic houses.

The newest kinds of houses such as experimental houses and solar houses are also discussed. Finally, we include in this chapter information about barrier-free design in the single-family residence, which can be a part of any house intended for use by the elderly or handicapped.

CONDOMINIUMS

In the past 20 years the condominium has firmly established itself on the American scene. Unlike other forms of ownership, it did not gradually evolve. It is a form of ownership that was created by special state real estate laws. All 50 states have passed some form of condominium legislation.

A 1963 amendment to the National Housing Act, extending government mortgage insurance to condominiums, helped condominiums to grow steadily in the marketplace in the 1960s. In the early 1970s there was a real boom which peaked in 1973 when about 350,000 individual units were created, either through new construction or conversion of existing units. There was a real slump in 1975 when only about 55,000 individual units were created and about 15,000 individual units were converted from condominium ownership back to other forms of owner-ship. From its bottom in 1975, the condominium market has come back and has experienced periodic ups and downs, but appears to have com-pletely recovered from the slump.

The word "condominium" is derived from the Latin and essentially means to have control (*dominum*) over a certain property jointly with (*con*) one or more persons. A popular misconception is that some partic-ular style or architecture or type of construction is a necessary part of being a condominium. This is not true. A condominium can be any style or type of construction. However, many of the new condominium de-velopments are good representations of modern design and construc-tion techniques.

Today, condos are available in a wide range of prices—from the afford-able starter homes suitable for young families with modest incomes and available down payments, to retirement communities designed for peo-ple who want a variety of social and recreational facilities, to town-houses and high rises in Washington, Chicago, New York and Miami that cost hundreds of thousands of dollars.

Actually, the condominium form of ownership is not limited to town-house construction, converted high rise apartments, or even residential construction. There are many detached single-family houses, duplexes, quadros, etc. that are set up in condominium form of ownership. Also, office buildings, warehouses, industrial parks and clubs can be owned in the condominium form of ownership.

Although condominium acts vary from state to state, many are quite similar because they are patterned after a uniform condominium act. They permit individual dwelling unit estates to be established within a total and larger property estate. In other words, each owner owns the fee (title) to his or her individual unit and a percentage of the fee of the common areas of the land and the improvements. The exact location of each individually-owned unit must be accurately spelled out in terms of both the usual horizontal description found in a deed and a vertical description as well.

Whatever is within the common area boundaries and not within any individual unit is considered common area. While owners of individual units may have exclusive use of some of the common areas such as basement storage and car storage areas, most condominium laws permit only the actual living area to be individually owned.

ADVANTAGES AND DISADVANTAGES OF CONDOS

An in-depth study as to what people like and dislike about condomin-ium living has been made by the Urban Land Institute.[1] Some favorable factors were:

---

[1] Carl Norcross, *Townhouses and Condominiums: Residents' Likes and Dislikes* (Washington: Urban Land Institute, 1973).

- Building up equity
- Not paying rent
- Lower cost than single-family housing
- Freedom from house and yard maintenance
- Better environment
- Recreational facilities

These factors point out why so many people are buying and moving into condominiums. In this era when house prices have increased so substantially in many areas, renters have felt that they have not shared in the profit made by homeowners. Many tenants have decided that the way for them to obtain their share of an equity build-up and to realize tax advantages is to purchase a condominium.

This choice is often made when the potential buyer discovers that with the cash he or she has available and with affordable payments, a more satisfactory living space can be obtained in a condominium than in a single-family dwelling or some other residence.

This is not the only reason that people elect to live in condominiums. Many people who can afford a detached, single-family home elect instead to live in a condominium. In fact, an important segment of the condominium market is composed of people who have sold their houses and have then bought a condominium. In addition to possible lower costs, these people are seeking freedom from house and yard maintenance and the better environment, social life and recreational facilities that the condominium they choose has to offer.

The Urban Land Institute study also identifies what people dislike about living in a condominium:

- Living too close together
- Noisy or undesirable neighbors and children
- Neighbors' pets
- Trouble with parking
- Poor association management
- Poor construction
- Dishonest salespeople who sold the units to them
- Negligent builders
- Renters in other units
- Thin party walls
- Long, identical rows of houses

This list points out some of the common problems which stem from the fact that people are usually living quite close together in a condominium complex. If you are used to living in a detached, single-family house in the country or suburbs and then move to a condo, you are going to have to get used to living close to your neighbors and hearing many noises that you are not accustomed to. You also will have to get used to the noise and mess of your neighbors' children. If you do not wish to live near young children, look for a condominium that either prohibits children or has attracted few families with children.

Pets are a constant source of problems in condominium management. It seems to be difficult, if not impossible, to enforce pet regulations in many condominiums. Some condominiums have regulations that prohibit pets. The history of these regulations is that they tend to be enforced when the project is new and being managed by the developer. However, when the owners' association takes over it runs into enforcement problems, and exceptions are often made for kittens that grow into cats and puppies that grow into dogs. When the association receives complaints about owners' roaming and barking dogs it often discovers it is too late to enforce the regulations since too many owners are violators.

FINANCING

A condominium unit is financed with a mortgage just as a detached, single-family dwelling is. These mortgages present some special problems for the lenders. Just as you, as a potential buyer should be familiar with the whole condominium development and how it is operating, so the lender must also be concerned. This means that in order to give you a mortgage on your individual unit, the lender must investigate and become familiar with the whole development. Usually, one or two lenders in the area have already become familiar with the development in which you plan to purchase. It often will be much easier to obtain a mortgage from these lenders than from a lender who is unfamiliar with the development.

CONDOMINIUM ASSOCIATIONS

When you buy a condominium you are buying more than just a simple place to live by yourself. What you are buying is part of a whole separate community within a neighborhood and municipality.

Just like a regular community, there is a special form of condominium government known by various names such as the "Owners' Association," "Condominium Association," "Homeowners' Association," etc., which is run by an elected board of directors. The responsibilities of this board are set forth under a set of bylaws recorded by the master deed. Usually a 66 or 75 percent majority of the owners must vote to change the bylaws, which in turn must always comply with the provisions of the condominium statutes of the state. It usually takes a 100 percent vote to change the master deed.

Typical responsibilities of the board of directors are the control of the use of the common areas and the maintenance of all those parts of the building, grounds and recreation areas that are not specifically required to be maintained by the individual owners.

According to one judge, a condominium is a "little democratic sub-society."[2] This judge went on to point out that owners in a condominium give up some of their freedom for the advantages of group living just as they do in the larger community.

Generally speaking, part of the condominium association's duty is to control the use of the common areas and maintain the improvements, grounds and other commonly-owned facilities. The association pays for these functions by assessing each individual owner his or her share of the costs. This assessment is often known as the common charges. The condo association also has the power to make "house rules." Some typical things it does is hire a management company to perform the routine functions of collecting common charges and assessments, handling reports of needed repairs and complaints from the individual owners, hiring, supervising and paying employees and outside service people.

The board of directors, besides having the power to maintain the property, also may make capital improvements up to some specified amount set forth in the bylaws without approval of the owners. Furthermore, the board can assess each individual owner for his or her share of the improvements even if the individual owner was opposed to the capital improvements being made.

The courts have ruled that the board of directors can make a variety of house rules, some of which may be very unpopular with some of the individual owners. However, these rules must be reasonable and not interfere too greatly with the private lives of the owners.

For example, the courts have ruled that the board of directors can reasonably regulate the hours that the pool, tennis courts and other recreational facilities can be used. They can permit or not permit the consumption of food, beverages and alcohol in the recreational areas but cannot control the use of these items within the individual units.

MANAGEMENT

Association management itself is often an ongoing problem. When the condominium is first developed, the developer is responsible for running the association. Usually, when a specified number of the individual units have been sold, the association is turned over to the individual owners who elect directors. The association often discovers that the day-to-day operation of the condominium is best left to professionals, and a management company is hired. It seldom works out well when an association tries, with the use of non-paid members, to run the project, except when the number of units is very small.

It is worth repeating here that it is very important to look into how the association in the condominium you are planning to acquire operates. It is very common to see two developments in the same neighborhood

---

[2] Will Bernard, "The Family Lawyer," *Naugatuck News,* Naugatuck, CT., Oct. 25, 1977.

which look physically very similar that are actually quite different. One will have an effective association with an active, capable board of directors that is providing for good management. The other will have a less effective board of directors which is providing poorer management. The result is that the common charges in the two similar developments may be quite different, as may be the level of maintenance, rule enforcement and the quality of the recreational facilities and activities.

When poor construction results in the need for many repairs, it is often the directors (unless there is still a developer warranty in effect) who must assume the responsibility of making the needed repairs and assessing the individual owners for the cost in the form of either increased common charges or special assessments.

When the developer starts to market individual units, a projected operating budget for the completed development is required. From this operating budget the monthly common charges for unit owners are projected. In a period of rapidly rising costs, it often turns out that the projected common charges are well under what they actually turn out to be. The problem is further compounded if the developer has underestimated what they will be in order to sell the individual units. As previously stated, poor construction that has to be corrected and which causes excess maintenance charges will cause the common charges to exceed original projections.

Since the directors have to live with their neighbors, the whole problem of rule enforcement is difficult. It also presents special problems when some of the units are occupied by tenants rather than the individual unit owners. Although there are many good, responsible tenants, there is likely to be more rule enforcement problems with tenants who are living in the condominium for relatively short periods of time than there is with permanent unit owners or long-term tenants. Often there is an aura of poor feelings between the unit owners who occupy their own units and the tenants.

KNOW WHAT YOU ARE BUYING

As a potential condominium buyer you should be sure to request and receive a copy of the current operating budget of the owners' association. You should also obtain a history of the past common charges including any past special assessments or any pending or upcoming special assessments.

Before you buy an individual unit, you should inquire about the community lifestyle of the owners. In some condominiums there are very little informal or organized community activities. In other units, there are almost daily activities that are an important part of the lives of the owners. You should know what the lifestyle is and whether it is the lifestyle you wish for yourself and your family.

Many condominiums seek to attract a special segment of the population such as retired couples without children, singles, young married families with many children, etc. Some condominiums actually are re-stricted to families in one of these or some other category. Many condo-miniums have strict rules about pets. You should check to be certain you will be permitted to keep or obtain the type of pets you wish to have.

Finally, be careful, if you are buying a used unit, to judge its value based on what other used units in the same condominium have recently sold for. You can be misled as to the value of a used unit by comparing it to the sale price of a new unit in the same condominium or a used unit in another project that looks to be similar but actually may be quite different.

For a complete Condominium checklist, see Checklist 42, page C-91.

COOPERATIVE APARTMENTS

In some parts of the country a property that would have been owned in the condominium form of ownership is instead owned as a cooperative. Actually, the cooperative has been around much longer than the condo-minium, and in a way, was the predecessor to the condominium. It has been, and remains, a very popular form of ownership in the New York City area.

Technically, owning a share in a cooperative apartment is not the same as owning a single-family residence or condominium. However, in the marketplace, cooperative shares are often bought and sold in a manner very similar to condominium units. In fact, in some markets, the public is only vaguely aware of the difference between them.

COOPERATIVE OWNERSHIP

A cooperative apartment is owned by a corporation. The corporation sells shares to buyers who wish to occupy the premises. Along with the ownership of the share goes the exclusive right of occupancy for some of the space in the building (the apartment) and the nonexclusive right to use other areas of the property. The stockholders in the corporation elect officers and directors who run the affairs of the organization. They have the power to assess the shareholders for the operating expenses.

The cooperative corporation raises the money for the construction, conversion or purchase of the apartment building by the sale of the shares and by giving a mortgage on the entire premises, usually to a lending institution. The amount of money the shareholders invest in the corporation plus the proceeds of the initial mortgage(s) are used to build, convert or buy the project.

When an individual owner wishes to sell his or her interest, including the right to exclusively occupy a unit, he or she can do so. Some co-operative corporations have built into their bylaws a provision that the shares must first be offered back to the cooperative corporation, some-times at market value and sometimes at a predetermined price.

ESTIMATED VALUE OF COOPERATIVE APARTMENTS

As a cooperative grows older, the value of the unit usually increases and the overall mortgage(s) becomes smaller because it is being amortized.

Here is an example of a typical 200-unit project converted to a cooperative in New York City 10 years ago:

Initial Cost of Project	$10,000,000
Initial Mortgage at Time of Conversion	$ 7,500,000
Stockholder Equity	$ 2,500,000
Value of Each Stockholder's Share ($2,500,000 ÷ 200)	$ 12,500

(In this example, the value of all units is equal.)

The initial stockholder in this project purchased a share for $12,500. Their common charges would have included payments on each stockholder's share of the mortgage ($7,500,000 ÷ 200 = $37,500). What they purchased was roughly equivalent to a $50,000 unit had the project been converted into condominium form of ownership. The amount of cash invested was about 25 percent of the free and clear value of what they were buying.

Today, 10 years later, the project may have doubled in value and the mortgage reduced to $5,000,000. The price of the original $12,500 share will now be $75,000. What is meant by doubling in value is that the unit that was roughly equivalent to a $50,000 condominium unit is now equivalent to a $100,000 condominium unit.

If this project were in condominium form of ownership, the original shareholder, or unit owner, as he or she would be called, would sell the unit for $100,000 (See Figure 78). The new buyer could get a new $75,000 mortgage of 75 percent of the value and would need $25,000 cash.

However, because the form of ownership is a cooperative corporation the old mortgage will not be paid off and the new owner cannot obtain a regular $75,000 first mortgage. He or she will either have to pay $75,000 cash for the share in the cooperative or obtain some other type of financing. Fortunately, what has happened in the markets where cooperatives are popular (especially New York City) is that lenders are willing to make special long-term loans at terms similar to mortgages, taking as security the stock in the cooperative. There is also a special HUD program available to insure the loans.

Here is more of the same example:

Present Value of the Project 10 Years After Conversion	$20,000,000
Present Balance on Mortgage	−5,000,000
Stockholder Equity (Value of all Shares)	$15,000,000
Value of Each Stockholder's Share ($15,000,000 ÷ 200) (Again, the value of all the units is equal.)	$75,000

FIGURE 78
ILLUSTRATION OF THREE HYPOTHETICAL 200-APARTMENT
PROJECTS (IN SIMILAR NEIGHBORHOODS
SHOWING THE AMOUNT OF CASH REQUIRED)

	Project A	Project B	Project C
Number of units:	200	200	200
Form of ownership:	Cooperative	Cooperative	Condominium
Total value of project:	$20,000,000	$20,000,000	$20,000,000
Blanket mortgage balance:	$ 5,000,000	$10,000,000	—
Price units offered for sale on market:	$ 75,000	$ 50,000	$ 100,000
Available individual first mortgage:	—	—	$ 75,000
Cash required:	$ 75,000*	$ 50,000*	$ 25,000

* May be partially financed with special long-term loan which is made to cooperative shareholders who pledge their shares as security.

To carry this same example further, another very similar cooperative (see Figure 78) may have elected to refinance its overall mortgage three years ago. Again, let's assume that the value of each unit, if it were free and clear, would be $100,000 and since there are 200 units, all assumed to be equal in value, the total value is $20,000,000. The cooperative corporation obtained a new $10,500,000 blanket mortgage which now has an unpaid balance of $10,000,000. The approximate value of a share in this cooperative would be $50,000 as illustrated below:

Present Value of the Project	$20,000,000
Present Balance on Blanket Mortgage	− $10,000,000
Stockholders' Equity (Value of all Shares)	$10,000,000
Value of Each Stockholder's Share ($10,000,000 ÷ 200)	$50,000

(Again, the value of all the units is equal.)

Many other principles that apply to buying a condominium also apply to a cooperative. When the project is a conversion of an old building, a great deal depends upon the quality of the conversion. Anything that isn't repaired prior to the conversion will become the responsibility of the shareholders after the conversion is completed. The amount of the common charges and special assessments will be greater when the need for repairs is excessive.

SPECIAL DOCUMENTS

There are some special documents that are part of cooperative ownership. In many areas, instead of a sales contract a subscription agreement is used. Often the sale is conditioned upon the buyer being approved by the cooperative board of directors. There are no absolute guidelines about the power of the board of directors to approve or disapprove prospective shareholders, although it is clearly established that they cannot discriminate based on race or religion.

Another unique cooperative agreement is the occupancy agreement. This document (which is also known as a stockholder's lease, owner's lease or a proprietary lease) spells out what space the shareholder will have exclusive use of. It also binds the shareholder to pay monthly maintenance fees and sets forth what percentage of the total maintenance fees of the project will be the shareholder's portion. The formula that determines the percentage of the maintenance fees and other common charges a shareholder pays is set out in the by-laws of the cooperative corporation.

The occupancy agreement also contains the rules and regulations of the cooperative corporation and typically covers such items as pets, storage, use of hallways and use of other public areas. Cooperative buyers should review these regulations prior to buying into the cooperative corporation to be sure that there is nothing in the regulations that would interfere with their lifestyles.

When you buy a cooperative apartment, there is no traditional closing when everything is signed. Instead, when you are ready to take title, you pay the money either to the seller or the cooperative corporation office, or its transfer agent, and you are issued a stock certificate as evidence of your ownership of shares in the cooperative corporation.

As a shareholder you will have an opportunity to help determine the policies of the cooperative. You can vote for directors, attend general stockholders' meetings, serve on committees and run for the board of directors if you desire.

Special tax regulations provide cooperative shareholders with the same tax deductions that condominium owners enjoy. That portion of the monthly maintenance charge that consists of the owner's share of the property taxes and interest on the blanket mortgage may be taken as a deduction on the owner's individual tax return.

ECONOMIC FACTORS

Cooperatives seem to offer one solution to the troubled housing problems of our large cities. In some areas it is unprofitable for landlords to own large apartment buildings, because of restrictions in raising their rents (rent control) and other economic factors. In many cases, such landlords make only essential repairs. There has also been increasing unrest among the tenants who often organize and negotiate with the landlord as a group. It is not uncommon for the tenants, when dissatisfied, to withhold the payment of rents. Landlords who wish to sell under these circumstances have the choice of an outright sale, conversion into a condominium or conversion into a cooperative.

Often the cooperative route is selected because the tenants are already organized. Sometimes they can take over an existing first mortgage or often are able to get a second mortgage for the new cooperative corporation but would be unable to get second mortgages as individual owners if the project were in a condominium form of ownership. Individual tenants can obtain loans when needed (there is a special HUD program to insure some of these loans).

Most cooperatives are conversions of existing apartment buildings in large cities. However, there are some new units and scattered cooperatives in many small communities. In all, there are about one-half million individual units in cooperative-owned buildings. They are a small but important part of our American housing stock.

**For a complete checklist on Cooperative Apartments,
see Checklist 43, page C-93.**

TIMESHARING

Timesharing,[3] also known as interval ownership, allows a resort home (or any property for that matter) to be purchased by several owners, each of whom has the right to the exclusive use of the property for a predetermined period of time each year. The property can be a detached, single-family dwelling, a townhouse, a high rise apartment or other type of property.

For example, 10 owners may buy an apartment in Florida. Each owner shares the cost of the property either equally or based on a formula that is tied to his or her period of exclusive occupancy. (Often as part of this arrangement the apartment will be rented to nonowners part of the year.) The owners each share in the acquisition costs and all income and expenses. In this example each owner has exclusive use of the apartment for two weeks during the peak winter season. Therefore, all the owners would occupy the apartment for a total of 20 weeks of the year. Here are some hypothetical figures that further illustrate this example:

Acquisition cost of condominium apartment		$100,000
First mortgage		75,000
Cash required		$ 25,000
Each owner's share ($25,000 ÷ 10)		$ 2,500
Annual cost to operate the apartment		
Taxes	$3,000	
Insurance	1,000	
Utilities	2,000	
Cleaning service	3,000	
Management and rental expense	4,000	
Repairs	1,000	
Condominium common charges	1,500	
Miscellaneous expenses	1,000	
Mortgage payment	9,000	
Total Expenses	$25,500	
Income from rental during non-owner occupancy 32 weeks	− 20,000	
Total annual operating costs and mortgage payments less rental income		$ 5,500
Each owner's annual share of the operating costs and mortgage payment		$ 550

---

[3] Stuart Marshall Bolch and William B. Ingersoll, ed., *Timesharing* (Washington: Urban Land Institute, 1977).

In this hypothetical example, an owner would pay $2,500 down and $550 per year. In return he or she would receive use of the apartment for two weeks during the peak season.

The popularity of this type of ownership was accelerated when the tax regulations were changed, severely limiting the tax losses available to owners of second homes used for recreational purposes. Previously, it was possible to own a second home in a resort area, use it when it was convenient and rent it out for the remainder of the year. As long as a bona fide effort was made to rent the property in those periods when it was available it could be classified as a business property. If the property lost money, the loss, together with the other permitted deductions of depreciation, taxes, interest and operating expenses, could be taken as deductions on the owner's individual tax return. Tax laws now limit the number of weeks the owner can occupy the premises and increase the burden on the owner to substantiate that the property is really intended to be a business property. Timesharing became a good alternate method of attracting buyers to second home, resort properties.

INVESTIGATE ALL DETAILS

A potential owner of a timesharing residence must take special care to determine exactly what is being bought. If the residence is an apartment in a condominium development (which is the most common situation found for timesharing) a buyer should take all the necessary steps recommended earlier in this chapter for the purchase of an individual condominium.

In addition, it is necessary to investigate the special aspects of the timesharing arrangement. For example, it must be determined if the use of the apartment during the last two weeks of December is considered to be a better time selection than the last two weeks of each November. If so, it must be determined precisely how each owner gets his or her time assignment. Another concern is who the other owners are, especially as it pertains to their ability to honor their financial commitments and how they will care for the apartment during their period of exclusive occupancy.

What the actual costs will be must be carefully explored. It may cost substantially more to keep the apartment in good shape, because of the heavy use by many families, than the original cost projections.

A common area of miscalculation is the rent to be received from non-owners. In our hypothetical example, the unit owner's annual expense would be substantially greater if the property brought in $15,000 per year in rental from a nonowner rather than $20,000 as projected and as illustrated below:

Annual cost to operate the apartment	$25,000
Annual rentals received from nonowners	15,000

Total annual operating costs and mortgage payments, less rental income	$10,500
Each owner's annual share of the operating costs and mortgage payment	$ 1,050

This illustration points out that if the rental income goes down 25 percent, the owner's annual expense doubles.

It is very difficult to estimate the value of timesharing units. Often they are sold by developers with large advertising budgets and highly trained salespeople. When an owner goes to resell, the amount he or she will receive may be substantially different from what was paid. The best evidence of value is what used units in the same development sell for.

TIMESHARING ORGANIZATIONS

National organizations have been set up to help swap the use of timesharing apartments among owners in many locations. For example, an owner of our hypothetical Florida apartment may wish to spend two weeks on the French Riviera instead of in Miami. Through an international timesharing organization, a family who owns a condominium in France makes it available to the owner of the Miami apartment for two weeks in return for being allowed to use the Miami apartment.

Timesharing is new, and there is little long-range experience to go on. It does have unique advantages, however, and for some families seems to offer a good solution to their vacation problems.

For a complete checklist on Timesharing, see Checklist 44, page C-95.

RESIDENCES ON LEASED LAND

When people who have formerly owned a home on the American mainland move to Hawaii they are surprised to learn that many of the properties in the Hawaiian Islands are built on leased land.

Although many of the leases are for 99 years, others are for much shorter periods. To protect the mortgagee, there is sometimes a provision in the lease that subordinates the fee (title) owner's interest to that of the mortgagee (lender). More commonly, the lease gives the mortgagee the right to take over the land rent payments in the event that the owner defaults. The mortgagee usually also has the right to find a new owner who will continue the lease payments. At the end of the lease the improvements become the property of the landowners, who may extend the lease, modifying it to reflect current market conditions.

When comparing the value of one residence against another similar residence in the same neighborhood, an adjustment must be made for any differences in the rental and the term of the lease.

Outside Hawaii there are only a limited number of areas where the concept of residences built on leased land is widely accepted. Outside of these areas, the market may penalize a house just because it is on leased land even though for all practical matters it makes little or no difference to the owners of the improvements.

For a Leased Land checklist, see Checklist 45, page C-97.

RESORT AND RECREATION HOUSES

About one out of every 35 homeowners also owns a second house which is occupied on a seasonal basis and used for recreational purposes. Over two million families now own recreational homes. These homes come in a variety of forms, ranging from expensive mansions like those found in Newport, Rhode Island; Palm Springs, California; and Palm Beach, Florida, to small cottages huddled together close to the edges of lakes, rivers, bays, sounds and oceans.

Since World War II there has been extensive development of resort homes by large builders and corporations who often develop attractive recreational packages. Homeowner associations are very common in resort areas. Often they own or control the recreational facilities or beach. The trend has been away from conventional fee simple ownership toward condominiums and most recently, timesharing (see pages 306 and 317).

Buyers of resort and recreational homes must exercise special care to ensure they will have long-range satisfaction from what, for many families, is a substantial commitment of funds and will require a large amount of the family's free time.

One of the major complaints heard from owners of resort and recreation homes is that they feel under tremendous pressure to use the facilities. For example, take a family who buys a home in a ski resort when their three children are 10, 13 and 15 years old. For a few years everybody is excited about going skiing and are pleased to depart for the resort whenever there are forecasts of good skiing conditions. Three years later when the children are 13, 16 and 18, a variety of conflicting interests develop and resistance develops to too-frequent trips to the mountain.

Earlier in this book we advised that the entire family be consulted about what they want in a house. This advice is doubly true for resort houses. There is nothing worse for a family than to have a teenage daughter or son protest each time the family plans to leave for its second home, basing their complaint on the fact they were never consulted about acquiring the resort home in the first place.

New resort communities are usually well merchandised by trained salespeople using attractive brochures, model homes and other advertising devices. It is only natural that they play up the good points and play down the poor points. For example, in one recent winter there was almost no snow in most of the Western ski resorts. Florida can have some very cold winters and some summers the sun rarely shines in Cape Cod, Massachusetts.

The best evidence of what a resort home is worth is what used homes resell for rather than what new homes are sold for by the developer. The value of resort homes in some areas can be very volatile. They are affected by economic conditions, weather, fuel prices and shortages and sometimes by nearby competitive developments. If you elect to sell your resort home in the future you will be doing so without the aid of the heavy promotions used by the developer. One apparent trend in many areas, however, is for properties on or near water to increase in value faster than properties without the water amenity.

Recent changes in IRS regulations about deducting the expenses and losses incurred from the ownership of second homes have also affected the value of many of these homes. If you plan to rent the home out part of the time, you should be sure you understand the IRS requirements in order to classify it as a business property on your tax return. Generally speaking, in this situation you will not be able to occupy the house more than five weeks a year.

For a complete Resort and Recreation Houses checklist, see Checklist 46, page C-99.

HOUSING FOR THE ELDERLY

A substantial amount of housing for the elderly is in rental apartments and other multi-unit buildings, a category of housing which is beyond the scope of this book. We are concerned here with the many single-family units, townhouses, condominiums and other forms of housing where the occupant can be the owner.

Some housing developments become housing for the elderly just because the developers elect to market the project to this segment of the population. Up to now the courts have upheld the legality of restricting sales in a development to senior citizens, who are usually defined as couples without children living with them, where one of the couple is over 55 years old. Some developments are designated housing for the elderly primarily so the occupants can receive government subsidies towards rent or mortgage payments.

Housing that is truly developed for the elderly should be specially designed. Often the units can be smaller than they would be otherwise.

There should be emphasis in the design and layout upon ease of egress, safety features and carefree maintenance.

True housing for the elderly may be more expensive, if compared on a cost per square-foot basis, than conventional housing. The higher costs are attributed to higher fire rating of materials used in construction and the costs of special equipment and design features. These higher costs are often offset by the smaller size of the residences.

Condominiums and cooperatives are very popular with senior citizens because they offer homeownership with less concern about maintenance and upkeep. The group social life that is often a part of condominium living also is appealing. And since people who are retired have substantial spare time, recreational facilities are very appealing to them.

The current capital gains tax laws permit people over 55 to sell their homes and buy less expensive homes more suitable for their needs without paying capital gains tax on all or part of the profit realized on the sale of their original homes. This profit can then be invested to produce income. However, this is a one-time only allowance.

Low and moderate income potential buyers often look for government subsidized projects. Unfortunately, demand for these units usually exceeds their supply. Since there is often a waiting list of many years to get into subsidized projects, it definitely pays to plan ahead and make the necessary applications as far in advance as possible.

Some families have the economic freedom to choose alternate geographic locations. They should study those climates and locations that seem to have qualities that they desire. If at all possible, a family should try a new location for a year or more before buying a retirement home there. Many people who have vacationed in particular places find it quite different when they move there permanently.

For a complete checklist on Housing for the
Elderly, see Checklist 47, page C-101.

MANSIONS

With many extra rooms for recreation, entertaining, guests and servant quarters, mansions were usually individually designed to reflect the special tastes of the owner, whose goal often is to enhance family prestige. A few mansions are still being built today. These are large houses often on large tracts of land with ample rooms for entertaining large groups of people and usually with rooms for guests and live-in servants.

Most mansions, when they are sold, are converted into some alternate use such as multi-family dwellings, schools, health institutions, monasteries, offices, and research laboratories.

HOMEOWNERS' ASSOCIATIONS AND PLANNED UNIT DEVELOPMENTS (PUDs)

HOMEOWNERS' ASSOCIATIONS

Many homeowners' associations organized prior to World War II often were in coastal communities or around lakes and other recreational facilities. The developer would deed the beach or lake front to the association which in turn would maintain and control it for the benefit of the association members. Associations were also formed to maintain and guard exclusive subdivisions that had common grounds, parks, courts and limited access. Often a major function of the association, in addition to maintaining the common facilities, was to hire guards to keep uninvited guests off the association's property.

Some of the typical functions of the early homeowners' association were:

1. Maintain commonly owned land, beaches, courts, pools, clubhouses, golf courses.
2. Collect rubbish and garbage, remove snow, sweep streets.
3. Provide and maintain sewer disposal systems and water supply systems.
4. Provide police and fire protection.
5. Provide lifeguards on beaches and waterfronts.

Often associations tried to exercise substantial control and did so by enforcing the private covenants and restrictions that gave them the right to approve the transfer of title or rental of property and to approve the style and size of new buildings. When these controls concerned race, religion or national origin they became unenforceable.

PLANNED UNIT DEVELOPMENTS

After World War II there was a demand for better use of our land and less restrictive ways for developers to create subdivisions. The Planned Unit Development (PUD) concept became more popular. At the outset, most of these would dedicate the extra land in a development to the community for use as parks and open space. This did not work out well, as the community did not want the responsibility of caring for the land and the individual property owners did not want to lose control of the land near their homes. A much better alternate arrangement was for the developer to dedicate the land to a homeowners' association. With the advent of the condominium the same concept was adopted for maintenance for the common land, recreational facilities and also the common areas of the buildings, which are all part of a typical condominium development.

Planned Unit Developments are a zoning alternative. They represent a different way to use land. Housing built in PUDs can be in fee simple or condominium ownership. The housing may be in the form of single-family residences, townhouses or multi-family buildings. PUD developments may also include commercial and industrial areas. In essence the PUD concept permits the grouping of housing units on lots smaller than usually allowed for residential construction. As a trade-off for being allowed to build on smaller lots, the developer sets aside some unused land to be dedicated to the community or to a homeowners' association. PUD developments can provide for flexible designs for streets, landscaping and public facilities that are impossible in conventional neighborhoods.

A Planned Unit Development has an owners' association which maintains and controls the commonly owned land. Sometimes the association's function is broadened to ownership and control of the recreational facilities. The association also may contract to perform services for the individual property owners such as ground care, exterior building maintenance, Cable TV or TV antenna, etc. The directors of the association also have the right to make the rules as to how the common areas will be used and to assess individual owners for their fair share of all the expenses they incur in behalf of the members of the association. It pays to investigate the owners' association of the PUD into which you plan to buy. Most of the same problems exist as exist with owners' associations in condominiums. You should be certain that the rules and regulations of the association are compatible with your lifestyle.

For a complete checklist on Planned Unit Developments, see Checklist 48, page C-103.

MOBILE HOMES

The pre-World War II trailer (the forerunner of today's mobile home), of which there were about 250,000 in 1936, was typically six to seven feet wide and from 12 to 27 feet long. The interior space was between 100 and 180 square feet. Until 1940 annual production was about 10,000 units and these were used primarily by vacationers or working people temporarily located in out-of-the-way places. Many had neither bathrooms nor kitchens.

Today's mobile homes are only distant cousins to the "trailers" of the 1930s and 1940s. Today most homes are at least 14 feet wide and there are models being sold that are 24 feet wide and 68 feet long which have three bedrooms and two baths. They contain modern appliances, built-in furniture, ample cabinets and counters and such exotic features as sunken living rooms, wet bars, imitation fireplaces and sunken bathtubs. Outside they are embellished with carports, porches, storage sheds, enclosed patios and imitation roofs that make the mobile home look more like a conventional house.

The trailer, as it was known in the early 1940s, was used by the government during World War II to house defense workers. After the war the acute housing shortage which lasted until 1951 laid the foundations for the mobile home industry as we know it today. New manufacturers were producing what then became known as mobile homes at a rate that peaked at 85,000 units per year. In 1955 the larger 10 and 12-foot wide models were introduced which were too large to be towed by an automobile.

The next 10 years was a period of major change in the industry and by 1965 the emphasis was on stability rather than mobility. Mobile homes have accounted for a high percentage of all the new single-family homes being built in the U.S.

Since June 15, 1976, all mobile homes built have been required to conform to the national standards established by the U.S. Department of Housing and Urban Development. These mobile homes all must have:

- Two exterior doors remote from each other
- An egress window in each sleeping room
- Smoke detectors wired to the electrical system with audio alarms outside of each bedroom
- Tie-down systems (strapping cable devices designed to tie the unit to an anchoring system so it cannot move in heavy winds or flooding)
- An electrical system that conforms to the National Electric Code (same as for on-site built houses)

The HUD standards also require an increase in the fire retardant rating for the surfaces of the furnace and water heater and the area adjacent to the cooking range.

If you buy a unit that was built before June 15, 1976, there is a good possibility that it will not have all of these features that HUD feels are essential for safe living in a mobile home.

Today mobile homes (or manufactured housing as the industry would like them to be known) are an important part of the American housing stock. At its peak in 1972 and 1973 over 500,000 units were produced each year, dropping to the current level of under 400,000 units a year, which still represents a substantial percentage of all the new housing units built each year. There are about 5,000,000 mobile homes in use today. The industry predicts that the nearly 300 mobile home manufacturers in 1980 will again be producing over 500,000 units annually. In 1979 there were over 18 million people living in mobile homes.

The manufacture of a mobile home is very different from the manufacture of conventional housing. It takes months to build a conventional house, but it takes hours to build a mobile home. Of the total cost of a conventional home over 50 percent is usually labor. The average labor factor in a mobile home is about 11 percent. In a period when the average cost to build a conventional home is around $35 per square foot, the cost to build a mobile home is under $15 per square foot.

In addition to offering low initial costs, mobile homes also have lower maintenance costs. Many mobile homes come complete with furniture. The monthly payments on that portion of the mobile home loan that financed the furniture is probably a lot less than what the payment would be for a similar amount of furniture purchased from a furniture store. This is so because the length of the mobile loan is usually longer than the typical installment loan contract used to finance the purchase of furniture.

Some people buy their own lot, build a concrete slab (called a pad), provide for utilities either by digging a well and installing a septic system or by connecting to municipal utilities and have their mobile home installed on the site. These mobile homes then become very similar to any small home on a similar lot.

MOBILE HOME PARKS

Many mobile homes are located in parks which range from barren lots with 12 or more homes per acre to elaborate mobile home parks with beautiful landscaping and many recreational facilities. Available social activities range from none at all to parks with almost continuous social activities for their residents.

Privacy also varies from park to park. A well laid out park with three mobile units to an acre provides a lot more privacy than a typical condominium apartment. On the other hand, a park with 12 or more units to an acre all lined up in rows provides little privacy.

Some parks are designed for senior citizens without children and are very quiet and peaceful. At other extremes are parks next to major highways, railroad tracks or in commercial or industrial areas that contain hundreds of mobile homes jammed together. When these parks attract young families with many children and pets the concept of peace and quiet is unknown.

The process of choosing a mobile home and a park should be similar to the process of choosing any other type of housing. The family should reach a consensus as to what region and communities within the region it wishes to locate in. It is important to remember that fewer than two percent of the mobile homes are now moved within 10 years of their being located on their first pad. It is a mistake to think that you can easily move a mobile home you find in one spot to a mobile home park at another location that suits your family better. With today's manufactured homes, this is expensive and cumbersome.

Select the best park you can afford. Unless you have no choice, you should avoid old, small parks. Generally they are very crowded and seldom do they provide the services available in newer, larger parks (of course there are some exceptions and a few small, old parks are excellent places to live).

A good mobile home park has paved streets, landscaping, street lights, underground utility lines and laundry facilities in addition to substantial recreational facilities.

Mobile home parks often have extensive rules and regulations similar to those of condominiums and cooperative apartments. There may be restrictions on pets, children and parking for guests.

There are sometimes also special regulations that are unique to mobile home parks such as what is permitted on the outside of the home, the age of mobile homes permitted to locate in the park and restrictions on freedom to sell a mobile home. It is important to check the regulations to be certain these will not interfere with your lifestyle.

Another unique feature of the mobile home park is that you pay rent for your site. Rental costs for park sites range from $45 to $125 per month.[4] Unlike the common charges of a condominium or cooperative apartment, which can be raised only to offset higher operating costs, the rent in a mobile home park can be increased at the whim of the owner(s) of the park. Therefore, just as when you move into an apartment you need a lease to protect yourself against arbitrary rent increase, so you need a lease for your site in a mobile home park. The need for a lease is more acute in a mobile home park in the event there is an excessive rent hike or a failure to provide satisfactory services. The cost of moving your mobile home is usually much greater than the cost of moving your furniture to a new apartment. In addition to monthly rent some mobile home parks charge a substantial one-time entrance fee. If you move you may also have to pay one of these again.

WHAT TO LOOK FOR IN A MOBILE HOME

If you are considering buying a used unit, the best place to start looking is in the park or parks you have selected as good places to live. In any given park you may find that some units are being offered for sale by the park owner, some by real estate salespeople and some by individual owners. You should explore all these sources for potential sellers.

Unlike conventional homes over the past few years, mobile homes still go down in value as they got older. A study done by the Texas Real Estate Research Center showed that when a mobile home is five years old it is generally worth about 60 percent of the initial price and thereafter depreciates at a rate of about 10 percent per year.[5] Other studies have shown that with average maintenance the typical mobile home depreci-

---

[4] *REALTORS® Review,* May, 1978.

[5] George Bloom and Henry S. Harrison, *Appraising the Single Family Residence* (Chicago: American Institute of Real Estate Appraisers, 1979).

ates approximately 10 percent the first year (based on wholesale value) and between five percent and six percent per year thereafter.[6]

One guide to the value of a used mobile home is the valuation books that are prepared by national publishers who collect sales data from mobile home dealers all over the country. These books are similar to the books car and truck dealers use to appraise used vehicles. They are a useful tool but they have some important limitations. The basis of their figures is averaging sales prices in many different mobile home parks. Built into this concept, however, is the assumption that mobile homes can easily be moved from one park to another while the fact is that fewer than two percent are moved and moves are costly and difficult. Actually, like a conventional residence, the value of a mobile home will vary from location to location. You may be well justified paying more for a mobile home located in the park of your choice than buying a similar unit in a less desirable park.

The older the mobile home is, the more careful you must be in making your selection. The first thing you should do when you are considering a used unit is to determine from its documentation when it was built. As we previously explained there may be a distinct difference between a unit that was built prior to June 15, 1976, and one built after that date because of the national standards that went into effect on that date. If possible, try to purchase a unit built after that date. If you elect to buy a unit constructed prior to June 15, 1976, you should inspect it to determine if it has the features listed on page 325 which are now required to be built into every unit being constructed. If the unit is missing any of these items, you should explore the possibility of having them installed and find out what the cost would be.

Another problem to consider with used units is that in the event you want to move the unit to another park you may be severely limited to where you can go. Many mobile home parks will not admit a unit that is over five years old.

Unlike a five-year-old conventional house which is considered to be relatively new at that age, a five-year-old mobile home is considered to be an old unit. In a unit of this age there is a substantial possibility that some of the mechanical systems and structural parts will soon be in need of repair.

When you buy a used unit you should obtain advice about the value of the unit from someone who will consider the value of the location as well as the published value in a national cost service. In many areas there are qualified appraisers who can perform both of these services.

Do not buy a used mobile home without the aid of an attorney who is familiar with the laws that apply to title transfer of mobile homes in the

---

[6] Bloom and Harrison

area. These laws vary from area to area. There is often a question as to whether the mobile home is considered real estate or personal property. This definition will determine what type of documents will be needed to transfer title and what steps need to be taken to assure that you get a clear title to the mobile home you are buying.

FINANCING

Another factor to be considered in buying a used (or new) mobile home is how it will be financed. Sometimes it is possible to assume the payments on an existing loan. This is especially desirable if the existing loan is at lower than current interest rates and you have sufficient cash available to pay the difference between the amount outstanding on the existing loan and the purchase price of the unit.

One of the factors that has kept the mobile home industry from developing even faster than it has is the problem encountered in financing. Recent studies show that about 25 percent of all mobile homes are paid for in cash. This high percentage is attributable in part to the many mobile home purchases by retired families who have sold their homes and have sufficient cash available to purchase their retirement mobile home. However, a substantial portion of the rest of the mobile homes purchased are also bought with substantial down payments. This is especially true for used units.

VA and FHA insured mortgages are available for the purchase of mobile homes. However, the amounts of the loans are limited and usually the mortgage term is limited to 12 years. Conventional mortgages are available in some areas that run as long as 15 or 20 years but these often cannot be obtained on used units. All things being equal, the rate of interest on a mobile home loan tends to be higher than the rate of interest on a loan on a conventional house.

Buying a new mobile home presents some different problems. It is hard not to be influenced by the attractive decorating you find inside some of the model units being offered for sale. But expertly conceived interior decorations are not the best criteria for selecting the best-built unit. (This is no different from being unduly influenced by the beautiful furnishing in model homes.)

Some of the quality features to look for in a mobile home are thick walls, good insulation, thick roof and floors, large capacity water heater, good heating and air conditioning, wood cabinets and trim rather than cheap plastic, doors and windows that are well weather stripped and carefully caulked.

If you choose to buy a new or used unit from the mobile home park owner where you intend to locate, this should give you a substantial bargaining advantage when it comes to rent and lease terms. Often it is to your advantage to pay a little more initially to buy from the park owner because in the long run what you will save in rent and other costs may far outweigh the initial additional cost. It is only human nature for a park owner who has just sold you a unit on which a profit has been made to treat you better than if you had just come into the park and started paying rent.

Finally, a word of caution about buying a mobile home as an investment rather than a place to live. Based on what has happened in the past, mobile homes (with some exceptions) have not made very good investments as compared to other forms of residences. Spokespeople for the mobile home industry say this will change in the future, but there is no way to determine if their prediction is accurate.

For a complete Mobile Homes checklist, see Checklist 49, page C-105.

MODULAR AND PREFABRICATED HOUSES

In theory it should be cheaper to build substantial portions of a house in a factory-like setting than on a site. However, to date the number of failures has far outweighed the successes, except in the case of the mobile home industry (see previous section). Mobile home builders can produce a house for less than half of the cost to produce a house of similar size on a conventional basis, when compared on a cost per square-foot basis.

MANUFACTURED HOUSES

The mobile home industry has officially changed its name to the manufactured housing industry. Much of the products it is turning out are looking more and more like modular housing. A single unit mobile home that is 14 by 69 feet (a very popular size being manufactured today) offers 966 square feet of living space. Now there are larger multi-sectional models known as "Double Wide" being made which are transported to the site separately and bolted together, making housing units that are 28 feet wide and 69 or 70 feet long. These units contain almost 2,000 square feet of living space. These larger units are usually called manufactured houses rather than mobile homes.

It is not hard to project into the future when many developers will buy tracts of land and erect on them large numbers of manufactured houses. It will not be fair to classify these developments any longer as mobile home developments. What they are in reality is modular housing.

According to the Manufactured Housing Institute a major reason more modular home development has not taken place is local zoning regulations that limit their development. The MHI argues that with all mobile homes being built to specifications set by HUD, the industry now actually has a national building code.

PREFABRICATED HOUSES

There is another segment of the manufactured housing industry that has been successfully selling its products in limited numbers for many years. These companies produce houses with unique styles such as log cabins, barns, contemporary style, etc. Such houses are usually shipped in less of a state of complete assembly than the product being shipped by the mobile home manufacturer. Often they do not contain any mechanical systems, appliances or furniture. Usually, however, they require a full foundation.

Once these units have been erected it is hard to tell them from conventionally built houses. Often they are marketed on the basis that they save money, but actually most are probably bought for their convenience, style and speed of availability.

MILL MANUFACTURED PARTS

The third way manufactured housing is creeping into the housing construction industry is through mill manufactured parts. For example, builders can buy whole wall, ceiling and floor sections that are mill assembled using panelized construction systems. Trusses, windows and doors, fiberglass bathrooms, kitchen cabinets and counters, staircases, fireplace mantels and a variety of other parts are available in various forms of preassembly to builders. The use of these preassembled parts makes the home builder more and more like the automobile assemblers in Detroit. Modular houses and houses that are wholly or partially prefabricated should continue to become a larger segment of all new homes being built.

The construction of conventional single-family houses has changed less than almost any other major item manufactured in this country. The efficiency of the assembly line and mass production methods should be applicable to housing, and the manufacturers of modular and prefabricated homes are trying to do this. Speed of construction is an important reason for this system of producing housing units. The on-site assembly of a factory-produced modular or prefabricated home is often as little as a few days. Another advantage is that the owner of an individual lot can choose from complete model houses. This is not possible of a house constructed from a set of house plans unless the builder has a similar house available for inspection. Also, lot owners may feel more confident they will get a house that is truly similar to the model they have seen when they buy from a large, established company rather than buying from a confusing set of plans and specifications.

If you decide to buy a modular home that a builder has erected on a site, you should be sure you are getting the advantage of the cost saving to the builder. Although it is impossible to predict the future based on the past there is a possibility the house will not appreciate at the same rate as conventionally built housing.

If the prefabricated house you buy is not erected, you need a good general contractor to supervise its assembly. Some prefabricated home companies encourage the home buyer to act as the general contractor. This makes the prefabricated house appear to cost less than a comparable house of standard construction. However, do not act as your own general contractor unless you have the experience, time and an even temperament. Most people who try to do so are sorry in the end.

For a checklist on Modular and Prefabricated Houses, see Checklist 50, page C-107.

HISTORIC HOUSES

Many houses in America are of major historic significance. Many other houses built before the turn of the century and much earlier in the United States are still in habitable condition. Some of these are considered to be part of the country's national heritage because of special architectural design or other historic note, and public interest groups have formed in many parts of the country to see that such houses are preserved.

Houses designated as historic landmarks are governed by special legislation, at either the national, state or local level. Such legislation is concerned primarily with the control of the exterior appearance of these structures. Most of these regulations provide for an administrative body which is charged with approving or disapproving any proposed exterior renovation. In the long run, such regulations and restrictions may enhance the value of such properties, although some property owners feel that these restrictions limit their ownership freedoms and thereby decrease the value of their property.

To encourage the preservation of historic homes, special tax legislation has been passed that benefits property owners who give historic easements (restrictions which restrict and control exterior and interior renovations). Most states have historic preservation organizations qualified to accept historic easements. The National Trust for Historic Preservation operates in the same capacity on a national level.

The advantage to the property owner for granting such an historic easement is twofold. He or she may be permitted to deduct the value of the easement as a gift for income tax purposes. And some communities have special provisions in their property tax laws that lower the property taxes when historic easements have been granted.

Location is very important in determining the value of historic houses. For example, consider two reasonably similar historic houses in a community. One may be in a neighborhood that is part of a redevelopment program. A neighborhood association is being formed, houses are being renovated, exterior appearances are being controlled and the sidewalks and streets are being rebuilt. The other house is in a neighborhood that is reaching the end of its economic life. The exteriors of nearby houses are in need of repairs and paint, several houses have had serious fires and are unrepaired, the area is primarily tenant-occupied, and many nearby homes are for sale although few sell. The first house usually would be more valuable than the latter. A house of major historical importance, however, may be less affected by its neighborhood than a nonhistoric house in the same area. But even historically important houses usually cannot completely escape the effect of their neighborhoods.

For a Historic Houses checklist see Checklist 51, page C-109.

COLONIAL REPRODUCTIONS

Americans have always liked antiques and styles that recall our past. The same feeling prevails about Colonial-style homes. There are not nearly enough original Colonial houses to satisfy the demand, and those that are available are often in the wrong location.

As Colonial and other historic houses have gained popularity, a revival of interest in authentic reproductions has occurred. The advantage of this is that the owner hopes to enjoy the amenity value of the old style without the inconveniences associated with an older home.

Colonial reproductions can be built by developers just as any other conventional house. Some new homes just have a touch of Colonial styling. Others are the result of extensive research and look very similar to the authentic homes of the past. Log cabins are a good example of this trend. Several companies have developed a complete set of materials for building reproductions of log cabins and are successfully marketing their products. Modern plumbing and heating systems are among the benefits of choosing a reproduction rather than an original. In Santa Fe, New Mexico, there are many excellent reproductions of adobe houses constructed with synthetic adobe materials. Other examples of reproductions of regional historic styles exist throughout the United States.

HOUSEBOATS

An owner of a marina on Long Island Sound where there are over 50,000 pleasure boats told us that on the best day of the season less than 10 percent of the boats in the marina leave the dock. What this points out is that most people use their boats while they are moored or docked to live and entertain on.

If that is the primary purpose of your boat you may be able to better accomplish this goal with a boat designed primarily to be a good place to live on rather than to be seaworthy in a gale. Today's houseboat closely resembles a mobile home. The principal difference is that it floats.

Today houseboats range in price from as low as about $25,000 for a used, not very large and not very fancy model, up to hundreds of thousands of dollars for some of the floating palaces that are moored for miles along Collins Avenue in Miami Beach, Florida.

An important consideration in buying a houseboat is finding a suitable place to moor it. In desirable locations the moorings are often very scarce. As with a mobile home, a houseboat moored in a desirable spot with a long-term lease on the mooring is worth more than a similar boat without a desirable mooring that has to be relocated.

Buying houseboats is not for the novice. At a bare minimum, your experience should include living on one for an extended period of time. Experienced boat-owners who think they would enjoy houseboat living often find that long exposure to motion, moisture, insects, lack of privacy, lack of storage space, etc., overcome the amenities.

If you do decide to buy a houseboat, you should make the sale conditional upon it being inspected by a boat surveyor (a boat appraiser and inspector) and obtaining a lease on a mooring of your choice.

SOLAR ENERGY HOUSES

Every civilization since the beginning of time has recorded in one form or another its recognition of the importance of the sun. The Egyptians, Mayans, Etruscans, Greeks—back to those peoples who are recorded in the Old Testament—all of them and more paid homage to this force through their art, on coins and often in religious rites. Although the sun and its relationship to their "universe" was little understood, it was fully respected. In fact, a total eclipse of the sun was viewed with awe and not a little fear.

As knowledge of the solar system evolved so too did dreams of the sun's potential uses. Foremost among them was (and still is) the harnessing of this vast storehouse of power as a source of energy for our civilized needs. The sun's endless energy can be converted into electricity by modern windmills and hydroelectric dams, many of which are already operating very efficiently here and in various other parts of the world.

Referring to "solar energy" as something new is naive. Actually, solar energy is the earth's oldest and most basic source of energy. Absorbed and converted by plants, shrubs and trees into food and fuel for all humans, its energy has converted wood and plant remains into the fossilized residuals which are our prime sources of fuel, namely coal, oil and natural gas.

The sun shines somewhere in the world every day. In that sense it is "free." In that sense, you won't get a bill for your sun tan or for the warmth the eager flowers turn their faces up for.

But collecting, storing and using the sun's energy is far from free. Whether the expensive equipment and adaptations in house design necessarily involved in home solar usage can compete with the cost of conventional fuels still remains to be seen. Indications are that fuel prices will rise, and solar equipment costs will come down. After the initial cost, the sunshine is free. When it's available!

According to the government, solar energy appears to be in the forefront of the possible energy systems which will have the power to heat homes and buildings and hot water systems. The subject of photovoltaics, which means simply that solar energy can be used to generate electricity directly by photovoltaic "solar cells," is mentioned here only in passing, as the method probably will not be feasible for a long time.

However, solar homes are here, now; they are "alive," and while not thoroughly "well," they have a favorable prognosis according to the government. In essence, the two chief advantages of using solar energy—its abundance and total lack of pollutants—have already been proven and found moderately successful. The chief disadvantage of a home solar energy system is its initial cost. However, this may not be an inordinate amount to the homeowner for very long if oil and gas prices keep rising. The cost of solar energy may indeed become competitive with those traditional sources of our home heat and hot water.

ADVANTAGES AND DISADVANTAGES

Before you consider building or buying a solar home or modifying an existing dwelling, you will need to explore its advantages and disadvantages to you and your family's lifestyle. When you are about to invest anywhere from $2,000 to $19,000 you will want some answers. Bear in mind at all times that while there are many solar systems installed and working successfully right now, there is *not a single one* that we know about that provides more than 75 percent of the family's heating and hot water needs. Therefore it is imperative that you have a back-up auxiliary heating system, such as a standard furnance fueled by oil, coal or gas, or electricity. Solar heating does not mean just installing a lot of collecting panels on the roof of your house. It is a *total* system which, in design and construction, combines the solar and back-up equipment in the production of affordable heat and hot water for your home.

Incorporating the solarization equipment into the design and planning of a new home is the key factor to efficiency, lower initial cost *and* appearance. Attractiveness is not so easily achieved in an existing house.

There are some who feel that a solar home will have a higher resale value as conventional energy prices increase. Long-term savings is another so-called advantage which is debatable. At present, the indications are that solar energy heating and hot water systems will be less expensive than gas, oil, or electricity in the long run. You will have to examine carefully the trade-offs between the high installation and equipment costs and the potential savings you *might* realize due to decreased use of conventional fossil-fuel. It bears repeating that the higher the conventional fuel prices go, the greater the possibility that you will save eventually with a solar system.

For the homeowner, there are four major applications of solar heat:

- Heating the hot water supply year-round
- Heating a home during cold weather
- Heating swimming pool water in season
- Heating an indoor swimming pool year-round

All four, but most likely only two or three usages may apply to you. What really should precede any personal applications is some specific definitive information on "HOW DOES IT WORK?" and "HOW CAN IT WORK FOR ME?"

HOW A SOLAR ENERGY SYSTEM WORKS

A solar energy system works like this: The heat (radiation) from the sun is absorbed by metal panels (collectors) installed usually on the roof of the house and ultimately stored, usually, in the basement. This storage process may or may not be accomplished with the assistance of a transfer medium which can be either water or some other liquid, or air or some other gas. The liquid or gas is forced through the collectors where it is heated, then carried to storage where it is distributed to the living spaces of the house. (With liquids, a pump and pipes deliver the liquid to the house spaces. With air, delivery is directly from the collectors or from storage via a forced air system.)

Storing the collected heat still leaves a great deal to be desired for at least two reasons. With fossil-fuel (oil-gas-coal) millions of BTUs (British Thermal Units, a measurement of heat) are stored for use in a very small "package" and released on very short notice by various means of combustion, "on demand." Try that with the sun! It's impossible, since with solar energy we have to store the BTU *after* release, and this requires bulk—lots of bulk in the form of panels, pipes, tanks, bins and various other equipment. Unlike the bulk problem, which one day may be resolved, the second major deficiency of using the solar energy system will always remain a certainty: the sun only shines for half a day and sometimes it chooses not even to be that generous. There could be no collection in the storage tanks for days while that "lucky old sun" is roaming around heaven all day somewhere other than over your house.

Well-insulated storage that holds more than one day's usage and back-up equipment are therefore necessary.

Basically, there are two solar energy heating systems (both work on the *same* principle of collection and storage as just described): active and passive. See Figures 79 and 80 for illustrations.

The active system uses collectors and has automatic controls to move or transfer the heat to storage via air or water, then to the living space. This system, while more complex than the passive one, can be used in either new or existing houses and lends itself to remodeling. You should upgrade *all* insulation—storm doors and windows and weather stripping—and put into practice every other energy conservation method which will tighten up your house simultaneously. *And* (this is a big one), unless your house has a good southern exposure, you probably should not consider going the active solar route at all.

A passive system uses the wall of the house or a separate stationary structural wall as both collector and storage medium. Movable wall panels or flaps are often used to direct the heat throughout the living space of the house. The south side of the house in a passive system should have lots of double glazed windows—or a glass wall—vinyl coated, if the budget allows. A "greenhouse" effect can be achieved which is aesthetically appealing as well. *All* glass should be double glazed with inside triple glazing on windows which are sunless from November through March. Draperies with sealable thermal liners, insulated shutters and other similar devices can be used effectively to contain heat. There should be insulation in any solid walls and in the wall between the "greenhouse" and the living space. Black painted drums of water or some type of masonry floor will absorb the sun's heat during the day and release it slowly at night.[7]

You can best incorporate the passive system when you are designing a new house. This requires meticulous placement of your house on the site, using the correct north-south orientation, and incorporating principles of landscaping as protective barriers. For peak efficiency an architect would not draw in any windows on the north side at all. The use of concrete in floor and walls (to absorb heat and then release it) will undoubtedly be part of the architecture. Still another approach to the collecting and storing of solar heat is through water bags on the roof which are covered with movable insulation and uncovered to welcome the sun's rays.

In both systems, active or passive, heat is stored two ways—in a tank or bin of gravel or rocks. In the space heating system that uses liquid as the transfer medium (from collectors) the storage system is usually a large tank (or tanks) which can hold from 600 to 1,000 gallons. The tanks

---

[7] Construction details for this greenhouse-type of system are presented in the book *Solar Room* (Charlotte, VT: Garden Way Publishing).

FIGURE 79
ACTIVE SOLAR ENERGY SYSTEM*

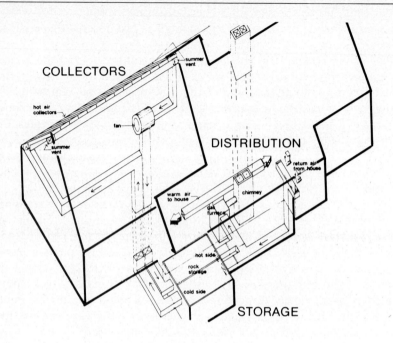

* Note: This is one possible active solar energy system; there are many possible variations.

Source: *Solar Heating and Cooling Demonstration Program—A Descriptive Summary of HUD Cycle 3 Solar Residential Projects* (Washington: U.S. Department of Housing and Urban Development Office of Policy Development and Research, Summer, 1977).

FIGURE 80
PASSIVE SOLAR ENERGY SYSTEM*

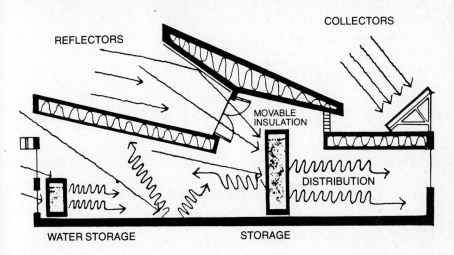

* Note: This is one possible passive solar energy system; there are many possible variations.

Source: *Solar Heating and Cooling Demonstration Program—A Descriptive Summary of HUD Cycle 3 Solar Residential Projects* (Washington: U.S. Department of Housing and Urban Development Office of Policy Development and Research, Summer, 1977).

may be in the basement, underground or outside the home. Bear in mind that liquids are heavy, which dictates the placement of the tanks—but wherever, they take up a *lot* of space.

For example, to store hot water from at least one day of the sun's largesse, you will need one to two gallons' storage space for every square foot of collector area. There are seven and one-half gallons of water in one cubic foot of space. A relatively small tank of 120 gallons occupies a space two by two by six feet and weighs 1,200 pounds! Since each person in a household uses an average of 20 gallons a day (excluding dishwasher, etc.) you can figure what your family's requirements might be.

In the system which utilizes air as the heat transfer medium, the heat is usually stored in a specially constructed bin of large gravel or rocks. Again, a problem of bulk. With this in mind, the bin has to be about two and one-half times as large as a tank used in the water system in order to store the *same amount* of heat. The "equation" is one-half cubic foot of gravel/rock for every square foot of a collector on the roof.

Estimates of the cost of a combined solar heating and hot water system for a single-family unit range from $5,000 to $19,000 according to the U.S. Department of Housing and Urban Development, (HUD), depending on variables like house style, climate, and design type and the size of the system needed. Many people who are interested in using solar energy in their homes have opted for the system designed to provide hot water alone, to begin with. The domestic hot water system is relatively small, requiring only simple installation, and in most cases can be connected to the present system. HUD estimates that this will cost about $2,000. (See Chapter 9 for information on solar hot water systems.)

If you are considering just the solar hot water system, you may obtain a helpful booklet entitled, *Solar Hot Water and Your Home.*[8] In it you will find these suggestions:

1. Get independent engineering advice first.
2. Get all performance claims in writing.
3. Ascertain who will service the system after installation. Find out if the system has a full or limited warranty and what parts, labor and services it covers.
4. If possible, check on reliability by visiting someone who is using the system. Select a firm whose reputation for knowledge and expertise in handling problems responsibly is well established. Some distributors have failed to honor warranties or to fulfill maintenance contracts, but worse, are so inexperienced that they have installed sys-

---

[8] *Solar Hot Water and Your Home* can be obtained from the Consumer Information Center, Dept. 605F, Pueblo, Colorado, 81009.

tems improperly. You COULD be stuck with a lot of equipment that doesn't function, even if the sun is shining.

INCENTIVES AND INFORMATION

With several thousand solar-heated homes on record in the United States and probably more which are being experimented on in a limited "do-it-yourself" style, there are currently at least 14 states which give homeowners a tax break for installing solar heating systems. In a program authorized by HUD, the agency can give approval for a $400 grant towards setting up a solar system in your house.

With all such innovative programs, there are bound to be discrepancies and a lot of loose statistics. Backers of the solar loan bill which has been approved by the U.S. House of Representatives say there are 500 or so companies in the field who are "starved for capital to expand production and services."

The National Solar Heating and Cooling Information Center (Box 1607, Rockville, Maryland, 20850), established by the Environmental Research Development Administration and HUD, will be pleased to answer any questions on solar energy for your home. Anyone—homeowners, contractors, community planners, zoning officials, architects, building code officials, bankers and others concerned with housing—may avail themselves of this service. Before a consumer can qualify for a HUD grant, the state must approve both the manufacturer and the system itself. State inspectors check the system to make sure it has been properly installed. The problem is that everyone is a pioneer at this point.

In some states, solar investments will not be subject to property tax for several years, and it is hoped that the resale value of such property will have been improved simultaneously. You can also get credits on your state and Federal income taxes to offset the cost of solar heating.

The 1978 Revenue Act provides for a nonrefundable credit for installations of solar (wind and geothermal) energy equipment in a principal residence of 30 percent of the first $2,000 and 20 percent of the next $8,000 spent on approved equipment. The maximum total credit is $2,200. This credit is effective as of April 20, 1977. The credit for equipment purchased between April 20, 1977, and December 31, 1978 is taken on the taxpayer's 1978 tax return. According to the present legislation the credit terminates as of December 31, 1985. Until that time, the credits are taken on the tax returns of the year in which the equipment is purchased.

The field of solar energy remains largely virgin territory, but it is beginning to arouse a great deal of curiosity and interest. Magazine and newspapers are devoting much space to the subject.

Solar energy is not quite ready to take over—we still have to cope with partial daytime sunshine, clouds, short winter days, wind, rain and "acts of nature." And as in any new field, interest ranges from skepticism to hostility to intense curiosity.

For a complete Solar Energy checklist, see Checklist 52, page C-111.

EXPERIMENTAL HOUSES

The largest number of experimental homes are solar homes with passive or active solar systems which were covered in the previous section. There are a variety of other types of experimental homes, using new materials such as plastic, metals, fiberglass, foams and other nonconventional building products.

Other experimental homes use both new and old designs. There is a renewal of interest in "cave" homes and other designs that are primarily below ground level. These designs in some ways resemble the original homes our forefathers built at Jamestown in 1607.

The value of an experimental home depends on the validity of the experiment and often the fame of architect, contractor and others involved in the experiment. As they did with mansions, many builders of experimental homes are using the home as a vehicle to express their individual ideas, feelings and creativity. For instance, the Geodesic Dome has received a lot of publicity as a house because it was developed by R. Buckminster Fuller.

Buying an experimental home is an unusual event. The buyers should be attracted to the experimental home because they are interested in becoming part of the experiment. For example, a disciple of R. Buckminster Fuller may wish to live in a Geodesic Dome home. Someone interested in the whole concept of inground living may elect to buy a below-ground home.

If you are considering building an experimental home, you should do so for the same reasons. You should keep in mind that unless you or the architect are famous, or the experimental home is uniquely successful it probably will not be worth as much as a conventionally built house of the same cost. In general, builders and buyers of experimental homes should be prepared to lose money.

BARRIER-FREE DESIGN

In a society where such great emphasis is put on being young, healthy, slim and unflawed, we have been discreetly ignoring that large segment of our population which is often none of these—the physically handicapped. It is estimated that one out of 10 persons (of *every* age) has limited mobility, and one out of seven has that physical disability permanently. Improved medical techniques which provide longer life and some mobility where it was not possible previously and the ever-growing population of older people increase those statistics each year.

While it is not within the scope of this book to be concerned with barrier-free architecture in publicly owned buildings or large commercial and office buildings that are privately owned, the passage of local, state and federal legislation to make these buildings accessible to the handicapped has in effect called attention to the plight of the handicapped in the private home.

Suffice it to say that the Federal Architectural Barriers Act of 1968 which states that "any building constructed in whole or in part with federal funds *must* be accessible to and usable by the handicapped," was a major breakthrough. This piece of legislation was strengthened by the Rehabilitation Act of 1973, and in that same year a survey of state laws to remove barriers indicated that nearly every state in the union had statutes on architectural barriers. Today, all do.

The handicapped citizen has benefited immeasurably by the research conducted by government organizations, veterans' rehabilitation centers, colleges and by architects who design hospitals and similar facilities. Nearly everything implemented in public buildings can be adapted and modified for the single-family home.

How ironic it is that only a few years ago, thousands of dollars may have been spent on the psychiatric care of a handicapped person, when a mere few hundred dollars might have been better spent on carpentry to adapt a home and remove some barriers which could provide that person with some mobility. More often than not, when physical barriers are removed, mental barriers disappear simultaneously. Everyone needs a degree of independence and comfortable self-esteem—a feeling of participating within the home and of being a part of society without.

In earlier chapters it has been emphasized that whether you buy or build, you should select a house which suits your family's needs. This is especially important if there are handicapped people in your family.

To get some idea of what a wheelchair-confined housewife (or anyone "keeping house") has to contend with in just the simple task of doing dishes, take a chair and place it in front of the sink. Sit in it. The first thing you'll discover is that you can't sit very close to the sink because there are cupboard doors underneath, and even if you turn side-ways, it is equally awkward. The second barrier is that the sink is too high. Your arms and shoulders would be weary within minutes, even if you could reach everything including the faucets, which you probably couldn't. This is, as the expression goes, just the tip of the iceberg.

Those individuals with restricted knee, ankle or hip movement who must wear prosthetic devices such as artificial legs, leg braces, back braces or comparable aids, find it difficult, hazardous and sometimes impossible to use steps with a nosing overhang, as illustrated in Figure

81. They can however, maneuver safely and with a minimum of discomfort and difficulty using the alternate type of step illustrated.

Below are some critieria for a freer, more accessible environment. The list is by no means complete. You may be able to improvise and adapt some of these ideas beyond what has been suggested. Bear in mind that these are criteria for structural measurements only. No attempt is made to suggest standards for appliances.

EXTERIOR

- The garage door should be a minimum 14-feet wide.
- An electric door opener is an asset.
- Entrance from the garage or carport should be covered.
- If the entrance is not at ground level, this entrance should be ramped in a gentle slope not exceeding a one-foot rise every 12 feet, (about eight and one-third percent) or a five-degree slope.
- If the ramp exceeds 20 feet there should be a five-foot landing every 20 feet.
- Ramp should be a minimum four-feet wide.
- Handrail should be mounted on at least one side of the ramp at a height of 32 inches.
- Threshold of door should be flush or have no more than one-half inch differential.
- The doorway should have an unobstructed view and should be a minimum 32 inches wide. The door should open easily, with the strength required of a person who has lost partial functioning of the arms.
- The landing adjacent to the door should be five foot square. It should extend at least one foot on either side of the door, so that the person can enter without rolling backward.
- The ramp should be constructed on nonskid material.
- Easily manipulated doorknobs or lever type handles should be installed at a height of no more than 36 inches above ground level.
- The door should have a sturdy kickplate.
- If the ramp is not covered, the entrance should be well sheltered by a roof overhang and should be well lit.

INTERIOR

- Once inside the home, there should be an avenue 32 inches wide for wheelchair passage to the handicapped person's room or to an area where the person is usually situated.
- For the ambulatory, steps and stairways should have rounded nosing and sloping risers, as indicated in Figure 81. Each step should be no more than seven inches high and no less than ten inches wide.
- Stairs should have a handrail (or two) 32 inches high from the tread at the face of the riser.

FIGURE 81
TRADITIONAL AND RECOMMENDED STAIR DESIGNS

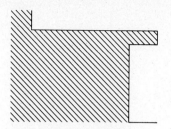

**TRADITIONAL STAIR DESIGN
WITH NOSING OVERLAY**

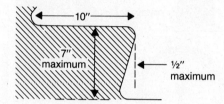

RECOMMENDED STAIR DESIGN

FIGURE 82
BARRIER-FREE DESIGN

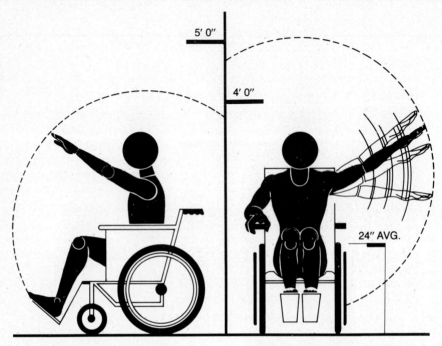

**5' 0" AVERAGE MAXIMUM REACH
FOR ADULTS IN WHEELCHAIRS**

**4' 0" MAXIMUM HEIGHT FOR
SWITCHES, LEVERS, HANDLES, ETC.**

- Floors should have a nonskid surface. Carpeting should be low-pile as deep shag is difficult to maneuver. Small scatter rugs are a hazard as are too highly waxed floors.

FURTHER AREAS OF CONCERN

- Wall height of lights, switches and controls (for heat, draperies, etc.).
- Doorways at least 32 inches wide.
- Floors same level, thresholds flush.
- Kitchen sink and oven of appropriate height.
- Space under sink with a minimum width of 28 inches for person's legs.
- Safety frame around toilet.
- Space in bathroom to make complete 180 degree turn in wheelchair; grab bars; height of toilet set at height of sink; unglazed tile floor; nonskid bath surface.
- In the bedroom, dressing table of correct height; closet with sliding doors preferred. Lower clothes rods to suit individuals.
- Some lowered counter space and storage.
- A minimum of five feet between counters and walls for ease in turning wheelchair.
- Plenty of toe space under cabinets—six inches deep and nine inches high suggested.
- Installed faucets and spray to one side of the sink rather than in the back, and a stove whose controls are in front and do not have to be reached across the burners from a sit-down position.

Other physically impaired people such as the deaf and blind are often overlooked when we think of barrier-free design but they surely have long been frustrated by the many barriers in their environment. Consider that the deaf person needs a visual counterpart of some kind to warning bells and sirens. The deaf person can't hear the alarm of a smoke detector, or even a telephone ring as most of us can. Therefore flashing lights should be connected to these devices. This is just one small area of concern which is vital to the welfare of the deaf. Blind people also have needs for special warning devices.

For a complete Barrier-Free Design checklist, see Checklist 53, page C-113.

CHAPTER 17
BUILDING OR BUYING —
A NEW HOUSE

In a typical year about 1.5 million new, single-family houses are built and sold, representing about 35 percent of all the houses sold during the year. What this means is that about 35 percent of all the people who buy single-family houses buy a new house. As you can see, if you want to own a new home instead of a used one, you are far from alone.

In this chapter we will focus on only those items that apply uniquely to new homes.

We will cover the various ways you can obtain a new house, how to deal with architects and contractors, how to decide what work to do yourself, what most people want in a house and how to cut costs.

FIRST STEPS IN BUILDING A NEW HOUSE

One of the surest ways of getting more free advice than you'll ever need for a lifetime is to announce at a family gathering or cocktail party that you have decided to build your own house. Be prepared for comments which will run the gamut from "you've got to be crazy" to "the best of luck" uttered with awe and respect.

Pay heed to none of it, as well intended as it may be. You'll have enough problems; solving them will be your concern once you are determined to take this step. The most expedient way to begin is by calling a family powwow with those people who will share your concern and your home. List everything you wish to have included and discuss each idea as you jot them down. Listen to everyone and consider no detail frivolous or ridiculous. After all, the very idea of building your own home implies that you can have specific amenities, tailored to the needs and desires of your family. Some may be found to be too sophisticated for the budget, but now is not yet the time to approach that problem. Meanwhile, get excited and be optimistic. For a brief while, at least on paper, nothing will be too expensive or too insignificant for your home. You will soon establish your priorities.

If your family is oriented to outdoor life, which means acreage for gardening, several pets, entertaining at barbecues, areas for sports practice and games or a pool or tennis court, you very well may have to sacrifice some interior facilities for those priorities. Perhaps you prefer all your comforts, conveniences and amenities to be interior-centered, in keeping with your preference for a more private existence. A sensitive stereo, banks of books or a custom kitchen in which you can create gourmet dishes may fulfill all your needs.

With this preliminary planning fairly fixed in your family's collective "mind," you are ready to embark on your adventure.

The information in Chapters 4 and 5 will help you select a suitable location for your home. When you have selected a site be sure that your purchase contract contains a provision permitting you to make the necessary tests to ensure the soil is suitable for waste disposal and has good bearing qualities.

Before we get further into details, here are the basic pros and cons of building.

ADVANTAGES OF BUILDING A NEW HOME

- You have a house which is of your own design.
- You have the excitement and satisfaction of creating a house which is unlike any other.
- You can adapt the house to your needs and lifestyle.
- Choice of location.
- Choice of materials.
- Landscaping is done to your taste and to meet your requirements.

DISADVANTAGES OF BUILDING A NEW HOME

- Frequent cost overruns.
- More expensive than an old or used house with the same number of square feet.
- Architect's fee may run as high as 15 percent of the total cost.
- Unknown factors in digging foundation such as water and poor bearing.
- Risk of creating a house tailored so well to fit your family that it may be difficult to sell eventually even at cost, let alone profit.
- General maintenance costs, once the house is no longer brand new, will be higher. Grounds work will cost more.

WHAT MOST PEOPLE WANT IN THEIR HOUSES

One of the advantages of designing and building your own house is that you can have exactly what you and your family want in it, subject only to the limitations of your budget. Knowing what many people prefer in their homes may provide you with a guide to making some decisions. Here are some highlights from a national survey on housing.[1]

Class of House. The overwhelming majority of those surveyed said they would prefer a detached single-family home.

Basement. Most people prefer a house with a full basement. This desire is strongest in the Northeast and weakest in the West and South.

Type of House. Almost twice as many people preferred a single level house to either a split level or two-story house. Less than 10 percent said they preferred a one and one-half story house.

Bedrooms. The majority want three bedrooms, except in the $65,000 to $85,000 price category where four bedrooms were preferred. Over that price range, again the preference was for three bedrooms. Four bedrooms were also desired by the 35 to 44-year-old buyers and buyers with large families (less than 10 percent of the families surveyed).

Bathrooms. Two bathrooms was the choice of slightly more families than those desiring one and one-half bathrooms and two and one-half bathrooms. Few would be satisfied with one bathroom or indicated a need for three or more.

Garage. Most people want a two-car garage.

Eating Area. There was little preference indicated between a combined kitchen and family dining room, full dining area for table and six chairs and an area for a small table. However, few people preferred a counter top with stools for eating or a food preparation area only without eating space.

Cost Reducers. Most people indicated that the best way to hold the cost down on a house was to design it so that it can be expanded at a later time, if so desired. They also indicated they approved of the use of standard designs which save money because of uniformity of construction.

General Space Desires. With the exception of very low-priced houses, the majority of people want separate dining rooms and separate family rooms. On the other hand, only a minority wanted a separate den/guest room, an enclosed or screened porch or a patio.

Appliances. A substantial majority wanted a home that included a range hood with a fan, a built-in stove or range, a built-in dishwasher and a garbage disposal in the kitchen sink. Interestingly, except in the most expensive houses, less than a majority wanted a refrigerator, clothes

---

[1] Summaries are based on national averages. There are significant geographic and demographic variances. Excerpted with permission from 1978 National Consumer/Builder Survey on Housing, *Professional Builder and Apartment Business Magazine*, December, 1978. All rights reserved.

washer, clothes dryer, trash compactor, microwave oven or food mixer center.

Exterior Finish. Brick and masonry are by far the most preferred exterior finishes, being more popular than all the other exterior finishes combined. Running far behind in overall preference are aluminum and other metal sidings, stucco, wood siding, wood shakes and shingles and vinyl siding. In the South more than three-quarters of the buyers prefer brick. However, in the Northeast and West more than 60 percent prefer some other type of siding.

Roofing. Asphalt shingles are the national favorite and are three times as popular as wood shakes and shingles. Aluminum roofing and tiles appeal to just a limited segment of the market.

Windows. Aluminum has surpassed wood in popularity for new homes.

Living Room Flooring. Carpeting is the big favorite. Even in the very expensive homes less than one-third of the buyers prefer the second favorite, wood. Practically nobody wants tile in the living room.

Bedroom Flooring. Again, carpeting is the big favorite with wood flooring wanted by less than 15 percent.

Kitchen Flooring. Vinyl sheet or vinyl tile are still the most preferred flooring with everything else running far behind.

Bathroom Flooring. Preference is about evenly split between ceramic tile and vinyl tile or sheets. Carpeting is preferred by about one-third of the people who acquire attached units.

Family Room Flooring. Carpeting is now the favorite covering except in low-priced homes.

Living Room Walls. Painted walls are preferred by the majority over all other kinds of walls. Less than 20 percent prefer paneling, wallpaper or fabric.

Bedroom Walls. Again, painted walls are the preference of the majority but about a third of the people want wallpaper or fabric.

Kitchen Walls. Paint shares the consumer preference with wallpaper and fabric. Brick and masonry, ceramic tile, mirrors and paneling run far behind.

Bathroom Walls. Ceramic tile is the narrow favorite; wallpaper and fabric are also preferred by about one-third of the consumers.

Family Room Walls. Two-thirds of those surveyed prefer paneling and less than one-third paint, wallpaper, fabric and all other covering combined.

Living Room Ceiling. A majority of buyers in all categories preferred painted ceilings. Wood beams were also preferred by about one out of five. About 10 percent preferred ceiling tile in low-priced homes.

Bedroom Ceiling. A large majority of people prefer painted bedroom ceilings. The preferences for ceiling tile is substantially less. Only a few surveyed prefer anything else.

Kitchen Ceiling. Again, a big majority prefer painted ceilings, a small group prefer ceiling tiles and only a few anything else.

Bathroom Ceiling. Almost the same preferences as for bedroom and kitchen ceilings.

Family Room Ceiling. Beams are desired, especially in the higher-priced homes. Painted ceilings are also popular.

Kitchen Preferences. Natural wood cabinets are the overwhelming favorite. So are stainless steel sinks, which are preferred two to one over enamel and procelain sinks. The majority also prefer sinks with one faucet handle. Colored appliances are preferred over white two to one.

Bathroom Features. The following items, listed in order of preferences, are features people feel should be included as standard items in bathrooms:

- Medicine cabinet
- Linen storage cabinet
- Exhaust fan
- Vanity with one bowl
- Tub/shower door
- Colored fixtures
- Safety features

Less than half of those surveyed felt the items below should be standard items. They are listed in descending order of preference:

- White fixtures
- Vanity with two bowls
- Bathroom heater
- Dressing area
- Mirrored wall
- Skylight
- Bidet
- Sauna
- Whirlpool

Other Features and Products. Here is a list, in general order of preference, of other features and products people would like to have included with the home they are buying:

- Fireplace—A majority of all classes of buyers want a fireplace. Over 90 percent of people who buy expensive homes want them
- Insulated windows (double glass)
- Smoke and fire detectors
- Storm windows and screens (except in West and in expensive homes)
- Patio and sliding glass doors (most wanted in the West and in attached units)
- Heavy duty security locks (most wanted in attached units, the West and in high value homes)
- Air conditioning—Just about half of the people surveyed wanted air conditioning. The demand ranged from about 75 percent in the South and high-priced homes to less than 20 percent in the Northeast
- Power attic ventilator—Only a majority of the people in the South want this item
- Garage door opener—The demand ranged from 55 percent of the $100,000 home buyers to 3.7 percent of the low-price buyers. Overall, less than 20 percent wanted the openers.

The balance of the list showed a low percentage of demand for:

- Clock-controlled thermostat
- Water softener
- Power humidifier
- Central vacuum system
- Intercom system
- Electronic air cleaner

ARCHITECTS AND CONTRACTORS

The best way to create the house you desire is to select a good architect to design it and help you get the house built.

THE CONTRACT

It is always best to have a written contract with the architect that clearly spells out what the architect is going to do for you and how you are going to pay for the services you receive.

Some architects are willing at first to be paid a fee by the hour, the amount to be applied later to the total contractual fee. Others prefer to sign a contract at the outset before any work is done. Contracts vary with the situation and the people involved. The only thing that you should insist remains firm is that an architect is paid *only* for the work actually done. These payments should occur at set times during the building process, as agreed to in the contract.

HIRE AN ARCHITECT EARLY

Whatever your agreement and financial arrangements are, the important element is that the architect be in on the very conception of your brainchild. Often the architect is brought in too late. It would be prudent to hire your architect at that moment you start looking at a lot and prior to actually putting cash on the barrelhead for it. Since architects are trained in every facet of building, literally from the ground up; they can tell you if the house you have in mind is going to fit the topography or not. You may have to change your house design or select another site with which it is compatible. Architects are experts at recognizing drainage problems and they may call in landscape architects to assist them. They know how to best situate your house on the site and will suggest ideas long after you thought you had included everything.

Architects perform a myriad of services, not the least of which is running interference with your contractor. As a less subjective third party, the architect is able to deal with the contractor in an atmosphere free of emotion. Together, they will position themselves to guard your interests against inferior work and code violations. And they will save you the inconvenience of dealing with local regulatory officials and the attendant piles of paper work.

In choosing an architect, it is best to rely on the advice of knowledgeable people you trust. The best recommendation is from someone who has worked with a particular architect and is satisfied with the results. Also, look around at homes which were designed by specific architects; question the owners about quality of work and services rendered.

WORKING WITH THE ARCHITECT

Once you have selected an architect you will work together translating the wishes of your family into a set of house plans. (Refer to earlier chapters in this book which explain in detail the elements of house design and construction.)

Be sure to allow the architect sufficient time to do a good job. It does not pay in the long run to rush the making of house plans. Remember, too, that the house is supposed to be for all the members of your family to enjoy. Hopefully, you have told the architect what your family desires in a house, based on the family meetings you had at the beginning of this process. Let everyone look at the plans in the early stages. It is much easier to make changes early rather than later on.

If money is a consideration (and it almost always is), items are going to have to be assigned according to priority. With the architect, develop a project budget. Based on your desires and the available budget, the architect can present you with alternatives as to what can be included and what will have to be left out in order to stay within the budget.

Family consensus is the best way to arrive at this decision. If a consensus is not possible, one member of the family must take the responsibility for making these final decisions. The architect should be notified, preferably in writing, who has the final authority to make decisions. Serious problems arise when the architect and contractor blame problems on the fact that they received instructions from various members of the family whom they *thought* were authorized to make decisions.

CONTRACTORS

Often the architect has worked successfully with a contractor in the past and recommends this contractor. You should not select a contractor solely on the architect's recommendation, however. It is best to ask for a list of other houses the contractor has built and also for an introduction to the owners. You should benefit tremendously by what these owners tell you about their experiences.

When a contractor has been tentatively selected talk to him or her and discuss what you have in mind and how much you wish to spend. A good contractor will be able to judge whether it is possible to build the house you desire within your budget.

DUTIES OF THE ARCHITECT AND CONTRACTOR

If you have not signed the contract with your architect because of prior arrangements, now is the time to do so. Once the lot is purchased, the architect will begin to draw up your plans and specifications. A standard form contract between owner and architect is published by the American Institute of Architects, outlining the architect's duties and responsibilities, method of payment and other responsibilities which are yours. The two of you may wish to write additional, individualized provisions into the contract.

Many of the duties have already been delineated (if not performed already) and others will be referred to as they become pertinent. Basically, the architect will now start on the line drawings of your house. Upon completion of that phase, the architect will be in a better position to give you an estimate of costs. If costs are really excessive for your budget, the architect and contractor will help you get nearer your mark with suggestions as to substitute materials and methods of cutting down but not necessarily "out." Then it will be back to the drawing board. Should you be fortunate enough to find their estimate to be less than you plan to spend, congratulations! But unless there is a large discrepancy there, don't try to spend it by adding wildly to your plans. It is doubtful that even *one* single house has ever been built without a cost overrun, however slight, in the entire history of building. Be inclined to feel that you're not going to be the first exception!

After the initial estimate, more detailed plans will then be drawn, these in consultation with the contractor and/or building supply houses. If you are still within your budget and your requirements are being met, you will give the architect the go-ahead on the final working drawings. Once drawn these final plans and specifications are for the builder's use.

Instead of using the contractor who has been working with you and the architect during the process of drawing the plans you may wish to put the job out to bid. If this was your intention from the beginning you should tell the contractor who has been working with you right from the start what you are planning to do. Many contractors are still willing to work with you during the planning stages under these circumstances. They know from past experience that if they are familiar with the job and have had input which allows them to select the materials and designs they are most familiar with, then there is an increased possibility of them being the low bidders. They also know that even if they do not come up with the lowest bid, they still may be selected for the job if they have developed a good relationship with the owner and architect.

Your architect has probably already advised you that three bids are the very least you should ask for from builders, and five are better. There is a standard contractor's form which many builders use and which, with the help of your architect, should expedite your discussion with potential contractors.

Several weeks should be adequate time to allow the bidders to check out costs, subcontractors and availability of time and materials. The contractors will also have to study alternates to some of your more ambitious plans which they recognize will cause an overrun of your budget. Remember that the American Institute of Architects publishes a standard form which outlines the duties and responsibilities of each of the major parties in a house-building project—owner, architect and contractor.[2]

ATTORNEYS, BONDS AND INSURANCE

If you have not already engaged the services of a lawyer, this is a good time to do so. It is not wise to sign a contract for the construction of a house without using a lawyer.

Your lawyer and architect have probably already recommended that you have your contractor post a completion bond. In all probability you will have to bear the cost of the premiums but it will be a small price to pay for peace of mind, knowing that you are guaranteed the contractor's completion of your contract (or the money to have it completed). This will also get you a speedy resume of the contractor's character and reputation. If a bonding firm turns the contractor down, you probably should too. There are some good small contractors who can't get bonds, but you substantially increase the possibility of serious trouble when you use an unbonded contractor. (Before signing anything, of course, you, your lawyer and your architect should go over the contractor's certificates with "magnifying glass" scrutiny.)

From now on, you and your builder will have certain joint responsibilities as well as individual ones. Although not one nail has yet been driven you should take steps immediately to insure against all hazards

---

[2] American Institute of Architects, 1736 Stockton St., San Francisco, CA 94133.

and catastrophes from fire and vandalism to the furies of the weather. Confirm with the insurer that this insurance also covers the contractor and any subcontractors and the materials on your premises. Ask your builder to present a certificate of coverage for the builder and any workers under Workmen's Compensation. Other necessary certificates will cover liability on vehicles, property damage and public liability. You and your lawyer may think of other protective measures, peculiar to your situation. *Now* is the time to discuss, agree on them or discard them.

SELECTING A CONTRACTOR BY NEGOTIATION

An alternate method of selecting a contractor is by negotiation. One or more contractors are invited to negotiate with you and your architect. Often part of the negotiation process includes suggestions from the contractor on how to cut costs.

SIGNING THE BUILDING CONTRACT

Now, you are ready to get down to serious building business. Sign a contract with your builder in the presence of your lawyer and architect. Have your lawyer check *all* contractual documents before signing anything. You may feel perfectly confident to handle these transactions yourself, but there are situations in which you shouldn't take a step alone. The escrow clause will demonstrate this.

For your own protection, it is advisable that your final payment to the contractor be held in escrow until your final acceptance of the house. The escrow agent is a third party entrusted by you and the contractor. Often the architect acts as the escrow agent. This is usually done without charge. Or you may wish to have your attorney hold the money and documents in escrow for you.

"Who" is not nearly as important as "why." If for any reason your contractor is unable or refuses to complete the bargain, the funds withheld in escrow will never pass into the contractor's hands. Thus you will be assured enough money to hire someone else to complete your home to your satisfaction. You might even have enough left over for legal action against the contractor if there have been contractual violations.

BUILDING FROM STOCK MAIL ORDER PLANS

One way to get a set of house plans is to buy a set of stock plans by mail. Many magazines and newspapers regularly carry advertisements showing a wide variety of plans. Many of the companies who sell these plans produce large, very informative catalogs of their plans. There are even monthly magazines that are primarily devoted to describing the various plans that are available. Plans can cost from about $25 to $200.

Some people buy plans and then work with an architect and modify the plans to their individual needs. The fee the architect charges should be much less than if the work was started from scratch. Not all architects are willing to use somebody else's plans, but in most communities you should be able to locate architects who do not object to doing this type of work.

One of the major objections to using mail order plans is that they do not take into consideration your special needs or the special conditions found on the particular lot you are planning to use. The argument advanced is that no two families' needs are the same and no two building lots are the same. The use of an architect to make whatever modifications are necessary goes a long way to overcome these objections.

After you have selected a plan that you like (and modified it to suit your family and your lot) you can order extra sets (which will also have to be altered) and go through the process of either putting the job out to bid or trying to negotiate a satisfactory price with a selected contractor.

If the price you first receive by negotiation or bid is too high, do not despair. This often happens. You should then get together with the contractor and architect (if you are using one) and discuss what might be done to reduce the cost.

REDUCING COSTS

Cost reduction starts with careful planning. If you have been proceeding as outlined in this chapter you probably are carefully planning what you propose to do.

The next step is to eliminate any expensive "frills" that have crept into the design. Many of these can easily be eliminated without sacrificing any significant amount of living comfort or efficiency.

Another way to cut the cost down is to do some of the work yourself. We will discuss this alternative in more detail towards the end of this chapter.

It is a mistake to think that steps you take towards economical construction necessarily mean inferior construction. On the other hand, don't be tempted to permit poor workmanship and the use of shoddy materials. In the long run this will just prove to be false economy. What you will save initially will shortly be lost on high maintenance and repair costs, plus the diminishment of the pleasure you and your family will receive from the home.

SITE COSTS

A major factor in the cost of a house is the site on which it is located. The ideal site is one that has good drainage and slopes gently away from where the house will be located.

The drainage of the lot, if natural, will forestall the necessity of costly storm sewers, expensive drain tiles around the footing and under the basement floor, and extra costs to prepare an absorption field for the septic system. If the lot has special drainage problems, it may be necessary to construct a more expensive foundation, put a sump pump in the basement and provide other extra waterproofing measures.

UTILITIES

The availability of public utilities including gas, water, electricity and municipal sewers substantially reduces the cost of the total project. It costs thousands of extra dollars to drill a well together with its pump and possible water softening system, but it is relatively inexpensive to hook up to a public water supply.

Septic systems, even under the best of conditions, are expensive to install and maintain. When the soil conditions are poor, extra initial charges and maintenance costs will be incurred.

Other site problems that can add to overall construction costs are rocks which will have to be removed, long electric lines, long driveways, sidewalks, difficult landscaping problems and a filled lot that will require extra deep footings.

CONFIGURATION AND SIZE

The next element to consider is the basic configuration of the house. Exotically shaped houses, while appealing to some, are a lot more expensive to build than houses of simple shapes. A simple rectangular one-story house or a box-like two-story house is the least expensive to build. Simple gable roofs are the most economical. Flat and shed roofs are also initially economical to build but they tend to develop problems sooner than other roof styles.

In most parts of the country basements are considered to be an economical way to add low-cost space to a house. If they are dry, well lighted and have direct access to the outside, they are more useful. Attics also add low-cost space to a house and dormers further increase the usable space.

Porches are costly because they often are used only seasonally.

A good way to reduce the cost of a house is to reduce its size. A good way to do this is to have rooms serve multipurposes. For instance, the kitchen, dining room and family room can be combined into one area.

Often by carefully reviewing the overall layout you can reduce the amount of circulation area (hallways) and even improve traffic patterns.

KITCHEN

Almost 10 percent of the cost of a typical house is spent in the kitchen area. When surveyed, people complain more about their kitchens being too large rather than too small. The key to good kitchen design is compact size and ample counters and storage cabinets. Standard one-piece oven-range units are least expensive and do not require cabinets or counters. Keep the work triangle under 22 feet (see Chapter 6).

PLUMBING

One way to save money on plumbing is to group it together. In two-story houses this means putting one bathroom above the other. Consider the possibility of one well-planned, compartmented bathroom with the tub, shower, toilet and lavatories separated from each other, rather than building two separate bathrooms.

It is usually cheaper to locate laundry equipment in the basement, attic or garage rather than in the more expensive living area.

CLOSETS

Careful placement and design of closets can save money. It is cheaper to store infrequently used items in the basement or attic. Deep closets waste space. Walk-in closets should be wide enough to provide storage on both sides of the aisle.

MATERIALS

It is false economy to buy cheap materials. Especially do not compromise on the plumbing fixtures, electric switches, heating and domestic hot water systems and well pumps. Cheap lumber and paint will end up being costly in the long run. Try to limit the variety of materials being used. Interestingly, most award-winning house designs have only one exterior wall covering and usually the covering is a kind that does not require painting.

New wall sheathing materials are available that have very good insulation properties. This is an economical way to increase the insulation of your house.

Hardwood floors are attractive but very expensive when they are compared to other floor materials. It is wasteful to cover a hardwood floor with a carpet.

There is a tremendous range in the cost of floor tiles. Many moderately priced tiles have good wearing qualities. What you often pay for in high price tile is design rather than wearing quality.

It seems that almost everyone wants to have a fireplace. Unfortunately these are expensive. Adding raised hearths, fancy mantels and expensive brick and stone all increase the cost. Prefabricated fireplaces, chimneys and flues are less expensive than custom-built ones.

It takes a skillful mason to make a custom-built fireplace that will work satisfactorily. When you give out your building contract you should have in it a provision that you have the right to approve the fireplace mason. Before you approve anyone, check on the mason's reputation for being able to construct a fireplace that works.

The secret to keeping costs of doors and windows down is to use standard factory-assembled units of standard sizes that come all ready to drop into rough openings in the framing.

OTHER COST-SAVING IDEAS

The National Association of Home Builders Research Foundation, Inc., in a project sponsored by HUD, has developed "The Optimum Value Engineered Techniques." [3] Known as OVE, this is a complete collection of related cost-cutting ideas, arranged in a whole sequence of planning, engineering and construction techniques that complement each other. However, it is not necessary to adopt the whole system in order to use some of its cost-saving techniques. Here are some highlights from this manual of items not already covered in this chapter:

- To save on materials costs, use two-foot, or better still four-foot, modules in planning your home. This means that the outside dimensions should divide evenly by either two or four. An ideal outside wall dimension would be 4, 8, 12, 16, 24, 20, 30 feet, etc. A 17-foot wall will waste a lot of material.
- Use a 24- inch on-center framing system if it is permitted by the building code in your area, not only for the walls but also for the floors and roof.
- Require that the design of your footings take into consideration the soil conditions and the size of your house. Many architects and contractors do not know how to design footings, so they specify maximum sizes which are unnecessary and expensive. The same is true of foundation walls.
- Consider using new framing techniques that eliminate wood sills on top of the foundation walls. The joists bear directly on the foundation and are tied to the foundation with perforated strapping or anchor straps embedded in the foundation and nailed to the side of the joists. These new systems also call for the elimination of the band joist, the use of joists laid in an in-line arrangement with off-center splices, glue nailing the subflooring and the elimination of cross bridging.

The OVE system also suggests a variety of techniques for building the walls that will save money. For example, it recommends the elimination of extra joists under non-load-bearing partitions because five-eighth-inch or three-quarter-inch plywood floor is strong enough to support these non-load-bearing partitions even if they fall right between two joists that are 24 inches on center.

Two ways to eliminate some wall studs are suggested. One is at the corner of two walls where it is claimed that two studs will do the job of three just as well. The third stud is only used to back up the drywall and this can be done much more cheaply with metal drywall clips, plywood cleats or a one-inch by three-inch wood strip nailed to the back of the

---

[3] The complete system is described in the OVE manual, *Reducing Home Building Costs with OVE Design and Construction,* available from the National Association of Home Builders Research Foundation, Inc., Rockville, MD 20850

inside corner stud. The other place to save a stud is where an interior wall runs into an exterior wall. The extra stud is not needed structurally. It is used to attach the walls together which can be accomplished cheaper by the use of a mid-height nailing block between the studs of the exterior wall together with the use of drywall clips, plywood cleats or lumber strips.

The OVE manual also recommends that the use of some headers can be eliminated. It points out that the purpose of a structural header is to carry roof or floor loads over an opening in a wall. Therefore, if there is no load no header is needed. An example would be in an interior non-load-bearing partition or even in the exterior end non-load-bearing walls of a truss-roofed house. When windows are placed between studs that are 24-inches on center you eliminate the need for both headers, jack studs and cripple studs. Where headers are needed they can be made out of plywood that is glue-nailed to the framing at the opening. The width and thickness of the plywood is determined by the size of the opening and the load it will carry. Often you can make this type of header out of scrap material found on the site.

Ceiling heights are recommended to be seven-feet, six inches, for a variety of reasons. The OVE manual claims this height creates a better scale, especially in smaller houses, and makes the rooms seem larger. However, the house is smaller (in cubic footage) and therefore cheaper to heat and cool. In two-story houses, the lower ceiling means one less step in the staircase and a reduction of total stair length. This leads to other space savings in the design as well. The OVE manual goes into other complex advantages and disadvantages of this ceiling height but concludes that the advantages and cost savings outweigh the disadvantages.

Another cost-saving suggestion is that roof trusses be used and that the roof design be a rectangular gable shape. Trusses often come preassembled from the mill. They are made of light pieces of lumber called chords and fastened together with a variety of different types of inexpensive metal fasteners. They are easy to erect so the house is enclosed quickly.

Other suggestions for economy are the reduction of trim detail, reduction in the use of moldings and natural finished hardwood trim. Later in this chapter we will cover additional cost saving ideas.

MAKING CHANGES

It is almost inevitable that as you watch the house being constructed you will want some changes. Changes are more costly for the builder to make than many people often realize. When you want a change, discuss it with the contractor and get a price to do the work. If you agree, then authorize it in writing. Many contracts call for all changes to be authorized in writing. However, this procedure is often not followed and many agreed-upon changes are authorized verbally.

Later a dispute arises about a change which the owner claims was not authorized or the price not agreed upon. The owner says this particular change was not authorized as called for in the contract. Unfortunately, this often will not work when the builder is able to claim successfully that a pattern was established of authorizing changes verbally even though the contract called for written authorization. Changes are by far the major cause of problems between owners and contractors.

FINISHING

Until now you have been paying your contractor at fixed intervals and, as the house nears completion, you owe the final payment. Hang on to it with a tight fist until you have checked and rechecked everything. You have to get the certificate of occupancy from the contractor who gets it from the local building inspector. Once you have that, you can move in. It is a myth that a contractor so loves his or her creation that there is a reluctance to complete it. If you find this to be true, obtaining the certificate of occupancy is a quick and painless way of severing the "Pygmalion romance."

Sit down with the contractor and architect and reexamine all the warranties and written agreements. Be sure all specifications have been met and that the warranties are in effect—those which apply to the built-in appliances, furnace, air-conditioning system, automatic garage door opener, a sauna and other warranteed structural components such as roofing.

The contractor should also present you with a warranty on the house itself. The usual agreement is for a period of one year during which time the builder is legally responsible to fix or replace that which needs fixing or replacing.

Finally, secure from the builder a written guarantee that all workers, subcontractors and supply houses have been paid and that there is a signed waiver of liens from all of them, lest they claim later not to have been paid. At this point you have probably spent more money than you ever dreamed you would when you first conceived the whole idea. The last thing you need now is a lien against you for an "unpaid bill" which you assumed had been paid.

Assume nothing. When you and your lawyer are completely confident, then, and only then, make your final payment to the contractor.

ACTING AS YOUR OWN CONTRACTOR

A way to reduce the cost of your new house is to act as your own general contractor. You can use the plans of an architect or stock mail order plans or a combination just as you would if you were to have the house built for you by one contractor with whom you either negotiated an agreed-upon price or arrived at a price by bidding.

When you act as your own general contractor you can elect to do as little or as much of the actual work yourself as you desire. The more work you do yourself the more money you will save. If you don't want to do any of the work yourself it is possible to find subcontractors who will, between them, do the required work. In this case your only function would be to act as coordinator. More likely you will elect to do some of the work yourself. For example, you may elect to buy all or some of the materials yourself and then hire roofers, carpenters, plumbers, and electricians to install the material. Or you may elect to do some of the easy carpentry and painting yourself. There is no rigid formula as to how you divide up the work.

Sometimes acting as your own contractor turns out to be false economy. Even if you attribute no value to your time and labor, you may discover when the house is completed that the total of all the bills you receive from the subcontractors plus the bills for the materials and supplies you purchase exceed what it would have cost you to have the work done by a general contractor. If you assign a fair value to your time and labor plus something for the risk you have taken you will discover that it may have been a better idea to have the house built by a contractor.

MANUFACTURED HOUSING

MOBILE HOMES

(See Chapter 16 for a complete discussion of mobile homes and their role in the market today.)

PANELIZED HOUSING

A panelized house is not like the mobile home or manufactured house that comes in one or two pieces complete with mechanical systems and, often, furniture. A panelized house consists of preassembled parts such as wall panels, roof panels, floors and walls. A panelized house consists of many two-dimensional parts which are assembled at the site into a three-dimensional house.

Transportation of panelized parts is expensive. It rarely pays to ship them more than 500 miles. Panelized housing is excellent for a do-it-yourself oriented owner. It takes much less skill to assemble a panelized house than it does to build an individual custom-made house.

PRECUT HOUSES

Precut houses differ from panelized houses in that the builder or owner must do a great deal more of the assembly work than in a panelized house. A well put-together precut home package provides most of the parts to build a house (except the mechanical systems) together with complete instructions on how to assemble the house.

GEODESIC DOMES

One type of precut home that is gaining in popularity is the geodesic dome. It is so unique that we have placed it in a category of its own. The geodesic dome is philosopher Buckminster Fuller's invention. It is not, according to Fuller, supposed to have any separate walls or ceilings. When separate areas are wanted, this is accomplished by connecting more than one geodesic dome together.

LOG CABINS

In the past few years the log cabin has returned as a popular style. They now comprise almost one percent of the new houses being built. Most of them come in kit form and are designed to be constructed by the non-professional builder. Besides being a style with an interesting history, then can be rapidly constructed, are easy to maintain and are durable.

BARNS

Based on their sales, barns seem to appeal to a great many people. Barns come in precut kits and factory-made panels.

PUTTING UP A MANUFACTURED HOUSE

When you buy a manufactured house you have a wide variety of choices available as to how you will have the house erected. Some of the dealers are also builders. They will assume as much or as little of the responsibility for the erection or completion of the house as you wish.

Other buyers of manufactured houses buy only the shell from the dealer, arrange to have their own foundation constructed on their lot and then when the shell is erected either install the mechanical systems themselves or arrange for some or all of the work to be done by subcontractors. (See Chapter 16 for more information on manufactured housing.)

BUYING A HOUSE IN A NEW DEVELOPMENT

A wide variety of different tract or development houses are offered for sale to the public. At one end of the scale is the small contractor who obtains a suitable piece of land to subdivide into lots and proceeds to build a small number of homes. The contractor sells the houses with the help of the contractor's own sales staff. Other times, the contractor elects not to do the marketing and turns the task over to a real estate broker who does the marketing for a fee or commission.

At the other end of the scale are the big development corporations that buy large tracts of land. They hire planners, landscape architects and various other experts who develop hundreds, thousands of homes and sometimes whole cities. They hire contractors, marketing organizations and anyone else needed to develop the project. These developments often include multi-family dwellings, office and commercial buildings and sometimes industrial and other special purpose buildings as well.

Between these large development companies and the small contractor, there is an endless variety of development operations of all sizes.

STEPS IN THE NEW HOME-BUYING PROCESS

Before you weigh the advantages and disadvantages of a new house in a large housing development or a single unit in a small tract, there are certain logical steps which you and your family must take in the new home-buying process.

First is the selection of the region, then the community, then narrowing down to neighborhood, and finally choosing the exact site where the house is located within the neighborhood. The principles described in Chapters 4 and 5 will help you select a satisfactory location.

The second step is narrowing the price range to exactly how much you can afford to spend. (See Chapter 1). By using the formulas and guidelines in Chapter 1, you will know fairly well in which price direction you can go.

Having done your homework will eliminate a lot of time and many problems as you approach the third step, which is selecting the class, type and style of house. You may have very definite ideas already conceived and that too eliminates a lot of time. If your heart is committed to a Spanish Hacienda, then that is that and the best of luck. Your dream house, on the other hand, may be a white Colonial—which brings us to the subject of definitions.

DESCRIBING HOUSES

Describing and classifying houses by precise names such as the much abused "Colonial" has long been a problem to the real estate industry. An examination of the forms used by the government, both local and federal, lending institutions and real estate practitioners throughout the country confirmed that there was no uniform system to describe and classify houses, which created a series of problems. For instance, a salesperson may have a buyer who seeks a "Colonial style" home which, by the buyer's definition, is a modern house that looks like one built in the early part of our history. Unfortunately in many areas the word "Colonial" is used to describe almost any two-story house. Therefore, the salesperson must screen many more listings than would be necessary if the term "Colonial" were applied only to a Colonial American style house. If the salesperson is using a computer sorting system there is no simple way to know if the "Colonials" selected are the style the buyer seeks.

The CTS System (Class, Type, Style) was developed in response to this need. Its components are:

- *Class*—Denotes the number of families a unit will accommodate and whether it has a detached or a party wall.
- *Type*—Refers to the structural nature of the house (one-story, one and one-half, split level, raised ranch. . . . .)
- *Style*—Refers to the design of the house, based on historical or contemporary fashion (Colonial, Oriental, nineteenth century American. . . .)

(See Chapter 7 for a complete description of this system.)

LOOKING AROUND

It is at this point where you will take step four—looking for the house you want, at a price you can afford, on a particular site which appeals to you.

This is an area where information from many quarters is desirable. There are many sources of information which you can and should seek. And there are sources which will seek you out, once it is known that you are "in the market."

Your best single source of information is the local or area newspaper. These are definitive in their listings, and you'll get some idea about prices. Careful perusal of the weekend real estate section can save you much valuable time by "semi-shopping" at home. Some Multiple Listing Services publish a monthly brochure listing area brokers' names, photographs of new homes available and other pertinent information. They are available free in supermarkets, drug stores and similar outlets.

Contact the Chamber of Commerce. This will prove to be a wellspring of information. And when your schedule permits, take a ride around town. Often there is a "For Sale" sign on a house that is not currently advertised or whose advertisement did not catch your eye.

ADVANTAGES AND DISADVANTAGES OF BUYING A HOUSE IN A DEVELOPMENT

Advantages

- Lower price—approximately 15 percent less than a comparable custom-built house even for the same house plan.
- You can customize your house later as you can afford it, thus eliminating a large initial expense and mortgage.
- Often the developer has made many of the arrangements with a lending institution. Mortgage applications and details are simplified and expedited for you. The interest rate may be lower than the current rate you would have to pay if you built the house yourself. There can be significant saving here.
- The home comes with builder's warranty that is good for a period of at least one year from purchase. It covers structural defects and the me-

chanical systems. The developer will also obtain and pass on to you the warranties (usually also good for one year) on all the included appliances.

- It is often a great advantage to have recreation areas within the development. These range from a simple park with a few benches, tennis courts and golf courses to sophisticated indoor swimming pools.
- The latest equipment in heating, kitchen and laundry appliances is often included (and in more than 53 percent of new homes being built, full air conditioning is installed and can indeed be tested usually before buying). Mass buying permits large developers to purchase these items for less than you could individually.
- Usually the street and sidewalks are paved and the driveway is already blacktopped.
- Storm windows and screens are installed.
- You can nearly always decorate as you wish and adapt *some* of the house to your needs although it isn't custom-tailored.
- Much of the landscaping is done but not completely, allowing you to place your patio and pachysandra where *you* wish.

Disadvantages

- Often all units fall within a narrow price range; therefore regardless of what you do to customize or add to the landscaping, "communal parity" will prevent you from ever selling beyond the price range of the other units.
- Frequently, you must buy the unit before it is built, on the strength of viewing a display model. Naturally, the model is in its "Sunday best," very probably decorated professionally with expensive paper and, paint and beautiful furniture. The appliances are the best and most expensive and not necessarily the size and quality which will be standard in the sale units. The model is also likely to be professionally lighted to enhance it and the furnishings.
- Expensive landscaping around the model home may bear little resemblance to what will be around the unit you buy.
- Taxes may remain a mystery figure until you have lived in the house. You cannot be sure the estimate you have received will be accurate in years to come.
- Location is limited to what is available at the time you decide to buy, and in large developments is usually limited to a small area.
- Every feature from room arrangements to appliances to topography must be accepted as is—or the cost will be higher. Changes that you ask for will usually be extra even if they do add value to the house.
- Zoning and other community regulatory restrictions are already in effect as well as any private deed restrictions which the developer may have included.

- If the developer runs into financial problems, the development may not be finished as originally planned.
- The majority of families in the development will tend to be the same age and within the same income bracket. However, these may not be disadvantages to many.
- You may have to buy features you don't want (full air conditioning, for one example). Usually you will receive only a small credit if the item is eliminated.
- Purchase of a house may require you to join the homeowners association which owns the recreation facilities and the common land. This will most assuredly mean added dues and periodic assessments to finance upkeep.

For a complete checklist on Building or Buying a New House see Checklist 54, page C-115.

CHAPTER 18
RENOVATION AND HOME IMPROVEMENTS

RENOVATING OLD HOUSES

Long ago Americans discovered that many houses built before World War II make excellent places in which to live. They are now discovering in vast numbers that the same is true about houses built before the turn of the century. Back in the "good old days" houses were built differently than they are today. This certainly seems to be true when you compare an 1880s Queen Anne home with a 1970s split level tract home. Of course there were many cheaply constructed homes built on small lots in the 1800s, too, but most of them aren't around anymore.

The fad of many young professionals today is to find an historic house, move in and spend the bulk of any spare time for years to come restoring it back to its original state. These people are attracted by the large amount of living space, sturdy construction, fireplaces, interesting moldings, high ceilings, big windows and bays, beautiful hardwood floors and the feeling of being anchored to our heritage by the home in which they live.

The rehabilitation of historic homes has been getting a big push from the federal government. One special program available to owners of

---

[1] Renovation and home improvements are general words that apply to any work done on a home. The words rehabilitation, modernization and remodeling have special precise meanings:

Rehabilitation. The restoration of a property to satisfactory condition without changing the plan, form or style of a structure. (In urban renewal, the restoration to good condition of deteriorated structures, neighborhood and public facilities.) Neighborhood rehabilitation encompasses structural rehabilitation and may extend to street improvements and a provision of such amenities as parks and playgrounds.

Modernization. Taking corrective measures to bring the house into conformity with changes in style, whether exterior or interior or additions necessary to meet your needs and wishes. This nominally involves replacing parts of the structure or mechanical equipment with modern replacements of the same kind.

Remodeling. Changing the plan, form or style of a structure to correct functional or economic deficiencies (i.e., moving the "back" door to the side by the driveway and garage and adding a breezeway).

From Byrl Boyce, ed., *Real Estate Appraisal Terminology* (Chicago: American Institute of Real Estate Appraisers and the Society of Real Estate Appraisers, 1975).

historic homes is the Department of Housing and Urban Development (HUD) Title 1 Home Improvement Loan Program. This program allows for special financing for the rehabilitation, preservation or restoration of an historic residence.[1]

There are also special tax benefits for those who renovate historic homes. (See the section in Chapter 16 on historic homes.)

URBAN HOUSES

For the third consecutive year, the 1978–79 sales of old houses will surpass three million units and no one will be surprised if it hits the three and one-half million mark soon. This trend is indicative of a change in attitude on the part of the American home buyer. Realizing that most of the existing housing available is in urban areas, buyers have realized at the same time that this is often a better buy, not for everyone, but for many. Because prices of these existing houses vary greatly for a variety of reasons both obvious and sophisticated, there is a wide range to choose from.

For the young couple, single person, several friends or whatever the "family" make-up, the older urban house may be the only way they can realize their shared American dream. Where the cost of a new house might be prohibitive, the broad range of costs for old housing provides something for everyone. In addition to being initially affordable, other expenses are frequently not included as they might be in a brand new home. Sewer and water connections are in. Transportation is at hand. Municipal services are provided. Sidewalks, curbs and storm drains are all installed.

Not only has the young American home buyer become aware of urban housing as a possible bargain, but so too have the lending institutions. In fact, the United States League of Savings Association, whose nearly 5,000 member associations are the chief source of residential mortgage money in the U.S., feels that there now needs to be more emphasis on rehabilitation and less on new construction. There is a feeling that cities can best be revitalized by a coordinated neighborhood approach involving local government and civic leaders, community residents, financial institutions, school administrators, insurance underwriters and fire officials.

An old or used house can be anywhere from a year to 300 years old. However, there are six distinct eras which categorize "old":

1. *Almost new.* (usually one previous owner) one to 10 years old
2. *Used.* From 10 years old back to World War II
3. *Pre-World War II.* 1930s and 20s ("featuring" old mechanical systems)
4. *Vintage Housing.* 1920–1900
5. *Houses of the 1800s.* Victorian era

6. *Authentic Historic Homes.* 1600s, 1700s and early 1800s

When you are looking for a house to rehabilitate there should be some prime considerations in your search.

The first is the location. The neighborhood either must be suitable currently for you and your family and appear that it will continue to be in the forecastable future or the neighborhood should be in a state of upward transition with good prospects of becoming a suitable neighborhood.

The conclusion of a recent study of the problems of urban rehabilitation[2] was that there was no significant urban rehabilitation industry existing that was comparable to the new home construction industry. Most rehabilitation is taking place in selected neighborhoods in some cities and it is primarily being undertaken by owner-occupants.

Some general patterns emerge, according to the study, indicating the importance of neighborhood pride and confidence in successful rehabilitation. A high degree of motivation in the people is also apparent.

HOUSES WITH RENOVATION POTENTIAL

AUTHENTIC COLONIAL HOMES

These houses, for the most part, were built before the Civil War. They include the Colonial homes of New England, such as the multistory Federal style houses, the simple New England Farmhouse, Adams Colonial, Garrison Colonial, New England Colonial, Dutch Colonial and the Salt Box Colonial (or Cat Slide Colonial). Garrison Colonials are found all over the East and throughout the Midwest.

Around Philadelphia, there are authentic Pennsylvania Dutch Colonials (or Pennsylvania German Farmhouses). Thomas Jefferson's Monticello was a classic Colonial built in 1772. Other old Classic Colonials and Greek Revivals are found in small numbers in a wide variety of locations.

George Washington built Mount Vernon in the Southern Colonial style in the 1700s. There are thousands of historic Southern Colonial mansions throughout the South. Those built before the Civil War are called Ante Bellum and those built after the Civil War, Post Bellum.

Log Cabins were first extensively used in America by the Swedish immigrants. They became the favorite house of the early pioneers. The Latta House in Arkansas is a beautiful example of a restored log cabin. Many others exist all over the country. The favorite European style of

---

[2] "Urban Rehabilitation: A Yes Vote for Cities," *Savings and Loan News*, December, 1977. Article quotes Nathaniel H. Rogg of the National Association of Home Builders.

the Colonial times was the English Georgian style. Because these houses were usually very well built many are still lived in today.

Around New Orleans the Creole or Louisiana or New Orleans style developed in the late 1700s. The French Quarter in New Orleans has many beautifully restored examples.

There are other authentic Colonial houses throughout the U.S.A., including an Adobe house in Santa Fe, New Mexico, which is claimed by its owners to be the oldest house in the United States. (See Chapter 7 for illustrations of many of these house styles.)

Many authentic Colonial homes are considered to be part of our national heritage. Special tax benefits are available to property owners who restore them. (See Chapter 16 for information on historic easements and other benefits.) Owners of an historic home can often receive renovation help in the form of planning assistance and sometimes outright grants and low cost loans from local, state and national historic organizations. Tax relief may be available by granting historic easements.

HOUSES OF THE 1800s

Most of the pre-Civil War homes built in the 1800s are very similar to the authentic Colonial home just discussed. After the Civil War there was a substantial change in our houses. This was the beginning of the true machine age. The public became fascinated with what could be built with precut parts produced on the power lathe and with a power gouge and band saw. These precut parts became widely available and were used extensively in house construction.

Some of the styles that became popular at this time and which are now often lumped together and called Victorian styles were the Gothic Revivals, Egyptian Revivals, Roman Tuscan Mode, Octagon Houses, Italianate and Italian Villas, American Mansard or Second Empire styles, Stick Style or Carpenter Gothic, Eastlake, the Shingle Style and the Romanesque style. The most popular style of the period was the Queen Anne style. In the eastern cities blocks of row houses were built of brownstone and brick, while in the western cities the row houses with their individual looking facades used a wide variety of building materials. The Mission style, with its stucco walls and red tile roof, was developed in the 1800s when the people in the West began to become aware of their architectural past. (Again, See Chapter 7 for illustrations.)

Most of these houses are located in the cities. Many of them are in neighborhoods that have been in a state of decline for many years. Unlike the early authentic Colonials which have always been in demand, these houses fell out of favor with the public and many have received little or no maintenance for many years. When the trend back to the cities which began in the 1960s increased in the 1970s, these old houses began to regain popularity. A very popular monthly newsletter, now available to owners of these houses, is called *The Old House Journal*. It is full of advice about how to restore an old house and where to obtain the needed supplies, materials, services and anything else needed to do the job.

The Old House Journal makes an important distinction between the words restoring or rehabilitating an old house and remodeling the structure which it calls, "remuddling." One important piece of advice given again and again in *The Journal* is that once you've immersed yourself in the history of the house (something that is highly recommended that all owners of old houses do) it acquires a new personality. You feel differently about the house—and what you want to do to it. Usually, the desire to remodel decreases and the desire to restore increases. You become less eager to make drastic changes in a house that has meant so much to so many.[3]

Remember that rehabilitation is defined as the restoration of a property to satisfactory condition without changing the plan, form or style of a structure.

Aficionados of old houses highly recommend that you do as little work as possible to the house before you move in. They realize, of course, that a certain amount of work must be done to make the house habitable but they advise, when in doubt about any work, to postpone it. They recommend you live in the house for at least six months before you do any serious rehabilitation. During this time you will get the "feel" of the house and learn where everything is and what does and does not work. You also will, hopefully, have the time and desire to do some research about the house and how it looked in its original condition. A trip to your local historical society may turn up an old picture of your house which will be good to refer to as you do your renovation.

OLD NONHISTORIC HOUSES (VINTAGE HOUSES)

There are millions of houses built since 1900 with little or no historic significance that can be renovated into good livable homes.

The Forest Products Laboratory of the U.S. Department of Agriculture has been researching and experimenting on the renovation of old homes for over 60 years. Its publication, *Renovate An Old House?*[4] is the primary source of much of the following material.

The primary considerations in the selection of an old house to renovate are its location (See Chapter 4) and its suitability for potential renovation.

A well-built home that has been reasonably well maintained has many parts that will not be worn out even if the house is 50 to 75 years old or

---

[3] *The Old House Journal*, Brooklyn, NY
[4] Gerald E. Sherwood, *Renovate an Old House?* (Washington: U.S. Dept. of Agriculture Forest Service, 1976).

older. This is true of both wood and masonry structures. Wood will not deteriorate in strength or stiffness from age alone. It takes several centuries for wood even to lose some of its shock resistance. However, wood can be destroyed by decay, insects, rodents, the elements and physical abuse.

Whether a house is worth rehabilitation can be determined by a systematic inspection of the structure and comparing of the cost of the renovation plus the initial cost of the acquisition with what the value of the house will be when the renovation is completed.

Generally, if the foundation, floors, walls and roof framing are structurally sound the house has a good potential for economically feasible rehabilitation.

Many old houses will require substantial repair and possible replacement of their heating, plumbing and electrical systems. It is almost always physically possible to do this work; however, it can be very costly. Unless you have the special skills necessary to examine these mechanical systems you should seek professional help. You should ask whomever is helping you to indicate what work must be done immediately and what work can be postponed. You should also try to estimate what potential problems and future repairs and replacements might reasonably become necessary to these systems in the next five years or so.

SELECTING A HOUSE TO RENOVATE

When a house that can be purchased at what appears to be a reasonable price has been located you should then consider some key points:

1. Can you visualize the house renovated in your mind's eye and does it appear to be a home you and your family will be happy living in?
2. Does the basic structure seem to be sound? Unless the foundation and framing are sound, the house probably is not worth rehabilitating. If the house is masonry or masonry veneer the condition of the masonry is also very important. Walls that have settled and are out of alignment or which have major cracks may be so costly to repair that their renovation will not be economical. Loose and crumbling mortar is a common defect that can often be repaired. If the framing has been seriously damaged by termites, other insects or wood rot, it may be beyond repair economically.
3. Is the layout of the rooms in the house such that the house can be made livable? Sometimes the layout is so poor and so difficult to change that a renovation is not practical at least by you for your family.
4. What will have to be done in order to make the house comply with the local building code and other applicable governmental regulations?

5. What work will have to be done to the mechanical systems? Will you be satisfied with the end result?
6. Are the other repairs and renovations you will have to do to make the house acceptable to you and your family economically feasible?

VISUALIZING THE HOUSE RENOVATED

People vary substantially in their ability to visualize in their mind's eye the results of a renovation. Unless you are able to visualize reasonably well what a house is going to be like after you complete its renovation, you probably should not get involved in the renovation project. Sometimes you may just be unable to visualize the end result of a particular house. If this is the case, you should try to find a house where you will be able to visualize the end result. You may discover you are never able to visualize how a house will look after it is renovated. If this is true, renovating is probably not for you.

DETERMINING IF THE STRUCTURE IS SOUND

The entire foundation should be checked to determine its general condition. Look carefully for signs of uneven settling. You will find some evidence of settling in almost every old house you examine. Some settling, especially if it is relatively even, is natural. Large amounts of uneven settling may distort the house frame or even pull it apart. It may distort window and door frames, loosen interior finish, loosen or cause exterior masonry or other siding to crack or create cracks in the walls of the house. When a solid masonry house has serious settling, the problems are compounded.

It is sometimes possible to compensate for small amounts of localized settling by adding support to beams and joists that have been affected by the settling. A careful judgment must be made, often with the help of a qualified builder or mason, about the degree of settling that has taken place, whether it is still going on and what needs to be done to correct any damage caused by the settling to date. If the damage has been extensive and the problem seems to be ongoing it suggests that a new foundation would be required to solve the problem. More often than not this would be too costly to do, so the house may not be suitable for rehabilitation.

A damp or wet basement may be caused by settling or some other problem. If the basement foundation is poured concrete, small hairline cracks often develop, usually with little effect on the structure. They alone do not cause dampness. Large open cracks are a sign of trouble and could be the source through which water is entering. Repairing these cracks is not an easy job. If the settling is still going on any repairs to the cracks will soon become damaged.

Other possible sources of basement dampness which have nothing to do with settling are open or broken exterior doors and windows or doors and windows with missing caulking. Clogged drain tiles, clogged or broken down spouts, lack of slope away from the house of the finished grade next to the foundation (a very common problem) all may permit water to enter. When surface water is allowed to accumulate around the foundation wall it will find its way into the basement through very small cracks.

Sometimes the wetness is caused by high pressure in the water table under the house which is not being relieved by operational drain tiles. This is an expensive repair and it is often not economically feasible. If the wetness is not caused by settling you should decide how you would feel if you are unable to correct the problem and will have to have a wet basement permanently. Some people are willing to accept such a condition. Others are not. If the wetness is caused by settling, the problem probably is very serious and the house may not be suitable for rehabilitating.

The building frame should be carefully examined. You should look for signs of sagging roof ridge, bulging walls, slanting, lack of squareness, eaveline distortion, loose fitting doors and window frames and binding windows. When any of these problems is evident you should try to locate its source.

Prolonged dampness will cause serious permanent damage to wood. It will lose its hardness and toughness. You should look for places in the house where it appears the wood may have been exposed to prolonged dampness such as where the wood is close to the ground or in an unventilated area such as under a porch or crawl space or air space under a room addition.

A good way to estimate the extent of the damage is to prod the wood with a sharp tool to see if it mars easily, or to pry out a splinter to check on the wood's toughness. When the toughness has been greatly reduced by decay, the wood may break across the grain with little splintering and lift out with little resistance. When the decay is far advanced no test will be needed as you will see evidence of the decay when you make your visual inspection.

Every house (except in those few northern areas that are still unaffected) should be professionally inspected for termite damage and the presence of termites. These wood-attacking insects can do a substantial amount of damage that is often difficult to detect by anyone without special training. A professional termite inspector will also provide an estimate of what it will cost to free the structure of the vermin so they will do no further damage. If the termites are well established, their extermination can be very costly.

Most houses with a basement are wide enough to require at least one main beam supported by wood, steel or masonry columns to support the first floor joists. These supporting posts should be examined. If they are wood they should be free of decay and supported on pedestals, rather than embedded in the basement floor where they may take in moisture that will cause them to decay eventually. Steel posts should be supported on metal plates that rest on separate footings.

The girders or beams should be checked for sagging and major cracks. Some sagging is natural. Excess sagging will require that additional columns be installed to provide additional support.

The sill plates, floor joists and any other framing member that rests directly on top of the foundation wall should be checked for signs of decay. They are exposed to moisture from the foundation wall and are especially vulnerable to decay and termite attack.

When the floor seems excessively springy when you walk on it, you must determine if this is caused by sagging of the foundation or a defective carrying beam. If neither is the case, you may elect to add an extra girder, support column or floor joist to provide extra stiffness.

Many houses have inadequate framing around the stairs. Additional support may be needed. Most stud walls will not fail unless there is some other problem such as settling, a defective main beam or girder, termite damage or decay or a defective header. When a distorted wall is discovered by its lack of squareness, slanting, bulging or binding doors and windows, the source of the problem should be located.

When a sagging roof ridge is observed it should be checked for cracking and poor support as well as for decay and signs of termite damage. Rafters will also sag due to inadequate stiffness or because they were not well seasoned. If the roof sheathing sags, it may indicate that the rafters are too far apart, the strip sheathing is too thin or the plywood is too thin or has delaminated.

ANALYZING AND CHANGING THE LAYOUT

It is unreasonable to expect that any house you did not design yourself, much less a house 50 to 75 years old, will have a layout that is exactly as you wish it would be. In fact, even people who design new houses for themselves with the help of skilled architects usually discover, once they move in, that the layout is not precisely what they wanted. On the other hand the layout of the house will substantially affect your convenience and pleasure of using it over many years.

If you conclude that changes in the existing layout will improve the livability of the house, you will have to determine if they are both physically and economically possible. Generally, it is much easier to estimate what it will cost to add a wall than it is to estimate what it will cost to remove one.

First of all, you must determine if the house has or can be made to have the basic features your family will require. For example, if you will need four bedrooms and two baths, a house with three bedrooms and one bath without room for the addition of these needed rooms probably will not be satisfactory. Likewise, if some member of your family cannot easily go up and down stairs you won't want a multi-story house unless everything the handicapped member of your family will need is on the first floor.

You should study the traffic pattern of the house. In many older houses it is very poor. Often you could get to one room from another only by passing through another room rather than by a hallway. This is especially bad when the room that is being passed through is a bedroom. In old houses the bathrooms are often in inconvenient places, such as off the living room or kitchen. Doors tend to be put in the middle of rooms which route traffic through the center of the room rather than around the edges. These door locations also make the placement of furniture difficult. Sometimes just by moving a door the layout can be greatly improved.

Ideally, when a house is well laid out the rooms will be grouped together into three zones which will be connected together with halls that act as the circulation paths. (See Chapter 6 for more information on interior zones.)

In the final analysis you will have to decide if you and your family are going to be happy living in the house as it will be laid out.

COMPLIANCE WITH LOCAL BUILDING CODES AND OTHER GOVERNMENTAL REGULATIONS

In many communities when you set about to rehabilitate a house you are required to take out a building permit from the local building department. This may trigger a variety of inspections from different government agencies. Some typical inspectors who would be involved are the building department's building, electrical and plumbing inspectors; the health department, the zoning enforcement officer; and environmental inspectors. In many communities these inspectors are very knowledgeable about rehabilitation and can be very helpful.

You should try to have as many of these initial inspections as possible made prior to your final commitment to buy the property. You may, for example, find you have underestimated what the cost of upgrading the electrical system will be when you discover the number of additional electrical outlets that are going to be required and the larger electrical service that will be needed to supply power for the additional required outlets.

If the house has a septic system, you often will find that the local health officer is very knowledgeable about both septic tank problems in the neighborhood and even about your own septic system.

It is always a good policy to check with the zoning enforcement officer in your community before you make any major changes to a building. It is much better to find out before you start, rather than after you have spent a lot of money, whether your plan conforms to all the zoning restrictions.

For the same reason you should check with any environmental agency that may have jurisdiction over your property. The building inspector can usually tell you if there are such agencies. They would usually have jurisdiction if you were near any water or watershed or if your land was classified as an inland or tidal wetlands.

If you approach these inspectors with a positive, open-minded attitude you usually will find they are helpful. On the other hand, if you approach them with a negative attitude and a closed mind, you will find them difficult to deal with.

REPAIRING AND REPLACING MECHANICAL SYSTEMS

Unless the house has been previously modernized, there is a strong probability that repairs will have to be made to the mechanical systems.

ELECTRICAL SYSTEMS

All except the smallest houses need 100 amperes and 220 to 240 volt electrical service or more to provide adequate power for the needs of a typical family today. The previously acceptable standard of 60 amperes just is no longer adequate. Current electrical codes often require an outlet on every wall and two on long walls except in the bathroom which has its own special need for a plug above the lavatory for electric shaver, hair dryer or other electrical appliance to be used in the bathroom.

You should examine the house to determine what kind of wiring it has. If it is the old knob and tube wiring, you will want to replace it with modern, safer wire.

If the house is wired with B.X. cable and the wire is in good condition, it will not have to be replaced. However, even B.X. cable gets rusty and wears out. Likewise, if the building has B.X. cable then you probably will just have to supplement the existing wiring. The same is true if the existing wiring is a plastic type that is Underwriters Laboratories-approved and is in good condition.

If you want to add many new outlets or branch circuits you may need a new or additional distribution panel.

Many older houses have few ceiling lights. Often there is no wall switch near the entrance to each room. Rooms without a ceiling light should have a wall switch near the room entrance that will control at least one wall duplex outlet in the room.

You may also wish to add wiring for doorbells or chimes, television, inter-communication systems, burglar and fire alarm systems or for other special needs your family may have.

PLUMBING SYSTEMS

Old houses often require major rehabilitation of their plumbing systems. A good place to start is with the water supply. If it is from a well, the quantity and quality of the water should be checked, together with the condition of the pump (which should supply 40 to 50 pounds of pressure) and water softening equipment, if it exists. When the water comes from a municipal supply, the service line should be checked to determine its condition and whether, over the years, it has become clogged with mineral deposits and needs to be replaced. The shutoff valve should also be checked to see if it is operational.

If the water supply is sufficient and the pressure is high enough, there should be adequate water available at the uppermost faucet in the house. A good test is to go into the upper bathroom and run both faucets in the sink, turn on the tub and flush the toilet all at the same time. A large pressure drop in the faucets indicates potential problems, while a good supply under these conditions is a positive sign that the water supply and pipes are adequate.

Old galvanized iron pipes often require replacing. Copper pipes that are not green in color and free of white or greenish crusting at the joints are probably in good condition. The condition of the pipes is important because it is difficult to replace them without considerable cutting of wall surfaces and in some situations structural framing members.

Old-fashioned plumbing fixtures that are in good working order have become very popular and bring a premium in the used plumbing fixture market. You may decide to replace some of the old fixtures because they are cracked and stained or just because old fixtures are not your cup of tea.

The waste pipes and vents also need to be checked for condition and adequacy. The waste system of many old houses do not meet the current plumbing code especially as to their venting and trapping requirements. By running the water for a few minutes you can check for clogged drains.

Houses that are not on municipal sewers must have an adequate septic system or other approved waste disposal system. Many septic systems are so constructed that they do not meet the current code and do not function adequately on a year-round basis. A new system, or repairs to the existing system, may be very expensive and the possibility exists that they cannot be made at all. If a new drainage field is needed there must be a plot of available land that will pass a percolation test (see Chapter 9). This is a test that shows in the wettest month of the year whether the water in a hole in the ground will be absorbed at a rate of at least one inch every 30 minutes.

DOMESTIC HOT WATER

Old domestic hot water systems that produce hot water from a heating coil in the hot air or hot water furnace often are not adequate or economical. A 30-gallon gas hot water heater or a 50-gallon electrically heated tank is the minimum size the average family needs. Larger tanks are desired by many homeowners.

HEATING SYSTEMS

When you find an old "octupus" gravity warm air heating system in the basement you must figure on the cost to install a new heating system. You may elect to use this old system to see if you are satisfied with its heating ability. Many people feel that since it is only a matter of time before they will have to replace it, it is better to do it as part of the general rehabilitation rather than do it later and have to tear up the house a second time.

When the system is relatively new it is hard to determine how adequate it is and how well it will operate without actually using it through a heating season. However, you can tell a little about a system just by looking at it and observing its general appearance which is often reflective of its actual condition. If you suspect there may be a problem with the existing heating system, you should seek the help of a professional.

OTHER REPAIRS AND RENOVATIONS TO THE EXTERIOR OF THE HOUSE

Exteriors of houses, be they wood or masonry, will last for long periods of time. One of the major causes of exterior damage is moisture. It may be moisture in the wood or it may be moisture from poor ventilation, lack of vapor barriers or contact with the wet ground. It can come from both the inside and the outside of the house. One main contributor is the lack of a sufficient roof overhang. This allows the rain to run down the face of the exterior wall. Vapor can also enter the wall from the inside when the wall lacks an adequate vapor barrier.

When the wall has siding made of horizontal boards they should be checked for gapping, looseness, cracks, warping and decay. Some of these defects, if not too far advanced, can be corrected by the replacing of a few siding boards, renailing where needed and caulking. If the damage is very extensive new siding will be required which is an expensive repair.

Many old houses have wood shingle siding. Shingles that are in good condition will have the appearance of a perfect mosaic. Worn shingles in need of replacement will have a ragged appearance. Many individual shingles will be broken or warped or upturned. When many of the shingles are damaged the exterior will have to be reshingled or recovered with some other suitable siding.

Some old houses have brick or stone veneer exterior walls. Small cracks can be repaired by regrouting and repointing of the joints. When the house has settled the cracks may be large and difficult to repair. Some people feel the appearance of old brick or stone walls can be improved by sandblasting. Others feel this spoils the appearance of the house and should be avoided. Before you do any sandblasting you should live in the house for a while to give yourself time to decide if you really want to have this work done or if you would rather leave the surface alone.

Water flowing over the surface of masonry walls is undesirable just as it is for wood walls. Sometimes a masonry wall will become porous. After all the cracks have been repaired and the joints repointed, it is desirable to coat the masonry surface with a clear water repellent material.

Solid masonry walls can last hundreds of years. But like masonry veneer walls they can suffer from cracking and loose mortar joints. They can be repaired much the way masonry veneer walls are repaired. When the house's foundation settles it can do serious and often irrepairable damage to a solid masonry wall.

You are fortunate, indeed, if you locate an old house that has its original decorative trim in good enough condition so that it can be restored to its original beauty. It should be closely examined for decay, cracking and missing parts. You should think twice before you remove old trim. You may wish later on that you had left it intact so you could have restored it.

When you make your exterior inspection you should examine all the flashing and caulking wherever the trim projects from the wall, around the coping, sills and at the intersections of the roof and walls. Plan to repair any of these places where flashing or caulking is not provided or where the need of repair is apparent.

ROOFS

A good roof that does not leak is an important part of any house. About the only roof that has the potential of lasting since the 1800s is a tile or slate roof. With these exceptions most of the roofs you find on houses of this age that are still in repairable condition will not be the original roofs. If you are lucky enough to find an old house with its original roof you should think long and hard before you replace it. A new slate or tile roof is very expensive and substitutes usually detract from the original beauty of an old house.

Many roofers do not want to be bothered repairing and restoring an old roof. They would much rather sell you a new roofing job. Therefore, you should investigate and find a roofer who has a record of successful repair of old roofs before you accept poor advice and remove a repairable roof based on the recommendation of the wrong roofer.

It is not hard to determine if a roof is leaking, even in dry weather. The leaks should be obvious from the damage they have caused to the inside of the house. Looking in the attic and around the upper story of the house will reveal water stains on the rafters. Not all water damage is attributable to poor roofing as it may have been caused by damaged flashing or condensation. Also it is possible that the leak that caused the damage has already been repaired.

A common replacement roof is made of asphalt shingles. These roofs rarely last more than 20 years. You can detect an asphalt roof that is nearing the end of its life by signs of brittleness, curling, missing shingles and loss of surface granules. Signs of wear can also be detected in the narrow grooves, between the tabs or sections of the shingle, or between two consecutive shingles in a row. When the wear is extensive it may extend completely through to the roof boards.

Another common replacement roofing material used on old houses is wood shingles which are often made of cedar. You can tell a wood shingle roof that is ready for replacement by looking for broken, warped, upturned and missing shingles. When only a few shingles show signs of these problems it may be possible to repair the roof. A good wood shingle roof can last up to about 30 years.

Some old houses have roofs that are flat or with gentle slopes. You can often safely climb up on the roof to check the built-up roof covering (these types of roofs should not be covered with shingles, tiles or slate, which require a good pitch to be effective). Bare spots, separations of the seams, breaks in the felt, bubbles, blisters and soft spots are all signs that the roof needs repair and possible replacement. A good built-up roof can last up to 30 years.

All roofs, no matter what type they are, require flashing made of sheet metal or other materials at its intersections with the walls or other roof components to prevent water from leaking in through these intersections into the house. Corroded flashing must be replaced.

When you are checking a house's roof you should at the same time check the leaders and downspouts. When the leaders are made of wood they are subject to cracking, warping, rotting and all the other problems other wooden parts of the house are subject to. When the damage is moderate they can be repaired or just small sections replaced. Often it is possible to prolong their life by coating the inside lining with metal or some other waterproof material. When they are made of metal their life can sometimes be extended by painting.

Finally when the house has no roof overhang or leaders and gutters the addition of these items should be considered. Keeping large amounts of water off the exterior walls and trim will extend their life.

WINDOWS AND EXTERIOR DOORS

The windows and exterior doors have the potential of being serious problems in old houses. Often they are loose fitting, rotted, cracked or have damaged or missing weather stripping. A window in poor condition lets the cold air in and causes heat loss and uncomfortable drafts. Windows should be checked for these defects. The sills should be checked at the same time. Only by taking the time to check each window will you know for sure about its condition and whether it opens and closes without binding.

It is very difficult to make satisfactory repairs to window sashes that have big cracks or suffer from any serious amount of decay or warping. Often it is less expensive to buy a replacement sash. If your window openings are not standard size you should compare the cost of reframing the opening to accept a standard size window sash against the entire cost of non-standard windows. If you are buying new windows you should consider double glazed panes to reduce heat loss.

Exterior doors should also open and close without sticking. When the door frame is out of square due to foundation settlement or shifting in the house frame, the doors will usually have to be rehung. Doors also tend to decay along their bottom edges. Check each threshold as many old ones may be worn, weathered or decayed and require replacement.

Sometimes the fit of the doors and windows is loose but otherwise they are in good condition. Storm windows and doors may be the most economical solution to this problem.

PORCHES

Porches were a popular feature of old houses built long before air conditioning was invented. Over the years they have lost much of their original popularity and many have been torn down or enclosed to make an extra room.

Often porches were built without foundations. They were very vulnerable to decay. When the framing members touched the ground they soon decayed and had to be replaced. If they were not set on masonry footings or piers the decay process would repeat itself. Poor ventilation under the porch will cause the subflooring to decay. Whenever you buy a house with a porch that is not over a basement the whole substructure should be carefully examined for signs of decay and rot.

INTERIOR STRUCTURE

Most old houses have interiors that have suffered damage over the years due to wear and tear, distortion of the structure and the presence of moisture.

Sometimes the original interior was made of good materials which were properly installed. In other old houses cheap or improper materials were used and poorly applied.

The most common situation found in old houses is that the original interior was well-made of excellent materials. However, over the course of years additions and alterations were made to the house and these were made of inferior materials that were poorly applied.

Beautiful natural woodwork is covered with cheap paint, walls are covered with layers of cheap wallpaper and magnificent hardwood floors are painted and covered over with a variety of inferior materials. If you are lucky the original materials will not be permanently damaged and can be restored to their original beautiful condition.

FLOORS

Unfortunately wood floors which have not been cared for over the years often suffer from buckling, cupping of the boards and wide cracks between the boards caused by their shrinking.

If you are lucky you will find floors that are generally smooth and without excessive separation between the boards. If these floors have not been refinished too many times in the past and are still thick enough to permit sanding, they can be refinished and their original beauty restored. Wood floors that cannot be restored will have to be replaced.

Tile floors should be carefully checked for loose tiles, broken corners and chipped edges. Look along the surface to see if there are any ridges or signs of unevenness or if the tiles are thin and the underlayment is showing through. Most old styles are no longer being manufactured. Therefore, if you have to replace any of the tiles it probably will be necessary to replace all the tiles in the room.

WALLS AND CEILINGS

Most original walls and ceilings in old houses are made out of plaster. Newer walls and ceilings in additions or in rooms where the ceiling has been replaced are often made of gypsum board. Occasionally wood paneling and other materials are also used.

Even plaster in good condition will have some small cracks and holes. These are easy to patch up. When a plaster wall or ceiling has large cracks and holes, or if the surface is uneven and bulging, or if it is loose it will have to be removed and a new wall or ceiling covering applied.

When the walls are in good condition and covered with wallpaper, a new layer of wallpaper of the color and pattern of your choice can be applied if the old wallpaper is adhering tightly to the wall. If the old wallpaper is loose or more than a few layers thick, it should be removed before the new wallpapr is applied.

When the old wall or ceiling has been painted, the old paint should be checked before another layer of paint is applied. If the paint has built up to excessive thickness over the years or is chipped, it will have to be removed. This is a job that takes time and a lot of work. Sometimes it is easier to cover the old surface with a new panel material.

INTERIOR DOORS, CABINETS AND TRIM

Some of the attractions of old houses that appeal to many new owners are the beautiful doors, cabinets and trim. It takes a lot of work to remove the old finishes and restore the wood to its original beautiful appearance but many people think it is worth the effort.

Today there are companies that make trim in many old styles and the cost of getting replacement pieces is not as great as it used to be. *The Old*

House Journal[5] is a good source of places to obtain these replacement parts.

Often interior doors made of beautiful solid wood (unlike our hollow doors of today) have been painted. When stripped of all the old paint and refinished, they become almost natural works of art.

For a complete checklist on Renovations, see Checklist 55, page C-117.

HOME IMPROVEMENTS

Typically new homeowners will plan ways to make their homes better places to live, even with brand new houses. Millions of home improvements are done each year. Below is a list, in order of popularity, of the major home improvements done in 1979 in this country.

- 1,740,000 insulation jobs
- 1,170,000 storm window and door jobs
- 1,100,000 roofing jobs
- 1,050,000 siding jobs
- 577,000 window replacement jobs
- 461,000 kitchen cabinet and/or kitchen counter top jobs
- 407,000 kitchen added or remodeled
- 355,000 major room additions
- 345,000 baths added or remodeled
- 191,000 attics/basements remodeled
- 187,000 garage/carport jobs
- 162,000 porch enclosures
- 115,000 wall paneling jobs[6]

Some home improvement jobs are necessary because a house lacks something the family needs or wants (like a garage or carport). Some are needed to bring the house back to good condition when some part has been damaged or worn out. The third item on the above list, roofing, often falls into this category.

The question most asked by homeowners who are considering making a home improvement is will it "pay for itself," or put another way, is the value created by the improvement equal to or greater than its cost. Unfortunately quite often the answer is no. This does not in any way

---

[5] *The Old House Journal*

[6] *The Green Book of Home Improvement Contractors,* 1980–81 edition (Crofton, MD: Construction Marketing Research Associates, Inc. and New York: National Home Improvement Council, Inc., 1980). This list is based on information compiled from a sample of 3000 contractors. As such, it represents work done nationally by 35,000 home improvement contractors and does not reflect do-it-yourself work done by amateurs.

mean that the improvement should not be made. First of all, when a repair is needed such as one to the roof, it may be more economical in the long run to replace the roof with a new one rather than to repair the old roof again and again.

INSULATION

The most common improvement is insulation. It has been estimated that a homeowner can recover anywhere from 20 to 100 percent of the cost of making an insulation improvement at the time the home is sold, depending on the area of the country.[7] A home without at least the equivalent of six inches of rock wool (R22-24) over the ceiling of the upper floor or under the attic rafters (or between the trusses) is losing a lot of heat and thus costing a great deal extra to heat and cool. This simple home improvement will, in fuel savings alone, usually pay for itself in two or three years. It requires only minimum skill to install overhead insulation and many homeowners can do it themselves or with just a little help from their friends. With few exceptions this important insulation should be installed when it is missing. Weather stripping the doors is another fuel saver that will pay for itself in a few years and is easy to do.

The subject of wall insulation is a more complex matter with more things to take into consideration. PostWorld War II houses with thin walls are often good candidates for insulation, especially in northern climates. It is usually relatively easy for a professional insulation installer to blow insulation into these walls or put in foam. It is a difficult job for anyone not familiar with how it is done and without the special equipment that is needed.

Wall insulation saves on fuel and increases comfort in two ways: first, it stops heat from escaping through the wall and reduces the cost to heat the house. It also increases the body comfort of the people in the insulated house during cold weather.

Human beings are most comfortable in cold weather when they are in an environment with a temperature between 68 and 72 degrees and when their bodies are not losing heat by radiation. When the body, which is a heat-producing mechanism, is near a cold, uninsulated wall, heat will radiate from the warm body to the cold wall. When this radiation is taking place it requires a higher room temperature for maximum comfort than when there is no body heat loss by radiation. What this means is that a person who is comfortable in a 68-degree room in a well-insulated house will require about 72 degrees of heat to obtain the same amount of comfort in an uninsulated house. Therefore, the fuel cost in the house with uninsulated walls will be greater both because it will take more fuel to heat it to any given degree of heat and also because

---

[7] According to a survey of five appraisers in different parts of the country reported in "Is That Home Improvement a Good Investment?" *Changing Times*, May, 1979.

people will require the house to be warmer than they would if the house were insulated.

Typical effective wall insulation is three and one-half inches of rock wool, the amount that will fit in a wall built with two-inch by four-inch studs (which are actually only about one and three-quarter inches by three and three-quarter inches). Don't make the mistake of trying to put more than this amount of insulation in this size wall by compressing the insulation. This will not increase the effectiveness of the insulation; in fact it will decrease its heat resistance as insulation depends upon the air inside it to give it its insulating properties.

There is an alternate way to construct a wall using two by six-inch studs. This permits more insulation to be installed in the house. These are known as super-insulated walls. In most markets only a small part of the extra cost of these walls will be recovered upon resale of the house. The same is usually true of an extra six inches of insulation over the ceiling or under the roof. The cost of other types of insulation such as storm windows and doors (which is second on the list of home improvements) weather stripping, caulking and underfloor insulation probably also can be recovered by the homeowner. The recovery comes from fuel savings, higher resale value and tax credits.

SIDING

New exterior siding is relatively high on the list of improvements. There is a possible recovery at resale of 25 to 60 percent of the cost of siding[8] Freedom from the cost and bother of repainting is another economic benefit of siding and the reason that many people decide to do it.

At the time new siding is put on it is also a good idea to install wall insulation if the house is without it.

Again, there is no clear cut answer whether new siding will pay for itself. The changes are greatest if you are going from a material that needs painting to one that does not. The fact that almost two percent of all houses were resided last year shows that the market is in favor of this type of home improvement which probably indicates that people will also be willing to pay for the benefits.

BATHROOMS

About 345,000 bathrooms were added to American houses in 1979.[9] This reflects a definite shift in the public's desire for more bathrooms. Experts believe stongly that a high percentage of the cost of an additional bathroom will be recovered when the house is sold. This will be especially true if the house does not contain the number of bathrooms and/or lavatories the market prefers in the type of house yours is. For

---

[8] *Changing Times*
[9] *Green Book*

example, if you are living in or buying a two-story house with only a single bath on the second floor in a market that expects at least a lavatory and preferably a full bath on the ground floor as well, you should try to add the second bath or lavatory. The chances are, unless there just is not any space available or any way to add space, that the recovery cost will be greater than the installation cost. Add this potential profit to the convenience you will have created by the addition of the bath or lavatory and you have a strong reason for making the improvement.

On the other hand, if you have a Ranch style house with two bathrooms in a market where most Ranch houses like yours also have two bathrooms then the additional value of a third bathroom may not equal the installation cost. Of course, it still may be a good idea to install it anyway just for the extra convenience and pleasure it will produce for you and your family. Since the market seems to want more and more bathrooms it is quite possible by the time you sell your house you will recover 100 percent of its cost[10] (or even make a profit).

Although the law of diminishing returns does apply, there is general agreement that the addition of a bathroom or lavatory is one of the best home improvements in a great majority of the real estate markets.

WINDOW REPLACEMENT

Window replacement has become a very popular home improvement, with more than half a million jobs done in 1979.[11]

If the windows in your house are old with sashes in poor condition, they should be replaced. Common sense indicates that a substantial portion of the cost would be recovered on the sale of many homes in many markets. An additional saving will also be realized from the fuel savings caused by the better fitting sash and higher insulating properties of the replacement glazing.

KITCHENS

Close behind replacement windows in popularity as home improvements comes new kitchen cabinets and counter tops. Here there is a tendency for homeowners to create an overimprovement or to select materials and colors based on their own tastes and desires rather than what will create maximum resale value. Keep in mind that the total cost of a kitchen remodeling should be in line with the total value of the home if maximum cost recovery is to be obtained. It is up to you to determine the relative importance of your color and material preference and how they will please you while you live in your house as weighed against the eventual resale cost recovery.

About 400,000 families do a major remodeling of their kitchens in a

---

[10] *Changing Times*
[11] *Green Book*

typical year and another half a million replace kitchen cabinets and/or counter tops.[12] Estimated cost recovery ranges from 25 to 75 percent of the remodeling costs.[13] This is not surprising when you consider that people have very strong feelings about what they like in their kitchens and these preferences vary significantly from family to family.

Again, when you plan a major kitchen modernization you must decide whether you are going to design it to suit your individual tastes or the tastes of the general public. Keep in mind, too, that it is very easy to spend a lot of money on a kitchen to obtain all the available kitchen appliances and decorator cabinets and counters that are available. What you will recover may be 100 percent-plus of your costs if you have replaced an out-of-date kitchen that is a minus factor in the sale of a house with a modern, well-planned kitchen that contains those items that appeal to the general public.

Kitchen remodeling has the potential of being either the best or the worst home improvement investment you can make depending on how you do the job. A final rule of thumb to keep in mind is that if you invest more than 10 percent of the total value of your home in a kitchen modernization you almost certainly are creating an overimprovement the cost of which you will not recover 100 percent.

ROOM ADDITIONS

If your house is short a bedroom, i.e., a two-bedroom house in most markets or a house with too few bathrooms as previously discussed, you probably are on sound ground making a room addition, as some 355,000 families did in 1979.[14] You may even recover more than your cost, according to the surveyed appraisers. They also reported that the addition of a family or recreation room or a dining room is often a wise decision when cost recovery is your prime consideration.[15]

A good way *not* to recover your costs is to convert a garage into a family room. This may even result in a 100 percent loss of your improvement costs. Other room additions that are nice to have but don't add much value to houses are hobby rooms, darkrooms, saunas and greenhouses. The same is often true when you enclose an existing open porch. Another room that has fallen out of favor in many markets is a finished recreation room in the basement. The same is true of small paneled dens which were quite popular not very many years ago. On the other hand, a room that has been gaining popularity in many markets recently is a ground floor recreation room especially when it opens up onto the portion of your lot used for outdoor entertaining and eating.

---

[12] *Green Book*
[13] *Changing Times*
[14] *Green Book*
[15] *Changing Times*

BASEMENTS AND ATTICS

About 191,000 basements and attics were finished in 1979.[16] This is not a large number of jobs when you consider that there are almost 70 million houses.

Only in New York, where space is at a premium, do the surveyed appraisers feel such an improvement will add even 50 percent of the cost to the house's value.[17] In spite of this, it is not hard to understand why people do this kind of work when in many instances this is the only way they can feasibly obtain the additional space that they need for their family. Often it is far less expensive to obtain needed space this way than it would be by selling the family home and replacing it with a larger home that already contains the needed space.

OTHER IMPROVEMENTS

The bottom three jobs reported on the list of popular major home improvements are garages and carports, porch enclosures and wall paneling jobs. The first, which we have not previously discussed, may have good cost recovery potential if economically accomplished and are in areas where garages especially are a wanted feature. This, of course, tends to be the case more frequently in colder climates.

Several other home improvements should be considered even though relatively few of them are made. One is the addition of a fireplace, or the opening up of a closed fireplace in an older home where one previously existed. A very high percentage of the buyers of expensive homes want a fireplace. An expensive home without at least one fireplace is often at a substantial disadvantage when it competes in the resale market. A good majority of home buyers in all classes of homes indicate that they would prefer a house with a fireplace. Therefore, it is really not a question whether buyers want a fireplace (it is almost universally agreed that a majority do) but rather will they pay a sufficient extra amount to add one to an existing house where there was none in the original design. This is a difficult judgment to make which must take into consideration both the cost of installing the new fireplace, or the cost of opening up and making operational an old fireplace, compared with how much extra the market will pay for a house with a fireplace.

HOW TO MAKE HOME IMPROVEMENTS

Unfortunately, the home improvement business is rampant with gyp specialists. It is a large industry with a volume of over $30 billion per year. There are many good, legitimate home improvement contractors

[16] *Green Book*
[17] *Changing Times*

but it is estimated that one out of every 15 dollars goes straight into the pockets of dishonest contractors.[18] In this section we will suggest various ways you can have your home improvements done, how to cut costs and how to avoid crooks.

DO IT YOURSELF (WITH SOME HELP FROM YOUR FRIENDS)

If you are all thumbs, can't change a washer, saw a board, drive a nail or even change a light bulb without breaking it, you should skip this section.

Another consideration is your available time. If you earn $50 per hour in your career and have all the work you can do, you should not be doing home improvements to save money. However, you still may elect to do some because the work will be a form of relaxation and enjoyment.

Most home improvements consist of 50 to 75 percent labor. Therefore, when you do the work yourself there is a big potential for savings. Many home improvements are well within the scope of what many amateurs can do. The main difference between the amateur and the professional is that the amateur often takes considerably longer to do the job. On the other hand, the amateur homeowner will often do a much more careful job—paying attention to many small details the professional would skip over.

Not all improvements can be done by amateurs. By law, in many communities, major plumbing, heating and electrical work can be done only by a licensed professional.

Selling materials and supplies to people who do their own home improvements has become a big business. Many communities have large home improvement centers. These are one-stop outlets where you can buy everything you need. They have many products especially designed for the amateur such as prefinished plywood panels, prepasted wallpaper and tiles with self-adhesive backs. Like anything else you buy, you should do some price checking before you select a vendor. Many home improvement products are also available at hardware stores, discount outlets and at commercial specialty outlets that serve primarily the building trade such as electrical, plumbing and roofing supply houses. Some of these outlets will sell to amateurs too but you may have to ask for discounts in order to get the best price.

If you don't have the necessary skills, it is possible to learn them if you have the time and the talent. There are a variety of books available which are excellent. The bibliography at the back of this book lists some of them. Many stores and supply companies offer free demonstrations and even formal classes on a variety of subjects such as how to lay a floor, paper a wall, shingle a roof and how to use power tools.

---

[18] Richard George, *The New Consumer Survival Kit* (Boston: Little Brown & Co., 1978).

Your local high school or community college probably offers courses in a variety of do-it-yourself subjects. Often these courses are quite inexpensive. They often draw on professionals in the community who act as instructors. For example, a local plumber, electrician, bricklayer, carpenter and other professionals will each be invited to teach the class how they can do for themselves some of the same work the professional does. Usually they give actual demonstrations of their skills and then the students have an opportunity to try to do the work themselves and ask questions.

Another thing that makes do-it-yourself home improvements much easier than it used to be is the proliferation of good, reasonably priced power tools. If you are going to do your own work, you should find a place in your house that will be your workshop. Here you should have a workbench and a place to store your tools and supplies.

No workshop should be without a good power drill. If you are doing only light repair work a one-quarter-inch model will do. For more substantial work a three-eighths-inch or one-half-inch model will work better. Besides drilling holes these tools can be used for sanding, grinding, polishing and driving in screws.

Another very useful power tool is a saber saw (also known as a portable jig saw). These tools can be used for a wide variety of sawing tasks.

It is also nice to have a variety of other power tools but unless you are doing a lot of work, they are probably more of a luxury than a necessity.

It is beyond the scope of this book to instruct you on how to actually do the many home improvements you may elect to make. Based on the millions of people who are doing their own work and the size of the home improvement supply industry that has developed to help and supply them, one has to conclude it is a good way to get the work done.

HOME IMPROVEMENT CONTRACTORS

For a variety of reasons you may elect not to do some or all of the work yourself. You will then need to hire professionals.

It is much easier and safer to hire specialists than it is to hire a general home improvement contractor. However, if you hire specialists you will have to do part of the work yourself and act as supervisor and coordinator. You may not have the skills or the time needed to act in this capacity.

In most communities you can locate good electricians, plumbers, roofers, siding installers, carpenters, masons, etc. By carefully checking with your friends and suppliers you stand a good chance of finding professionals who have been around for a while and who probably will continue to stay around in the future. The electricians and plumbers must have a license in your community.

A good professional will be willing to give you an estimate of what it will cost to do the work you want. Keep in mind that in a remodeling job you must allow the contractor some flexibility in the cost estimate. This is especially true if the work involves tearing something down or working on old walls, floors and ceilings where unexpected obstacles and problems may be encountered. If possible, try to get two estimates.

Before you ask for an estimate you should carefully decide exactly what you want done, including what kinds of materials you want used. You are not obligated to hire the person who gives you the lowest estimate. You should consider when they say they will do the work, how they want to get paid, their reputation and your own reaction to them. Sometimes it becomes apparent from your initial contract with the professional that there is going to be a personality conflict or the opposite— that you are going to get along well together. This is a very important consideration and often is more important than the estimated price.

HIRING A GENERAL HOME IMPROVEMENT CONTRACTOR

Many times, because of the size of the job as compared to your skills and time availability, you will need to find a general home improvement contractor to do your work.

The best way to start looking for the right firm is to check with your friends and neighbors who have recently had similar work done. A word-of-mouth recommendation from someone you know is still the best type of recommendation you can get.

Don't act hastily in your selection of a contractor. Carefully go over the proposed work with the contractor and get a written estimate. It is always better to get more than one estimate.

When you have received what you feel is a satisfactory estimate, before you sign a contract you should check with both your local building inspector and Better Business Bureau to be certain there are not unresolved, outstanding complaints against the contractor. Also, you should see if the contractor is a member of either the National Home Improvement Council or National Remodelers Association. Membership in these organizations does not necessarily guarantee good work or a good reputation but it is generally a good sign.

CONTRACTS

Except for very small jobs you should have a written contract with your home improvement contractor. It is always a good idea to have a lawyer check the contract. If the job is over $1,000 it is particularly foolish to bypass legal advice.

The contract should contain a detailed description of what is going to be done by the contractor and what materials are going to be used. A major cause of dispute between homeowners and home improvement contractors is about what work the contractor was supposed to do. Often the problem is caused by poor communications and a lack of understanding about what is to be included in the job, rather than poor intentions on the part of the contractor. If the job is a large one, the best way to ensure there will be no misunderstanding about what is to be done is to have an architect draw a set of plans and provide specifications.

The contract should also state when the job will be started and approximately when it will be completed. Home improvement contractors have a problem of insuring an even flow of work. What they like to do is to start several jobs and string them out over a long course of time. This is fine for them but not very good for you if you are anxious to have the work completed. Unless the contract provides for some type of a significant penalty if the work is not completed, there is little you will be able to do when the contractor starts to drag out your job. This is a very common, serious problem many people have with home improvement contractors. It is best to discuss the matter with the contractor before you make a final commitment. If you can't work out a satisfactory arrangement you should seek another contractor.

When the job calls for the contractor to supply appliances and fixtures, you should agree as to exactly what will be provided by brand name and model. Later, if the contractor wants to use a substitute you will have the authority to accept or reject the proposed substitute. The contract should also require the builder to install the appliances and fixtures in such a way as their warranties will be valid.

Another important provision is how the contractor is going to be paid and how the contractor is going to pay the subcontractors. Most contractors will require some type of advance payment. Around 10 percent is customary. When large down payments are required, you, in turn, should seek some guarantee that the work will be completed. The best guarantee is a performance bond but usually only the very large contractors will provide them. When you give a large advance deposit to a contractor who is not very well established in your community or who does not provide a performance bond you are taking a big gamble that you will not lose your money.

Many states have mechanic's lien statutes, some of which provide that a subcontractor who works on a job is entitled to be paid by the property owner for labor and materials even if the property owner paid the general contractor who, in turn, for some reason such as bankruptcy did not pay the subcontractor. This alone is reason enough to use a lawyer in order to find out the best way in your state to handle payments to afford you the maximum protection from having to pay for the work twice.

Most remodeling contracts will provide for cost overruns to cover the unexpected cost incurred by the contractor. There should be some percentage limit such as 10 to 15 percent without your written approval.

The most common cause of additional costs are changes ordered by the homeowner after the contract is signed and the work is underway. Every time you want a change you should find out how much it will cost and if you agree to have it done, a written amendment should be attached to your contract. This has always been a major source of problems between contractors and their customers. Customers order changes which they think will be inexpensive without getting a cost estimate for the change. When they get a bill at the end of the job for an amount much larger than they expected they become angry and frustrated. Unfortunately there is little they can do at this time except pay the bill.

Another good clause for the homeowner to have in the contract is a "hold back" clause. This provision allows you to not pay the last 10 percent or more of what is due until some time like 30 to 60 days after the completion of the job. The purpose of this "hold back" is so the contractor will be forced to come back and complete any work left undone or correct any deficiencies that develop.

The contract should also specify that the contractor will remove all materials or debris from the site when the work is complete and that the premises will be left "broom clean." People who have never done an alteration are amazed what dirty jobs they are. Unless you can seal off parts of your house, be prepared to do a lot of heavy cleaning when your home improvement job is completed. Most contractors do not consider this to be their responsibility.

The contract should also require that the contractor carry Workmen's Compensation insurance and bodily injury and property damage insurance. The contractor should be required to provide you with valid certificates showing this insurance is in force and provide that you will be notified, in advance, if it is going to be cancelled for any reason. This insurance will protect you in case anyone is injured on the job or if the contractor damages your house accidentally.

At the same time you should notify your own insurance agent about the proposed work. Some homeowners insurance policies and fire insurance policies require that you notify the insurance company whenever you do any alterations to your premises.

It is very expensive and time-consuming to have to sue your contractor if a dispute arises, especially if it is not a large item. A much better way to settle this type of problem is through arbitration. This is a procedure that provides for a third party to listen to the dispute and make a decision as to how it will be settled.

An arbitration clause in the contract will make this method of settling disputes mandatory and will state who will be the arbitrator. Often it will state that the American Arbitration Association will provide and supervise the arbitrators. Remember both you and the contractor will be bound by the decision of the arbitrator even if you do not like the results of the arbitration. The arbitrator has the power to make you pay more money than you expected to if the arbitrator feels you caused extra expenses to be incurred by the contractor.

Many contracts also require that the property owner sign a completion certificate when the job has been satisfactorily completed. It affirms to both the contractor and the lender that all the work has been satisfactorily performed. It goes without saying you should not sign the certificate until you are satisfied the job is 100 percent complete.

THE GYP ARTISTS

As we mentioned in the beginning of this section, there are a lot of con artists and marginal operators in the home improvement business. It is reported that one out of three home improvement contractors goes out of business within three years. Here are some of the common techniques used by less than reputable home improvement contractors:[19]

1. "Just in the neighborhood finishing another job and have leftover materials."
2. Itinerants with out-of-state license plates who will work "cheap" to earn money to get to wherever they are going.
3. Scare tactics used by a solicitor who tells you your roof is about to blow off in the next high wind.
4. The "direct" factory representative who sells roofing and siding at less than regular prices.
5. Your home will become the "model home" in the neighborhood; the contractor will obtain more work, therefore your job will cost less.
6. Quick estimates which usually indicate fly-by-night operators. Legitimate contractors take their time and usually have to get supply prices before they can give you cost figures.
7. High pressure tactics which imply that the only way to get the low price is to sign right away.
8. People without proper identification (they usually have something to hide).
9. Basement waterproofing firms offering quick miracle cures. It is often difficult, if not impossible, to fix a wet basement. A guarantee from a firm that won't be around to make good on the guarantee is worthless.
10. Driveway resealing firms which use cheap materials. A good job that will last requires first-class materials installed as recommended by the manufacturer. Cheap products soon wash away.
11. "Bait and switch" advertising. Some of our largest retailers have a record of using this technique. They advertise some low-priced product which brings you to the store where the salespeople upgrade you to a more expensive item.
12. Easy contests where you win something at a discount price rather than getting it completely free are almost always just sales gimmicks.

---

[19] *Changing Times*

One advantage of dealing with a contractor who is a member of the National Home Improvement Council[20] or the National Remodelers Association[21] is that you can seek help from these organizations if you run into problems. Some states have a licensing commission that has jurisdiction over home improvement contractors. Other states have different agencies that help protect the consumer. Problems should be reported to your local Better Business Bureau and to your local consumer protection agency, if one exists.

For a complete Home Improvements checklist, see Checklist 56, page C-119.

ENERGY SAVINGS

Almost 20 percent of all the energy consumed in the United States is used in our residences. Of this energy, about half is used for heating and cooling and about 15 percent for domestic hot water. The remaining approximately one-third is used for our lights, cooking, refrigeration and miscellaneous appliance operation.

A substantial amount of this fuel can be saved by some affordable renovations according to government publications[22] such as the inexpensive caulking and weather stripping of doors and windows. Many people are capable of doing this work themselves. The total savings possible is over one-half million barrels of oil daily during the cold weather, enough to overcome most of our current heating fuel shortage.

INSULATION AND VENTILATION

Most homes built before World War II do not have adequate vapor barriers and insulation. Good insulation cuts heating costs and adds to comfort by making the temperature in the house more uniform and reducing body heat loss by radiation to cold wall surfaces.

Insulating an old house that was not previously insulated is a complex matter and should not be attempted by anyone who is not familiar with the problems it creates.

The main problem is one of moisture condensation. When a large difference in temperature exists between the outside air temperature and the temperature inside the house, moisture is forced out through the walls and condenses on the insulation inside the walls wetting the insulation and the exterior siding. This problem can be controlled by the installation of vapor barriers but this is a difficult thing to do in an old

---

[20] National Home Improvement Council, 11 East 44th St., New York, NY
[21] National Remodelers Association, 50 East 42nd St., New York, NY
[22] *Tips For Energy Savers*, (Washington, D.C.: Federal Energy Administration).

house. In spite of the problems created in cold climates vapor barriers should be installed as part of the renovation.

Probably the most effective potential heat-saving work you can do is to install six and one-half-inch mineral wool, glass fiber or cellulose insulation in the attic either over the ceiling of the top floor or under the roof between the roof rafters or trusses. Many millions of our homes lack this insulation. This insulation should reduce a home's fuel consumption by over 20 percent. The cost of the insulation will be recovered in just a few years.

Again, adequate ventilation and vapor barriers are essential and unless they are properly installed and located, damaging condensation will occur in the attic on the cold framing members. When the vents are properly installed in the correct locations they not only help keep the attic dry in the winter but they also keep hot air moving from the attic during the summer and help keep the house cool.

It is also very effective to install insulation in those exterior walls which are not presently insulated. In addition to making it less costly to maintain the house at the desired temperature, this also makes people feel comfortable at lower temperatures. For example, as explained earlier, a person who normally feels comfortable in an insulated room at 68 degrees of temperature may feel uncomfortable at 68 degrees in an uninsulated room and raise the temperature to 72 degrees in order to obtain the same level of comfort.

The installation of insulation in walls is not easily done by the homeowner. It usually requires special equipment and professional help when done in existing homes.

Another effective way to conserve energy is by the installation of storm windows. The most popular types are combination storm windows and screens because they do not have to be removed when temperatures are moderate and open windows are desirable.

A temporary substitute that works quite effectively are clear sheets of plastic film tightly taped to the inside of the window frames.

Another fuel-saving device that can be installed is an automatic flue opener and closer. This device closes the furnace flue when the furnace is off and stops the heat from going up the chimney.

ENERGY CONSERVATION TAX CREDITS

The following residential energy-conservation measures now provide eligibility for the tax savings benefits in the 1978 National Energy Act:

- Caulking and weather stripping of doors and windows
- Clock thermostats or automatic energy-saving setback thermostats
- Insulation of floors, walls, ceilings and attic
- Water heater insulation
- Storm windows and doors

- Multiglazed windows and doors
- Special heat-absorbing and heat-reflecting window and door glazing
- Electrical demand regulating devices
- Solar energy devices for heating and cooling
- Wind power devices for heating, cooling and power generation
- Replacement furnace burner that reduces fuel consumption as a result of increased combustion efficiency
- Automatic flue openers and closers
- An electrical or mechanical furnace ignition system that replaces a gas pilot device
- A meter that displays the cost of energy usage

In order for any of these items to be eligible for tax credit they must reasonably be expected to remain in operation for three years. The purchase of used equipment does not qualify for tax credit. Nor does the remounting of storm windows and doors taken down at the end of the previous heating season.

The tax credit allowed for the listed items (except those that qualify for the special "Solar and Wind-Energy Tax Credit") is 15 percent of the first $2,000 expended after April 19, 1977, and before January 1, 1986, for a maximum credit of $300.

Expenditure for eligible items qualifies for tax credit only in the tax year in which the installation of the item is completed regardless of when it was paid for. A credit cannot be claimed for qualified expenditures on vacation homes or rental properties or for expenditures on residences substantially completed after April 20, 1977. Tenants are eligible for expenditures they make.

A special tax credit is provided for those items that are classified as solar and wind-energy items. The credit is 30 percent of the first $2,000 expended and 20 percent of the next $8,000 expended. The maximum credit is $2,200. The solar-wind credit is available for expenditures in both new and existing dwellings that are the taxpayer's original residence. A purchaser of a newly constructed residence is eligible for the solar-wind credit in the year the taxpayer moves into the residence, regardless of when the solar equipment was actually installed. To be eligible, the equipment must have an expected life of at least five years.

For an Energy Savings checklist, see Checklist 57, page C-121.

ECONOMIC FEASIBILITY

Before you decide to do any renovation or home improvement, you should make an estimate as to whether the project is economically feasible. You may decide to proceed even if the work is not economically feasible because you want to do it for the way it will improve your way of life and the pleasure derived from living in your home. We are in no way recommending that the only renovations and home improvements that should be made are those that are economically feasible. We only suggest that you understand the true cost of what you plan to do; then if you wish to go ahead you will be doing so with eyes wide open.

COSTS

It is much more difficult to estimate renovation or rehabilitation costs than that of new construction. Unit-in-place costs for new work, plus an additional allowance for the normally higher cost of repair work, go into making renovation estimates. Rehabilitation estimates frequently may be based upon actual recent costs for the same or equivalent work performed on the property or on similar properties. This information may even include bids for specific items that have not been accomplished in the rehabilitation, such as exterior painting, roof repair or interior decorating.

The cost of some rehabilitation work may approximate that for similar work in new construction. However, the cost of modernization or remodeling work is almost invariably higher than that for new construction for several reasons. Although the quantity of material may be the same as for new work, more labor is involved and the conditions are different. The alteration of a structure usually involves tearing out old work and performing small portions of new work under conditions not conducive to the degree of efficiency attainable on new construction. If the estimate made by the contractor is on a flat fee basis, the charge may be substantially higher than the cost of identical work in new construction, in order for the contractor to be protected against complications that may develop as the remodeling progresses. Such unforeseen complications may involve the placement of existing conduits, pipes, and structural load-bearing members.

Other costs to be considered are those that may be incurred by the owner rather than the contractor. These include such items as the architect's fee, the owner's cost of supervision and loss of use of the house while the work is being done.

PROCEDURES

Whether rehabilitation, modernization or remodeling is involved, the justification for any renovation program depends upon the answer to the basic question: what constitutes the highest and best use of the property? The study that the appraiser gives to this question produces the cost estimates necessary for a program to achieve such use, which in turn provides the basis for a decision as to its economic justification.

If the property is old but in sufficiently sound condition for remodeling, if the neighborhood standards and trends are materially higher than the property's present status, and if the prospective value increase is substantial, a comprehensive program may be feasible.

A wide range of potential programs may justify consideration, but there is only one satisfactory way to select the final plan. That is to explore the alternatives, estimate the cost and potential value increases, and then be guided by the results of a comparison of the data. For example, assume that a brownstone townhouse is available in a neighborhood going through a period of redevelopment. The house can be purchased for $15,000. It is estimated that it will take about $10,000 to rehabilitate the house to meet the minimum code requirements. The estimated value when the rehabilitation is completed is $30,000. Based on these figures, the rehabilitation to meet minimum standards is feasible.

The other possibility is to restore the house to its original historical appearance and do a much more elaborate renovation. The estimated cost of this renovation would be $30,000, but the final value would be $55,000.

Example No. 1:

Acquisition Price	$15,000
Renovation Cost	+ 10,000
Total Cost	$25,000
Estimated Value After Renovation	30,000
Estimated Profit	$ 5,000

Example No. 2:

Acquisition Price	$15,000
Renovation Cost	+ 30,000
Total Cost	$45,000
Estimated Value After Renovation	55,000
Estimated Profit	$10,000

FEASIBILITY

Both of the above programs are feasible. However, the second example represents the highest and best use of the property since it produces the maximum profit. In some cases where the profit potential due to a rehabilitation, modernization and remodeling program is substantial, the "as is" value estimate for the property under appraisal should be modified upward. In many cities properties have been purchased at relatively low prices by imaginative investors who have undertaken programs of selective modernization, sometimes involving new exterior ("skin") treatment and other major expenditures. Modernized and attractive properties thus created have become marketable at levels substantially higher than the investments involved. Whether this is practical in any specific situation can only be ascertained with a feasibility analysis.

ADVANTAGES AND DISADVANTAGES OF RENOVATION

In any appraisal of older houses you should consider the possibility that additional value might be created by well-advised renovation. Rehabilitation costs are normally a simple deduction from the value indicated by the usual approaches to the value estimate, if the final outcome is predicated upon the building being just what you and your family want.

However, modernization and remodeling may create additional value, prolong the economic life of your house, and thus produce an economic margin of value over and above the cost of the work. You should anticipate a substantial profit as an "entrepreneur" to justify undertaking such a renovation program (with incumbent headaches). The method for determining whether a remodeling program is suited for your particular property includes estimating value "as is", cost of the work, and value after completion. Then consider whether there is sufficient profit incentive or increased value to warrant the indicated cost.

In the final analysis, the appraiser's estimate of a feasible rehabilitation, modernization or remodeling program is part of the process used to arrive at a value estimate for the property. Whether or not the owner actually carries out such a program, the value of the property in its existing state may be influenced by its potential for increased value under a feasible renovation program.

Advantages of Renovating (Compared to Buying a New House)

- Cheaper than total cost of new house and lot.
- Landscaping already completed—trees, shrubs, lawn, patio established.
- More space—living and storage.
- Character of neighborhood is evident. You know what you're getting by way of schools, stores, churches, and how well neighbors care for their homes and property.
- Transportation easily accessible, or, in a majority of cases, shopping and activities are within walking distance.
- Cost of taxes is known. You probably can find out what heating bills and other similar yearly costs are from previous owner or real estate broker. (Tax information at city hall.)
- Threat of special levies such as for sewers is virtually eliminated since they are already in.
- *Sometimes* the current mortgage of the owner can be assumed by you, the buyer, at a lower-than-current interest rate. These are often GI or FHA mortgages.

- Additional value can be created by well-advised renovation. The pride of possession and in creative remodeling to one's taste can offset or even surpass the thrill of buying a new house.
- You may "inherit" some expensive feature such as a greenhouse, darkroom, carpeting, lighting and bathroom fixtures.
- The trend seems to be toward vintage houses such as the Queen Anne as being very "in". Thus you are considered avant garde in an old castle!
- Higher quality materials and workmanship than in the average new house. (Marble, vitreous china, ceramic tile, solid doors, hardwood flooring and baseboards.)
- Whatever flaws there are are fairly obvious and can be dealt with. You don't have to play the "guessing game" of the new house.
- Prices vary greatly on a wide range of old/used houses. Therefore, just about anyone can afford something to call his or her own.
- Some intangibles: Charm, elbow room, comfort.

Disadvantages of Renovating

- Location. You have to take the house you like where you find it.
- Wasted space. You may get more space than in a new house, but not all space is well utilized. There may be large foyers, halls, attic, high ceilings, non-usable areas.
- You miss the thrill and excitement of planning and executing an "original" house plan of your very own with your architect and your family.
- No protection of the one-year warranty which is inherent in buying new.
- Possibility of declining neighborhood or zoning changes.
- Initially, general housecleaning.
- Great possibility of little or no insulation with resulting heat loss in winter.
- Termites or wood rot.
- There is no central air conditioning and probably the cost of its installation would be prohibitive.
- The exterior design, such as stucco, is "dated" and although you may like it, it could be difficult in a resale.
- You may inherit some absolutely useless (to you) features which you can live without, i.e., a mud room, sauna, root cellar.
- Upkeep. Maintenance costs are greater overall and will remain so. (However, taxes and amortization should be lower.)

CHAPTER 19

NOISE, SAFETY,
FIRE PROTECTION AND
SECURITY

We are covering the subjects of noise, safety, fire protection and security in a separate chapter because they are of concern to all home buyers. Because this is the last chapter in the book does not mean it is the least important. If the chapters were arranged in order of importance this chapter might indeed be Chapter 1.

NOISE CONTROL

Until recently we always considered loud or unusual noises to be a nuisance but we never realized it was also a danger to our health. Now hearing experts tell us that the noise from jet planes, loud music and any other loud noise to which we are exposed for long periods of time will do permanent damage to our ears and our ability to hear.

Noise control is definitely not a frivolous matter. The federal government recognized that fact officially in 1972 with the passage of the Noise Control Act. This law directed the Environmental Protection Agency (EPA) to set noise limits for those many products which emit noise in their usage and which are manufactured in the United States. The 1972 Noise Control Act also gave the EPA authority to act jointly with the Federal Aviation Agency in establishing noise control standards for aircraft.

We are primarily concerned here with protection from noise as it pertains to the average homeowner. Before discussing the methods with which you can defend yourself against the onslaught of undesirable noise, it is important to define noise—simply because what may be noise to you may literally be "music to the ears" of your neighbor.

Noise is uninvited, unwanted sound; unwanted in that it interferes with talking, listening or the thinking process. Noise annoys, disturbs and distracts (detracting as well) and it may ultimately cause physical or emotional damage. Technically, anything which interferes with normal communication processes, such as static or a hum, is noise. It may be a quiet hum but it is insidious noise nonetheless.

A decibel is a unit for measuring the relative loudness or intensity of sounds. Zero decibels is approximately the least intensity of sound the average normal ear can hear—not an *absence* of sound, but the least you are aware of. To illustrate more practically, we speak ordinarily at about the 60 decibel level.

The control or channeling of these decibels so that they either please or cease to interfere in some fashion with the sensibilities is a condition of a civilized society. Classic no-no's include 1) practicing your snare drums at midnight in a condominium; 2) allowing a youngster to ride a skateboard on the asphalt under someone's bedroom window at 8 a.m. and 3) throwing a New Year's Eve-type party *every* Saturday night.

Where there is legitimate noise such as that caused by industry, traffic, schools or whatever, there are diverse ways of preventing its intrusion into your home. As in choosing parents whose ancestors were "long livers," you would be fortunate to have bought a house with thick exterior walls, strongly constructed. If your house is less than ideal in this respect, there are things you can do to alleviate "noise pollution" in your immediate environment.

NOISE INSULATION

If you are building a new house, discuss the exterior wall framing with your architect and contractor. Sound will easily penetrate inferior construction and thin materials.

The newest framing in what is loosely termed a "super-insulated" house has two by six-inch studs instead of the conventional two by four's. In this way it is possible to get in six inches of sound insulation instead of three and one-half. Since many new homes are incorporating electric heat, it is much better to use the two by six studs as they provide space for more insulation which will keep out noise as well as reduce heating costs.

Snug-fitting flooring is helpful in reducing noise transmission between floors in a multiple story house. The better the quality and the better the construction, the less noise transmission. The recent practice of using plywood as subflooring and then covering it with carpeting provides a good sound barrier between stories.

After other necessary refinements in the construction, the soundproofing starts with the incorporation of the insulation into the wall and ceiling areas. Naturally it is easier to install the insulation during the first stages of construction, but many thousands of already-built homes are being insulated daily. Indeed, home insulation has become the most popular home improvement project in this country (see the section in

Chapter 18 on home improvements and the section on insulation in Chapter 8).[1]

Some types of insulation soundproof better than others alone and in combination with some wall "finishes." It would be a good idea to discuss the latest in finishing materials with your architect and building supply dealer.

Good quality, custom-fitted storm windows and doors are beneficial for fuel economy, comfort and the reduction of loud noise from outside.

The interior walls which cover the insulation and studs are usually made of materials such as plaster, drywall construction, wallboard and hardwood paneling. It is not unusual to find entire walls consisting of glass doors or an expanse of window in contemporary houses. All these "finishes" by themselves, and in addition to other hard surfaces in a room, not only reflect but amplify noise. Glass and slate are particular villians.

Generally, brick (unglazed), stone or similar substances produce much less vibration and therefore are desirable acoustically as well as aesthetically when incorporated into a house design. Flooring of carpets, rubber tile, linoleum, cork and other types of porous material help to absorb and deaden sound. Indoor-outdoor carpeting is also successful. It is especially effective around the swimming pool, an area which is conducive to noise because of the nature of the materials used in its construction and because of the nature of the relaxed atmosphere. Recent interior room designs, both new and in renovations, feature "astroturf" as a floor covering. Even without a stadium and 65,000 people, this too is effective in absorbing sound.

INTERIOR NOISE CONTROL

Noise and vibrations can be controlled in several ways. The first is obviously by diminishing the source of the noise. The second is by baffling the sound so that it cannot travel from one place to another, and the third is by absorbing the noise into something else.

We all have sound-producing mechanisms which run constantly in our homes—the refrigerator, furnace, dishwasher, air conditioning unit, washing machine, hair dryer, kitchen fan and a myriad of others. Most of the noise produced by these aids and appliances, fortunately, has been greatly reduced for us by modern engineering. Further sound reduction can often be accomplished by enclosing some of these appliances within a closet, under a staircase or in other available space.

"Baffling" the noise so it doesn't know which way to go and thus eventually goes nowhere, as you would suspect, takes a little more

---

[1] Detailed descriptions of various types of insulation are included in Henry S. Harrison, *HOUSES—The Illustrated Guide to Construction, Design and Systems* (Chicago: REALTORS NATIONAL MARKETING INSTITUTE®, 1976).

doing. You can put your washing machine in the basement, your freezer in the garage; you can enhance your picture window with draperies which soak up the sound of the air conditioning's hum, but what do you do for example with interior noises of a defective plumbing system? If you are building a new house, insist that the plumber take great care about the installation of the plumbing system. An effective well installed system should *not* be noisy.

A high-pitched whistling sound when the toilet is flushed may be caused by the valve in the toilet closing too slowly. A simple adjustment by a plumber will eliminate the noise. A sucking sound when the water runs out of a fixture is often made by a siphoning action in the trap caused by improper venting of the waste stack. If unclogging the vent doesn't work, only a major change in the vent system will eliminate the noise.

A hammering noise in the water pipes when the water is turned off is caused by a buildup of pressure in the pipe. In high pressure areas, air chambers, which are pipes filled with air, are installed at the fixtures connected to the water line. They provide a cushion of air which lets the pressure build up more gently. Pressure buildup is a serious problem which, if gone uncorrected, will result in broken or leaking pipes. It may be possible for a plumber to install one or two large air chambers in the system or a variety of other mechanical devices designed to correct the trouble.

The sound of running water is caused by undersized pipes and pipes that run in walls that are not sound-insulated. Wrapping the pipe with a noise insulation material may help. If the noise is very objectionable the pipe may have to be replaced with a larger one.

Often the plumbing system is noisy because the pipes are loose. Installing brackets and supports can eliminate the vibrations. Occasionally the temperature of the hot water is too high, with resultant hammering sounds within the pipes. Keeping the water control temperature setting at about 140 degrees nearly always solves the problem, and in addition has energy saving advantages. Noisy faucets may need only a matter of washer replacement or a set-screw adjustment.

If your septic tank system is blocked or flooded, that may cause noise in the drainage pipes (to say nothing of the noise it will cause when you discover it). The best thing you can do is call in professional help to remedy the problem. This is no time or place for do-it-yourself experimentation.

There are a variety of noises and sounds in home heating systems. Most are harmless and we ignore them after a while. They're just part of the family cacophony. One typical noise is often in the heating ducts. Noisy hot air heating ducts are caused by having direct connection to the furnace without a short piece of canvas between the furnace discharge and the beginning of the ducts. Any really mysterious, unusual or disturbing noises within your furnace or its system should be thoroughly investigated by *experts.*

The noises of everyday living within a house, while necessary and welcome, require some civilizing. Consideration of one another can be enhanced further by good interior layout. If you're buying an existing house, particularly an older one, you may be able to achieve more favorable soundproofing with remodeling or renovating some of the interior.

A good way to think about the interior layout of a house is to divide it into zones (see Chapter 6). The private/sleeping zone contains the bedrooms, bathrooms and dressing rooms. The living/social zone consists of the living room, dining room, recreation room, den or enclosed porch. The working/service zone consists of the kitchen, laundry, pantry and other work areas. In addition to the three zones there are circulation areas consisting of halls and stairs plus guest and family entrances. The three zones should be separated from each other so that sounds and activities in one zone do not interfere with sounds and activities in another.

In a two-story or split-level house this can be accomplished by putting these zones on two separate levels or floors. In a two-story house it is easier to isolate the zone visually than it is to keep out the noise. Noise transmission from the working and living zones to the private/sleeping zone through the floor and ceiling is one of the major disadvantages of a two-story house. It can be minimized with heavy carpeting (with underlay, so much the better) and where possible, installation of acoustical tile on the ceiling below.

The separation of rooms with the careful use of closets, bathrooms and hallways is effective. A stairway can be a buffer zone as well.

The judicious placing of rooms away from the street or from other foreseeable exterior noises is also important.

Use of furnishings is probably the most easily attainable and successful mode of subduing the interior noise level. Rugs, draperies, curtains, wall hangings, some types of wallpaper, upholstered furniture, plants— all these drink in the decibels while serving their functional and decorative purposes.

It is sometimes overlooked that people absorb noise as well. Scientific testing has produced evidence that one person absorbs about as much noise as a heavy three by four-foot rug. (The larger the person, of course, the more sound absorption.) It is not recommended here that you fill your rooms frequently with people *just* to soundproof them. Somehow there is an inverse ratio as to how much sound people *produce* versus what they "absorb" at a party!

EXTERIOR NOISE CONTROL

Aside from whatever protection your federal, state and local government affords you against unwanted noise, there are things you can do to further quiet your surroundings, by going to the exterior. You may feel that the services of a landscape architect will be worthwhile and a good investment. Plantings of trees, shrubs and gardens all soften, deaden or divert noise. Fences and hedges are useful as baffles where they don't create more of a problem (from neighbors) than they eliminate. The correct placement of the garage can be advantageous as a noise barrier.

In summary, prerequisites to soundproofing a house are:

1. Solid basic construction
2. Wall, ceiling and attic insulation
3. Tightly fitted pipes and mechanical systems without noise producing defects
4. Snug fitting flooring
5. Generous use of draperies, carpeting and furnishings
6. Exterior landscaping techniques

For a complete Noise checklist see Checklist 58, page C-123.

SAFETY

We are a country of people which opts for safety glass and the safety belt in cars, the safety razor in the bathroom and child-proof safety tops on medicine containers. We invented the safety match which lighted the way to the safety warning on book matches—"close cover before striking." That modern miracle of design, the safety pin, like the mousetrap, has yet to be improved upon.

We seem to care for our physical being routinely when we close our front doors and step out into the world each day. But how well do we care for our physical being on the other side of that door, within the "safety" of our own homes? We care extremely well for our creature comforts but often sacrifice safety for it. What we do to safeguard ourselves from accidents in the average home leaves much to be desired. The slogan "Safety First" does not seem to apply in most of the country as evidenced by the startling statistics on accidents, injuries and deaths in the home directly attributable to carelessness and unsafe conditions.

Accidental deaths in the home rank second only to deaths on the highway. Approximately 27,000 Americans lose their lives in home accidents in a typical year. Just as solemn a statistic is that nearly 4.5 million other Americans are injured annually in home accidents to the point of becoming disabled. It is not farfetched, then, to parallel a household which has unsafe conditions and hazards with that of a speeding car or one being driven by someone who is intoxicated. You certainly wouldn't knowingly subject yourself to such a situation, yet you are in just as much jeopardy within your own house if you don't constantly monitor the situations and areas which could cause mishaps.

It stands to reason that a house which is relatively "safe" overall is a better buy than one which is unsafe and will have to be made safe. The general areas to be concerned with are the *interior* of your home from cellar to attic, the *exterior* of your home including the landscaping, and the *environment* around you. Another area of concern, and one which we include a special section on, is *child safety*.

INTERIOR

Basic Construction. Floors that were either laid improperly or which have buckled, separated, pulled away from the wall, or in some other manner become uneven are a menace.

Wood rot or damage from termites can cause a sudden collapse of floor sections. Often the damage is done long before it is noticed, particularly to homes that have no basements and are built over a crawl space. If you have the slightest doubt, call in professional termite inspectors.

Windows which are not well-puttied and have loose glass are a threat, particularly to very old people who require more strength to open a window. They face the danger of accidentally forcing the glass from its frame and of being cut on the face, arms and hands. Putty is cheap and easy to apply. (But don't fall off the ladder while doing it!)

Nine out of ten deaths from accidents within the home occur in the age 65 and over group. This is the group which also suffers the most serious and crippling injuries. A preponderance of falls, which is the most common of all accidents, occur in the bathroom due to the nature of its construction and function. Water, soap and tile is a deadly combination particularly for the elderly and the very young. Bathtubs and shower walls should be equipped with strong hand bars in strategic places. These should be applied to the wall with long screws. Cemented-on soap trays do not make good "grab rails" as they frequently pull away from the wall when undue pressure is put on them. The tub should have a nonskid surface applied if it is not the newest texturized type. A slanted grab rail beside the toilet steadies an elderly person as he or she sits and rises. No electric pull chains or switches should be located where they can be reached from the tub.

Many post-World War II homes were designed with windows high up on the walls. This was thought to be good for privacy and for better furniture arrangement. While that may or may not have proven true, one thing is obvious. It is not a good design in case of fire. For safety reasons, there should always be at least one bedroom window placed not more than three feet from the floor.

The kitchen, for all its association with warmth and pleasure, can easily be the arena of disaster as well. A highly waxed floor may look beautiful but is about as harmless as walking on a beautiful ice pond in January. It is better to achieve a nonskidding surface in any one of several ways available to you.

All kitchen areas, particularly sink, stove and entrances should be well lighted. Most accidents occur because people either don't look where they are going or cannot see where they are going. Wall switches at door entrances should be standard. It is dangerous to walk into a dark room. The stove and electrical equipment should be kept in good repair and all those exotic and efficient small appliances should be returned to their cabinets or drawers as soon as possible after use.

Stairs. Although a fall on a level spot may be as dangerous as a fall downstairs, it is unlikely that you'd choose the latter given a choice!

The objective of a well-planned stairway is to provide ascent and descent, plus a design and arrangement of stairs which assures adequate headroom and space for moving furniture and equipment. Particularly treacherous are the one and two-step stairs between rooms which change the floor level only slightly.

Stairways need to be treated with healthy respect. They should have sturdy, well-attached railings with brackets securely screwed or lag bolted on at least one side and which run the length of the staircase, be it a straight one, broken or curved. The handrail may also be supported by posts (balusters). Stairways should be well lit, with a switch at both top and bottom.

Any treads which squeak or feel loose should be checked and repaired. It is wise to inspect stair carpeting periodically so that a tight installation can be maintained and to ensure that no tacks or nails have worked loose. Stepping on a small tack could easily cause a fall.

The treads themselves should be at least ten inches wide and the risers approximately six inches high. (The maximum riser height condoned by the FHA for interior stairs is eight and one-quarter inches). Most importantly the risers should each be of uniform size. Even small variations cause missteps and loss of balance.

Not having enough headroom can be another cause of accidents. Lack of headroom most frequently occurs on the attic and/or basement stairs. Here, too, a continuous handrail should be installed on at least one side of each flight of stairs. Stairs which are open on both sides, including basement stairs, should have a continuous handrail on one side and a railing on the open portion on the other side. Railings should also be installed around the open sides of all other interior stairwells including the attic, which has traditionally held a fascination for children. The best lighting standards should be followed in the basement and attic areas regardless of how infrequently they are used.

Electrical. The danger of fires of electrical origin has been greatly reduced in the past decade as knowledge, techniques and new materials have evolved. But in no way are we 100 percent free of them.

The old system of wiring a house was to run two insulated wires parallel to each other from the panel box (usually in the cellar) to the outlets and fixtures. A separate pair of wires was run for each circuit, a few inches apart and attached to the house with white procelain insulators called knobs. When the wire passed through a wall or joist, it went through procelain tubes (hence referred to as knob and tube wiring). This system, while obsolete, is still in existence. Replacing it is a major expense. Knob and tube wiring must be viewed very suspiciously. Its insulation tends to crack with age, leaving exposed wires which are very dangerous.

In building, the wire choices today are:

1. Non-metallic cable (cheapest system available)
2. Armored cable (the popular name is B.X.)
3. Flexible steel conduit
4. Rigid steel pipe—most preferred and expensive

Another item which needs close scrutiny, especially in an older house, is the fuse box. All the fuses should be the right size so that the various circuits in the house are protected from being overloaded. The circuit breaker (or fuse) cuts off the electrical curent when the circuits become overloaded, thus preventing the wiring from becoming overheated and potentially dangerous.

Each general circuit should serve no more than 360 to 500 square feet of floor area. A 1,500 square-foot house could meet minimum standards[2] with three general circuits, but really should have five. Special circuits for small appliances are protected with 20-ampere fuses and cannot be used for large appliances. There should be at least two special circuits for heavier electric use.

Large appliances such as clothes dryers, water heaters, ranges, dishwashers, freezers and large window air conditioners require large amounts of watts and often 220 to 240 volts and special three-wire circuits using wire from No. 12 to No. 6 size (the lower the number the larger the wire). These circuits are protected with 30 to 60-ampere fuses or circuit breakers.

If the size of the wire used in a circuit is too small, the light and appliances do not work at peak efficiency. The bulbs shine dimmer than they should and the appliances do not work as well or get as hot as they are designed to do. The same amount of electricity comes through the electric meter and is paid for even though the electricity is not providing maximum performance. This is because the undersize wire itself is creating extra resistance and turning the electricity into heat.

Inadequate Wiring. The problem of inadequate wiring starts with inadequate voltage and amperage coming into the house. A minimum 220 to

---

[2] National Electric Code and FHA standards.

240 volts and 100 amperes should be supplied, more if the house is large, has many major electric appliances (especially ranges and clothes dryers) or has electric heat and air conditioning.

Lack of sufficient branch circuits to the various appliances and rooms of the house can be corrected by installing a bigger distribution panel and additional wiring. Use of fuses that have higher ratings than called for is a sign that the wiring is under the needed capacity. Having insufficient wall outlets in rooms leads to the use of dangerous extension cords and monkey plugs. Lack of outside outlets is an inconvenience.

The duplex receptacle was, until 1960, the most common type of household outlet used. It accepts a two-prong plug, the type most often found on lamps and small appliances. In 1960 the National Electric Code and the FHA Minimum Property Standards (MPS) required that all receptacles be the grounding type designed to accept a three-prong as well as a two-prong plug. Many small appliances are wired with a third ground wire that is attached to the frame or metal housing of the appliance. The third slot in a grounded outlet is connected to a water pipe or other grounding metal. Grounding of an appliance by using a three-prong plug and receptacle reduces its shock hazard.

Switches. Wall switches are used to control permanently installed light fixtures and may also be used to control wall outlets. Rooms without permanent light fixtures are becoming very common as ceiling fixtures in some rooms continue to go out of style and lamps gain in popularity. However, it is dangerous to have to walk into a dark room to turn on a lamp. A wall switch near the door that controls the wall outlet into which a lamp is plugged eliminates this problem.

A good indication of an adequate switching arrangement is being able to walk anywhere in the house and turn on a path of light and then turn off the lights without having to retrace steps or walk in the dark. This includes getting in and out of bed or entering and leaving the house by both entrances and through the garage.

Glass. It is appalling that thousands of people were injured last year by walking into or through nonsafety glass in the form of patio doors, storm doors, picture windows, tub enclosures and other panes used in residences. The irony is that these architectural glass panes were installed to enhance and beautify the home and instead became the instruments of mutilation and horror.

Most states have implemented the provisions of the safety standards for architectural glazing materials issued by the Consumer Product Safety Commission which became effective July, 1977. "The standard applies to glazing material and architectural products incorporating glazing materials that are produced or distributed for sale to or for the personal use of consumers in or around a permanent household or residence, or in recreational, school or other buildings or parts thereof open to the public."[3]

If you buy or build a home which will use glass panes functionally (other than windows) you should use some sort of device such as a decal as a warning against potential accidents. If you have very young children, put something on a glass door at *their* eye level so that they will not walk into it.

The use of laminated glass, acrylic plastic and polycarbonate plastic are definitely your best choices because it is more difficult to break them.

Be especially cautious if you have an older house since virtually none of them will have any type of safety glass. Storm doors are particularly "vicious."

Federal Regulations. Happily, along with all the other new safety regulations now in effect, we have the government ruling that all glass replacement for storm doors be of approved safety glass.

Not all architectural glazing materials are subject to new federal standards. Only those intended for use in products which have the greatest injury potential have been included. Even within these products there are certain exceptions. The following list describes which products are subject to the standard.

1. Storm doors or combination doors
2. Other doors intended for human passage
3. Bathtub doors and enclosures
4. Shower doors and enclosures
5. Sliding glass doors (patio type)
6. Certain glazed panels (only these which present a high risk of injury)

Gas (Natural and Manufactured). Many American homes use natural or manufactured (liquefied petroleum gas) to supply power for a number of home appliances, mainly the furnace, hot water heater, space heater, stove, refrigerator, fireplaces and clothes dryers.

The local gas company or supplier will service the systems in most areas. If you suspect a gas leak, call them immediately. If it should be at a late hour or for some reason they are unavailable, do not hesitate to call your local fire department.

Meanwhile, no matter where you smell the gas, you should check the pilot lights on all the gas appliances. Also check the stove burners. Someone may have turned one on, which for some reason was left open and unlit. Children occasionally do this. Or someone's clothing may have brushed against a stove knob.

---

[3] *Explanatory Bulletin on Safety Standard for Architectural Glazing Materials* (Washington: Consumer Product Safety Commission).

After a quick check, if you can't locate the source of the escaping gas quickly, open windows and turn off the main gas shutoff valve which is located near your gas meter. In the event that you are using bottled gas, you will find a different shutoff arrangement. In fact, don't wait for an emergency to locate these valves. Acquaint every member of the family with their locations as part of your family fire drills. Above all, while waiting for the service representative or fire department, do not light your cigarette or pipe to relieve the tension. You are very likely to relieve yourself of more than tension if you do.

The first thing to do when an emergency has passed and the gas is turned on is once again to check all pilot lights to see that they are properly lit. Should there be a malfunction in a pilot light, your gas company is usually happy to repair it or make the necessary adjustment. If not, you'll have to call your own repair person. Don't hesitate for any reason.

Caution, common sense and cleanliness are three necessary ingredients in cooking. If your gas stove burner is clogged with spilled-over food, it will not ignite. If the spills get to the pilot light, it will be quenched. Some burners are removable and can be cleaned or soaked clean at the sink. A non-removable burner will have to be cleaned with a stiff brush, lifting food particles up and out, or in some other manner.

Miscellaneous Interior Hazards

- Throw rugs and scatter rugs can be very dangerous, especially on steps. Each one should have an inexpensive nonslip pad under it.
- Many cleaning aids are poisonous. They must be kept in places that are inaccessible to children.
- Insecticides must also be kept where children cannot get at them.
- No empty refrigerators should be kept on the premises. Children can get into them and lock themselves inside.
- When you are cooking care must be taken not to leave the handles of pots and pans hanging over the edge of stoves. Children can grab them and be burned by the contents spilling on them.
- Power mowers, snow blowers and other yard equipment that is stored in the basement or other parts of the house must be so stored that children cannot get at them.

EXTERIOR

It is truly a tragedy that many of the home casualties, deaths, injuries and disfigurements would never happen if families had a policy of regularly inspecting their homes' exteriors.

Stairs and Porches. The exterior stairs and porches seem to be "favorite" spots for accidents. Stairs and railings should be inspected regularly for structural defects, rotting or looseness. Where no handrail exists, one should be installed, so that it runs from the top level to the edge of the first step on porches, terraces, stairwells or any other change in levels. It is particularly important, as with interior stairs, that the risers be of uniform height (no more than seven and one-half inches) and the treads of all the same width. Any unevenness invites trouble.

Overhanging shrubbery or branches cut down visibility and impair vision. They should be eliminated. Structural weaknesses are often aided and abetted by termites or carpenter ants which can undermine an entire porch before the danger is noted.

Walks and Driveways. Sidewalks should be kept in good repair. Cracks and holes should be filled, with the surface kept as even as possible. In colder climates, frost heaves should be levelled as soon as the "season" is past. Walks should be free of obstructions such as overhanging branches or a post placed too closely to the walk. They should be well illuminated if used at night. Flagstones, brick walks and terraces are often uneven and slippery when wet. In these areas, special care in walking is about the only accident prevention measure possible. Many homeowners appear to be willing to run the risk, in exchange for the beauty of these areas.

On driveways, which in many instances also serve as the walkway to the back or side entrance of the house, cracks and holes should be filled as they appear. Grease and oil spots should be removed regularly. Northern winters are especially rough on asphalt driveways, due to salt and various additives used in road sanding. These substances are tracked in by the tires and undercarriage of cars and deposited on the asphalt surface. Periodically, driveway sealer has to be applied. This has the added advantage of looking nice, as well as preserving the surface of the driveway and hence its life.

If your driveway needs a major overhaul, by all means consult a reputable firm. Do NOT hire anyone who comes to your door because he "happened to be in the neighborhood" and is therefore willing to install a new one or resurface this one, for "almost nothing."

When you do hire a reliable person, get a contract listing each specification of work and materials, the completion date and finally, a written guarantee of the life expectancy of the driveway.

Garages. There are far more hazards in the average garage than there are in your living room. To minimize the dangers inherent in our two-car garage society, follow several simple precautions:

- Keep the floor area free from clutter. Trite and true, "everything in its place. . . ."
- Keep flammables in safety cans—the kerosene for your patio lamps

and gasoline for your mower should be tightly capped and instantly recognizable. Store safely away from children. Don't smoke nearby.

- Store your garden sprays in their original containers. If the label is not intact, prepare a new one. Store these preparations on a high shelf, and *do* always empty your spraying equipment when a job is completed.
- Make regular and routine checks of the hinges between the sections of overhead doors, searching for signs of loose screws, rust in hinges or cracks in the metal.

There should be no low projecting eaves on the garage overhang where you walk to enter it or your car; no obstructions of lamp posts or branches to block your vision. If you have a sidewalk in front of your home which is intersected by the driveway, that intersection should be kept particularly shipshape as it is more likely to suffer from the ravages of constant traffic. Most sidewalks are simply not built to withstand the pressure which a driveway undergoes.

Hedges, in all their glory, unless carefully pruned and trimmed, are a menace to driver and pedestrian alike. They should do nothing to obstruct vision—yours or your neighbors'—when driving in or out.

The usual winter admonitions bear repetition. Keep porches, handrails, steps and sidewalks clear of snow and ice. Sprinkle sand, chemical de-icers, sawdust or other suitable substances on the ice also. Sand and wet leaves are treacherous underfoot especially on an incline, and should be removed.

Swimming Pools. In the "active-age" groups, drowning ranks second in fatalities only to motor vehicle accidents, and the majority of the fatal water accidents occur in the pursuit of recreational play or leisure-time activities, according to data released by the American Red Cross. When you consider that almost 15 million families in the United States own a pool of some type (including the inflatable wading variety), you can see the ease with which an accident can occur. Ironically, about a third of the nearly 300 deaths due to pool drowning annually occur in a neighbor's or relative's yard and not at home.

For these reasons alone, the installation of residential pools is a growing concern to neighbors, communities and their safety officials. Most municipalities have a list of regulations and specifications which must be met by the homeowner who has an in- or above-ground pool. Constant vigilance and supervision is the unwritten Rule No. 1.

Fencing or an enclosure of some type is required by law in most communities, primarily to protect against small children or trespassers. The use of filters and drains is also governed. In those areas where there is no such requirement, the pool owner shouldn't wait for such legislation. Every possible protective measure should be taken, from the fencing to the self-latching gate and lock, to the easy availability of a "reaching" pole, lifesavers, cushions and similar devices. Some owners install float lines and other aids. Small wading pools should *always* be emptied after use and then up-ended.

It is expensive, but an excellent idea, to install an alarm system which will apprise you of any uninvited guest in the pool area or water. Pool covers are also desirable.

Good maintenance and regular inspection is both safety-wise and economically prudent. Winter draining presents different problems in different parts of the country. If you "inherited" a pool with the house you bought, try to find out who installed it, and contact the firm if any maintenance or repair problems arise. Some repairs are simple to make. Cracks or breaks in concrete pools can be patched fairly easily—left too long, they are unsafe and become more expensive to correct. There are many types of plastic materials available.

Above all, each family member should be impressed (as young as possible) that a knowledge of the dangers inherent in swimming and general enjoyment of the pool plus being able to swim and to handle oneself well are basic to safety in the pool or relaxing beside it.

MISCELLANEOUS HAZARDS TO YOUR HOME SAFETY

The majority of other hazards to your safety within your own home environment are due to carelessness, naiveté or ignorance. Some of the most common are reflected in this checklist of do's and don't's:

1. Keep walking areas and doorways clear of furniture or other obstructions.
2. Screen your fireplace when in use, and put the fire out before retiring or leaving the house. Installing protective (and incidentally, attractive) Pyrex-type glass doors is a safeguard.
3. Have many well-spaced electrical wall outlets on each wall to avoid doubling up (or tripling) connections.
4. Provide yourself with a rack or cabinet in which to store your gun collection under lock and key. Lock away the ammunition separately somewhere else.
5. Keep stairways clear of objects. Teach children never to leave toys on stairs or in the traffic pattern in your house.
6. Take clotheslines down when not in use. A child running could be severely hurt if playing near one. An adult getting the night air or walking the dog in the dark could walk into it as well.
7. Fill potholes and depressions in your lawn. Clear debris after storms as soon as possible. Remove (or have removed) dead tree branches, which are a threat to your property, wires or house.
8. Follow directions explicitly in the use of outdoor equipment, from

tractors to grass edgers. Never use any of these appliances in your bare feet and never leave any of them running or plugged in, unattended.

9. *DO* take one of the many courses on safety and first aid available to you. Do take another member of the family along. Urge each family member to enroll in at least one of these courses sometime.

10. Keep a list of emergency numbers near each telephone.

For a complete Safety checklist, see Checklist 59, page C-125.

CHILD SAFETY

Since children are in the care of grown-ups (parents, teachers, grandparents, sitters) for the major part of their young lives, it is very clear where the responsibility for accident prevention and of safety education lies. It is therefore up to the adult to provide safe conditions and make safety a household word and family affair and to set a good example in obeying the rules of safety at home.

The following checklist for child safety in your home is a comprehensive outline of positive and preventive measures which can surely avert needless tragedy.

Kitchen

- Be sure that matches and cigarette lighters are out of sight and reach.
- Keep young children away from the stove whether it is turned on or not.
- Do not leave appliances (toasters, irons, blenders) on counters or a board, plugged in and/or with cords dangling.
- Keep pans on back of stove, and others with handles turned in.
- Keep knives and sharp utensils out of reach; poisons and cleaning aids locked up.
- Allow no flammable material in the vicinity of the stove.
- Keep the kitchen clean; free from moisture on the floor.
- Be a good housekeeper and sweep up spilled foods or broken china immediately. Discard cracked or chipped glasses.

Bathroom

- Never leave water in a tub or sink.
- Never leave a child alone in a tub or on a bathing table.
- Lock up all medicine. Keep cosmetic aids, razor blades and sharp toiletry instruments out of reach.
- Keep electrical equipment (razors, electric curlers and irons, radios and massagers etc.) away from sink and tub when not in use.

Bedroom

- See that toys are put away where they can't cause falls.
- Secure windows and screens, less a child fall out.
- Supply plenty of light.
- Have adequate fire escape routes; a window low enough for egress.
- Have fire drills.
- Never use lead paint on furniture.
- Buy only flame/fire retardant sleepwear.

Yard

- Keep power tools inaccessible to curious youngsters.
- Use garden tools and sharp objects only for their intended purpose. Keep them properly stored.
- Teach your child never to run carrying sticks, rods or bottles and never to put similar objects in the mouth, even while walking.
- Store ladders safely away, especially stepladders which ingenious small fry find intriguing to play on and under.
- Keep your yard free of hazards such as boards with nails in them, broken glass and litter. Store rubbish in tightly covered containers in a separate, specific area for this alone. Make it off limits.
- Do NOT have low clotheslines, and remove any others when not in use. Have no loose ropes available.
- Never leave lighted grills or fireplaces unattended. Do not dispose of live coals; douse them thoroughly.
- Remove doors from old freezers and refrigerators. And, preferably, get rid of them entirely.
- Keep driveway clear for full visibility in order to better see small children. Have safety rules agreed upon with your children if the drive area also doubles as a basketball court, bicycle drive or skateboard area. Maybe some children still play hopscotch, too!
- Do have a complete pool and water safety program with your family. Have discussions and drills. Hold practice sessions. Try to take water safety courses. Consult the section in this chapter on swimming pools.

Other

- Use doorgates for toddlers at top or bottom of stairs.
- Know and train your baby sitter. Leave a list of emergency numbers, instructions and regulations.
- Provide yourself with a liquor closet or storage area which can be locked away from youngsters.
- Instruct (and oversee) young children not to play near fans, television sets, sewing machines or the ironing board.

- Never allow children to play with fireworks and chemistry sets except under adult supervision.
- The workshop, laundry and places where things are stored have a magnetic effect on young children. Render them inaccessible.
- Don't leave croquet wickets up after dusk!
- It is also possible for a young toddler to get violently ill or even die from eating the leaves of poisonous house plants or berries from shrubs. Teach your children early that *nothing* but the good food and drink you provide for them should enter their mouths.

For a complete Child Safety checklist see Checklist 60, page C-127.

FIRE PROTECTION

Even as you read this, somewhere in the U.S. a fire has just started. By the time you finish the chapter, at least 300 fires will be raging somewhere across the land and at least one death will result, not to mention scores of injuries and devastating property loss.

Of the approximately 10,000 victims of building fires in a typical year, almost nine out of ten will die in home fires. It is inconceivable that there is one school in our nation which has never conducted a fire drill, yet there are fewer than 100 school fires a week as compared with thousands of dwelling fires every day, which account for approximately 87 percent of all fire deaths in buildings!

The tragedy, suffering and property damage could be greatly lessened if every householder took steps to eliminate potential home fire hazards and to develop a plan of escape with the family. We need sound practices in the home, starting *with* the home, and we must be educated to react properly when fire threatens. These criteria can be met by 1) ensuring that your home is built with fire-safety consciousness in mind; 2) eliminating fire hazards; 3) developing a plan of escape—Operation EDITH (Evacuation Drill In The Home); and 4) installation of smoke detectors and extinguishers.

FIRE-SAFE MATERIALS

Ensuring that your home is fire-safe must start literally from the ground up. If you are building a new house, you, your architect and contractor should discuss the materials and construction methods which will be used.

The impact of new materials and systems should be assessed very carefully during the design and planning of a new home, long before you move in. All of your appliances should bear the label of Underwriters Laboratories (UL), American Gas Association or other recognized major testing laboratory. Your new furnace, hot water heater, air conditioner and various other systems and major appliances should be installed and wired only by a *licensed* electrician, not by a handyman or a friend. Defective and inadequate electrical wiring and other equipment is one of today's major causes of fires.

Asphalt roofing is most commonly used today in new home construction. Other popular materials, more expensive than asphalt, are (treated) cedar shakes, tile and slate. Fortunately, the Underwriters Lab tests and rates most of the roofing being produced today for fire resistance, wind resistance and other factors.

Most asphalt shingles are made to meet tight fire-safety standards. Asphalt shingles with a Class C listing have been tested to make sure they will not ignite easily and will not spread fire rapidly. Shingles listed as Class A offer protection against severe fire exposure. Needless to say tile and slate go beyond that in their fire protection properties. If you have questions about the flammability characteristics of any of the materials which will go into your house from the paint to the paneling, call upon your local fire marshall's office. No house is completely fireproof but you must do all within your power to minimize the risks.

It should be a relatively simple matter in buying a new house to contact the builder and get most of your answers about construction, materials, fixtures, wiring, warranties, guarantees, plumbing, electrical and heating systems, insulation and UL or other fire test labels on appliances. Some new homes are now coming equipped with smoke detectors. If you don't see one, ask for it. They don't cost a lot of money, and the builder might include it free if you ask for one.

Next, look at the house very objectively, as to exit. How would you and your family get out of each room? Are there obstacles?

The older, previously owned house particularly requires close inspection. It would be good insurance for you to engage the services of a qualified inspector who can evaluate the condition and quality of the old wiring, the furnace and hot water heater, fireplace and chimney and fuse box circuits.

There are now home inspection firms in many cities that provide complete and unbiased inspection, not only reporting on the condition of the home, but also suggesting the cheapest and best means of correcting defects and hazards. The average cost for this service is $100 to $200 depending upon the value of the house, its age and location.

Faulty wiring; chimneys without flues or damaged flues; a crack in the heating system; defective ducts; tinder-like joists, studs and rafters; infrequent or inadequate fire stops; dried-out, nonfireproof roofs are all conditions which exist to some degree in many old houses. Furthermore, many old house attics were insulated with sawdust and occasionally wood shavings or newspapers. The use of fire resistant materials or fire retardant paint was rare. The practiced eye of a professional inspector can evaluate all of these hazards and aid you in achieving maximum safe conditions.

But this is just the beginning of what should be a total program of fire prevention in your home. It matters not if you live in a mansion or a cottage, a brand-new or a vintage house—all the ingredients for a fire are there: fuel, heat, oxygen and chain reaction.

Once a fire starts, it builds up heated gases very quickly and can produce temperatures of 800 degrees in a very short time. Bare wood will then ignite in a few seconds and spread its flames by contact with any combustible material and by the hot air and gases that rise and surge through open doors, up stairways, through halls and wall spaces. The speed at which this can happen might be just a matter of minutes.

If there are no fire stops between the wall studs, the devastating gases will travel between floor joists and into any wall spaces available; they are able to burst furiously into flame far from the original source of the fire. Fire stops between wall studs, particularly in the basement where many fires originate, can deter the rapid growth of a fire. Installing a basement ceiling of fire-resistant material is also an excellent preventive measure. Gypsum board has a low surface flamespread rating and is good material for this purpose.

A FAMILY ESCAPE PLAN

The majority of all fire deaths (80 percent) are due to *smoke* and *deadly gases*. This danger can be greatly lessened in several ways, with emphasis on the first priority—a family fire escape plan:

1. Sit down with the family and draw a floor plan of your home, labeling the bedrooms, hallways, stairways, room doors, exit doors to outside and windows. Depict roofs, decks, balconies or other areas which might provide escape from the upper floors. You needn't worry if your plan doesn't resemble a rendering by Frank Lloyd Wright. It only matters that you get the point across: *How Best To Get Out.*
2. Mark the normal exit route with heavy arrows. Next, plan and mark an alternate route from each bedroom with a different color arrow. Halls and stairways are often blocked by heat and smoke, so it is imperative to have an alternate exit.
3. Impress upon everyone that smoke and deadly gases kill 80 percent of fire victims, and that they must get to fresh air very quickly. If the smoke is heavy, the face should be covered. Since smoke tends to rise, the air at the floor level is more breathable. It is best to crawl, not walk, out of a smoke-filled room.
4. Designate a prearranged spot where everyone can meet outside the

house. In conjunction with this step, plan on how you will evacuate infants, invalids or anyone else who is helpless. If the family pets can be rescued without endangering a life for one second, all well and good. But stress that once outside, forget valuables. Do not reenter. Stay at your meeting place.

5. A rope or chain ladder should be kept on an upper floor where there is no other possible way of escape except through a window, should the door be blocked. Discuss how to drop from a window or roof, if necessary, by backing over the edge, holding the sill or gutter and then dropping down with knees slightly flexed.

6. Practice removing a storm window or screen, with children. If this becomes a problem during an emergency, urge everyone to break the glass with a chair or any other object, taking care of course not to be injured by the glass.

7. Familiarize each family member with the location of the fire alarm box nearest your home and how to operate it.

8. At least once a week have each family member take a turn reciting the procedure:
   a. When fire is suspected or discovered, alert everyone in the house
   b. *Get out of the house*
   c. Meet at the designated spot
   d. Notify the fire department through neighbors or alarm box
   e. DO NOT reenter the house

9. Go through your EDITH (Evacuation Drill In The House) several times at first and then routinely at least once a year. Surprise the family now and again by calling a drill. Hold at least one of your fire drills in the dark. It is wise to keep a small flashlight in each bedroom. These may be used for the night fire drills as well as for other purposes. Invite your regular baby sitter to one of your sessions. Discuss escape routes with any other sitters, and impress on them the importance of getting everyone out quickly, and of *staying out* of the house.

It should become increasingly apparent that getting out of the house very quickly into fresh air should be your first priority. Again, only 20 percent of fire victims are burned to death. Eighty percent die of smoke or gas inhalation.

SMOKE AND HEAT DETECTORS

Once you have your family well acquainted with Operation EDITH, there are additional precautions to be taken. The most inexpensive and dependable way to protect your family is with the installation of home smoke detectors. There are several types of detectors which are easily obtainable. You will have to decide which kind of detector best suits your purpose: smoke detector alarms, heat detection alarms or a combination-type alarm. Your local fire department is the best source of information on the relative advantages and disadvantages of these various alarms and detectors.

OTHER PREVENTIVE MEASURES

Additional protection from the horrors and hazards of fire can be gained by having a fire extinguisher handy. Probably the best place to keep an all-purpose type of extinguisher, which is designed specifically for home use, is near the kitchen. Additional ones would be best hung in the garage and basement/workshop area. To be effective, a fire extinguisher has to be easily reached, maintained in perfect operating condition, inspected frequently and recharged according to directions. Its operation must be made familiar to all members of the family who might be responsible for its use.

The installation of a lightning protection system is often advisable. The natural fear that humans and animals alike have of lightning is well founded and not to be taken lightly. The powerful discharge of atmospheric electricity can kill, shock and burn and bring destruction. Lightning storms annually account for many deaths and injuries, the ignition of forest fires that burn thousands of acres of timber, and many residential fires and deaths.

Homeowners can protect their property with properly installed and maintained lightning protection systems (rods). Consult a licensed electrician. Look for the "Master Label " plate issued by Underwriters Laboratories (UL) as an assurance of quality and efficiency.

It is also an excellent precautionary measure to have a garden hose hooked-up permanently to a special faucet in the basement for extinguishing wood or paper fires. Chemical fire extinguishers are necessary for other flammables such as oil and electrical fires. A garden hose connected year round outside, if elements permit, also gives protection.

WOOD-BURNING STOVES

Wood-burning stoves are a recent addition to many households. The combination of the energy crunch and Bicentennial-inspired nostalgia have been major factors in the sky-rocketing sales across the land, primarily in the North.

The Ben Franklin stove and the classic potbelly, as well as several variations, have been popular. As romantic and thrifty as this is, installing a cast iron stove is not just a matter of bringing it into the house and putting it where you want it for decor, or simply where you have room for it.

A wood-burning stove is capable of giving off a tremendous amount of heat in and around itself and up through its smoke pipe. In some models, coal may be used as the fuel. In no case should you burn charcoal *inside* your home, in the stove or fireplace. This gives off a noxious gas. The heat produced has the real potential of setting fire to the floor, wall and ceiling.

The length of pipe from stove to outside is also of utmost importance. Smoke pipes should extend at least two feet above any part of a roof or roof ridge if not vented into a chimney. The smoke pipe should be constructed of a fireproof material equivalent to U.S. Standard 24-gauge steel. Factory-built chimneys should be listed by Underwriters Laboratories and installed in exact accordance with the listing, If it says to lay a piece of protective sheet metal under the stove area, do it! Fires get hot and sparks fall out onto floors as the fire is being stoked, poked and played with.

Never connect your stove to the flue for the central heating unit (furnace) of the house. Each piece of equipment must have its own flue.

GENERAL FIRE PREVENTION PRACTICES

- Have a fire escape plan, and regular drills with the family.
- Install a fire alarm system.
- Install a lightning protection system.
- Have heating equipment (furnace) cleaned and checked annually.
- Keep space heaters and smoke pipes away from combustible walls, furniture and storage closets.
- Use correct fuses and circuit breakers and do not overload wiring; label them for identification.
- Care for and clean your fireplace regularly. Do not burn charcoal in it as this is a hazard indoors. Screen it.
- Have chimneys cleaned and checked regularly.
- Replace worn out wiring and fixtures.
- Use drywall or plaster when remodeling.
- Be sure that your hot water heater has a pressure relief valve, piped near the floor (and toward it).
- Determine the cause of a blown fuse before it is replaced or a circuit restored.
- Know the location of your main electric switch and how to turn it off before doing even the slightest electrical work. Apprise your family of its location.
- Dispose of trash and rubbish. Store flammables in metal containers.
- Be fire-safety conscious at all times.

For a complete Fire Protection checklist see Checklist 61, page C-129.

HOME SECURITY

"Home Security Starts At Your Door"[4] is the title of an interesting pamphlet which will suggest to you many ways of making your home more resistant to forced entry. The information in this pamphlet resulted from research performed by the Law Enforcement Standards Laboratory, National Bureau of Standards, under the sponsorship of the National Institute for Law Enforcement and Criminal Justice, U.S. Department of Justice. In a sentence, the Laboratory's finding is that if you want to protect your home against burglary, the place to start is literally at your door.

If you are worried about the increasing threat of having your home burglarized and possessions stolen, you have every reason to be! According to FBI statistics, a burglary takes place on an average of once every 13 seconds. *No other criminal activity occurs more often—or threatens so many people.*

In the past decade, night time residence burglaries have increased by 95 percent; daytime residence burglaries by 300 percent. The average family therefore is running an ever-increasing risk of being victimized by criminals. But why start at the door?

DOORS

Statistics compiled in case after case of burglary across the land indicate that almost all "intrusions" were made through doors, or attempted at doors, before resorting to the windows. "The right kind of doors, locks, frames and hinges can greatly increase your chances of keeping burglars out—and your valuables in," according to the National Bureau of Standards report.

Most professional thieves will get into a house no matter what kind of locks there are and what other precautions have been taken. And unfortunately, no one—and nothing—is safe from professional burglars and thieves today. However, many burglars are "bunglers"—that is, not professionals; therefore good hardware with locks that are difficult to pick, force or break will often act as a satisfactory deterrent. A solidly constructed door, hung with a well-fitted frame and secured with a good deadbolt lock, along with windows that will resist forced entry, together offer substantial protection for your home.

In some cases you may have to correct door construction problems in order to make your home more resistant to forced entry.

The most vulnerable of all, sliding glass doors, are particular favorites of the burglar. There are many ways to break in through them and, be

---

[4] "Home Security Starts At Your Door" (Washington: U.S. Dept of Commerce, National Bureau of Standards).

assured, the burglar in his versatility knows every one. Here are some methods of breaking in through glass doors and some suggested deterrents.

Methods

1. Doors can often be removed by lifting them from the track they slide in, even from outside the house.

2. Weak latches can be easily pried from the frame. Frames, usually of aluminum, have a great amount of "give".

3. Most of the hardware, such as the locks on average priced glass doors, is not very strong. The glass itself, however, is usually of satisfactory quality.

4. Some doors sold currently may be "in-stock" inventory and could be plate glass. Don't touch them at any price! They are extremely unsafe and a hazard to everyone (even to the burglar!).

Deterrent

1. Install spacers of some type—or screws with the heads left protruding in the grooves (track) above the doors so that they cannot be lifted.

2. Place a long enough piece of pipe or stick such as a broom handle in the bottom groove, so that even if the latch is broken, the door will not slide open.

3. Install one of the special sliding glass door locks which are very strong and specifically designed to prevent the door's removal.

4. Purchase *only* glass sliding doors which have a permanent label of the manufacturer, attesting to its being safety glass. This label may be affixed by means of etching, sandblasting, firing of the glazing material, hot-die stamping or other means, but it should be legible and visible.

For additional protection, many homeowners are turning to a home security alarm system. These systems are discussed later in this chapter.

LOCKS

We see it all the time, in movies and on television: The thief takes a plastic credit card, a thin metal strip or plastic bank calendar and slips it between the door and the frame to open the latch bolt. In some cases this is an education to juveniles.

The best kind of latch bolt on a lock has a spring plunger which will automatically lock the latch when it goes into the strike. If you do not have this type, consider getting one. A replacement is worth the small investment.

The addition of a good deadbolt lock to the automatic latch bolt will increase the security you are seeking. A deadbolt is a straight bar, usually rectangular, squared off at the end and locked only by turning a key or knob. The vertical bolt lock (which is especially good for double doors) is particularly effective against burglars who try to force the door from the frame.

A chain lock is desirable as it allows you to see who is at the door without fully opening it. But, it should NOT be your *only extra* lock. There are too many "weaknesses" in this link chain. You would be better off to have a peephole in your door. These are inexpensive to buy and fairly easy to install.

There are several kinds of "peepholes" (the more familiar term for optical viewers), ranging in diameter from a fraction of an inch to three inches. You have a choice of one-way glass, plastic glass and wide angle glass, in some combination.

The danger underlying the larger viewers is that there is a possibility that a burglar could break the glass and insert a tool with which to open the door from the inside. However, the new type of glasses make this extremely difficult to do.

The wide-angle peephole made of double glass allows maximum visibility and maximum safety conditions simultaneously.

Some doors merely have a pane of one-way glass which allows the homeowner to see out only. Unless the glass is one of the newer safety versions, however, it would be relatively easy for a burglar to gain entrance. This feature negates any advantage one-way glass offers.

Beware of having too many locks. It adds nothing to your security, for instance, to have four instead of three adequate locks—and you may even be locking yourself IN as you lock others out. This is particularly true if one of your locks is the type that requires a key to unlock it from the inside. If you have such a lock, be certain that the key is always accessible to everyone in the family, preferably in a place right at the door. Have duplicate ones made also, and tell family members where they are kept.

You should also have strong hinges, hung with long screws which go into good wood. The door hinges should be on the inside of the door so that the hinge pins are inaccessible to intruders. Some hinge pins are nonremovable. Most interlock when the door is closed, another good security value.

The ultimate in "security at your doorstep" would be a combination of 1) a wooden door with a solid core, approximately one and three-quarter inches thick (metal doors are preferable but are not aesthetically desirable for the single family residence); 2) a well fitting door in a strong frame with good quality hinges; and 3) a good deadbolt lock. But remember, the most ideal conditions in the world will not prevail if you leave your doors unlocked even for a moment.

GARAGE DOORS

Electrically operated garage door openers are no longer a rarity; and with the increase in numbers has come a decline in the cost. The "automatic" system provides good security because its motor is controlled by either a key switch inside the garage or by a low-power radio transmitter.

Because the garage usually houses more than just the average two cars today (cars are more often than not nestled between bikes, tools, a barbecue grill, a freezer, a lawnmower and even an occasional sailboat wintering in the rafters), it is evident that good security is all the more imperative.

If your garage doors operate manually, a slide bolt on the bottom section that is key operated should give adequate security. Again, that is, if you keep the doors closed!

FENCES

The use of security fences around the typical house is uncommon and unpopular. Only occasionally will you find a yard entirely fenced in with one or two gates which lock. There is an awareness that when you fence the world out you are also fencing yourself in, which is more or less self-induced isolation. Most people are not that antisocial.

If there is considerable property or if an estate must be protected for any number of reasons, there are modified and sophisticated forms of fencing to ensure the desired security. Or a home security alarm system can readily solve the problem.

The usual single home fence is more likely to consist of a hedge, a picturesque low picket fence, a split-rail cedar fence or a border of rambling roses—"token" fences.

The only means of security accomplished here is that such fencing does define the borders of the property, indicating to an outsider that this is the territory which belongs to that particular house and subtlety suggests that an intruder would be "noticed" within its confines.

HOME SECURITY ALARM SYSTEMS

One of the most effective deterrents to burglary is to install a reliable residential burglar alarm system.

Installing a burglar alarm system doesn't guarantee that burglars won't attempt to break into your home. But police officials tell us that an effective alarm system is the *single best deterrent* against burglary and robbery. And the logo of the alarm company, on a sticker which is displayed in a prominent place such as a living room window, seems to have a lot of clout on its own.

Like so many other things, an ineffective or unreliable alarm system is worse than no alarm at all. Before you purchase an alarm system be sure to check the company's professional credentials. Ask your local police officials and your Better Business Bureau. If you know of anyone who has a system, you might question them about the service and satisfaction with a particular company. The cost will be in the vicinity of $500 to $2,000-plus, depending upon the size of your house and other variables.

Regardless of the number of security firms now in business, or of the quality of the system, all security alarms are comprised of three basic parts: the detectors or sensors; the unit which controls it; and the actual alarm itself.

The detectors are electronic devices which detect the presence or activity of an intruder. The control unit is just that. It receives the proper "signals," then transmits them to the signal that triggers the alarm somewhere designated. There is also an auxiliary connecting system which can be activated manually by the homeowner (or anyone in the house) pressing a panic button, usually located in the area of the front door or bedroom.

Finally, the alarm is sounded when it "realizes" that one or more of the sensors has been disturbed. The alarm can be set to sound in the home or transmitted to a remote location such as to a police station or to the security company which monitors the system.

The most common detectors are:

1. Switch sensors: These are electromagnetic devices which are placed at each entry point of the house which is considered at all accessible to the ground, or, on a balcony door or window which could be reached from a tree branch or low roof.
2. Pressure mats: These devices are designed to protect specific areas. They are hidden under carpeting where there is a natural "traffic" flow in the residence, or near objects of value such as a wall safe, stereophonic system, or expensive photographic equipment.
3. Ultrasonic motion detectors: With this device, ultrasonic sound waves are caused to fill the room (or rooms). Movement within the room triggers the alarm by disturbing the sound wave pattern. Someone descending uninvited from a roof skylight would cause havoc with this type of sensor, where obviously a pressure mat would be useless. A skylight can be covered with metal bars or a grill, but purists find that distasteful, not wanting anything to mar the open view. A padlock will add to the security buy only in the event the glass isn't broken.
4. Photoelectric sensors: An infrared light beam is projected between two points such as on the opposite ends of sliding glass doors or across the foot or top of a staircase. The alarm is triggered by anything which interrupts the light beam. This type of detector is particularly effective at entry points, interior *and* exterior.

It is only sensible to familiarize each member of the family with the operation of the system. Once it is installed, maintain it exactly as the manufacturer and installing firm suggest. Don't try to test it yourself! The police department in one New England city took a dim view of the man who decided to test how quickly the local police could arrive at his house if he triggered his alarm. Not only did he find that out, but he also discovered—as would happen with a real intruder—that he was under arrest!

Above all, if you are in the house when the alarm goes off, stay out of the way. If possible lock yourself in a bedroom or bathroom. Make no move to retrieve your valuables or detain the burglar! When the alarm sounds, your intruder will have but one thought, and that is to get out of there as fast as possible. If the intruder is confronted he or she may cause harm. Remember, there is no need for you to be a hero!

SECURITY PRECAUTIONS

Not everyone wants or can afford a home security alarm system. But whether you have one or not, there are some basic practices and precautions which, in the final analysis, are just good common sense.

While on vacation:

- Have someone mow your lawn—or shovel the walks.
- Stop mail, newspaper and milk deliveries. Have someone (perhaps the person who cuts your grass, etc.) check the entrances to see that there has been no tampering, or no mail, papers or milk left accidentally.
- Inform your local police department of your departure and return date. Leave a key with a trusted neighbor or friend, along with a phone number where you can be reached.
- Follow instructions of your security alarm system which are clearly spelled out for the eventuality of a vacation away.
- Have several low wattage bulbs connected to automatic timers in various parts of the house set to go on when you ordinarily turn your lights on in the evening.
- You may wish to leave a radio turned on near one of your doors if you will be away for a brief time.
- Always leave your telephone connected and functioning.
- Keep the news of your trip quiet, except to close friends, and then, politely inform them not to do you any nice favors by having the news of "your cruise" put in the newspaper as a surprise for you. It may result in a "surprise" not anticipated.

Burglars breed on fortune, good and bad. If you are going to a family wedding, rely on the services of a friend or other reliable person to be your "house sitter"—and similarly for the misfortune of a family funeral. Since these affairs are routinely announced in the newspapers, burglars know exactly what time the family will be away from home. They peruse these and similar announcements very carefully.

Record the serial numbers of your valuables including your stereo equipment, camera, typewriter, television sets, calculator, small appliances and bicycles. In some instances your municipal police department or perhaps a local service club might loan out an instrument which can etch your name (or some predetermined number) onto this equipment for identification purposes.

With today's high incidence of crime, each precaution you take, however small and seemingly insignificant, should serve to strengthen the security of your home and provide you with peace of mind.

For a complete Home Security checklist, see Checklist 62, page C-131.

BIBLIOGRAPHY

How To Buy a House

Agan, Tessie and Luchsinger, Elaine. *The House—Principles/Resources/Dynamics.* Philadelphia: J. B. Lippincott, 1965.

Better Homes and Gardens. *How To Buy a House.* Des Moines, IA: Meredith Corp., 1978.

Biesterfeldt, R. C., et al. *Finding and Keeping a Healthy House.* Washington, DC: U.S. Dept. of Agriculture, Forest Service Misc. Publication 1284, 1974.

Callender, John. *Before You Buy a House.* New York: Crown Publishers, 1953.

Case, Fred E. *The Investment Guide To Home And Land Purchase.* Englewood Cliffs, NJ: Prentice-Hall, 1977.

Chicago Title Insurance Company. *The House Hunter's Guide.* Chicago: 1977.

Coppock, J. T. ed. *Second Homes: Curse or Blessing.* Oxford, England: Pergamon Press, 1977.

Davis, Joseph C. and Walker, Claxton. *Buying Your House.* New York: Emerson Books, 1975.

DeBenedictis, Daniel J. *The Complete Real Estate Adviser.* New York: Simon and Schuster, 1969.

Denton, John H. *Buying or Selling Your Home.* New York: Barrows and Co., 1961.

Duncan, Kenneth. *Home Builders and Home Buyers—The Blue Print for Happy Home Ownership.* New York: Funk and Wagnalls Co., 1951.

Eldred, Gary W. *House For Sale.* Columbia, SC: Harbour House, 1976.

Fowler, Glenn. *How To Buy a Home—How To Sell a Home.* New York: The Benjamin Co., 1969.

Griffin, Al. *So You Want To Buy a House.* Chicago: Henry Regnery Company, 1970.

Hess, Nancy. *The Home Buyer's Guide.* Englewood Cliffs, NJ: Prentice-Hall, 1976.

Indiana Association of REALTORS®. *Your Housing Preference Profile.* 1971.

Irwin, Robert. *How To Buy a Home at a Reasonable Price.* New York: McGraw-Hill, 1979.

Johnson, B. Kenneth, et al. *Building or Buying a House, a Guide to Wise Investment.* New York: McGraw-Hill.

Kilpatrick, W. A. *The House of Your Dreams*. New York: McGraw-Hill, 1958.

Lass, William M. *Lawyer's Title Home Buying Guide*. New York: Popular Library, 1969.

Lee Institute, *How To Choose Your House—And Live Happily Ever After*. Brookline, MA, 1965.

McCarthy, Kevin F. *Housing Search and Mobility*. Santa Monica, CA: Rand Corporation, 1979.

Mencher, Melvin, ed. *The Fannie Mae Guide to Buying, Financing and Selling Your Home*. Garden City, NY: Doubleday, 1975.

Moger, Byron. *How To Buy a House*. New York: Lyle Stuart, 1967.

Mork, Lucile F. and Cooper, Mary Lou. *Selecting and Financing a Home*. Washington, DC: U.S. Dept. of Agriculture, 1977.

Mortgage Bankers Association of America. *Buying a House*. Washington, DC: 1980.

Murray, Robert W. *How To Buy the Right House at the Right Price*. New York: Collier Books, 1965.

Perl, Lila. *The House You Want, How To Find It, How To Buy It*. New York: David McKay Co., 1965.

Peters, Frazier Forman. *How To Buy a House—And Get Your Money's Worth*. New York: Garden City Books, 1950.

Phipps, Anthony A. and Moseley, Norman F. *The Home Buying Guide*. Cambridge, MA: Abt Books, 1979.

Reiner, Laurence E. *Buying or Building the Best House for You*. Englewood Cliffs, NJ: Prentice-Hall, 1973.

Rogers, Tyler S. *The Complete Guide to House Hunting*. New York: Avon Books, 1963.

Scher, Les. *Finding and Buying Your Place in The Country*. New York, Collier Books, 1974.

Schuler, Stanley. *Homeowner's Directory. A Complete Guide to the Best Equipment Available for Building, Remodeling and Repairing Your House*. New York: Simon and Schuster, 1978.

Schwartz, Robert and Cobb, Hubbard H. *The Complete Homeowner*. New York: Macmillan Company, 1973.

Shanley, Michael G. and Hotchkiss, Charles M. *How Low-Income Renters Buy Homes*. Santa Monica, CA: Rand Corporation, 1979.

Sleeper, Catharine and Harold. *The House For You To Build, Buy or Rent*. New York: John Wiley and Sons, 1948.

Smith, Don and Jo-an. *The Home Buying Check List*. New York: Avon Books, 1975.

Springer, John L. *The Home You've Always Wanted at a Price You Can Afford*. Englewood Cliffs, NJ: Prentice-Hall, 1962.

State Farm Fire and Casualty Company. *Finding the Right Home for You*. Bloomington, IL: 1973.

Sumlchrast, Michael and Ronald G. Shafer. *The Complete Book of Home Buying* (A Consumer's Guide For Today's Inflationary Housing Market). Princeton, NJ: Dow Jones Books, 1979.

U.S. Department of Agriculture. *Handbook for the Home*. Washington, DC: 1973.

U.S. Department of Housing and Urban Development. *Rent or Buy*. Washington, DC: U.S. Government Printing Office, 1974.

U.S. Department of Housing and Urban Development. *Wise Home Buying*. Washington, DC: U.S. Government Printing Office, 1972.

Valorie, Carl M. *A Dream House Without a Nightmare*. New York: Vantage Press, 1970.

Veteran's Administration Pamphlet 26-6. *To the Home Buying Veteran—A Guide for Veterans Planning To Buy or Build Homes with a G.I. Loan,* revised. Washington, DC, March, 1977.

Watkins, A.M. *Building or Buying the High Quality House at the Lowest Cost*. New York: Doubleday and Co., 1962.

Watkins, A.M. *How To Avoid the Ten Biggest Home Buying Traps,* rev. ed. New York: Hawthorn Books, 1972.

Wren, Jack. *Home Buyer's Guide*. New York: Barnes and Noble, 1970.

Renovation

Labine, Clem, ed. *The Old House Journal*. Brooklyn, NY: Old House Journal Corporation.

Stephen, George. *Remodeling Old Houses—Without Losing Their Character*. New York: Alfred A. Knopf, 1972.

"Urban Rehabilitation: A Yes Vote For Cities." Chicago: *Savings and Loan News*, December, 1977.

Architecture and Historic Buildings

Camesascz, Eltore, ed. *History of the House*. New York: G. P. Putnam's Sons.

Fletcher, Sir Banister, *A History of Architecture on the Comparative Method*. London: B. T. Batsford, Ltd.

Foley, Mary Mix. *The American House*. New York: Harper and Row, 1980.

Lockwood, Charles. *Bricks and Brownstone: The New York Row House, 1783–1929—An Architectural and Social History*. New York: McGraw-Hill, 1972.

Maass, John. *The Gingerbread Age, a View of Victorian America*. New York: Bramhall House.

Nelson, Lee H. *Nail Chronology*. Technical Leaflet #48. Nashville: American Association for State and Local History, November, 1968.

Old House Journal Corporation: *How To Date an Old House*. Brooklyn, NY: 1978.

Whiffen, Marcus. *American Architecture Since 1780—A Guide to Styles*. Cambridge, MA: M.I.T. Press, 1969.

Home Construction and Home Repairs

Boaz, Joseph N. ed. *Ramsey and Sleeper's Architectural Graphic Standards*, 6th edition. New York: John Wiley and Sons.

Ching, Francis D. K. *Building Construction Illustrated*. New York: Van Nostrand Reinhold.

Complete Do-It-Yourself Manual. Pleasantville, NY: The Readers Digest Association.

Dietz, Arthur G. H. *Dwelling House Construction*. Cambridge, MA: The M.I.T. Press, 1971.

Harrison, Henry S. *Houses—the Illustrated Guide to Construction, Design and Systems*. Chicago: REALTORS NATIONAL MARKETING INSTITUTE®, 1973. Revised 1976.

Hotton, Peter. *So You Want To Build a House*. Boston: Little, Brown and Company, 1976.

How Things Work in Your Home (And What To Do if They Don't). New York: Time-Life Books.

National Association of Home Builders Research Foundation, Inc. *Reducing Home Building Costs with Optimum Value Engineered Design and Construction*. Rockville, MD: 1977.

Schuler, Stanley. *Homeowner's Directory. A Complete Guide to the Best Equipment Available for Building, Remodeling and Repairing Your House*. New York: Simon and Schuster, 1978.

Swezey, M. Kenneth (update: Scharff, Robert). *Formulas, Methods, Tips and Data for Home and Workshop*. New York: Harper and Row, 1979.

The Way Things Work. New York: Simon and Schuster, 1967.

University of Illinois: *Circular Series*. Urbana, IL. Including the following pamphlets:

B3.0	Fundamentals of Land Design
C1.1	Hazard-Free Houses for All
C1.5	Living with the Energy Crisis
C2.5	Split-Level Houses
C5.1	Household Storage Units
C5.32	Kitchen Planning Standards
C5.4	Laundry Areas
C5.6	Bedroom Planning Standards
C5.9	Garages and Carports
C7.3	Pressure Treated Wood
D7.0	Selecting Lumber
D7.2	Plywood
F2.0	Basements
F2.5	Termite Control
F3.0	Wood Framing
F4.4	Crawl-Space Houses
F4.6	Flooring Materials
F6.0	Insulation in the Home
F6.2	Moisture Condensation
F9.1	Counter Surfaces
G5.0	Plumbing
G4.2	Electrical Wiring
G6.0	Summer Comfort
G6.1	Cooling Systems For The Home
G3.1	Heating The Home
F12.3	Roofing Materials
F7.0	Chimneys And Fireplaces
C5.33	Separate Ovens
H1.0	Interior Design
F17.2	Brick and Concrete Masonry
A1.3	Financing The Home

A1.5   Maintaining The Home
G3.5   Fuels and Burners
F11.0   Window Planning Principles
F11.1   Selecting Windows
F11.2   Insulating—Windows and Screens
A2.0   Business Dealings With The Architect And The Contractor
Technical Note 1—Prevention and the Treatment of Construction Damage to Shade Trees
Technical Note 2—Built-up Roofing Details
Technical Note 3—Insulating for Heating
Technical Note 4—Converting a Concrete Slab to a Wood Subfloor
Technical Note 5—Planning for More Space
Technical Note 6—Investigation of the Mechanical Characteristics of Truss Plates on Fire-Retardant-Treated Wood

U.S. Department of Housing and Urban Development. *HUD Minimum Property Standards, 1973 Edition (Revision #8, May 1979), One and Two-Family Dwellings.* Washington, DC: U.S. Government Printing Office.

Energy

Killorin, Francis H. *Heat from the Sun: How To Get Your Share.* Duxbury, MA: Solar Seven, 1978.

U.S. Department of Housing and Urban Development. *Solar Energy and Your Home.* Washington, DC: U.S. Government Printing Office, May, 1978.

Architects

Dibner, David R. *You and Your Architect.* Washington, DC: American Institute of Architects, 1974.

The American Institute of Architects. *How To Find, Evaluate, Select, Negotiate with an Architect.* Washington, DC, 1973.

The American Institute of Architects. *Statement of the Architect's Services.* Washington, DC, 1971.

Appraising

American Institute of Real Estate Appraisers. *What To Look for in an Appraisal.* Chicago, 1979.

Bloom, George and Harrison, Henry S. *Appraising the Single Family Residence.* Chicago: American Institute of Real Estate Appraisers, 1978.

Friedman, Edith J. ed. *Encyclopedia of Real Estate Appraising.* (3rd edition-enlarged). Englewood Cliffs, NJ: Prentice-Hall, 1978.

Harrison, Henry S. *Harrison's Illustrated Guide, How To Fill Out a Freddie Mac-Fannie Mae Residential Appraisal Report* (FHLMC Form 70-FNMA Form 1004). New Haven, CT: Collegiate Publishing Co., Rev. ed. 1979.

Stebbins, Jr. H. Grady. *A Guide to Appraising Residences.* Chicago: Society of Real Estate Appraisers, 1969.

Real Estate Principals and Practices

Galaty, Fillmore W., et al. *Modern Real Estate Practice.* Chicago: Real Estate Education Company, 1978.

Ring, Alfred A. and Dass, Jerome. *Real Estate Principles and Practices.* Englewood Cliffs, NJ: Prentice-Hall, 1977.

Semenow, Robert W. *Questions and Answers on Real Estate.* Englewood Cliffs, NJ: Prentice-Hall, 1978.

Weimer, Arthur M., Hoyt, Homer and Bloom, George. *Real Estate.* New York: John Wiley and Sons, 1978.

Taxes

Higgins, Warren. *The Application of the Revenue Act of 1978 and the Energy Act of 1978 to Real Estate Decisions.* Storrs, CT: Center for Real Estate and Urban Economic Studies, University of Connecticut, December, 1978.

Master Tax Guide 1980, 63rd Ed. Chicago: Commercial Clearing House, Inc., 1980.

Financing

Hoagland, Henry E. and Stone, Leo D. *Real Estate Finance.* Homewood, IL: Richard D. Irwin, 1973.

Sirotz, David. *Essentials of Real Estate Finance* (2nd Edition). Chicago: Real Estate Education Company, 1979.

GLOSSARY-INDEX

A tax on real estate.

Attributes of a house or neighborhood that make the house or neighborhood more desirable, such as good design, view, beaches, fireplaces, etc.

One of the professional institutes affiliated with the NATIONAL ASSOCIATION OF REALTORS.®

A unit used to measure the amount of electricity that flows through a wire. Houses commonly have 30, 60, 100, 150, 200 or more ampere services.

A bolt set into the top of a concrete foundation that extends through the sill and holds the sill down.

A person who determines through experience and analysis the value of property

A type of wire often called "B.X." cable that consists of insulated wire wrapped in heavy paper and encased in flexible, galvanized steel covering wound in a spiral fashion.

A well drilled through impermeable strata deep enough to reach water that will rise to the surface by its own internal hydrostatic pressure. Named after Artois, France, where these wells were first drilled.

The value of a property the assessor in a community uses as the basis for property taxes. It is often a percentage of market value.

One of a string of small poles used to support the handrail of a stairway.

A type of framing system where the studs extend unbroken from the sill to the roof.

Special design features that permit access and
use by handicapped people.

A piece of interior trim laid around the walls of a
room next to the floor. Often it consists of three
pieces of moulding called the base, shoe,
baseboard and base moulding.

The number of linear feet of base cabinet in a
kitchen.

A horizontal or vertical load bearing structure made of wood, steel, concrete or other strong material.

A large piece of wood, steel, stone or other material used to support a house. It usually runs from foundation wall to foundation wall and is supported with poles or pillars.

A glass-enclosed small room on the roof of a house used as a lookout, often reached through a trap door.

A type of house siding which is thicker on one edge than the other when installed.

A water faucet on the outside of the house with a screwnose to which a hose can be connected.

A bathroom fixture used to wash the perineal area after using the toilet.

A type of house. It has two stories. The lower story is partially below ground. The level at the front entry is halfway between the two stories.

A preliminary agreement and down payment certifying the good faith of a purchaser.

A type of house siding that consists of wide boards butted together with a narrow board nailed over the joint.

The part of the furnace that holds the water being heated by the ignited fuel.

A contract for the transfer of property that binds the grantor to transfer the title some time in the future after the buyer complies with the conditions of the contract (usually the condition is a series of payments).

A covered passage between the house and garage.

A small piece of wood or strips of metal nailed between joists or studs to give them lateral rigidity.

A house style that became popular in the late 1800s in New York and other large Eastern cities. The brownstone row houses generally cover an entire block and have 4 or 5 stories with a stoop leading to the first floor. Each house has common side walls with its neighboring houses. Brownstones are characterized by their chocolate sandstone (brownstone).

A measurement of heating and cooling capacity. It is the amount of heat required to raise the temperature of one pound of water 1 degree Fahrenheit.

A house style based on the style of houses often found in Cape Cod, Massachusetts.

Gains realized from the sale of capital assets. Generally, the difference between cost and selling price, less certain deductible expenses. Usually mainly for income tax purposes. A profit from sale of a capital asset. Capital gains are taxed at a lower rate than ordinary income.

An open-sided, roofed shelter. Often it is made by extending the house roof to one side.

A type of window hinged to open at one of its vertical edges.

A designation awarded by the REALTORS NATIONAL MARKETING INSTITUTE.®

An air conditioning system in which air is cooled and treated in a central area and piped or blown into other spaces.

Part of a waste disposal system that functions similarly to a septic tank. A covered cistern of stone, brick, or concrete block. The liquid seeps out through the walls directly into the surrounding earth.

A permanent safety device used as a substitute for a fuse. It automatically turns off an electric circuit when it is overloaded.

In a hot water system, circulators are devices which pump water through finger-size tubes into radiators and baseboards.

A group of house styles based on Early American, French, English, Spanish and other historic styles.

A form of ownership in which each owner owns the fee to the individual unit and a percentage of the fee to the common areas.

The transfer of heat by the heating of the air which moves throughout the area to be heated either naturally or blown by fans.

These mortgage loans and mortgages are made by lending institutions without the guarantee of the FHA or VA.

A circle ideally about 10 feet in diameter in which to arrange furniture for easy sit-down communication. Standing conversation circles need only be 6 feet in diameter.

A written instrument that transfers an interest in real estate from one party to another.

A form of ownership in which each owner owns shares in the entire property and has the exclusive right to occupy part of the property.

One of the three traditional approaches to value used by real estate appraisers. It is the theory that value of a property is the sum based on the land plus the reproduction cost of all the improvements, less depreciation from all causes.

A new offer made to counter and cancel an original offer.

A concave or quarter round piece of moulding. Popularly, covenant is synonymous to contract. More specifically, a written agreement executed by sealing and delivering.

A designation awarded by the REALTORS NATIONAL MARKETING INSTITUTE®

A record of a loan applicant's past capability to pay installment payments.

A designation awarded by the REALTORS
NATIONAL MARKETING INSTITUTE.®
Class, Type, Style. A uniform method for
describing houses.
A house that is built to the owner's specifications
and purchased before construction begins.

A metal plate in a flue that can be adjusted to
regulate the draft. Also a device to control
vibrations.

A unit of measurement of the relative loudness of
sounds.

A legal document that is used to convey title in
real property.

A failure of the mortgagor to meet the obligations
of a mortgage such as making payments,
providing insurance, keeping the property in good
condition, etc.
A mortgage with very low initial payments based
on the deferred payment of all amortization and
part of the interest.

Alternate square blocks and blank spaces on a
cornice that give the appearance of teeth.
The Department of Housing and Urban
Development of the Federal Government is
responsible for the implementation and
administration of government housing and urban
development programs.
A sum of money offered by a potential buyer to a
seller in conjunction with an offer to purchase or
lease real estate.
An accounting and appraisal term that designates
how much a property reduces in value over a
period of time.

In an electric system, a metal box containing the fuses (fuse box) or circuit breakers. It is used to divide a supply line into branch circuits. In a septic system, an underground box which divides the waste flowing from the septic tank and distributes it to the laterals leading to the disposal field.

A portion of the sales price to be paid by the purchasers from their own funds, not from any financing they may have received.

A pipe used for carrying rain water from the roof of the house to the ground or into a dry well or sewer connection.

A system which removes surface water by tiles and pipes.

A type of tongue and grooved exterior board siding.

A masonry wall laid up without mortar. An interior wall finished with something other than plaster. Commonly used to refer to a gypsum board finished wall.

A hole in the ground lined with stone used to disburse waste or rain water into the ground.

In house construction, pipes of metal, plastic or other material used for distributing or collecting air.

The right of someone other than the owner of the fee to the limited use of a property for such purposes as crossing it with a utility line or crossing the property to obtain access to adjoining properties.

A channel of wood or metal on or at the edge of the roof to carry off water from rain and melting snow.

An improvement that illegally crosses over the border of one property onto an adjoining property. Items that affect or limit the fee simple title to property such as liens, mortgages, easements, etc.

A federal government agency that loans money for the purchase of homes in rural areas.
A device at the end of a pipe to control the flow of water.

A corporation specially authorized by Congress popularly known as Freddie Mac. It buys blocks of conventional mortgage loans from lenders. It guarantees their principle and interest and sells bonds to raise funds to finance the purchase.
A part of the Department of Housing and Urban Development. It insures mortgages and sets housing standards.

Mortgages granted by a federal government agency, the Farm Credit Administration, for the purchase of farm lands and the construction of farm buildings.

The maximum interest a private party can have in real estate.

A type of building board used for insulation, made of reduced fibrous material such as wood, cane or other vegetable fibers.

A piece of material, usually metal or composition, used to protect, cover or deflect water from places where two materials join or form angles such as roof valleys.

A roof having a slope just sufficient to provide water drainage and a pitch not over 1 to 20.

In consideration for receiving the mortgage, the seller is required to put part of the down payment in a savings account which is pledged to secure the loan.

A form of insurance that protects the property owner from losses caused by flood.

A type of heating unit that is installed directly under the floor with its grilled upper surface flush with the finished floor.

An enclosed passage in a chimney or any duct or pipe through which smoke, hot air and gases pass upward.

Footing and foundation 128
  and foundation 129(*i*)
  walls 128
For sale sign 46, 367
Foreclosure 212, 215

A concrete support under a foundation, chimney or column that usually rests on solid ground and is wider than the structure being supported.

The legal proceedings by which a mortgage, after default by the mortgagor, makes the mortgagor sell the property in order to recover his loan.

Forest Products Lab of the United States Department of Agriculture 374
Foundation 129–130, 250, 275
  basic forms 130
  cracks 129
  footings and 121, 128
Framing 132–135
  anchors 132
  checklist C-47
  defective 132
  exterior walls 132
  interior walls 44
  poor 29
  problems 134
  techniques, new 361
Freddie Mac *see* **Federal Home Loan Mortgage Corporation**
Freezer 194
  in garage 90
French Normandy style 112(*i*)
French Provincial style 111(*i*)
Front yard requirements 54
Frostline 128

A bearing wall below the floor joists or below the first floor or below the ground which supports the rest of the house.

A part of the building process that consists of putting together the lumber skeleton parts of the house.

The maximum depth under the ground in an area which freezes in the winter.

FSLIC *see* **Federal Savings and Loan Insurance Corporation**
Fuel 188–90
  checklist C-69
  comparison of costs 190
  conservationists 137
  consumption 135
  costs 137
  economy 408
  oil 189
  prepaid, adjustment 296
Fuel oil 189, 279, 288
Fuller, Buckminster 365
Functional modern/contemporary style 120(*i*)
Functional obsolescence 238
Furnace 149, 164, 190
Fuse box 414
Fuses and circuit breakers 193
Gable roof 106(*i*), 359

Gambrel roof 105(*i*), 106(*i*)

Garage door 91, 344, 431
  openers 95, 271, 344, 353
Garage 91–95, 255, 350, 392, 418
  accessibility to service area 90

A triangular gable formed by the ends of a ridged roof.
A two-pitched roof style which has its slope broken by an obtuse angle so that the lower slope is steeper than the upper slope.

A hemispherical dome often constructed out of prefabricated lattice modules and covered with plastic, metal or other thin material.

A large horizontal beam, often carrying other beams and joists, on which the first floor is laid.

A system of land description that is used extensively except in the 13 original states. Frequently called the Geodetic Survey System: Using meridians and base lines, it divides an area into quadrangles each of which is about 24 miles on each side. Each quadrangle is divided into 16 townships about six miles on each side. Townships are further divided into blocks that are about one square mile known as a Section.

A mortgage that has payments that are lower in the initial years and increasing in later years.

A figure used by appraisers that represents a ratio between the monthly rental of a house and its value. It is obtained by dividing the selling price by the monthly rent.

A framing member that goes across the top of an opening and carries the load above. In masonry, block or stone laid with its end toward the face of the wall.

The floor of a fireplace and the floor immediately in front of a fireplace.

A device used in a fire detection system that registers an alarm when subject to high heat.

A roof that rises by inclined planes from all four sides of the house.

An organization of homeowners (or condominium unit owners) of a designated development whose primary purpose is to control and maintain those facilities that are commonly used.

A multiple peril policy that provides a variety of coverages needed by property owners such as fire insurance, liability protection, theft and additional living expense.

A boat designed primarily for living upon on a permanent basis. Though mobile, it usually is docked at one place most of the time.

A hot water heating system.

One of the three traditional approaches to value used by appraisers. For a single-family house it is also called the Gross Monthly Rent Multiplier.

Any material used to reduce the transmission of heat and cold or to reduce fire hazard.

An equal undivided ownership of property by two or more people. The remaining survivors automatically take over the interests of a deceased partner.

Heavy pieces of timber laid horizontally on their edges to support the floors and ceilings.

The secret return of part of a fee or commission to someone who helped obtain the work.

A steel column, usually cylindrically shaped, used as a support for beams or girders. Often they are filled with concrete to increase their strength.

Also known as a "Contract for Deed." A special contract used when the purchaser has only a small down payment which specifies that the purchaser will make specified additional payments and when they are completed, title will pass to the purchaser.

(1) A room used for washing and equipped with a sink and sometimes a toilet. (2) A sink, basin or bowl usually permanently installed with water faucets and used for washing the hands and face.

A field of trenches dug into the ground and lined with tile, broken stone, gravel or sand, used to disburse waste water from a septic tank into the ground.

The vertical pipe that carries rain water from the roof gutters to the ground and/or sewer system.

A contract between a property owner and tenant containing the conditions and terms by which the landlord gives the tenant the right to use the property in return for the payment of rent or other consideration.

The description of the boundaries of a property which is used in legal documents.

A charge against a property that is made to secure the property as security for the payment of a debt or pending suit.

A wall that is strong enough to be used to support the upper floors and roof of the house.

A style of house made of round or square logs.

A system used in the original 13 states that identified property by delineating its boundaries in terms of a series of directions and distances called metes and bounds.

A designation awarded by the American Institute of Real Estate Appraisers of the NATIONAL ASSOCIATION OF REALTORS® to those who demonstrate the ability to make all kinds of appraisals.

A roof with two slopes on all four sides. The lower slope is very steep. The upper slope is usually not visible from the ground.
A house of considerable size or pretension.

A title to property that is sufficiently free of encumbrances to be considered salable.

A wall made of brick, stone, concrete, etc.

Special liens provided by specific state statutes that give priority claims to those who perform labor or furnish materials for the improvement of real property.

A type of counter surface of which Formica is a popular brand. It is a smooth, durable surface that resists stains. It scorches and dents easily, however.

The boundary lines of a property including terminal points and angles.

A rate of property tax expressed in mills (10ths of a cent) per dollar of assessed value. For example, a home assessed for $80,000 and taxed at 60 mills would pay $4,800 in tax ($80,000 × .060).

A type of insulation made by sending steam through molten slag or rock. Common types are glass, wool and slag wool.

A factory-built home (also sometimes known as a manufactured home) that is transported to a site in one or two pieces. The most popular sizes are 12 feet or 14 feet wide by 60 feet long.

Replacement or remodeling specifically designed to make the house meet current design standards.

A legal document that conditionally conveys title to a property to a lender. The actual conveyance only takes place when the mortgage is in default because the borrower failed to make timely payments or fulfill other conditions of the mortgage.

The largest private mortgage insurance company
that guarantees the payment of home mortgages
to lending institutions.

Life insurance on the life of the mortgagee (borrower) that pays off the unpaid balance of the mortgage
in the event of the death of the mortgagee.

A long, narrow strip of wood or metal, plain,
curved or formed with regular channels and
projections, used for covering joints and for
decorative purposes.

Lending institutions that specialize in savings
accounts and investing their money in mortgages.
Each depositor is an owner of the bank. Profits
are paid as dividends on deposits.

A national non-profit organization chartered by
Congress for the purpose of preserving historic
buildings.

Any separately identifiable cohesive area within a community with some community of interest shared by its occupants.

The upright post at the bottom of a stairway that supports the handrail.
Used bricks placed between the timbers of wall construction. Called covered nogging when covered with stucco and exposed nogging when visible.

A provision in a mortgage that prohibits the borrower from selling the property and having the new owner assume the existing mortgage.

A use that does not conform to current zoning regulations that is permitted because it existed before the zoning regulations became effective. Such uses preclude additions or changes without approval of the zoning authority.

A wall that supports only its own weight.

A cable whose wires, in addition to their own insulation, are wrapped with a paper tape and then covered with a heavy fabric and then treated to be made fire resistant.

A contract that grants the right to a potential buyer to buy the property at a specified time in the future at a specific price.

The part of the wall that rises above the roof line.
A coating of cement applied to the surface of a masonry wall to waterproof it.

A soil test made to determine the soil's ability to absorb water discharged from a septic system.
A bond that guarantees that a contractor will complete an undertaking in accordance with an agreement.

A special form of ownership developed for large parcels of land wherein owners have fee simple title to their individual parcel and a shared interest in common land that is controlled by a homeowners association.

A house that is manufactured in a factory and transported to a site either fully or partially assembled.

A square or nearly square cut stone with beveled edges, set in the corners of masonry and stone houses.

A way that heat is transferred from a hot surface to the surrounding objects.

A heating system that consists of pipes embedded in the walls, floors and ceilings.

A house type used to describe one of the nine major house types used in the CTS System to describe houses.

Any person, firm, partnership, copartnership, association or corporation which for a compensation sells or offers for sale, buys or offers to buy, negotiates the purchase or sale or exchange of real estate, leases or offers to lease or rents or offers for rent any real estate or the improvements on real estate for others as a whole or partial vocation.

A federal law for the protection of consumers that requires lenders to provide home mortgage borrowers with information about settlement closing costs.

The Institute of the NATIONAL ASSOCIATION OF REALTORS® which promotes educational services and publications in the areas of residential and commercial real estate brokerage and office management.

A fixture installed at the end of an air duct that directs and controls the flow of air into the room.

The restoration of a house without changing the plan, form or style of the structure.

Appraisal term that means the period of remaining time an improvement will continue to add value to the whole property.

The improving of a house by making improvements and alterations.

An appraisal term that means the cost to produce an exact reproduction.

A wall used to contain or hold back dirt, water or other materials of a similar nature.

The lender makes regular payments to the borower thus increasing the amount of the mortgage each time a payment is made.

The right of an owner of abutting land to water and land below water.

A variation of the variable rate mortgage. The interest rate is renegotiated at the end of a specified period of time. If agreement is not reached, the mortgage must be paid off without any penalty.

Thin pieces of wood or other material that are tapered and oblong in shape, used as wall and roof coverings.

A type of close rabbeted joint used to join two boards together.

A framing member placed on top of the foundation wall that serves as a level base for the wall studs and floor joists.

A quality toilet in which the flushing action is assisted by a jet of water.

A type of basementless foundation made by pouring concrete directly on the prepared ground surface and over the top of the footings.

A large space over the damper that prevents the smoke from backing up into the fireplace.

A part of a fireplace that prevents the cold air from flowing down the inside of the chimney into the fireplace.

A vertical waste pipe that receives waste from the toilet.

A vertical framing member in a wall or partition. Used in the CTS System to describe the design of the house based on historical or contemporary fashion.

A floor laid over the floor joist. The finish flooring is attached to the subflooring.

The equity an owner obtains in a property as a result of work he does himself to improve the property.

A tenancy shared by two or more parties.

An insect that resembles, but can easily be distinguished from, an ant. It lives underground and migrates into houses, eating wood.

A wide variety of building materials made of fired clay, cement, plastic, vinyl, stone, glass or other material used for floors, walls, drains and a number of other purposes.

A relatively new concept of ownership which is increasing in popularity. It is the purchase of an undivided interest for a fixed or variable time period.

A type of joint where one half has notches cut into it (grooves) and the other matching piece has tongues that fit into the grooves.

A bend in a waste pipe that remains filled with water, making a water seal that prevents sewer gases from backing up into the house.

The upper horizontal board on each step of a flight of stairs.

The part of Public Law 90–231 (Consumer Credit Protection Act) which requires the borrower to be informed of true credit costs being charged.

Material or paint applied to a wall to prevent the passage of moisture into the wall.

A mortgage agreement that calls for the adjustment of the interest rate in keeping with the fluctuating money market.

An exception to an existing zoning regulation granted to a property owner to overcome a claimed hardship caused by the zoning restriction.

A small, vertical pipe connected to plumbing fixtures that carries sewer gases through the roof to the outside air.

A system of circulating fresh air through a structure.

An agency of the federal government to administer a variety of veterans benefits. Their VA home loan guarantee program is designed to help veterans secure a home with a low down payment and at favorable interest rates.

Ceiling or roof beams that stick out through the exterior walls in Adobe style architecture.

A measurement of the pressure of electricity. Most houses use 110 to 120 volts or 220 to 240 volts.

Conveyance of title that contains certain assurances and guarantees by the seller that the deed conveys a good and unencumbered title.

A pipe that carries waste from a bathtub, shower, lavatory or any fixture or appliance except a toilet.

A mechanical device for removing minerals from water by circulating it through a solution of Zeolite.

(1) The depth from the surface to natural underground waters. (2) A ledge along a building designed to aid the run-off of water.

A measure of electricity. It is volts × amperes.

Treads of a curved staircase which are cut with one end wider than the other so they fit into place to make a curved form.

A storage area for wine. The cellar may range from a tiny closet to small room and may not be in the cellar at all. The most important condition is steady temperature which the connoisseur will provide with a cooling system. Proper lighting is essential to read the wine labels.

A chemical (hydrous aluminum silicate) used in water softeners which exchanges the minerals in the water for sodium chloride (common salt).

PART 5
CHECKLISTS

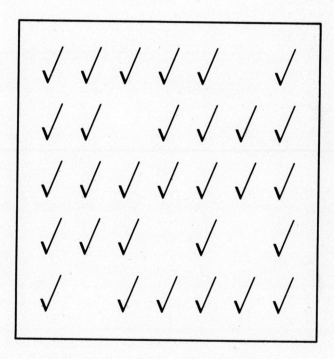

These 62 checklists are designed to offer you the maximum utilization of the material in this book. They are perforated for your convenience.

Also for your convenience, those checklists dealing with specific items you are likely to want to compare from one house to another (i.e. plumbing, heating systems) are designed to be used for three different houses.

Those checklists on subjects you will be dealing with when you have decided on a house (i.e., insurance, closing) are designed to help you attend to all the necessary details.

Family Annual Income:

Husband's	$_____
Wife's	_____
Total	$_____
minus income taxes	−_____
Total after-tax income	$_____
minus automobile payments	−_____
minus other long-term expenses	−_____
Annual income after taxes and payments	$_____
	× 40%[4]
Maximum income available for shelter	$======

Estimated Operating Expenses:

Property taxes[1]	$_____
Homeowner insurance[2]	_____
Trash & garbage collection[2]	_____
Repairs & maintenance	_____
Commuting cost[3]	_____
Heating, cooling, domestic hot water[2]	_____
Electricity[2]	_____
Grounds maintenance[2]	_____
Snow removal[2]	_____
Total	$======

Income available for shelter (see above)	$_____
minus estimated operating expenses	−_____
= Annual dollars available for mortgage payments	$_____
Divided by annual payment per $1,000 for mortgage payment[5]	÷_____
= Amount of mortgage feasible	$_____
Add amount down payment	+_____
= **Total Amount You Can Afford To Pay**	$_____

[1] If you are moving to a new community find out how the property taxes are charged. In some communities one tax covers everything. In other places, there are several separate taxes such as school taxes, water taxes, etc.

[2] Estimates for some of these costs—taxes, utility and heating bills, and others—can usually be obtained from your real estate agent or from the seller. If you wish verification of the property tax bill, you need only to go to your tax office in the city or town hall, as tax payments are a matter of public record.

[3] Some people might not include this as part of "housing" expenses—however, it is a fact of life and must be included somewhere.

[4] Maximum percentage of after-tax income many families can pay for shelter.

[5] Find amount on table shown in Figure 1.

CHECKLIST 1
CHECKLIST OF PEOPLE WHO CAN HELP YOU

	Yes	No
1 Have you considered getting advice from each of the following people?		
REALTOR®		
Attorney		
Home Inspector		
Architect		
Contractor		
Termite Inspector		
Septic Tank Inspector		
Well Expert		
Plumber		
Electrical Expert		
Heating System Inspector		
Roofer		
Insurance Agent		
Lender		
Relatives		
Appraiser		
2 Have you discussed with an attorney the following:		
a Who will represent you at the closing		
b The sales contract or binder you intend to sign		
c What type of deed you will receive		
d Title insurance		
e In what form of ownership you will take title		
f How the closing costs will be divided between the buyer and seller		
g What personal property will be included in the sale		
h How much the attorney is going to charge for services		
3 Have you obtained a list of REALTORS® in your area from the local Board of REALTORS®?		
4 Have you reviewed with a REALTOR® your feelings and needs concerning a community and neighborhood?		
5 Have you made sure that your sales contract or binder is conditional upon your being able to obtain all the inspections and appraisals you feel will be needed?		
6 Does your sales contract or binder include a list of personal property that will be included in the sale?		
7 Have you discussed with your accountant or estate planner the tax consequences of the purchase of a home?		
8 If you recently sold a house, do you know how much time you have to buy another house without suffering tax penalties?		

CHECKLIST 2
HOW TO RATE THE ECONOMIC HEALTH OF A COMMUNITY

	4 Very Good	3 Good	2 Fair	1 Poor
1 The ratio of gainfully employed community residents who work in industries, businesses and institutions which export goods and services outside of the community. **Very Good:** 30% to 40% or more				
Good: 20% to 30%				
Fair: 10% to 20%				
Poor: less than 10%				
2 The diversity of the industries, businesses and institutions which export goods and services outside the community. **Very Good:** 10% or less of the gainfully employed working in one industry, business or institution.				
Good: 11% to 25% of the gainfully employed working in one industry, business or institution.				
Fair: 26% to 49% of the gainfully employed working in one industry, business or institution.				
Poor: 50% or more of the gainfully employed working in one industry, business or institution.				
3 The stability of the major base employers is: **Very Good:** When the major employers in the community are government and institutions such as insurance, banking, etc.				
Good: When the major employers are stable industries and wholesalers.				
Fair: When the major employers are refining or extracting industries subject to depletion and cycles.				
Poor: When the major employers are military bases, industries that tend to have cycles; tourist and resort attractions that are affected by weather and availability of fuel.				
4 Population of the community: **Very Good:** When growing at an average rate of over 5% per year.				
Good: When growing at an average rate of 2 to 4% per year.				
Fair: When growing at a rate less than 2% per year.				
Poor: When not growing.				

To rate the Economic Health of a Community assign a number to each rating (Very Good = 4, Good = 3, Fair = 2, Poor = 1). When the total of the numbers is 14 or more, the economic health of the community is very good; 13 to 10, the economic health of the community is good; 9 to 6, fair and less than 6, poor.

COMMUNITY RATING CHECKLIST

	4 Very Good	3 Good	2 Fair	1 Poor

Education

1 How does the State Board of Education rank the school system against others in the state?
   Very Good: Top 25%

   Good: Upper middle 25%

   Fair: Lower middle 25%

   Poor: Bottom 25%

2 Condition of school facilities based on personal observation.

3 General reputation of school system in opinion of other educators such as college admissions personnel, teachers, librarians, etc.

Government and Community Services

4 Reputation of community government with respect to stability, honesty and ability to provide services.

5 Provision of free rubbish removal, streets in good repair, good fire protection and police protection, municipal sewers.
   Very Good: all of above are very good or good.

   Good: at least three of above are very good or good

   Fair: two of the above are very good or good

   Poor: only one of the above is very good or good

6 **Convenience of Services**
   Very Good: If community has a regional shopping center *and* a hospital.

   Good: If the community has either a regional shopping center or a hospital.

   Good: If a hospital and regional shopping center are within five miles and there are ample doctors' and dentists' offices within the community.

   Fair: If a hospital and regional shopping center are within 10 miles and there are ample doctors' and dentists' offices in nearby communities.

   Poor: If the nearest hospital is over 10 miles away and there is no convenient regional shopping center.

	4 Very Good	3 Good	2 Fair	1 Poor
7 **Availability of Recreational Facilities** **Very Good:** When there is a major recreational facility such as waterfront, ski slope, golf course, etc., that attracts residents to the community.				
Very Good: When the recreation facilities are better than those of the surrounding competing communities.				
Good: When the recreational facilities are typical of those of the surrounding competing communities.				
Fair: When nearby communities have available recreational facilities.				
Poor: When community lacks significant recreational facilities that are available in competing communities and these facilities are not available to nonresidents.				

Assign the number 4, 3, 2 or 1 to each item checked. Add up the total of all the numbers. The ratings for the community based on education, government and community services, convenience of services and availability of recreational facilities are: Very Good: 21 to 28 points; Good: 14 to 20 points; Fair: 8 to 13 points; Poor: 0 to 7 points.

CHECKLIST 4
NEIGHBORHOOD PHYSICAL AND
ENVIRONMENTAL FACTORS CHECKLIST

	4 Very Good	3 Good	2 Fair	1 Poor
1 Location Within the Community **Very Good:** You consider the location the best location in the community.				
Good: Not best location but convenient and in path of community growth.				
Fair: Many neighborhoods are in a better location but not the poorest location.				
Poor: Location is the poorest or one of the poorest in the community.				
2 Barriers and Boundaries **Very Good:** Good, natural and human-made boundaries on all sides.				
Good: Several boundaries vague and provide little protection from the outside.				
Fair: Most boundaries vague and provide little protection from the outside.				
Poor: All the boundaries are only vaguely defined.				
3 Topography **Very Good:** In hilly communities towards the top of the hill. In other areas the preferred topography of the area.				
Good: Topography typical of area in general.				
Fair: Flat (in area where other lots have rolling terrain).				
Poor: Steep slopes or other features that make entry to roads dangerous or construction of improvements extra costly.				
4 Soil Drainage **Very Good:** No flood hazard. Good natural drainage.				
Good: No flood hazard. Average natural drainage.				
Fair: No flood hazard. Poor natural drainage.				
Poor: Flood hazard. (Designated flood area.)				
5 Services and Utilities **Very Good:** All utilities available, i.e., telephone, electricity, gas, public water, sanitary sewers, storm sewers.				
Good: All utilities except one of the above.				
Fair: All of above except public water and/or gas.				
Poor: No public water or sewers.				

	4 Very Good	3 Good	2 Fair	1 Poor
6 **Proximity to Supporting Facilities** **Very Good:** Hospital, regional shopping center, public transportation within convenient distance.				
Good: Regional shopping center and public transportation within convenient distance.				
Fair: Regional shopping center within convenient distance.				
Poor: Regional shopping center and hospital beyond convenient distance.				
7 **Street Patterns** **Very Good:** Curved streets with cul-de-sacs at end of each dead end street.				
Good: Some curved streets, no through traffic.				
Fair: Checkerboard street layout but no heavy through traffic.				
Poor: Heavy transient traffic runs through neighborhood.				
8 **Patterns of Land Use** **Very Good:** Each different use well buffered from adjacent uses.				
Good: Unplanned but clearly defined uses.				
Fair: Poorly defined areas within neighborhood but no encroachments.				
Poor: Encroachments of commercial and industrial uses in residential part of neighborhood.				
9 **Conformity of Structure** **Very Good:** Reasonable conformity of structures but not monotonous similarity.				
Good: Stable level of care but either there is monotonous similarity or many diverse types and styles.				
Fair: Too many diversified styles and types of buildings and unstable levels of care.				
Poor: Widely diverse styles and levels of care which appear to indicate the neighborhood is moving toward change.				
10 **Appearance** **Very Good:** Well maintained, attractive houses with attractive open spaces and/or parks within the neighborhood.				
Good: Well maintained, attractive houses but few parks or open spaces.				
Fair: Some poorly maintained houses and yards.				
Poor: Many poorly maintained houses and yards.				

NEIGHBORHOOD PHYSICAL AND
ENVIRONMENTAL FACTORS CHECKLIST (continued)

	4 Very Good	3 Good	2 Fair	1 Poor
11 Special Amenities **Very Good:** Some special amenity such as waterfront, special view, recreational facility or other feature that gives the neighborhood a definite competitive advantage.				
Good: Some amenities that improve appeal of neighborhood but less important than the above.				
Fair: Lack of special amenities, which is typical of area.				
Poor: Lack of special amenities in an area where other competing neighborhoods have them.				
12 Nuisances and Hazards **Very Good:** Effective barriers against noise, traffic congestion, smoke and other nuisances.				
Good: Lack of any noise, traffic congestion, smoke or other nuisances.				
Fair: Some undesirable nuisances and/or hazards.				
Poor: Significant undesirable nuisances and/or hazards.				
13 Age and Condition of Improvements **Very Good:** Most houses under 10 years old and well maintained.				
Very Good: Regardless of age, most properties are well maintained.				
Good: Most of the new houses are well maintained; some of the older houses need renovation.				
Fair: Many buildings getting older and some are poorly maintained.				
Poor: Many older and poorly maintained buildings.				

Assign the number 4, 3, 2 or 1 to each item checked. Add up the total of all the numbers. The ratings for the neighborhood based on the physical and environmental factors are: Very Good: 42 to 52 points; Good: 28 to 41 points; Fair: 14 to 27 points; Poor: 0 to 13 points.

NEIGHBORHOOD SOCIAL FACTORS CHECKLIST

	4 Very Good	3 Good	2 Fair	1 Poor
1 Community and Neighborhood Associations **Very Good:** The neighborhood has a well-organized association that controls significant community-owned recreational facilities and/or open space land.				
and/or The neighborhood has a well-organized association that plays a significant role in the social interaction among the neighborhood or block residents.				
Good: The neighborhood has an association that is well organized and controls some community-owned recreational facilities and/or open space land.				
and/or The neighborhood has a well-organized association that plays some role in the interaction among the neighborhood or block residents.				
Fair: The neighborhood has an association that is interested only in activities that encourage neighborhood preservation or political lobbying.				
Poor: There is no well-organized neighborhood association.				
2 Crime **Very Good:** The level of crime in the neighborhood is low and there is very good police protection.				
Good: The level of crime in the neighborhood is average for the community and there is good police protection.				
Fair: The level of crime in the neighborhood is a problem and there is less than adequate police protection.				
Poor: The level of crime is high and there is inadequate police protection.				

Assign the number 4, 3, 2 or 1 to each item checked. Add up the total of all the numbers. The ratings for the neighborhood based on social factors are: Very Good: 7 to 8 points; Good: 5 to 6 points; Fair: 3 to 4 points; Poor: 0 to 2 points.

CHECKLIST 6
NEIGHBORHOOD ECONOMIC FACTORS CHECKLIST

	4 Very Good	3 Good	2 Fair	1 Poor
1 Relationship to Community Growth **Very Good:** Neighborhood is a portion of the community that is growing steadily in an orderly fashion.				
Good: Neighborhood is a portion of the community that is slowly growing, but in an orderly fashion.				
Fair: Neighborhood is a portion of the community that is not growing or the growth is not well controlled.				
Poor: Neighborhood is a portion of the community that is decreasing in population or where the growth is uncontrolled.				
2 Economic Profile of Residents* **Very Good:** The median income of the neighborhood residents is in the top 25 percent of the community.				
Good: The median income of the neighborhood residents is in the top 50 to 74 percent of the community.				
Fair: The median income of the neighborhood residents is in the lower 26 to 49 percent of the community.				
Poor: The median income of the neighborhood is in the lower 25 percent of the community.				
3 New Construction and Vacant Land **Very Good:** Very good zoning regulations and/or deed restrictions which are strictly enforced and which control the use of the remaining land in the neighborhood, plus a history of organized resistance whenever an undesirable change or non-permitted use is proposed by a developer.				
Good: Good zoning regulations and/or deed restrictions which are normally enforced.				
Fair: Good zoning regulations and/or deed restrictions which are not vigorously enforced and/or from which variances can often be obtained by developers.				

* Based on current U.S. Census figures.

	4 Very Good	3 Good	2 Fair	1 Poor
Poor: Poor zoning and/or deed restrictions and/or poor enforcement which often results in new construction that may be detrimental to neighborhood values.				
4 **Turnover and Vacancy** **Very Good:** Neighborhood is growing and tends to hold the majority of its residents. Few single-family residences are rented.				
Good: Neighborhood is stable and tends to hold the majority of its residents. Few single-family residences are rented.				
Fair: High turnover rate in neighborhood but marketing time short. Substantial number of rented houses.				
Poor: Many "For Sale" signs. Slow marketing time; many houses are rented.				

Assign the number 4, 3, 2 or 1 to each item checked. Add up the total of all the numbers. The ratings for the neighborhood based on economic factors are: Very Good: 13 to 16 points; Good: 9 to 12 points; Fair: 5 to 8 points; Poor: 0 to 4 points.

NEIGHBORHOOD GOVERNMENTAL FACTORS CHECKLIST

	4 Very Good	3 Good	2 Fair	1 Poor
1 Taxation and Special Assessments **Very Good:** The effective tax rate is low in relationship to the services being provided.				
Good: The effective tax rate is below average in relationship to the services being provided.				
Fair: The effective tax rate is above average in relationship to the services being provided.				
Poor: The effective tax rate is high in relationship to the services being provided.				
2 Public and Private Restrictions **Very Good:** There is a comprehensive plan and updated zoning regulations.				
Good: No comprehensive plan and updated zoning regulations.				
Fair: No comprehensive plan and outdated zoning regulations.				
Poor: No comprehensive plan or zoning regulations.				
3 Schools **Very Good:** Schools have best reputation in competitive communities.				
Good: Schools have best reputation in the community.				
Fair: Schools have a good reputation.				
Poor: Schools have a poor reputation.				
4 Planning and Subdivision Regulations **Very Good:** Strictly up-to-date subdivision regulations.				
Good: Somewhat up-to-date subdivision regulations.				
Fair: Outdated subdivision regulations.				
Poor: Poor subdivision regulations.				

Assign the number 4, 3, 2 or 1 to each item checked. Add up the total of all the numbers. The ratings for the neighborhood based on governmental factors are: Very Good: 13 to 16 points; Good: 9 to 12 points; Fair: 5 to 8 points; Poor: 0 to 4 points.

CHECKLIST 8
SITE CHECKLIST

	HOUSE 1 Yes No	HOUSE 2 Yes No	HOUSE 3 Yes No
Relationship to Surroundings			
1 Do proposed improvements (house and grounds) conform to other improvements in the neighborhood?			
2 Does proposed orientation of improvements conform to orientation of improvements on nearby sites?			
3 Is there no heavy traffic on street in front of site?			
4 Is there: a Good access from site by car to work?			
b Good access from site to shopping?			
c Good access from site to recreation?			
d Good access from site by public transportation to work?			
e Good access from site by public transportation to shopping?			
f Good access from site by public transportation to recreation?			
g Good access on foot to local grammar school?			
On-Site Physical Characteristics			
1 Is there a public water supply available?			
2 Is municipal sewer connection available?			
3 Is site suitable for septic system? a Water table below septic field level?			
b Soil has satisfactory percolation rate?			
4 Is subsoil bearing quality satisfactory?			
5 Is surface drainage satisfactory?			
Will soil support landscaping?			
6 Is site large enough for all planned uses?			
7 Street: a Public street			
b Sidewalks			
c Curbs and gutters			
d Street maintained by municipality			
e Street cleaned and/or plowed by municipality			
f Street fully developed			
g Street lighting			
8 Hazards: a Site out of flood hazard area			
b Site out of inland or coastal wetlands area			
c No earth or rock slide hazard			

	HOUSE 1 Yes No	HOUSE 2 Yes No	HOUSE 3 Yes No
d No earthquake hazard			
e Not near dangerous ravines or bodies of water			
f Not in high fire danger area			
9 Is there a special view?			
10 Are there no special climate or meteorological conditions?			
11 Are there no nearby nuisances?			
Economic Factors 1 Are the prices of nearby lots similar?			
2 Are assessments on nearby lots similar?			
3 Are utility connection costs similar to nearby sites?			
4 Are there no special private road maintenance costs?			
5 Are there no special rubbish removal costs?			
6 Are there no special garbage collection costs?			
Title and Record Data 1 Is a current survey available?			
2 Can the current assessment be obtained?			
3 Are there no special assessments?			
4 Do improvements conform to current zoning?			
5 Have setback requirements been met? a Front yard			
b Side yards			
c Rear yard			
6 Have building codes been investigated? a General building code			
b Electrical code			
c Plumbing code			
7 Are there no: Encroachments?			
Easements?			
Party wall agreements?			
Riparian rights?			
Environmental restrictions?			
Recent changes in zoning?			
Future zoning changes likely?			
Prohibited uses in deed?			
Special building requirements in deed?			

CHECKLIST 9
INTERIOR ZONING CHECKLIST

	HOUSE 1		HOUSE 2		HOUSE 3	
	Yes	No	Yes	No	Yes	No
1 Are the three zones (living/social, private/sleeping, work/service) separated from each other so that activities in one zone do not interfere with activities in another?						
2 Is the private/sleeping zone insulated from the noise of the other two zones?						
3 Can you control:						
a Family entrance						
b Guest entrance						
c Activities in sleeping/private zone						
d Activities in living/social zone						
e Activities on the porch, patio and backyard areas?						
4 Is there direct access from guest entrance to:						
a Living area						
b Guest closet						
c Guest lavatory						
5 Is there a noise and visibility barrier between the guest entrance and the sleeping/private area?						
6 Does the family entrance lead directly from the car storage area into the kitchen?						
7 Is it possible to carry the groceries from the automobile into the house without getting wet in inclement weather?						
8 Can you move from the work/service zone to the private/sleeping zone without going through the living/social zone?						

LIVING ROOM CHECKLIST

	HOUSE 1 Yes No	HOUSE 2 Yes No	HOUSE 3 Yes No
1 Is living room so located so that it is not a passageway for traffic?			
2 Is the living room at least 11 feet by 16 feet?			
3 If there is a picture window is it located in a way to ensure privacy and security?			
4 Is there adequate storage for books, radio, stereo, records, newspapers, magazines, ash trays, coasters, stationery and writing equipment?			
5 Does the window and outside door area equal at least 10 percent of the floor area?			
6 Can the furniture be placed in 10-foot diameter conversation circles?			

CHECKLIST 11
KITCHEN CHECKLIST

	HOUSE 1 Yes No	HOUSE 2 Yes No	HOUSE 3 Yes No
1 Is the kitchen located adjacent to or does it have a good view of the play area or family room?			
2 Does traffic bypass the kitchen work triangle?			
3 Is the kitchen at least 10 feet by 12 feet?			
4 Do the three sides of the work triangle total 22 feet or less?			
5 Does the window area equal at least 10 percent of the floor area?			
6 Is there a window over the sink?			
7 Is there a window over the range?			
8 Are there at least 8 feet of kitchen base cabinets?			
9 Is the kitchen free of these most common deficiencies? a Insufficient base cabinet storage space.			
b Insufficient wall cabinet storage.			
c Insufficient counter space.			
d No counter beside the refrigerator.			
e Not enough window area (at least 10 percent of floor area).			
f Poorly placed doors that waste wall space.			
g Traffic through work area.			
h Too little counter on either right or left side of sink.			
i No counter beside range.			
j Insufficient space in front of cabinets.			
k Distance between sink, range and refrigerator too great.			
l Range under window.			

CHECKLIST 12
DINING ROOM AND DINING AREA CHECKLIST

	HOUSE 1 Yes No	HOUSE 2 Yes No	HOUSE 3 Yes No
1 Does the house have a dining room or good size dining area?			
2 Is one wall free of windows and doors?			
3 Does the window area equal at least 10 percent of the floor area?			
4 Is the dining room or dining area at least 110 square feet?			
5 Is the room wide enough (10-foot minimum) so there will be 3 1/2 feet all around the table?			
6 Is the dining room or dining area big enough to hold all your furniture?			

CHECKLIST 13
BEDROOM CHECKLIST

	HOUSE 1 Yes No	HOUSE 2 Yes No	HOUSE 3 Yes No
1 Are there at least three bedrooms?			
2 Is each bedroom directly accessible from a hall?			
3 Can you reach a bathroom from each bedroom without being seen from the living/social area?			
4 Is the smallest bedroom at least 8 feet by 10 feet?			
5 Is the middle size bedroom at least 10 feet by 12 feet?			
6 Is the master bedroom at least 11 feet, 6 inches by 12 feet?			
7 Does each bedroom have adequate lighting?			
8 Does each bedroom have a closet that is at least 3 feet wide and 2 feet deep with a hanging rod and storage shelf?			
9 Is there a light in each closet?			

CHECKLIST 14
BATHROOM CHECKLIST

	HOUSE 1 Yes No	HOUSE 2 Yes No	HOUSE 3 Yes No
1 Does the house have a bathroom with a tub and shower plus a lavatory?			
2 If the house is two stories, is there a bathroom on each floor?			
3 Is each tub at least 5 feet long?			
4 Is there a vent fan in each bathroom and lavatory?			
5 If there is a window, is it away from the tub and toilet?			
6 Does each bathroom have the following: a Medicine cabinet with mirror			
b Towel racks			
c Toilet paper holder			
d Soap holder			
e Glass and toothbrush holder			
f Clean linen storage space			
g Dirty laundry storage space			
h Hooks for hanging clothes and robes			
7 Does each door lock have a device on the outside to permit entry in an emergency?			
8 Is there a solid grab bar in each shower?			

CHECKLIST 15
FAMILY AND RECREATION ROOM CHECKLIST

	HOUSE 1 Yes No	HOUSE 2 Yes No	HOUSE 3 Yes No
1 Is there a family room or recreation room at least 190 square feet in size?			
2 Is the smallest wall dimension at least 10 1/2 feet?			
3 Is there a closet in the family or recreation room?			
4 Are there adequate cabinets and counters?			
5 Is there adequate lighting?			
6 Does the window area equal at least 10 percent of the floor area?			

CHECKLIST 16
PATIO AND PORCH CHECKLIST

	HOUSE 1 Yes No	HOUSE 2 Yes No	HOUSE 3 Yes No
1 Is there a patio at least 100 square feet in size?			
2 Is the patio in a private area of the yard?			
3 Is the patio easily accessible from the kitchen?			
4 Is the patio easily accessible from the family room or recreation room?			
5 Is there a waterproof electrical outlet near the patio?			
6 Is there a closed-in porch?			
7 Is there a waterproof electrical outlet on the porch?			
8 Is there a spotlight for nighttime use?			

CHECKLIST 17
LAUNDRY AND STORAGE AREA CHECKLIST

	HOUSE 1 Yes No	HOUSE 2 Yes No	HOUSE 3 Yes No
1 Is there a laundry area or room?			
2 Is the laundry room or area properly ventilated?			
3 Is the dryer separately vented to the outside of the house?			
4 Is there adequate counter space?			
5 Is the floor able to withstand moisture?			
6 Is the wall covering moisture-resistant?			
7 Is there adequate light in the laundry area or room?			
8 If there is a basement, does it have its own outside entrance?			
9 Is there a convenient place to store the outside furniture and other outdoor equipment?			
10 Is the garage or carport extra wide or extra deep to permit its use as a storage area?			

CHECKLIST 18
GARAGE AND CARPORT CHECKLIST

		HOUSE 1 Yes No	HOUSE 2 Yes No	HOUSE 3 Yes No
1	Is there storage for at least two automobiles?			
2	Is each garage or carport at least 10 feet by 20 feet?			
3	Is the wall between the house and the car storage area fireproof?			
4	Are there adequate lights in the car storage area?			
5	Are the light switches for the garage inside the house?			

EXTERIOR DESIGN CHECKLIST

1 What is the CTS classification of the house being considered?

HOUSE 1	HOUSE 2	HOUSE 3
Class: _____	Class: _____	Class: _____
Type: _____	Type: _____	Type: _____
Style: _____	Style: _____	Style: _____

2 Is it a good example of one of the 58 traditional styles?

HOUSE 1	HOUSE 2	HOUSE 3
_____	_____	_____
_____	_____	_____
_____	_____	_____

3 What restoration could be made to improve or preserve its exterior style?

HOUSE 1	HOUSE 2	HOUSE 3
_____	_____	_____
_____	_____	_____
_____	_____	_____

CHECKLIST 20
GROUNDS AND SITE IMPROVEMENTS CHECKLIST

	HOUSE 1 Yes No	HOUSE 2 Yes No	HOUSE 3 Yes No
1 Do you have a clear understanding with the current owner about what shrubs and plants (if any) will be included in the sale?			
2 If the house is purchased from a builder, is there a written agreement that clearly sets out the builder's responsibility for landscaping and lawns?			
3 Have you had or are you planning to have a soil test made?			
4 Have you checked all the trees for damage and change of ground level around their bases?			
5 Are there no trees within 30 feet of the house which need to be removed?			
6 Are the sidewalks free of cracks?			
7 Is the driveway paving in good condition?			
8 If there is an in-ground swimming pool, has it been professionally checked?			
9 If there is an above-ground swimming pool, is there a clear understanding who will own it and if it is to be removed, what repairs will be made to the vacated site?			
10 Are there adequate outdoor electrical outlets and lights?			
11 Does the site have adequate storm water drainage?			
12 Are the dry wells used to collect rain water from the house at least 15 feet away from the foundation?			
13 Do the retaining walls appear to be properly constructed (at least one foot thick and set on a well-made footing) and free from tilting?			
14 Are all the fences and walls in good repair?			
15 Have you determined who owns the fences and walls on the boundary lines and who is responsible for their repair?			

SUBSTRUCTURES CHECKLIST

	HOUSE 1 Yes No	HOUSE 2 Yes No	HOUSE 3 Yes No
1 If cement is being poured, is the builder using the correct mixture of cement, sand and water?			
2 Is there a moisture/vapor barrier below the basement floor?			
3 Does the house have a partial basement?			
4 Is the whole basement floor cement covered?			
5 Are there no cracks in the foundation walls or the basement floors?			
6 Is the foundation wall made of cement block rather than cinder block?			
7 Are there no signs of powder-white mineral deposits a few inches off the floor?			
8 Are there no stains along the lower edge of the walls and columns and on the furnace and hot water heater which are indications of dampness?			
9 Is there a lack of mildew odor in the basement?			
10 Does the earth around the house slope away from the foundation wall?			

FRAMING AND EXTERIOR WALLS CHECKLIST

	HOUSE 1 Yes No	HOUSE 2 Yes No	HOUSE 3 Yes No
1 Do all the visible studs appear to be at least 2 inches by 4 inches?			
2 Do all the floor joists appear to be 16 inches on center?			
3 Are the wall studs placed with their narrow sides facing the wall surface?			
4 Is there a header beam over every door and wall opening?			
5 Are there no notches cut in load-bearing framing members to permit the passage of pipes or wires?			
6 When viewed along the edges, is there no sign of bulging of the outside walls?			
7 Do none of the windows stick?			
8 Are there no large cracks on the outside of the house between the chimney and the exterior wall?			
9 Are there no cracks running outward at an angle from the upper corners of the window and door frames?			
10 Are there no sloping or sagging floors?			
11 Are shingles or siding nailed with corrosion resistant nails?			

CHECKLIST 23
INSULATION AND VENTILATION CHECKLIST

		HOUSE 1 Yes No	HOUSE 2 Yes No	HOUSE 3 Yes No
1	Does the house have adequate under-roof or ceiling insulation?			
2	Does the house have adequate wall insulation?			
3	Does the house have adequate insulation under those floors that are not above a basement?			
4	Does the house have storm windows and doors or insulated glass?			
5	Are the doors adequately weather stripped?			
6	Are all ventilation openings covered with mesh?			
7	Are there at least four foundation ventilators in the basement or crawl spaces unless one side of such space is completely open to the basement?			
8	Is cross ventilation provided in any attic area or spaces between the roof and the top floor ceilings?			
9	Are ventilation openings designed to prevent the entrance of rain or snow?			

ROOFS, FLASHING, GUTTERS AND DOWNSPOUTS CHECKLIST

	HOUSE 1 Yes No	HOUSE 2 Yes No	HOUSE 3 Yes No
1 Does it appear that there is adequate flashing wherever chimneys and vents protrude through the roof?			
2 Are there "duckboards" or some other adequate protection wherever a flat roof is walked upon?			
3 Are there no signs of water stains on the underside of the roof?			
4 Are there no unusual newly painted ceilings?			
5 If the roof is asphalt-shingle covered are there no shingles cracked or broken, curling, tearing or becoming pierced with holes?			
6 If the roof is wood-shingle covered, are there no shingles curling, split or loose and broken?			
7 If the roof is metal-covered, is the metal not rusted, bent or pierced with holes?			
8 If the roof is flat and covered with roll or built-up materials, has none of the material become loose, torn, patched or worn through?			
9 Does the house have gutters and downspouts?			

INTERIOR FLOORS, WALLS, CEILINGS AND STAIRS CHECKLIST

	HOUSE 1 Yes No	HOUSE 2 Yes No	HOUSE 3 Yes No
1 If the subflooring is made of wood planks, are they laid diagonally to the joists?			
2 Is there bridging every 6 to 8 feet between the floor joists?			
3 Do none of the floor joists appear to be undersized or weakened with notches cut for wires or pipes?			
4 Are all interior load-bearing masonry walls at least 8 inches thick?			
5 Are the plaster walls free of bulging or cracking?			
6 Are there no signs of loose ceramic tiles around the shower or tub walls?			
7 Are the wood panel walls properly attached to the wall framing?			
8 Do the main interior stairs have at least 6 feet, 8 inches of headroom?			
9 Do the basement stairs have at least 6 feet, 4 inches of headroom?			
10 Is there a landing at least 2 feet, 6 inches deep at the top of any stair that has a door opening over it?			
11 Do all staircases of more than three stairs have hand-rails?			

CHECKLIST 26
FIREPLACES, CHIMNEYS AND VENTS CHECKLIST

	HOUSE 1 Yes No	HOUSE 2 Yes No	HOUSE 3 Yes No
1 Is the opening of each fireplace wider than it is high?			
2 Are the inside walls of each fireplace built at an angle so that the rear inside wall is at least 1 1/2 feet narrower than the front opening?			
3 Does each fireplace have a damper and an ash dump?			
4 Does each fireplace hearth extend at least 16 inches from the front of the fireplace and 8 inches to each side for fire safety protection?			
5 Is each fireplace set on its own footings?			
6 Is the smoke pipe that connects the furnace and hot water heater to the flue at least 10 inches below the ceiling or floor joists and further protected with plaster or a shield of metal or asbestos?			
7 Does the chimney extend at least 2 feet above the highest point on the roof?			
8 Are all prefabricated fireplaces and flues approved by the Underwriters' Laboratories?			

TERMITES AND OTHER VERMIN CHECKLIST

	HOUSE 1 Yes No	HOUSE 2 Yes No	HOUSE 3 Yes No
1 Are there no signs of living termites in the house?			
2 Is there no sign of termite damage?			
3 Has there been a recent professional termite inspection?			
4 Does the house have adequate termite barriers?			
5 Is all the wood that has not been specially treated 6 to 8 inches above the ground?			
6 Is the site graded so that the water flows away from the house?			
7 Are there no unscreened holes through which vermin can enter the house?			
8 Are all sources of food and water covered and vermin-proof?			

CHECKLIST 28
MISCELLANEOUS CONSTRUCTION DETAILS CHECKLIST

	HOUSE 1 Yes No	HOUSE 2 Yes No	HOUSE 3 Yes No
1 Is the moulding attractive and well installed?			
2 Do the doors open and close without sticking?			
3 Do the windows open and close without sticking?			
4 Are the windows in the children's rooms high enough to be safe yet low enough so a child can climb out in the event of a fire?			
5 Have you checked out the television reception and are you satisfied with the quality of reception available?			
6 Are there adequate cabinets and counters in the kitchen?			
7 Are the styles of the cabinets compatible with your furniture and decorating tastes?			
8 Is the paint on the exterior of the house in good condition?			
9 Are you prepared to repaint and paper all the rooms that will require it because of your taste in decorating?			
10 Are there no streaks or water stains around the window trim?			

HEATING SYSTEMS CHECKLIST

	HOUSE 1 Yes No	HOUSE 2 Yes No	HOUSE 3 Yes No
1 Are all the living areas in the house heated by the central heating system?			
2 Are any areas that are not heated by the central heating system adequately heated by a supplemental system?			
3 Does each room in the house have adequate radiators or air registers?			
4 Does the furnace appear to be modern and in good condition?			
5 Has an independent inspection of the heating system been made or ordered?			
6 Is there adequate means available to control the distribution of heat throughout the house?			
7 Are you satisfied with the type of heating system the house has?			
8 If the house has a solar heating system, do you thoroughly understand the advantages, disadvantages and cost of the system?			

CHECKLIST 30
AIR CONDITIONING CHECKLIST

	HOUSE 1 Yes No	HOUSE 2 Yes No	HOUSE 3 Yes No
1 Is the type of air conditioning in the house currently acceptable for this price house in your area?			
2 If there are any window air conditioning units, are they to be included in the sale?			
3 If there is a central air conditioning unit, does it cover the whole house?			
4 If the central air conditioning system is over five years old, or appears to be in poor condition, has it been professionally inspected or has an inspection been ordered?			
5 Is the attic fan rated large enough to remove air equal to the volume of the house once a minute?			
6 Is there a separate 220-volt electric line with a special plug near each window that has an 8,000 to 12,000 B.T.U. window air conditioning unit?			
7 If the central air conditioning system is connected through the heating ducts, have they been modified so they are large enough and have registers near the ceilings?			

PLUMBING CHECKLIST

	HOUSE 1		HOUSE 2		HOUSE 3	
	Yes	No	Yes	No	Yes	No
1 Does the house have an adequate water supply?						
2 If there is public water available, is the house receiving all its drinking water from this supply?						
3 Does the house have an adequate waste disposal system?						
4 If the waste disposal system is a septic tank or cesspool, has it recently been inspected or has an inspection been ordered?						
5 If a municipal sewer line is available, is the house connected to the municipal sewer system?						
6 Have all the brass, iron and steel water pipes been replaced with copper tubing or plastic pipes?						
7 If the water is hard in the area, does the house have an adequate water softener?						
8 Do all of the plumbing fixtures have the manufacturer's name stamped on them?						
9 Are all the bathtubs at least 5 feet long?						
10 Are the shower stalls at least 3 feet by 3 feet?						
11 Are all the toilets either the reverse trap or siphon jet type?						
12 Does each shower have an "automatic diverter" control?						
13 Are there at least two outdoor sill cocks on opposite ends of the house?						

CHECKLIST 32
DOMESTIC HOT WATER CHECKLIST

	HOUSE 1 Yes No	HOUSE 2 Yes No	HOUSE 3 Yes No
1 Does the domestic hot water heating system appear to be adequate for the needs of your family?			
2 Is there a hot water faucet on each sink?			
3 If hot water is supplied by the furnace, is there an auxiliary storage tank?			
4 If the electric hot water tank is the slow recovery type, is it wired and metered to take advantage of lower "off peak" electric rates?			
5 If there is a solar hot water system, are you aware of the advantages and disadvantages of the system?			
6 Are all of the hot water faucets or hot water-using appliances connected to the hot water source by pipes less than 15 feet long?			
7 If the pipes connecting the hot water source to the faucets and appliances are over 15 feet long, are they all wrapped with insulation?			
8 Does the hot water system use the fuel that is least expensive in your area?			

FUELS CHECKLIST

	HOUSE 1 Yes No	HOUSE 2 Yes No	HOUSE 3 Yes No
1 Does the house use the most economical fuel in your area for its heating system?			
2 Does the house use the most economical fuel in your area for its domestic hot water system?			
3 If the fuel used is oil, is there an outside tank with at least 550 and preferably 1,000-gallon capacity?			
4 If the house does not use the most economic fuel, are there other advantages that outweigh this deficiency?			

CHECKLIST 34
ELECTRICITY CHECKLIST

	HOUSE 1 Yes No	HOUSE 2 Yes No	HOUSE 3 Yes No
1 Does the house have at least a 100-ampere size electric service?			
2 Does the distribution box use circuit breakers rather than fuses as protection devices?			
3 Is there a special circuit installed for a laundry clothes dryer?			
4 Is the house free of knob and tube wiring?			
5 Are all the electrical outlets the new three-prong receptacles?			
6 Is there at least one special waterproof outside outlet?			
7 Are there adequate duplex outlets in each room?			
8 Are there two extra outlets over the kitchen counters?			
9 Is there an outlet near the mirror in each bathroom and lavatory?			

MISCELLANEOUS SYSTEMS AND EQUIPMENT CHECKLIST

	HOUSE 1 Yes No	HOUSE 2 Yes No	HOUSE 3 Yes No
1 Does the house have any of the following miscellaneous systems and equipment? Heat pump			
Humidifier			
Intercommunication system			
Built-in hi-fi sound system			
Burglar alarm			
Fire alarm			
Smoke detectors			
Automatic door opener			
Elevator			
Dumbwaiter			
Stair lift			
Incinerator			
Laundry chute			
Central vacuum cleaner			
Sauna			
Special tubs			
Exercise equipment			
Computer controls			
Darkroom			
Special hobby rooms and equipment			
2 If there is a heat pump, has it been professionally inspected or has an inspection been ordered?			

NEGOTIATING CHECKLIST

	Yes	No
1 Are you satisfied you know what the house is worth before you make an offer?		
2 Do you know how much the down payment will be increased and how much the monthly mortgage payment will be increased for each $1,000 (or fraction thereof) you increase your offer?		
3 Are you using a REALTOR®?		
4 Have you made a sincere effort to convince the salesperson or broker that you are ready to buy a home soon?		
5 Have you truthfully and accurately presented your financial situation to the salesperson or broker?		
6 Have you resisted letting anyone talk you out of using an attorney if you want to use one?		
7 Have you insisted upon immediately getting a copy of anything you sign?		
8 Does the contract or binder spell out what will happen to your deposit and who will hold it?		
9 When you make an offer have you:		
a Prepared a list of improvements and repairs that you feel will be needed together with their estimated cost to be shown to the seller?		
b Told the salesperson about other houses you are considering and how their prices compare with the house on which you are making an offer?		
c Submitted any appraisal report you have that supports your price?		
d Allowed a reasonable but short period of time for consideration of the offer so you will be free to make other offers?		
10 Have you resisted the temptation to tell anyone you might increase your offer?		
11 Have you limited the time the seller has to accept your offer?		
12 If your offer is rejected have you considered other concessions you may be willing to make instead of raising the offer?		
13 Have you inquired what other concessions the seller may want instead of a higher offer?		
14 Have you hired an attorney to represent you at the closing if you haven't one already?		
15 Have you considered recording the sales contract?		

CHECKLIST 37
FINANCING CHECKLIST

	Yes	No
1 Have you carefully estimated the amount of money you have available for a down payment?		
2 Have you shopped around for a mortgage, trying at least three different sources?		
3 Have you arranged for an attorney before you sign any mortgage documents?		
4 Has someone explained to you your additional obligations required by the mortgage besides just making timely payments?		
5 If you are a veteran, have you checked to see if you are eligible for a VA guaranteed mortgage?		
6 If you need a lower down payment, have you checked into a privately insured mortgage?		
7 If you are going to use a mortgage banker, have you checked on his or her reputation?		
8 Have you checked to find out what mortgage programs are available in your state?		
9 If the lender is offering you a Variable Interest Mortgage, is there a valid reason why you should accept it rather than the traditional terms?		
10 Have you looked into the possibility of obtaining a Graduated Payment Mortgage, Flexible Payment Mortgage or a Deferred Interest Mortgage?		

CHECKLIST 38
APPRAISAL CHECKLIST

		Yes	No
1	Does your proposed sales contract contain a provision that makes the sale conditional upon obtaining an appraisal that indicates the sale price is the market value?		
2	Have you selected an appraiser based on either a good recommendation or the appraiser's qualifications as indicated by his professional affiliations and designations?		
3	Have you requested information about the qualifications of the lender's appraiser?		
4	Has the lender agreed to let you review its appraisal prior to a final decision being made on your loan application?		
5	Do your appraisal and the lender's appraisal at least contain the minimum items required by the American Institute of Real Estate Appraisers?		
6	Are your appraisal and the lender's appraisal both based primarily on the Market Data Approach to value?		
7	Have you checked the appraisal upon which your tax assessment is based?		
8	Do you know how to make an appeal if you are not satisfied with the tax assessment of your house?		
9	Is the amount of insurance you plan to carry on the dwelling structure equal to at least 80 percent of its current replacement cost?		

INSURANCE CHECKLIST

	Yes	No
1 Prior to the closing have you arranged either to take over the existing home-owner's insurance policy or to get a new policy to be effective at the time of the closing or settlement?		
2 Have you become familiar with the various forms of homeowner insurance available (standard form, broad form and comprehensive form) and selected the form best suited for your budget and needs?		
3 Have you found out what the "replacement cost" of your house is and arranged to have the dwelling covered to at least 80 percent of that cost?		
4 Have you discussed with a professional insurance agent the many optional coverages available as part of a homeowner's policy and selected those needed by you and your family?		
5 Have you checked to find out if earthquake insurance is available as an endorsement to your homeowner's policy or if a separate policy is required?		
6 Have you checked to see if your home is in an identified flood zone and if so is flood insurance available in your community?		
7 Have you checked with your attorney about the need for title insurance?		
8 Have you considered buying title insurance that protects *you* as well as the lender?		
9 Have you found out from a reliable insurance agent the cost of a mortgage life insurance policy for the amount and term of your new mortgage?		
10 Have you found out from a reliable insurance agent the cost of various forms of income protection or disability insurance policies?		
11 Together with your attorney, accountant or other financial advisor have you discussed how mortgage payments can be made in the event of death or injury and whether mortgage life insurance or mortgage disability insurance is needed by you and your family?		
12 If you decide to buy an income protection or disability insurance policy, have you read the policy's definition of "total disability" and "partial disability" and are you satisfied that they are fair definitions?		
13 Is there a home warranty insurance policy, paid for by the owner or builder, available for this house and is the policy one that covers both structural defects and servicing of mechanical equipment?		

CHECKLIST 40
SALES CONTRACT CHECKLIST

everything line 1 – line 30	Yes	No
1 Have you consulted an attorney on all contractual matters?		
2 Have you checked to determine if the contract contains the correct name of the seller(s) (who should be the actual owners of the property) and the buyer(s)?		
3 Does the contract contain a description of the property detailed enough so there is absolutely no question what is being sold?		
4 Are the deposit requirements clearly spelled out: a Amount of the deposit(s)?		
b When is the deposit(s) payable?		
c Who holds the deposit(s)?		
d When is the deposit(s) turned over to the seller?		
e When is the deposit(s) returned to the buyer?		
f If there is a dispute about the deposit(s) how will it be settled?		
5 Does the contract contain a list of personal property or property that may be considered by some as personal property that will be included in the sale, such as: a Screens		
b Storms windows and doors		
c TV antenna		
d Drapes, curtains, blinds and rods		
e Carpeting and rugs		
f Shades and awnings		
g Domestic hot water heater		
h Window air conditioners and humidifiers		
i Heating equipment		
j Special light fixtures		
k Intercommunication and music systems		
l Garage door openers		
m Shrubbery and plants		
n Appliances		
6 Does the contract state the purchase price and how it will be paid		
7 Does the contract provide clear information about the closing? a Where it will be?		
b When it will be?		
c Who will search the title?		
d Who will provide the title insurance policy or certificate of title?		
8 Is there a clear provision who will pay the title closing costs: a Search of title		
b Title insurance or certificate of title		
c Drawing the deed		
d Preparing the mortgage(s)		
e Attorney's fees for holding a closing		
f Recording the documents		
g Other expenses		

SALES CONTRACT CHECKLIST (continued)

	Yes	No
9 Is there a clear mortgage clause:		
a That the agreement is conditional upon the buyer obtaining a mortgage(s)?		
b The term of the mortgage(s)?		
c What type of mortgage(s) will be applied for?		
d The interest rate of the mortgage(s)?		
e Who will pay any points or other charges by the lender?		
f What effort the buyer must take to obtain the mortgage(s)?		
g How long does the buyer have to obtain the mortgage(s)?		
h What happens when the mortgage is not obtained (including buyer's obligation to notify the seller)?		
10 Is there a provision that spells out what the condition of the property will be at the time of closing?		
a Will the property be conveyed "as is"?		
b Does the seller agree to make renovation and/or repairs?		
c Do you plan to inspect the premises immediately before closing?		
d Did the seller make any representations about the condition of the improvements or mechanical systems?		
11 Do the sellers make the following promises about the care of the property?		
a Except for normal wear and tear the property will be in substantially the same condition on the date of the closing as on the date of agreement?		
b That the seller will continue to maintain the lawn and shrubs and will attempt to keep them in the same condition as they were on the date of the agreement?		
c That the seller will deliver the premises, including the basement, attic and grounds in broom-clean condition and will not leave any rubbish or personal property anywhere on the premises or grounds?		
12 Does the contract contain a provision giving the right to reinspect the property immediately prior to the closing?		
13 Do the sellers make the following representations about the past history of the property:		
a That during their occupancy of the property they have never experienced any accumulations of surface or subsurface water in the basement of the premises (or if they have, details about the problem and how it was fixed).		
b That during their occupancy the property has never been damaged by fire or other perils covered by a standard homeowner policy (or if it has, the details about the damage and how it was repaired).		
c That the septic system is, to the best of their knowledge, in good working order and has never malfunctioned to the best of their knowledge in the past (or if it has, details about the current or past problem and how it was repaired).		
d That the well, well pump and water softening system, including the pipes, to the best of the sellers' knowledge, meet with all local health depart-		

	Yes	No
ment standards, and has never had any problems relating to the quality, quantity or flow of water furnished by the well (or if so, the details about the problems and how they were cured).		
e That there are no leased fixtures on the premises except as specifically stated in the contract.		
f That all of the improvements located on the premises are, to the best of the sellers' knowledge, free of termites, vermin or other infestation.		
g To the best of their knowledge all the improvements, appurtenances, systems, driveways and walks, fences and walls, septic system and leeching fields, wells and pipes are entirely within the boundary lines of the premises and that none of the above belonging to anyone else is within the boundaries of the property (unless noted in the contract).		
h That the well, well pipes, utility connections serve no other premises.		
14 Does the contract provide that marketable and insurable fee simple title to the premises (as defined by the Standard of Title of the Bar Association of the state in which the property is located) will be conveyed to the buyer by warranty deed (unless some other form of conveyance is stated)?		
15 Is there a provision that all the conveyance taxes will be paid and who will pay them?		
16 Is there a provision that all past due real estate taxes have been paid and that the current taxes due will be prorated between the seller and the buyer?		
17 Is there a clause stating that the conveyance will be subject to recorded easements, grants, rights of way and deed restrictions and that there are no known violations of these restrictions that are not stated in the contract?		
18 Is there a clause saying that the conveyance will be subject to all provisions of any ordinance, zoning regulations, municipal regulation, environmental regulation, public or private law, including building and health codes, inland wetlands, coastal wetlands and flood plain regulations, and that there are no known violations of any of the above known to the sellers that are not stated in the contract?		
19 Is there a provision that the seller will deliver to the buyer an affidavit stating no one has rendered services or delivered materials to the premises during the past 60 days (or whatever the period for recording mechanics' liens is in the state the property is located) who has not been paid in full?		
20 Is there a provision about the surveys: a Will a survey be made or updated?		
b Who will order that the survey be made or updated?		
c Who will pay for the survey or updating?		

	Yes	No
d That the seller will certify by affidavit at the closing that no structural changes have been made outside of the dwelling on the premises since the date of the survey?		
21 Is there a provision about real estate brokers or salespersons: a If some were involved does it state: Who were they?		
Who will pay them?		
How much will they be paid?		
When they will be paid?		
b If none were involved in the transaction, is there a statement to that effect?		
22 Is there a provision that clarifies that there will be a prorata adjustment of personal property taxes on items included in the sale and any other taxes that are customarily adjusted for in the area?		
23 Is there a provision that sets forth what items, other than taxes, will be adjusted for, such as: a Homeowner association dues.		
b Fuel oil.		
c Mortgage interest (when a mortgage is assumed).		
d Insurance premiums (when a policy is taken over).		
e Sewer, water, electric and gas charges.		
24 Does the contract contain a statement whether the contract is assignable or not assignable by each party to the agreement, and if it is assignable whether the other party has to consent to the assignment?		
25 Does the contract have a statement as to whether the agreement is binding or not binding upon the heirs and successors of each party?		
26 Does the contract have a statement that the agreement supersedes any and all prior understandings and agreements between the buyer and the seller?		
27 Is there a statement that the agreement constitutes (or does not constitute) the entire understanding between the parties?		
28 Is there a statement of what will happen if the buyer fails to live up to the agreement?		
29 Is there a statement of what will happen if the seller fails to live up to the agreement?		
30 Does the contract have a provision that requires the seller (or buyer) to insure the property from the date of the agreement together with a clear statement as to what kind of insurance will be carried, who will pay for it and who will receive the benefits in the event of a loss occurring?		

	Yes	No
31 Is there a provision that spells out whether the seller will occupy the premises beyond the date of the closing or vacate the premises prior to the closing? If occupancy is to be beyond the closing, when will the occupancy terminate? Is there an agreement of how much the seller will pay for occupancy beyond the closing date and how much extra the seller will pay if he or she stays beyond the agreed date to vacate the premises?		
32 Is there a provision that permits the buyer to occupy the premises prior to the closing? If there is such a provision, does the contract state how much the buyer will pay for this occupancy prior to closing?		
33 If the contract is written in the singular, masculine gender is there a clause stating that the singular, masculine gender is deemed to refer to the feminine gender and the singular will be deemed to refer to the plural, and vice versa, whenever the context so requires?		
34 If there is an addendum to the contract, does the main body of the contract contain a provision making the addendum part of the contract?		
35 Is there a provision that spells out that the terms, conditions, promises and representations contained in the agreement will survive the closing of title?		
36 Is there a provision that states that the date of the agreement will be the date it is signed by the last buyer (or last seller or some other date)? Also, does it state the contract is void if not signed within some fixed period of time by all the parties?		
37 Does the contract have a place for the signature of all the parties (and witnesses and notaries, if their use is customary in the area)?		
38 Is there a place to indicate separately the date the buyer and the seller signed the agreement?		
39 Does the contract contain a provision making the sale conditional upon the buyer obtaining an appraisal of the property indicating the sale price is not in excess of the appraiser's opinion of the value and/or inspections by whatever inspectors the buyer deems advisable (home inspectors, architect, contractor, termite inspector, septic system inspector, well expert, electrician, heating system inspector, roofer, insurance agent, lender, relatives, friends, others)?		
40 Is there a home warranty insurance policy covering the structure and the mechanical systems? If there isn't is there a provision in the contract allowing the buyer the opportunity to obtain a policy and making the contract conditional upon his or her ability to obtain the policy?		

CHECKLIST 41
CLOSING CHECKLIST

	Yes	No
1 Have you obtained a copy of the HUD booklet, "Settlement Costs and You?"		
2 Have you checked with at least three lenders to see who will give you the best mortgage?		
3 Have you checked your sales contract and prepared a list of items that will have to be negotiated at the closing?		
4 If you are going to use an escrow agent, have you checked on those available and compared their fees?		
5 If you can pick who makes the title examination, have you inquiried who does this work and compared their fees?		
6 If you are planning to buy title insurance, have you compared the costs of the different companies who write it in your area?		
7 If you are going to use an attorney, have you gotten recommendations from people you have confidence in?		
8 Have you asked the attorney you intend to use what the estimated fee will be?		
9 In addition to the amount of mortgage, interest and term they will give you have you asked potential mortgage lenders what their other loan-related charges will be?		
10 Is there a clear understanding between you and the seller(s) how each of the following adjustments will be made:		
a Prepaid taxes		
b Prepaid fuel		
c Prepaid association dues		
d Prepaid mortgage interest (if you are assuming a mortgage)		
e Prepaid insurance premiums (if you are assuming an insurance policy)		
f Prepaid sewer, water, electric and gas charges		
11 Do you know when your first mortgage payment will be due?		
12 Do you know if you will have to pay any mortgage interest at the closing and, if so, how much?		
13 Have you reviewed all the other possible charges you may have to pay?		
14 Have you requested a disclosure of settlement costs one day before the closing?		
15 Have you reviewed the completed disclosure of settlement costs using the material in this chapter as your guide?		
16 Did you reconcile the mathematics on the closing statement?		
17 Did you request and receive a federal Truth-in-Lending Statement?		
18 Did you arrange to have the needed additional cash available at the closing?		

CHECKLIST 42
CONDOMINIUM CHECKLIST

	Yes	No
1 Have you checked to determine what lenders are familiar with your condominium, and made a mortgage inquiry of them?		
2 Have you checked out the reputation of the directors of the owners' association?		
3 Are you willing to give up some of your privacy and freedom for the convenience of condominium living?		
4 Is there adequate parking for unit owners, tenants and guests?		
5 Is the condominium managed by a professional management company?		
6 Have you checked on the history of past assessments?		
7 Have you checked to determine if any special assessments are pending?		
8 Have you checked on the history of the common charges and what increases are pending?		
9 Have you asked some of the other unit owners how they like the development and what problems they have had?		
10 Have you checked the published house rules to determine if you are comfortable with them?		
11 Have you checked on the resale prices of other units in the condominium complex and other similar condominiums?		
12 Have you received a copy of the current operating budget?		
13 If you have a pet, have you determined that your pet will be welcome?		
14 If you have children, have you determined that children will be welcome?		
15 Have you made inquiry about the life style associated with the condominium and are you satisfied it is the type of life style your family desires?		

CHECKLIST 43
COOPERATIVE APARTMENT CHECKLIST

	Yes	No
1 If you are considering buying a condominium have you also considered a unit in a cooperative if they are available in your area?		
2 Have you checked what the mortgage balance is and how much is allocated to the unit you are considering purchasing?		
3 Have you reviewed all the rules and regulations to determine if they will interfere with your life style?		
4 Have you reviewed the history of repair costs of the cooperative corporation to see if they are increasing rapidly?		
5 Have you reviewed the history of the shareholders' maintenance costs to see if they are increasing rapidly?		
6 Have you compared the offering price of the shares with what shares in other units in the same cooperative apartment have recently sold for?		

CHECKLIST 44
TIMESHARING CHECKLIST

	Yes	No
1 Have you checked what periods of time will be available for your exclusive time?		
2 Do you feel the division of exclusive time between owners is equitable and fair?		
3 Do you think the projected rental charges, cost to clean and repair the units between occupants and projected general expenses are accurate?		
4 Is the projected rental income from nonowners borne out by the past experience in the same unit or other comparable units renting at comparable rents?		
5 Have you calculated what would happen if the projected annual rent received was 25 percent below the projected income?		
6 If the annual carrying cost doubled, could you afford to maintain your ownership?		
7 Have you compared the price of the unit you propose to buy with the resale price of other units in the same project or similar projects?		
8 When you compared the price of the unit you propose to buy against the resale value of similar units in other projects, have you made an adjustment for any differences in financing and carrying costs?		
9 Are you satisfied that the management company in charge of the timesharing project will maintain the unit so that when you occupy it during your exclusive time it will be ready for you when you arrive—clean and in good state of repair?		

CHECKLIST 45
LEASED LAND CHECKLIST

	Yes	No
1 Are residences on leased land well accepted in the area you are contemplating?		
2 Is the balance of the term on the lease you are purchasing acceptable to you?		
3 Does the lease contain a provision that subordinates the fee owner's interest to that of the mortgagee?		
4 Does the lease give the mortgagee the right to take over the land rent payments in the event the owner defaults on the mortgage payment?		

RESORT AND RECREATION HOUSES CHECKLIST

	Yes	No
1 Has every member of your family been consulted about your choice of a resort home?		
2 Are you satisfied that you are willing to make a substantial commitment of funds and time to your resort home and will continue to be willing to do so when the novelty has worn off?		
3 Have you checked on what the resale prices are of similar homes if you are buying a new home from a developer?		
4 Have you received competent advice from a tax expert about what expenses you will be able to deduct from your individual tax return?		

HOUSING FOR THE ELDERLY CHECKLIST

	Yes	No
1 Have you carefully considered the advantages and disadvantages of living in a setting restricted to elderly residents versus living in a nonhomogeneous setting?		
2 If you or your spouse is over age 55 or getting close to that age, have you considered selling your home and buying a less expensive home, condominium or cooperative apartment?		
3 Are you familiar with the special provisions of the IRS Regulations that provide for a once-in-a-lifetime $100,000 capital gain forgiveness?		
4 Have you checked to determine if you are eligible for any subsidized rent or mortgage payment programs?		
5 If any member of your family is handicapped, have you looked for housing that would be easier for him or her to live in?		
6 If you are considering changing your geographic location, have you explored the possibility of renting for a year before you buy in the new location?		

CHECKLIST 48
PLANNED UNIT DEVELOPMENT CHECKLIST

		Yes	No
1	Have you checked to determine what is owned in common by the owners' association?		
2	Do you know what form of ownership your individual unit will be?		
3	Do you know what recreational facilities are owned or controlled by the owners' association?		
4	Do you know what maintenance the owners' association will perform on your property and to your building?		
5	Have you reviewed the annual assessments and special assessments of the association?		
6	Have you inquired if any special assessments are contemplated in the future?		
7	Have you checked the rules and regulations of the owners' association to be sure they are compatible with your life style?		
8	Have you checked on the quality of the directors and management of the owners' association and how effectively they perform their functions?		

CHECKLIST 49
MOBILE HOMES CHECKLIST

	Yes	No
1 Have you consulted all the members of your family and reached a consensus about where you want to live?		
2 Have you examined all of the mobile home parks in those communities which you have selected as suitable places for you to locate?		
3 Have you considered buying your own lot or a lot in a special mobile home development rather than renting a pad in a mobile home park?		
4 After locating a potential mobile home park in which to live, do you plan to check the following: a Monthly pad rental		
b Entrance fees		
c Lease length and term		
d Services included in your rental charge		
e Recreational facilities available		
f Make-up of family attracted to the park		
g Amount and type of organized social activities		
h The rules and regulations		
5 Does the mobile home park have the following: a Good landscaping		
b Paved streets		
c Street lights		
d Underground utility lines		
e Laundry facilities		
6 If you are buying a used mobile home, have you examined the documents that show when it was built?		
7 If the mobile home was built before July 15, 1976, have you specifically examined it to determine if it has the following? a Two exterior doors remote from each other		
b An egress window in each sleeping room		
c Smoke detectors wired to the electric system with audio alarms outside of each bedroom		
d A tie-down system		
e Evidence that the wiring conforms to the National Electrical Code		
f Good fire ratings for surfaces of the furnace and hot water heater and area adjacent to the cooking range		
8 If any of the above items are missing, have you determined what it would cost to have them installed?		
9 If you decide to buy a used mobile home, have you obtained the services of an attorney to assure that you get a good title to what you are buying?		
10 Have you shopped around for the lowest interest rates and best loan terms available?		

MOBILE HOMES CHECKLIST (continued)

	Yes	No
11 Have you explored the possibility of obtaining a VA or FHA insured loan?		
12 If you are buying a new (or used) mobile home, have you checked it for the following quality features?		
a Thick walls		
b Thick floors		
c Thick roof		
d Good insulation		
e Large capacity hot water heater		
f Good quality heating unit		
g Good size air conditioning unit		
h Wood cabinets and trim rather than cheap plastic		
i Well-caulked and weather stripped doors and windows		
13 If you decide to buy a mobile home from the mobile home park owner where you plan to locate, have you tried to get some rental and lease concessions?		

MODULAR AND PREFABRICATED HOUSES CHECKLIST

	Yes	No
1 Have you considered buying a modular or prefabricated house?		
2 If you have decided to buy a modular house, does it appear that the developer has passed the cost savings on to you?		
3 If you decide to build a modular or prefabricated house, have you resisted the temptation to be your own general contractor (unless you are truly qualified to be one)?		
4 Have you considered the possibility that the rate of appreciation that will take place based on what has happened in the past may be less than that of conventionally built housing?		

HISTORIC HOUSES CHECKLIST

	Yes	No
1 If the residence you are considering was built before 1900, have you checked to determine if it has possible historic value?		
2 Has the house you are considering been designated as an historic landmark?		
3 Are there any public or private easements or restrictions controlling the exterior appearance?		
4 Are there any public or private easements controlling interior renovations?		
5 Have you checked to determine if the house you are considering is eligible for special lower property taxes?		
6 Are you aware of the special benefits other than financial that you will enjoy by living in an historic house?		

CHECKLIST 52
SOLAR ENERGY CHECKLIST

	Yes	No
1 Have you considered buying or building a residence with solar heating or solar domestic hot water?		
2 Do you know the difference between an active solar system and a passive solar system?		
3 If you are considering buying any solar equipment have you determined if the products are approved so you will be eligible for the tax credits provided for in the 1978 Revenue Act?		
4 If you are considering solar equipment, have you written to the Consumer Information Center, Dept. 605F., Pueblo, Colorado, 81009, for information?		
5 Before you purchase solar equipment or buy a solar house, do you plan to get independent engineering advice first?		
6 Have you insisted that all performance claims for the solar system you plan to buy are put into writing?		
7 Have you ascertained who will service the system after it is installed?		
8 Does the system you are purchasing or the system in the house you are buying have a solar system that is covered by a valid warranty?		
9 Have you visited and inspected a location where the solar system you are contemplating is already installed and in operation?		
10 Have you written to the National Solar Heating and Cooling Information Center, Box 1607, Rockville, Maryland, 20850, for information about the system you are contemplating buying?		

BARRIER-FREE DESIGN CHECKLIST

	Yes	No
1 If you are building or remodeling a residence, are you planning to make it as barrier-free as possible?		
2 Does any residence you are building, remodeling or buying have the following exterior barrier-free features?		
a Are the exterior stairs the type with a maximum riser height of 7 inches; a smooth nosing overhang of 1/2 inch and tread width of 10 inches?		
b Are the garage doors at least 14 feet wide with an electric door opener?		
c Is there an entrance ramp at least 4 feet wide which slopes at a rate not exceeding 1 foot rise every 12 feet (8 1/3% slope) with a 32-inch high hand rail if there is no ground level entrance? Are ramps of nonskid construction and sheltered by a roof or an overhang?		
d Are the thresholds of the doors flush or have no more than 1/2 inch differential?		
e Are as many exterior doors as possible 32 inches wide and easy to open?		
f Are the landings adjacent to doors at least 5 feet square and extending 1 foot on either side of each door at the top of the stairway?		
g Is the door hardware the kind with level-type handles or easily manipulated doorknobs installed not more than 36 inches high?		
h Do the exterior doors have sturdy kickplates?		
3 Does any residence you are building, remodeling or buying have the following interior barrier-free features?		
a Is there a 32-inch wide passage from a bedroom of a handicapped person to where he or she would sit and eat?		
b Are the interior stairs the type with a maximum riser height of 7 inches, a smooth nosing overhang of 1/2 inch and tread width of 10 inches?		
c Do the interior stairs have at least one handrail 32 inches high from the tread at the face of the riser?		
d Do the floors have nonskid surfaces?		
e Does the carpeting have a low pile height?		
f Is the residence free of small scatter rugs?		
g Is the residence free of slippery, highly waxed floors?		
4 If you have a handicapped person in your family have you planned for adapting at least part of your home to his or her special needs?		

BUILDING OR BUYING A NEW HOUSE CHECKLIST

	Yes	No
1 If you want to buy a new house have you considered:		
a Hiring an architect and designing a custom built house?		
b Building a home from a set of mail order stock house plans?		
c Buying a house in a development?		
2 Have you consulted with all the members of your family about what they would like in a new house?		
3 If you are going to use an architect have you:		
a Looked at other houses he or she has designed?		
b Talked with some of his or her clients?		
4 Have you considered including in your plans these features and items most people desire in their homes?		
a Full basement with an exterior exit		
b A one-story design		
c At least a two-car garage		
d Separate dining room		
e Separate family room		
f Fireplace		
g Brick or masonry exterior finish		
h Asphalt shingle roof		
5 If you are going to use a contractor, have you:		
a Looked at other houses he or she has built?		
b Talked with some past customers?		
6 Have you secured the services of a lawyer?		
7 Are you planning to sign a written contract with the:		
a Architect		
b Contractor		
c Developer		
8 Have you considered acting as your own general contractor?		
9 Have you considered doing some of the work yourself?		
10 If you are using a general contractor, have you insisted upon a completion bond?		
11 If you are going to use mail order stock plans, have you considered using an architect to modify them to suit your needs and site?		
12 If your house is turning out to be too expensive, have you considered the following cost reduction ideas:		
a Eliminate unnecessary "frills"		
b Plan to do some of the work yourself		
c Choose an alternate site that will be easier to develop		
d Simplify the basic configuration		
e Use a basement and/or attic to provide needed space		

BUILDING OR BUYING A NEW HOUSE CHECKLIST (continued)

	Yes	No
f Eliminate porches		
g Reduce the size of the house		
h Reduce the amount of hallways		
i Reduce the size of the kitchen		
j Eliminate some hardwood floors		
k Select less expensive tiles		
l Design windows and doors so stock prehung windows can be used		
m Use outside wall dimensions that are divisible evenly by 4 feet		
n Use a 24-inch on center framing system (if permitted by your local building code)		
o Reduce the size of the footing to the size actually required for your soil conditions and house design		
p Use the new framing systems and other cost-cutting recommendations developed by the National Association of Home Builders Research Foundation, Inc. (Optimum Value Engineering System)		
q Use trusses in your roof system		
13 Have you authorized changes to your signed contract only in writing with your contractor?		
14 Have you obtained from the contractor waivers of liens from all the suppliers and subcontractors?		
15 Have you considered buying a manufactured home?		

RENOVATION CHECKLIST

	Yes	No
1 Is the house structurally sound and suitable for renovation?		
2 Is the layout of the rooms such that the house can be made livable?		
3 Can you visualize how the house will look after it is renovated?		
4 Have you made the purchase of the house conditional upon a negative termite inspection?		
5 Have you inspected the house for the following major defects? a Wet basement		
b Defective main supporting beam		
c Cracked or decayed sill plates		
d Cracked or decayed floor joists		
e Cracked or decayed framing members		
f Defective floors		
g Sagging roof ridge		
6 Have you determined what will have to be done to make the house comply with the following local codes and other governmental regulations: a Building code		
b Electric code		
c Plumbing code		

d Health code
      Waste disposal
      Water supply		

e Zoning regulations		
f Environmental regulations		
7 Have you planned to have at least minimum electric service of 100 amperes and 220–240 volts?		
8 Is the heating system adequate and in good repair?		
9 Is the domestic hot water system large enough and in good repair?		
10 Is the exterior siding in good condition or repairable?		
11 Are the roof and flashing in good condition?		
12 Are the exterior doors and windows free of rot and in repairable condition?		
13 Are the porches free of rot and repairable?		
14 Are the interior walls and ceilings in good condition or repairable?		
15 Are the floors in good condition or repairable?		
16 Are the interior doors, cabinets and trim in good condition or repairable?		

CHECKLIST 56
HOME IMPROVEMENTS CHECKLIST

		Yes	No
1	Are you considering making any of the following most popular home improvements? a New roofing		
	b Insulation and weather stripping		
	c New siding		
	d Additional or remodeled baths		
	e Replacement windows		
	f New kitchen cabinets and counters		
	g Kitchen remodeling		
	h Major room additions		
	i Remodeling attics or basements		
	j New wall paneling		
	k Porch enclosures		
	l Addition of a garage or carport		
2	Are you aware that many home improvement jobs will not add value to your home equal to or greater than their cost?		
3	If your house does not have at least 6 inches of insulation over the top ceiling or under the roof, are you planning to add it as soon as possible?		
4	Are you aware of the many dishonest people in the home improvement business?		
5	If you are going to hire a home improvement contractor have you carefully checked on his or her reputation?		
6	If your home improvement job is going to be more than $1,000, are you planning to have a lawyer check the contract before you sign it?		
7	Does your home improvement contract contain the following items? a A detailed description of what is going to be done by the contractor		
	b What materials will be used		
	c When the job will be started		
	d Approximately how long the job will take		
	e Specifications as to what appliances and fixtures will be supplied		
	f Requirement that appliances and fixtures be correctly installed		
	g When and how the contractor will be paid		
	h A provision to hold back the last payment until after the job is completed		
	i A provision about cost overruns		
	j A provision that only changes authorized in writing will be charged for		
	k A requirement that the contractor will remove all materials and debris from the site and leave the premises "broom clean"		
	l A requirement that the contractor carry adequate Workmen's Compensation and liability insurance		
	m A clause specifying arbitration in the event of a dispute		

ENERGY SAVINGS CHECKLIST

	Yes	No
1 Have you considered the following potential energy-saving items: a Overhead insulation		
b Wall insulation		
c Weather stripping and caulking		
d Storm windows		
e Clock thermostats		
f Water heater insulation		
g Multiglazed windows and doors		
h Electric demand regulating devices		
i Solar domestic hot water system		
j Wind power devices		
k Replacement furnace burner		
l Automatic flue openers and closers		
m Electrical or mechanical devices to replace gas pilots		
n A meter that displays the cost of energy being used		
2 If you have done any approved energy saving improvements to your home since April 19, 1977, have you applied for a tax credit? (If you have not, you may be able to file an amended tax return.)		

CHECKLIST 58
NOISE CHECKLIST

		Yes	No
1	If you are building a new house, have you considered installing the following noise reduction items?		
	a 2 by 6-inch studs with super insulation		
	b Carpeting instead of hard flooring materials		
	c Soundproofing materials in the walls and ceilings		
	d Storm windows		
	e Baffling the areas in which the refrigerator, furnace, dishwasher, air conditioners, washing machine and other noisy appliances are located		
2	If the plumbing system is noisy, have you had it checked by a plumber for the specific goal of noise reduction?		
3	If the heating system is noisy, have you had it checked for the specific goal of noise reduction?		
4	If you are building or renovating a house, have you used the zone method of planning to help separate the zones from each other?		
5	Are the walls of the bedrooms soundproofed as well as they can be?		
6	Have you explored the use of furnishings such as rugs, draperies, curtains, wall hangings, upholstered furniture and plants for noise reduction purposes?		

CHECKLIST 59
SAFETY CHECKLIST

	Yes	No
1 Have you resolved to make your home a safe place for you and your family to live in?		
2 Have you checked all the floors for: a Buckling		
b Large cracks		
c Uneven surfaces		
d Slippery surfaces		
e Wood rot and termite damage		
3 Have you checked all the windows for: a Loose glass		
b Weak frames		
c Broken glass		
4 Are all your bathtubs and showers equipped with strong hand bars in strategic places and nonskid surfaces?		
5 Are all electric switches and pull chains located far enough away from the tubs and showers so they cannot be reached from them?		
6 Is the kitchen floor safe to walk on?		
7 Is the kitchen well lighted, especially around the entrances and near the sink and range?		
8 Are the stove and all the electrical appliances in good repair, especially their electric cords and plugs?		
9 Is there a sturdy, well-attached railing on at least one side of every stairway?		
10 Are all stairways well lighted with a switch at both the top and bottom?		
11 Are all the stair treads tight and free of defects?		
12 Is all the carpeting tight and free of nails and tacks?		
13 Are all the stairs on each stairway the same height (between 6 and 8 1/4 inches is the safest) and at least 10 inches wide?		
14 Does each stairway have sufficient headroom?		
15 Is the electrical system in good condition?		
16 Is the size of the electrical service adequate?		
17 Are there sufficient plugs throughout the house?		
18 Are all the fuses the correct size?		
19 Are there separate circuits for each air conditioner, clothes dryer, dishwasher or other appliances that are the proper size for the appliance?		
20 Are all the duplex outlets the new kind with a third grounding prong?		
21 Is there a switch at the entrance to every room?		
22 Does each throw rug and runner have a nonslip pad under it?		
23 Are cleaning aids stored in a safe place?		
24 Have the doors been removed from all nonused refrigerators?		

	Yes	No
25 Is there a safe place to store all power mowers, snow blowers and other yard equipment?		
26 Are all glass doors, storm doors, picture windows, tub enclosures and any other glass someone could walk into made of safety glass?		
27 Does everyone in your family know where the main gas shutoff valve is?		
28 Are all the gas stove burners clean and unclogged?		
29 Are all sidewalks and driveways free of dangerous cracks and holes?		
30 Is the garage: a Free of clutter		
b Free of low, overhanging eaves		
31 Are the garage doors in good repair?		
32 Are all flammables such as gasoline, kerosene and cleaning fluids stored in safe cans in safe places?		
33 Are all garden sprays, insecticides and other poisons stored in safe places?		
34 Is there good visibility around the driveway so nobody can suddenly step in front of a car without being seen and is it possible to see far enough for safe entry to the street?		
35 Is the swimming pool completely fenced in?		
36 Is the pool area free of all electrical appliances that are not battery operated?		
37 Is there a good screen and a proper size outer hearth for each fireplace?		
38 Are all guns in a locked cabinet and all ammunition in a separate locked cabinet?		
39 Are all stairways free of objects?		
40 Are all clotheslines and other low ropes and wires taken down when not in use?		
41 Are the grounds free of holes, storm debris, dead tree branches and fallen wires?		
42 Is there a list of emergency numbers at each telephone?		

CHILD SAFETY CHECKLIST

	Yes	No
1 Are all matches and cigarette lighters stored out of the reach of children?		
2 Are all electrical appliances unplugged when not in use?		
3 Are pans kept on the back of the stove, out of the reach of children?		
4 Are knives and other sharp utensils stored out of the reach of children?		
5 Are all flammable liquids kept away from the stove?		
6 Is the kitchen floor kept nonslippery?		
7 Is the kitchen floor free of broken glass and china?		
8 Does everyone in your family make it a practice not to leave water in the bathtub or in the sinks?		
9 Is it a rule in your family that children are never left alone in the bathtub?		
10 Are all medicines, cosmetic aids, razor blades and sharp toiletry instruments kept out of the reach of children?		
11 Is all electric equipment (razors, electric curlers and irons, radios, massagers, etc.) kept away from the sink and tub when not in use?		

FIRE PROTECTION CHECKLIST

	Yes	No
1 If you are building a house, have you arranged that the furnace, hot water heater, air conditioner and all major appliances: a Have an Underwriters Laboratories (UL) or the equivalent label?		
b Have been installed or wired by a licensed electrician and not by a handyman or friend?		
2 Is your roof covered with fireproof material?		
3 If you are buying an older house, have you arranged for a professional inspection of: a Electric system		
b Heating system		
c Hot water heaters		
d Fireplaces		
e Chimneys		
4 If the house is old, have you checked to be certain none of the insulation is paper or sawdust?		
5 Have you made a fire evacuation plan of your home: a With normal exit routes shown on it		
b With alternate exit routes shown on it		
c With a designated, prearranged spot for everyone to meet outside the house		
6 Have you provided at least a rope ladder to those places on upper floors without a second means of exit?		
7 Have you practiced removing the storm windows and screens with the children?		
8 Have you familiarized each member of the family with the location of the nearest fire alarm box?		
9 Do you conduct fire drills at least once a month?		
10 Have you installed smoke detectors in your home?		
11 Do you know what operation EDITH is?		
12 Do you know the difference between a smoke detector alarm and a heat detection alarm and how much it would cost to equip your house with either system?		
13 Do you or are you planning to have at least one fire extinguisher in your house?		
14 If the house has a wood burning stove, have you determined that it has been installed in a safe way according to manufacturer's instructions?		

	Yes	No
15 Have you checked the house to determine that no stove or heater is connected into the furnace flue?		
16 Have you checked the fuse box to determine that only correct size fuses are used and none have been bypassed?		
17 Have you checked your fireplace: a To determine its outer hearth is big enough		
b It is clean		
c It is never used to burn charcoal		
18 Is the basement, attic or garage free of accumulations of flammable trash?		

CHECKLIST 62
HOME SECURITY CHECKLIST

		Yes	No
1	Is each of the outside doors in the house:		
	a Solidly constructed		
	b Hung with a well-fitted frame		
	c Secured with a dead bolt lock		
2	Does the house have or are you considering a home security alarm system?		
3	Have you covered all glass in doors within three feet of the door knob with some nonbreakable material, or installed locks that can only be opened from either side with a key?		
4	Have you moved all mail slots away from the door knobs or installed locks that can only be opened from either side with a key?		
5	Have you taken the recommended steps necessary to make all sliding doors and jalousies break-in proof?		
6	Does your home alarm system have:		
	a Switch sensors		
	b Pressure mats		
	c Ultrasonic motion detectors		
	d Photoelectric sensors		
7	Have you considered an alarm directly connected to the police station or a security company?		
8	When you go on vacation do you take the following steps to decrease the exposure of your house to burglary:		
	a Will someone regularly mow the lawn?		
	b Will someone shovel the snow?		
	c Have you stopped mail delivery?		
	d Have you stopped newspaper delivery?		
	e Have you stopped milk delivery?		
	f Have you notified the police department that you will be away and when you will return?		
	g Have you arranged for lights to be turned on and off with automatic timers?		
	h Have you left a radio playing?		
	i Have you left your telephone in operation?		
	j Have you avoided publicizing your trip?		
9	Have you inscribed your name or a special number on your appliances and other valuables?		